SHAKESPEARE   SOPHOCLES   ARISTOPHANES
PLAUTUS   A MEDIEVAL PLAY   COMMEDIA
DELL'ARTE   MOLIÈRE   CONGREVE   SHERIDAN
WILDE   IBSEN   CHEKHOV   STRINDBERG   SHAW
O'NEILL   BRECHT   IONESCO   PINTER   VAN
ITALLIE

ACTING
The Creative Process

SECOND EDITION

ARISTOPHANES   PLAUTUS   A MEDIEVAL PLAY

COMMEDIA DELL'ARTE   MOLIÈRE   CONGREVE

SHERIDAN   WILDE   IBSEN   CHEKHOV

Hardie Albright

STRINDBERG   SHAW   O'NEILL   BRECHT

IONESCO   PINTER   VAN ITALLIE   ZINDEL

SHAKESPEARE   SOPHOCLES   ARISTOPHANES

PLAUTUS   A MEDIEVAL PLAY   COMMEDIA DELL'

ARTE   MOLIÈRE   CONGREVE   SHERIDAN   WILDE

IBSEN   CHEKHOV   STRINDBERG   SHAW

Wadsworth Publishing Company, Inc.
Belmont, California
O'NEILL

VAN

ITALLIE   ZINDEL   SHAKESPEARE   SOPHOCLES

ISBN: 0-8221-0046-0
Library of Congress Catalog Card Number: 72-90245

Printed in the United States of America
Printing (last digit): 10 9 8 7 6

The frontispiece is from the American Conservatory Theatre's production of George Feydeau's farce *A Flea in Her Ear*, Michael O'Sullivan and Herman Popp featured. Photo by Hank Kranzler.

End papers from a Hogarth engraving in the Henry E. Huntington Library and Art Gallery. Reproduced by permission.

Production editor: Janet Greenblatt
Copy editor: Marianne Polachek
Interior design: Kay Cole
Interior artwork: Michael Hobson
Cover design: Larry Byrd

Contents

CONTENTS

CONTENTS   ix

List of Plays

List of Exercises

Foreword

Sir John Gielgud, recently asked by an interviewer what the basic requirements were for an actor, unhesitatingly named three: "Imagination,
self-discipline, industry," and, as an afterthought, added quickly, "voice,
of course, is wildly important." How do young, talented people satisfy
these requirements? Mainly by hard work in steadily controlled training.

The conscientious student of acting, whether in high school, college,
workshop, or even working alone, will profit considerably from mature,
professional advice. A course of study offered with such hard-gained
authority may sometimes equal the knowledge acquired by working for
a long period with a professional company of actors.

When I first perused Hardie Albright's manuscript—actually his
lecture notes for a university extension course—it was this practical, truly
professional approach toward the education of prospective actors that
impressed me most favorably. Only an actor with a solid occupational
background—and a teacher of wide experience—could arrange a textbook
which so sensibly combines theory with ample practical exercise.
Mr. Albright succeeds in personalizing essential points of the acting process in order to free them from cold didactics. He always relates theories
to the thoughts of practicing successful actors. So when he quotes Alec
Guinness on voice training, or Laurence Olivier on the physical aspects
of acting—to cite only two of the numerous examples—he inspires the
student to relate any element of the acting process to something a fine
actor has said, as if the student had really talked to the actor about it.
Mr. Albright wisely avoids editorial bias. In this book, the reader is
allowed, even encouraged, to reach his own conclusions after hearing all
sides. All acting theories and methods, from Stanislavski and Bertolt
Brecht to the latest avant-garde, are discussed and skillfully applied to
exercise scenes selected from the master dramas in world literature.
The author is particularly lucid in defining the various styles of acting
that have developed out of historical and practical needs. Only an actor
who has done it himself can convincingly explain how to act Greek
tragedy and comedy, Commedia dell'Arte, Shakespeare, Restoration,

Ibsen, or the Theatre of the Absurd. It is this special quality that will separate this book from many others.

In a time when repertory theatres are being built all over the United States, there is one pressing need: to provide well-trained actors who will be able to perform the great plays of the past and the present. Every effort must be made to meet this challenge. Hardie Albright's book shows the way.

William W. Melnitz
Dean Emeritus, College of Fine Arts
University of California, Los Angeles

Preface

This second edition of *Acting, the Creative Process* has greatly benefited from suggestions contributed by many instructors who have used the first edition in actual classroom situations. It fulfills a long-felt need in blending the techniques, philosophy, and history of acting. A fresh approach has been taken to the material covered. It is written in a style which should appeal to both student and instructor.

It has been said that acting is believing, but believing, alone, will never make an actor. There must be a modicum of talent and the fortitude to spend hours in developing the body and voice as instruments of communication. This is exactly where this book begins. Next, the student is given the experience of creating pantomime and improvisation. From dealing with the theatre environment and its disciplines, he is led into building his own acting method for creating characterization and sensory experience. Much stress is placed upon present-day acting methods, physical-spatial-spiritual training, and upon creating fresh and original metaphors, as well as upon the more traditional Stanislavskian approaches for the realistic theatre. This inclusion of more modern acting approaches is mandatory for an actor contemplating work in today's splintered theatre world, where innovative and even revolutionary plays are offered along with traditional and classical dramas.

Throughout the book there are over one hundred exercises illustrating points made in the text. In the rich Styles in Acting section, which has been extensively used and highly praised, each great historical acting style is considered and explained. For example, in the chapter devoted to Greek drama, excerpts from *Oedipus the King, The Birds,* and *Lysistrata* are given. Moreover, discussions of Roman and Medieval drama have been added to this new edition, including play excerpts from these two historical periods of the theatre. Next come the chapters devoted to the Commedia, Shakespeare, Moliere, and the Restoration and the eighteenth century. The acting process is then considered in light of the nineteenth- and twentieth-century dramaturgy of Wilde, Ibsen, Chekhov, and Strindberg, and Shaw, O'Neill, and Brecht, with excerpts from such works as *The Ghost Sonata, Pygmalion, Long Day's Journey,* and *The Good*

Woman of Setzuan, just to name a few. The thrust of the final section is with the contemporary and innovative theatre, including excerpts from Ionesco, Pinter, van Itallie, and Zindel (best known for his Pulitzer Prize play *Marigolds*). Appendixes offer advanced voice and speech work as well as answers to questions most often asked by acting students.

I
The
Creative
Process

1
Discovering Yourself

The actor's art consists of making a disciplined instrument from an undisciplined human being. It is a very complex and absurd art which is only possible thanks to the duality of each individual: his profound being and his identity. It is an art which tears the actor apart since, on one hand, he must develop his power of sensibility to the extreme of hysteria, and, on the other hand, he must develop through will power a constant self-control.*

Jean-Louis Barrault
French producer-actor

*By permission of the Clarendon Press, Oxford, England. (Photo from *The Theatre of Jean-Louis Barrault*, used by permission of Barrie and Rockliffe, London.)

So great is the desire of some beginning students to act that, far too often, they begin by acting scenes from plays. This encourages them to use cliches or to mimic professionals they have admired. How much wiser they would be if they developed their own individualities, their own resources, and if they studied how their imaginations and physical beings affect their reflexes and emotions.

Other students might spend hours in psychological discussions about a play and a character. But the time always comes when they must get up on their feet—*and act*. So, why not begin that way? Unless study can be communicated physically, it has no value in theatre. Of course, an actor must study his character but it must be done first through his body and its spontaneous reactions to a given situation.

How many of us have seen something beautiful in nature and said, "Oh, if I could only paint!" The difference between us and the artist, who also appreciates beauty, is that the artist has learned to record his reactions by using colors and brushes to create certain effects. The actor-artist is in the same kind of situation. He must learn to use an actor's instruments skillfully in order to express his creativity.

First things must come first, and that is where we begin this book— by developing impulses, reflexes, and images. Then we learn to make these visible through body action and, ultimately, we achieve an automatism of our physical equipment which will promote integration of conceptual judgments and emotional responses.

A complete technique of acting cannot be mastered at one time. It must be studied in sections, sequentially; then, when all parts become

A STUDY IN ACTION-MOVEMENT BY THE BAUHAUS, GERMANY. (COURTESY OF FRAU TUT SCHLEMMER.)

DISCOVERING YOURSELF

organically assimilated, they can be combined into a creative acting process. And the study continues for a lifetime.

Movement is at the foundation of acting. All inner impulses must come through the body. Acting can be compared to a Pollock painting because *the meaning is the action.* If you watch children at play, you will see that they do not imitate reality, they create it. A cardboard box becomes a space vehicle, a broom handle a sword. It was for very good reasons that Shakespeare referred to actors as players.

Reactivating a joyful, childlike approach in adults may be the key to unlocking the acting mystique. A spontaneous human response to ideas or a set of circumstances, free use of the imagination, acceptance of an abstract fantasy world: these are elements in acting which are most lacking in the mature mind. Those incapable of accepting exercises we use to develop images, impulses, and imagination through physical training, may never accept such other elements as dedication, self-discipline, and devotion to ideas, which are absolute demands in acting.

The values in the exercises throughout this book are in their immediacy, and in their use of instinct and imagination. They will also help train both body and voice as receptive instruments. That bright American star, Ina Claire, once said, "If [an actor] has complete control of his body, his mind, his emotion and his will, he can make an audience react as he wishes it to react."[1]

Exercises should not be rehearsed over and over, as if preparing for an audience. That would interfere with their spontaneity. They are for use in private classes *as a learning experience.*

RELAXATION

Each exercise must begin in total relaxation. The more you can relax your body, the greater will be the synchronization between your physical and mental efforts.

When performing these exercises, wear anything that does not bind but allows free movement: T-shirts and Levi's for men, body suits or leotards for women; even bathing suits are suitable. No shoes should be worn as you will want to feel the security of the ground under you.

EXERCISE 1. STANDING

Stand at center stage, feet together with arms hanging easily at your sides. Keep your spine erect. Imagine that there is a wire attached to your breastbone, pulling you up. Or visualize a yardstick against your back, touching buttocks, kidneys (small of the back), and shoulders.

(To help correct posture, lie flat on your back, and adjust until you are unable to get your hands into any space around the kidneys.)

STANDING

[1]Morton Eustis, *Players at Work* (New York: Theatre Arts Books, 1937), p. 81.

THE CREATIVE PROCESS

At first, this position may seem stiff and wooden, but it will soon become natural, because it *is* natural. Slumping is unnatural—and unhealthy. Continue, that is, standing perfectly still and relaxed in front of the class. It should be easy. But standing calm and relaxed in front of an audience is *not* easy. But never *will* yourself to be calm. That, in itself, will produce tensions.

When you are on a stage, you are mercilessly exposing yourself. Theatre is not a private but a social place. Everything that *is* you is up for appraisal: your appearance, how you speak, what you feel, and even what you think. Perhaps the most harassing moment for a beginner is when he is first asked to get up alone on a stage and face fellow-students. True, there are those who enjoy this, but most people are basically shy. Good. Many fine actors are in reality very quiet, reserved, and thoughtful persons. They have learned to conquer their timidity by long and devoted training. And they have more or less conscious ways of relieving the tensions which cause stage fright.

When performing exercises, don't be concerned with how you look—only what you feel. Concentrate upon some reason why you are standing in front of these people. As an example, pretend you are looking for some familiar face in the audience, or imagine that you are at an airport waiting for some close friend to arrive at the passenger gate. Use your imagination to invent other circumstances. Actors need to approach all physical tasks not only with the body and voice but also through objectives and motivations that come from within. These inner ideas may originate from remembrance of personal experience or they may be completely imaginative. The most important point is that these *circumstances or images should always be fleshed out in detail before performing any physical act.*

Stanislavski, in *Creating A Role* (p. 55), gives an example of the importance of physical actions. He says, "When a person has been drowned,

(COURTESY OF THE LIVING STAGE, A PROJECT OF THE ARENA STAGE IN WASHINGTON, D.C.)

TRAINING IS A VITAL PART OF THE AMERICAN CONSERVATORY THEATRE'S PROGRAM. CLASSES IN PHYSICAL DEVELOPMENT, MIME, VOICE, AND THEATRE GAMES ARE INCLUDED IN THE DAILY SCHEDULE OF THE ACTING COMPANY OF THE CONSERVATORY. (PHOTO BY CLYDE HARE, COURTESY OF THE AMERICAN CONSERVATORY THEATRE.)

DISCOVERING YOURSELF

AT THE AMERICAN SHAKESPEARE FESTIVAL AND THEATRE ACADEMY, STRATFORD, CONNECTICUT, ACTOR'S TRAINING PROGRAM INCLUDES STRENUOUS PHYSICAL WORK. (COURTESY OF AMERICAN SHAKESPEARE FESTIVAL THEATRE AND ACADEMY.)

THE EGG

THE TRIPOD

others force him to breathe by resuscitation or mechanical means. As a result of the enforced oxygen, his heart beats again, blood circulates, and finally by sheer momentum of the living organism his inner spirit is revived."

EXERCISE 2. RELAXATION #1

All exercises work better when you are quiet in body, so that you you may think beyond yourself.

Stand next to a chair, so that it will be handy should you need support. Now, slowly raise your arms as high as possible. Reach! Stretch! Now slowly balance on the balls of your feet. Shout if you feel like it. Then relax slowly; bend over, allowing all the force and energy to pour out with your breath. Now raise your head slowly and imagine you are breathing country air. Smell the grass you lay down on when you when you were ten. Fill your lungs with it. Now relax again, exhaling slowly. Let your heavy head drop. Feel the muscles stretching at the back of your neck. Hold, turning the head slowly from side to side. Follow this routine as many times as you need to release tensions.

Now sit in the chair. Adjust your body until you feel comfortable. Let your arms fall to the side, with feet set forward comfortably so that your heels are touching the floor. Now lean back and think about lying on a sunny beach or sitting on the bridge of a ship, moving gently with the swell. Next, bend over until your head is near your knees. Blood is draining from those centers of tension in your neck.

Slowly get up and take a long deep breath. Bend your arms at the elbows, allowing the hands to hang limp. Now shake them. Stop. Stretch the fingers. Now, supporting yourself on the chair, raise your knee slowly; first the right, then the left. Do this several times, and stretch those knees up as far as they will go.

EXERCISE 3. RELAXATION #2

1. *The Egg.* Lie flat on the floor. Sit up. Then raise your knees and bend over until you can clasp your hands about your legs. Slowly lower your head, stretching the back of your neck. Stay in this position until you feel tensions lifting from your spine.

2. *The Egg Roll.* Without changing your position, begin a rocking motion, back and forth, until you roll back on your spine, then back down on your feet.

3. *The Tripod.* Now lie prone again. Begin by bending your knees up with back still flat on the floor. Allow the force of this movement to arch your spine, permitting you to place your hands under the hips, elbows on floor, to support the weight of your body. Now raise your legs straight above your head. Stay in this position for

6 THE CREATIVE PROCESS

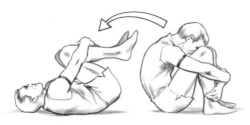

THE EGG ROLL

at least one minute, or until the blood can flow into the upper part of your body from the feet.

WARM-UPS

All sessions should begin with some limbering-up activity such as stretching, yawning, grimacing, stooping, squatting, etc. Warm-ups, as they are called, should be performed for five or ten minutes not only before each exercise session but also before rehearsals and performances. Warm-ups are no longer considered experimental, but are now standard procedure— even in the professional theatre.

EXERCISE 4. WARM-UP, BREATHING

The group stands erect and relaxed, facing a member who leads in deep breathing exercises.

1. Take in deep breath through nose only—hold—exhale, making the "OHM-m-m-m" sound.
2. Take in deep breath through nose and mouth—hold longer than before—exhale with a nasal sound.
3. Continue, each time holding breath longer than before and making different vowel sounds while exhaling.
4. End by shaking arms and body in short palsied movements, and twisting the muscles of the face into grotesque, masklike formations.

Exercises as described are movements only. *You* must supply the inner impulse for doing them. They are not to be thought of as calisthenics but as a means of stimulating ideas through physical actions.

EXERCISE 5. WARM-UP, THE CALCUTTA

This is one of the main exercises used by the cast of *Oh! Calcutta!* before every performance.

Perform to rhythm. Stand relaxed. Raise arms to shoulder height so that there is room between each performer. Now step forward twisting lower body while keeping head, neck, and shoulders as a unit. Center of balance should shift with each step from right to left as hips twist.

DISCOVERING YOURSELF 7

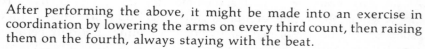

THE CALCUTTA

THE CIRCLE

After performing the above, it might be made into an exercise in coordination by lowering the arms on every third count, then raising them on the fourth, always staying with the beat.

Warm-up exercises should be given which are most applicable to the needs of the particular group and not necessarily in the sequence published here.

EXERCISE 6. WARM-UP, THE CIRCLE

1. Walk in time around a circle to some music. At a count or signal, rotate arms and hands, still keeping to the beat while walking.
2. Walk with knees bent, hands on hips.
3. Walk with stiff legs, pointing the toes on each step.

WALKING, LEAPING

4. Walk two steps, then leap for two counts. Repeat.
5. Rotate trunk from the waist upward with hands on hips, as you trot.

THE CREATIVE PROCESS

As in all exercises, the student should imagine some *reason* (real or imaginary) for his action; for instance, in the first problem of this exercise, you may be giving signals as an official might at a football game, or on an aircraft carrier. Use your imagination and think of images for all exercises.

THE PEANUT PUSH

EXERCISE 7. WARM-UP, THE PEANUT PUSH

Perform in place. Begin on hands and knees. Bend over, arms in front with palms flat on floor. At the signal, lower head to permit chin to push an imaginary peanut. Raise head and shift weight back to knees, then forward again to push the peanut. Do only a few times at first. Later, it can be performed up to fifteen times.

Do not use mirrors because, if you do, you will imitate what you see instead of what you feel.

Most people are constantly playing a part. This part may be the person they would like to be, the one others want them to be, or a sublimation for some failure. Before any creative acting can be done, all such pretensions must be removed along with the tensions causing them. An actor expresses things he would normally hide behind his defenses.

Training is hard work. It is mental as well as physical discipline. If you approach the exercises and problems in this book with sincere dedication, they will work for you as they have for others. They require no technique, no props or costumes, only a synthesis of imagination, instinct, and natural movement.

Some of the exercises are original, others are adaptations inspired by various authorities: Grotowski, Spolin, Stanislavski, Alexander, and others. But they have all been tested under workshop conditions. Begin each problem by creative rest and concentration. Start only when the action is sincerely felt; then, begin all movements in your body center.

As you do these exercises, do not work for *results* and don't worry about how you look. Exercises must develop spontaneously and organically and this approach will make them living experiences. Above all, do not think of these exercises as childish; they can be the beginning of your work on the creation of a character because they give you a direct line on how to express physical being and presence.

DISCOVERING YOURSELF

EXERCISE 8. VISUAL IMAGES, IMPORTANT AS WORDS

We begin by having everyone in the group take a place within a circle. The circle is the form used by tribal man for getting people together. It is the "all hands around" of folk dancing. The circle has a magic which shifts emphasis from the individual to more communal interests. The group revolves as a recording is played. Physical contact, action, and sounds are combined. Chants, cries, laughter, monosyllables, grunts, groans, and clapping of hands in rhythm are introduced with the hope that some kind of magic will occur wherein inner images and ideas, which cannot be verbalized, will emerge through externalizing them.

An imaginary object (a beach ball?) is tossed from one player to another as they continue walking or trotting around the circle. The imaginary object changes shape, weight, texture; sometimes it is hot or cold—or it may have various scents. Spontaneous reactions are encouraged, ranging from joy to terror, fear, disgust, etc., all timed in reaction to the recording.

Beginning with total freedom, players are using their bodies and senses as instruments of communication. Complete relaxation and a joyful spirit of child play are essentials; never forget that we are trying to reach inner feelings by first relating them to the physical act.

Some of the exercises which follow are training for the individual, others are oriented toward a group. Eventually, acting involves vibrations with others: players, director, and audience. By adjusting to a social situation, an individual experiences self-confidence and assurance through

(PHOTO BY FLETCHER DRAKE, COURTESY OF THE LIVING STAGE, A PROJECT OF THE ARENA STAGE IN WASHINGTON, D.C.)

THE CREATIVE PROCESS

the sharing of a common goal, and comes to consider himself as part of a select group with each member chosen for the special qualities he can contribute. This assures the student of the value of contacting others mentally, physically, and emotionally. In turn, such vibrations encourage individual spontaneity and fresh responses to problems.

In a group problem, a member is asked to look directly into the eyes of another, and describe in words what he sees as he touches the face of the other. After such tactile human contact, with its resultant lowering of barriers, it would be difficult for any individual to think only of himself and not think of the oneness of the group.

In ensemble exercises, gestures without words, movement without character, or other isolated problems, may be indicated. But all are meant to lead the student into self-discovery and to locate areas of deficiencies, so that he may correct them and improve himself as an actor. During physical exercises the atmosphere should be free and loose, one which fosters participation in game playing—unlike rehearsals which are held in a climate of dedication toward the opening of a play.

EXPRESSIVE MOVEMENTS

When you remember that walking is but one facet of acting, and that many other studies must be accomplished, such as gesture, speech, improvisation, characterizations, and emotions, you begin to understand why we must begin simply and develop our work in sequence.

EXERCISE 9. WALKING WITH IMAGES

The following describes only the mechanical actions. You should decide the impulse for each action, the ignition for the motor.

1. Walk, expressing calm and dignity. (Suggestion: visualize a coronation.)
2. Walk, expressing haste or impatience. (Do not think about hurrying, but about what is making you hurry.)
3. Walk, expressing opposition or uncertainity.
4. Walk, expressing fatigue. (What are the circumstances?)
5. Walk, expressing dread or fright. (What is frightening you? How does it look? Picture its size, color, shape, etc.)
6. Walk, expressing stealth. (What is the stimulus for such action?)

As in all exercises you are to begin with the impulse and allow it to flow organically to your body. Imagine you are:

7. Walking on a skyscraper girder.
8. Thirty years older than you are. Now, perform #7 again.
9. Walking in joy, anger, despair.
10. Walking against a strong wind, holding a large flag.

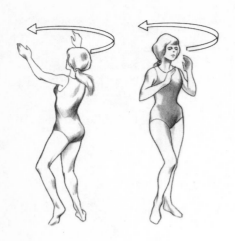

11. Walking blindfolded into a tunnel, with hands tied behind your your back.
12. Walking in a cloud or nightmare.
13. Walking in rubber boots in mud.
14. Walking in bare feet in the desert.

Before each exercise, close your eyes and concentrate. Feel the movement inside and act only when you are motivated, sincerely and definitely.

EXERCISE 10. SPACE EXPLORATION (A GROUP PROJECT)

With other members of the class, walk around the stage at will:

1. Pretend you are all in pitch dark by closing your eyes. When one player avoids colliding with another, he moves in a circle and claps his hands, once, to indicate success. Begin slowly, then increase tempo.
2. One player moves through a tightly packed crowd of noisy New Year celebrants.
3. A player brings news of a presidential assassination to various groups at a cocktail party (use gibberish sounds).
4. Several players are told they are in a small room and are sightless. Problem: by listening, touching, and receiving impulses from outside, they are to measure the confines of the space.
5. Two players are told they have long extended poles attached to their arms. They are to probe and discover the space of the acting area.

Ensemble playing is as valuable to the individual player as to a group. Each actor must be confident that he can depend upon others and that there is complete cooperation. This interdependence among a company of actors could be compared to the buddy system among skin divers.

THE CREATIVE PROCESS

EXERCISE 11. INTERDEPENDENCE

Five or six players form a circle and join hands. Another player stands within that circle; at a signal,[2] he stiffens his body and falls back. The others catch him and he continues falling to the right, left, and front, until he has complete confidence in his fellow-players.

Playwrights often use similes as a kind of shorthand to indicate the mood or feeling of a character; quite often these are based upon animals. For example, "she claws like a tigress"; "she moves like a snake"; a character is "mousey" or "he wolfs his food." The actor should learn to translate these similes into action and feeling.

Visit your local zoo and study the different animals. Note how their entire bodies contribute to a movement. They are superb at expressing emotions such as fear, love, hate, hunger, pain, fatigue, and boredom. The reactions of animals are not complicated by built-in repressions and censorship, as ours are, and are excellent teachers of conveying primary emotions through organic action.

The use of exercises in creating animal images has often been the butt of jokes made by those who do not understand the process of building a characterization. In the kangaroo, monkey, cobra, and cat exercises, we are trying to *feel* like the particular animal by assuming its physical attributes. Some day you may find that you can abstract something from such exercises in order to visualize and absorb simian or catlike qualities in a part.

CAT

EXERCISE 12. ANIMALS

1. Jump, imitating a kangaroo.
2. Walk on all fours like a cat, then strain chest, arms, and shoulder muscles by raising head, allowing pelvis to drop as back arches. Then drop head and tighten abdominals. Hold for count of three. Arch back again, while making catlike fricative sounds.
3. Walk on all fours like a rhesus monkey with bent rear legs, stiff arms supported on knuckles. Visualize a long tail at rear. Find the animal's basic tempo of movement; the short quick actions, sitting back on hind legs, then leaping again to action.

[2]In exercises, the go signal is often a click sound, such as a rider uses when on a horse.

DISCOVERING YOURSELF

13

COBRA

4. Cobra. From a horizontal position, face down, forehead resting on floor, bend elbows out so that flat palms are under the thorax. Slowly lift back the head only, straining neck muscles. Turn head slowly right and left. Gradually push up with the arms until they are straight, bending the spine back, stretching as far as possible. Hold. Return slowly to first position by bending arms at elbow, forehead on floor, palms under thorax. Repeat. (Lower body does not move in this exercise.)

FURTHER READING: DISCOVERING YOURSELF

Alexander, F. Matthias. *The Resurrection of the Body*. Edited by Edward Maisel. New York: University Books, 1969.

Artaud, Antonin. *The Theatre and its Double*. New York: Grove Press, 1958.

Birdwhistell, R. L. *The Kinesic Level in the Investigation of the Emotions*. New York: International University Press, 1963.

Brockett, Oscar G. *Perspectives on Contemporary Theatre*. Baton Rouge: Louisiana State University Press, 1971.

Brook, Peter. *The Empty Space*. New York: Atheneum, 1968.

Brustein, Robert. *The Third Theatre*. New York: Alfred Knopf, 1969.

Gardner, R. H. *The Splintered Stage*. New York: Macmillan, 1965.

Grotowski, Jerzy. *Towards a Poor Theatre*. New York: Benjamin Blom, 1969.

Houghton, Norris. *The Exploding Stage, An Introduction to Twentieth Century Drama*. London: Weybright & Talley, 1971.

Hutchinson, Ann. *Labanation*. Boston: Little, Brown, 1969.

Kerr, Walter. *God on the Gymnasium Floor*. New York: Simon & Schuster, 1971.

King, Nancy. "Theatre Movement: The Actor and his Space." 100 training exercises. *Library Journal* (1971).

Laban, Rudolf. *The Mastery of Movement*. London: Macdonald & Evans, 1960.

Lahr, John. *Up Against the Fourth Wall*. New York: Grove Press, 1970.

Kernan, Alvin, ed. *Modern American Theatre*. New Jersey: Prentice-Hall, 1967.

Kirby, E. T., ed. *Total Theatre: A Critical Anthology*. New York: Dutton, 1969.

Schechner, Richard. *Public Domain*. Indianapolis: Bobbs-Merrill, 1969.

THE CREATIVE PROCESS

Pasoli, Robert. *A Book on the Open Theatre*. Indianapolis: Bobbs-Merrill, 1970.

Roose-Evans, James. *Experimental Theatre*. New York: Universe Books, 1970.

Rostagno, Aldo; Beck, Julian; and Malina, Judith. *We, the Living Theatre*. New York: Ballantine Books, 1970.

RECORDINGS

These are used to stimulate moods, atmosphere, imagery, and metaphors. Any recordings will do as long as they are not popular rock, jazz, vocals, or hackneyed standards. Pure sounds are best, even a metronome or a drum may be used. Many of the exercises should create their own rhythms.

Albeniz. *Malaguena*. Columbia DX 1846.

Antheill, George, *Ballet Mechanique*. Urania: 1924. 134:5134.

Brant, Henry. *Angels and Devils*, Concerto for flute, Signs & Alarms. Galaxy, Columbia ML 4956 II. Lehigh University.

Cage, John. *Amores*, for prepared piano and percussion. Time: 580009. Stereo: 8000.

————. *Indeterminancy*, New Aspect in Instrumental and Electronic Music. 2 Folkways 3704.

Cage, John, and Harrison, Lou. *Double Music for Percussion*. Time: 58000. Stereo: 8000.

Copland, Aaron. *El Salon Mexico*.

de Falla. *Miller's Dance*. Columbia DX 1817.
       Danza Espanola. Columbia DX 1846.
       El Amor Brujo.

Delins. *Brigg Fair*.

Holst. *Planet Suite*.

Mossolov. *Steel Foundry*.

Saint-Saens. *Carnival of the Animals*.

Schuller, Gunther. *Seven Studies after Paul Klee*. Mercury 50283. Stereo: 90282.

The following sound effect records are obtainable through the Dramatist Play Service, 440 Park Avenue South, New York, 10016.

| Traffic noises | #5005 | Gunfire and Explosions | #5033 |
| Door buzzer | #5025 | Bus sounds | #5023 |

2
Mime

The pantomimist mimes the water and becomes fish, he mimes the wind and becomes tempest, he mimes the fire and becomes flame, he mimes the feelings and becomes passion, he mimes the thing and becomes object, he transforms himself into a tree and becomes a bird, he becomes animated nature.*

Marcel Marceau

*From foreword to *Le Mime Marcel Marceau*, Harald Von Pawlikowski-Cholewa, Paris: Overseas Publications Vaduz 1963. (Brown Brothers photo)

The man in the White House, the man in the street, we are all mimes. We shrug our shoulders, nod, shake our heads, point our finger, place our thumbs up or down, and replace speech with an ancient art known as pantomime, and pantomime is a concise and beautiful language.

When we see Marcel Marceau walking without moving, climbing invisible stairs, catching imaginary butterflies, leaning on nonexisting mantelpieces, or in performing any of his extraordinary mimes, few of us realize the antiquity of this art. For pantomime is the oldest form of dramatic expression and the most universal. It has occurred in all primitive cultures.

In ancient Egypt and India, pantomime had already developed artistic forms. In Greece, performers enacted fables of heroes and gods. Later, in fifth-century Rome, topical subjects were used and there was a special school for the development of pantomime. The Commedia dell' Arte amplified the form by adding improvisational dialogue. In England today, popular entertainments during the holidays are called pantomimes but they use music, dancing, songs, dramatic speech and slapstick clowning.

Mime, as we know the term, is language using no words. It is acting in which all physical images are stylized. Gestures are used sparingly but are intensified; each movement is completed before beginning another. The only sounds made by a mime are those of objects—the swish of bullets, the squeaking of doors, the pop of opening champagne bottles, etc. These are accepted conventions but the sounds typical of people are not. When a performer laughs, sneezes, or cries out, it is done silently and communicated only by movement. When he needs a mantelpiece to lean on, a chair to sit upon, he creates these out of air. When he handles imaginary objects such as bottles, teacups, flowers, or telephones, the mime creates for the audience a complete memory of the actual object: its size, shape, weight, color, smell, and touch. So that movements are interpretative of the size and shape of an object, the hand is opened as it grasps and, then encloses it. The mime must be careful not to violate the confines of imaginary objects which have already been established; that is, he must never "walk through" a table, a chair, or forget that he still holds a glass in his hand. He should put the glass down before beginning another action. All of his gestures are enlarged, bigger than life. This is a necessity in the large open theatres of today.

Although movements are enlarged, they are, as in all acting, stimulated from inside the actor. And like the verbal actor, the silent actor must have complete control over every part of his physical self. Indeed, physical training is much a part of present-day conditioning of all actors. Gilmor Brown, who trained so many well-known actors at the Pasadena Playhouse, once said, "The director's great problem is to get the actor to use his body as a metaphorical vehicle for the expression of a dramatic idea."

In devising mimes, we should remember to choose original and general themes in which there is universal interest. Avoid those mimes that are done frequently, such as the man shaving and the lady-and-girdle

SPRITELY STREET MIME, ROBERT SHIELDS PRACTICES PURE THEATRE ON THE STREETS OF SAN FRANCISCO TO THE DELIGHT OF HIS LOYAL LUNCH HOUR FANS. (COURTESY OF ROBERT SHIELDS AND LORENE YARNELL.)

routines. The story is less important in miming than the execution of physical images. They should be presented in their essence, precise, clean-cut and, as we have said, larger than life.

EXERCISE 13. HANDLING OBJECTS

Furnish a room from your imagination. Show the location, size and shape of tables and chairs by using them. Next, handle smaller objects, such as bottles, flower vases, plates, and show their weight, shape, and texture.

EXERCISE 14. BEING OBJECTS

WOMEN: Housecleaning.
You are to become the cleaner and also the objects used in cleaning—a dust cloth, a carpet sweeper, spray can, a squeegee for windows, etc.

MEN: Car or motorcycle.
You are to be the motor, the tires, the steering wheel or handlebars, and the highway.

EXERCISE 15. CHARACTER PANTOMIMES

TIME: One minute each.

MEN:
1. A retired scientist selecting fruit in a supermarket.
2. A golfer getting ready to make a shot and having trouble with a bee.
3. A doctor examining a ticklish patient. You are the patient.
4. A waiter carrying a tray and serving, hoping not to sneeze.
5. A cowboy in a lingerie shop.
6. A mechanic handling tools.
7. A musician fingering his instrument.
8. A father watching a little league game.

WOMEN:
1. A PTA speaker wearing tight shoes.
2. A typist having trouble with her machine.
3. A nurse examining a shy patient. You are the patient.
4. A waitress clearing a table and picking up an inadequate tip from a former customer.
5. A housewife knitting socks and listening to a TV soap opera.
6. A mother holding her own child. Someone else's child.
7. An old lady threading a needle.
8. A B-girl at a bar.
9. A mother at a little league game.

THE CREATIVE PROCESS

EXERCISE 16. EYES

Pretend to be gagged and bound to a chair. By use of your eyes only, inform someone where to look for an object.

The eyes of a mime are an important tool of communication.

EXERCISE 17. MIMETIC GESTURE.

By means of body gestures only, express the following phrases:

1. Please go away.
2. About this long.
3. I have a stomachache.
4. Get up and get out of here.
5. Come over here, I want to say something to you.
6. I won, I won!
7. He zigzagged all over the road, then fell down.
8. Pull over to the side and stop the car.

When communicating several thoughts, do each one, *and finish it* before introducing another thought. Do not blur all of your gestures together.

YOUNG AMERICAN HUSBAND AND WIFE MIMES, ROBERT SHIELDS AND LORENE YARNELL HAVE APPEARED AT FAIRS, IN CONCERT, AND ON MANY POPULAR TV SHOWS TO GREAT ACCLAIM. (COURTESY OF ROBERT SHIELDS AND LORENE YARNELL.)

EXERCISE 18. PANTOMIMES.

1. You are an army nurse, or a male medic, in a field hospital. You have accidently discovered a bomb. You try to get some native attendants to get the bomb squad, but they understand no English.
2. A deaf mute is about to touch a hot stove. You try to prevent this.
3. You are in a foundry where the noise is deafening. Warn a co-worker that he is in immediate danger.
4. You are in a TV studio, about to go on camera with the leading lady when you notice that the back of her dress is not zipped up. Your instinct is to fix it, but you feel she might misunderstand. You cannot speak or whisper, so you use gestures instead.
5. You are in a boat with your young son, fishing on a clear lake. You see a large bass and try to indicate that your son should put his line where you have seen the fish.
6. A lady tells a story to an old and a young man who sit at her feet and whistle their reactions. It is a story about a princess, a castle, and a handsome prince—but there are no words to it, only gestures because it is a memory.[1]

FURTHER READING: MIME

Aubert, Charles. *The Art of Pantomime.* New York: Benjamin Blom, 1970.

Barlanghy, Istvan. *Mime Training and Exercises.* New Rochelle, New York: Sportshelf & Soccer Associates, 1967.

[1]From Jean-Claude van Itallie's one act, *War* (New York: Dramatist Play Service, 1967), p. 13.

MIME

Broadbent, R. J. *The History of Pantomime.* New York: Citadel Press, 1965.

Bruford, Rose. *Teaching Mime.* London: Methuen, 1958. New York: Barnes & Noble, 1958.

Cage, John. *Silence.* Connecticut: Wesleyan University Press, 1961.

Cherry, C. *On Human Communication.* New York: John Wiley, 1957.

Dorcy, Jean. *The Mime.* New York: Robert Speller Sons, 1961.

Du Chartre, Pierre. *Commedia dell'Arte.* London: Peter Smith, 1965.

————. *Italian Comedy.* New York: Dover, 1965.

Enters, Agna. *On Mime.* Connecticut: Wesleyan University Press, 1965.

Hall, Edward T. *The Silent Language.* Greenwich, Connecticut: Fawcett World Library, 1959.

Huff, Theodore. *Charles Chaplin.* New York: Henry Schuman, 1951.

Hunt, David K. *Pantomime,* New York: Atheneum, 1964.

Hunt, Douglas and Kari. *Pantomime, the Silent Theatre.* New York, Atheneum, 1968. (Recommended)

Lawson, Joan, *Mime.* London: Pitman, 1957.

Marash, Jessie Grace, *Mime in Class and Theatre.* London: Harrap, 1950.

Mawer, Irene. *Art of Mime.* London: Methuen, 1957.

Nicoll, Allardyce. *Masks, Mimes and Miracles.* New York: Cooper Square Publications, 1964.

Sayre, Gweanda. *Creative Miming.* London: Herbert Jenkins, 1959.

Shawn, Ted. *Every Little Movement.* Published by author, 1954.

Shepard, Richmond. *Mime, The Technique of Silence.* New York: Drama Book Specialists, 1971.

Walker, Katherine Sorley. *Eyes on Mime.* New York: John Day, 1969.

THE CREATIVE PROCESS

3

The Actor's Voice and Speech

I think a classical background of acting gives a performer many things; he can stand well, walk well, speak well, be heard above all. I think all the great actors had good voices. There have been many glamorous-looking men and women in the theatre who have been matinee idols without being able to touch the higher reaches of their profession, because they have let down vocally.*

Sir Alec Guinness

*Reprinted by permission of Calendar magazine, *Los Angeles Times*. (Photo by permission of Columbia Pictures)

The way people speak reveals their background, education, and social standing as well as their state of health and emotion of the moment. To those we meet, we may sound friendly or persuasive, monotonous or affected. If one possesses a pleasant and convincing way of speaking, he has a lifetime asset. Conversely, poor speech can be a permanent handicap. For business executives, salesmen, teachers, politicians, and ministers, good speech is beneficial.

For the actor, good speech is a necessity. Standards in his profession are higher than in any other. An actor depends upon his voice to convey thought, emotion, and characterization. Voice has usually been the first-mentioned characteristic in descriptions of the celebrated actors of the past. It is gratifying to hear an actor who owns a resonant and flexible voice using it to transmit meaning and emotion to an audience.

Obviously, the first duty of the actor is to be *heard*, and yet he must sound conversational. The written speeches must seem to be spoken for the first time, but the use of the hesitations and corrections of everyday speech onstage seriously interferes with the flow of the play. There has been a notion among some actors that the training of the body and voice inhibited the expression of their artistic souls. Their fear was that they might become artificial or "hammy." The misconception brought with it slovenly, inaudible speech and ugly postures and movements. These actors overlooked the fact that nothing on the stage is real. It is the actor's magic which should make it all appear real. Fortunately, such views seem no longer fashionable.

The distinction between voice and speech should be clarified at once. While speech is an acquired skill, voice is instinctive. No baby needs learn to cry or croon, whereas speech is a difficult and complicated acquisition. To speak one word we might use a hundred muscles, and most of us take this skill for granted. Once it is learned, we must continue to practice our speech or it atrophies. Speech is affected by many factors: regional and family environments, physical and psychological conditions, and others too technical for our present consideration. Certainly body conditions can affect speech. Anxiety and tenseness could result in speaking too quickly. A phlegmatic attitude is evidenced in an indifferent or boring delivery. The actor can only be convincing in emotional moments when both his voice and body are coordinated.

Human speech is produced by:

1. A *motor*, largely composed of respirator muscles in the general region of the diaphragm. Its function in speech is to provide power for the expulsion, regulation, and control of air.

2. A *vibrator*, which is chiefly concerned with the vocal folds (or bands). Its function is to produce tone by sound waves and vibration of air.

3. A *resonator*, chiefly in the cavities of the throat, mouth, and nose. Its function is to re-enforce or amplify sound waves, giving them resonance.

4. The *articulators,* composed mainly of the lips, teeth, tongue, upper gums, hard and soft palate, the uvula, and lower jaw, functioning to give shape and character to each separate speech sound as the phonated or nonphonated breath stream is expelled through the nose and throat.

Let us begin at the beginning with respiration or the "motor" device.

BREATHING

Projection, sustained tone, and the timing of vocalization depend in most part upon control of the breath stream. The mechanism of breathing consists of the rib cage, diaphragm, lungs, and trachea which leads up to the larynx and vibrating folds.[1] As you inhale, the powerful diaphragmatic muscle which forms the dome-shaped floor of the thoracic cavity contracts and descends; air fills the lungs. When you are breathing quietly without speaking, the relaxation of the diaphragm and the rib cage slowly force out the air. In normal breathing, inhalation is active and exhalation passive; the time cycle is equal. But in breathing for speech, both inhalation and exhalation are *controlled,* as is the time cycle. This control allows the actor to sustain a tone, to exhale with economy while speaking, and to permit changes in timing of phrases and pauses. Skill in other phases of the speech process depend upon this breathing control, for it influences tone, resonance, articulation, and rhythm patterns. Faults in breathing include a rapid rate of speaking, broken phrasing, and unsteady tone. If you have any of these, work with the following exercises.

EXERCISE 19. BREATHING

1. *Clavicular breathing:* Stand and relax, then inhale and at the same time raise your shoulders and collarbone. Exhale. Breathe this way several times, then try speaking a sentence.
2. *Upper thoracic breathing:* Stand, relax. Place your open palm against your breastbone and raise the chest as you inhale. Repeat. Now read the same sentence.
3. *Medial breathing:* Relax again, and as you inhale this time, press your palms against the lower ribs, moving the ribs outward and slightly upward. Repeat, then try your control of breathing as you speak the sentence.
4. *Diaphragmatic-abdominal breathing:* Stand at ease and inhale as you place your right palm over the soft part of the abdomen just under the ribs and your left palm against the ribs and abdominal wall. Repeat, then try the sentence.

NOTE: Upper chest breathing (1) is to be avoided as it usually results in fatigue and lack of control. Because they are nearest to natural breathing, (2), and (3) are best for acting. The next time you engage

[1]From *Basic Voice Training For Speech* by Elise Hahn and others. (New York: McGraw-Hill Book Company, 1957), pp. 24-55. Used by permission.

THE ACTOR'S VOICE AND SPEECH

in a lively discussion, note which type of breathing you use. Note someone using clavicular breathing; do they tire easily?

5. *Deep breathing.* Take a deep breath, inhale to the bottom of your lungs; now exhale slowly by blowing through pursed lips. Repeat.

6. *Controlled breathing.* Take a full deep breath and count silently: IN, 1, 2, 3, 4, 5; HOLD, 6, 7, 8, 9, 10, and OUT. Now increase by two counts each time the exercise is repeated.

Exercises in natural breathing and control of breath are of value in avoiding stage fright when regular breathing rhythms are upset.

EXERCISE 20. DEVELOPING BREATH SUPPLY AND CONTROL

Study the three excerpts that follow and decide the meanings you wish to express.

Underline words to stress, and mark the pauses that best bring out meaning. *But also remember that you must renew your breath supply.* Try using this exercise on a stage or somewhere you can project.

> *Since brasse, nor stress, nor earth, nor boundless sea,*
> *But sad mortallity ore-swaies their power,*
> *How with this rage shall beautie hold a plea,*
> *Whose action is no stronger than a flower?*
> —From *Sonnet 65* by Shakespeare

> *I feel sorry for a commander like that—when maybe he had something big in mind, something they'd talk about in times to come, something they'd raise a statue to him for, the conquest of the whole world for example—Lord, the worms have got into these biscuits!—he works his hands to the bone and then the common riffraf don't support him because all they care about is a jug of beer or a bit of company.*
> —From *Mother Courage* by Bertolt Brecht

For eighty or ninety years, small waste cuttings from diamonds were secreted under the back steps of the Anderson's porch.

Other material to use for this exercise may be found in the speeches of Lincoln, Roosevelt, and Kennedy. The Bible is an excellent source for long passages or sentences demanding breath control.

PROJECTION

An inability to "speak up" seems a common fault of the beginning actor. In everyday conversation, psychologically he has set the receiving object at a few feet distant. But in the theatre, he must "throw" or project his voice. It may be that he need only adjust his thinking to correct the habit. If not, breathing exercises can be of great help in developing muscles and learning how to control the supply of air. Experienced actors seem able to project a whisper, which requires not only breath control and strong muscles but also precise, careful articulation.

It would seem obvious that if actors cannot be heard and understood, the curtain might just as well be dropped and money refunded to the audience. Projection is energy that can be controlled. Although related to loudness, projection is not loudness alone. An actor may speak very quietly and, by proper projection, be heard and understood by everyone "out front." On a stage, actors must seem to be speaking to each other but they should be conscious that their words must reach all over the house. An actor may identify or "point up" a particular word or phrase by suddenly speaking quietly, using a varied tone, or rhythm, or all three.

Intensity refers to the rate at which energy is given off from the motor source. When you prepare to shout, you automatically increase inhalation and exert pronounced pressure on the lungs. When this pressure is released through the trachea to the vocal folds, they are put into motion, vibrating in such a manner that the sound is louder than usual. If pressure is maintained to sustain this tone, release is controlled in the diaphragmatic-abdominal region, and not in the throat. Loudness and projection are not factors to be considered in isolation. To project, an actor must be in control of his physical activities and also be motivated by a wish to be heard.

EXERCISE 21. PROJECTION #1

Place someone at a distance from you, say fifteen feet, and speak some lines to him. If he is able to hear your every word, ask him to move back, and then continue. Repeat this until you become aware of the breath control needed. Be sure to use the diaphragm when projecting. When you can be easily heard and understood at a distance, try next to develop the impression that you are speaking conversationally. With practice, proper projection develops into a sixth sense and becomes automatic behavior, so you need not fear to practice consciously at first.

EXERCISE 22. PROJECTION #2

Turn up a rock recording to its highest sound level, and group around yourself members who shout. Note how much you must use your diaphragm and added breath to be heard at all. Pretend there is a person in the last row of the theatre you are trying to reach with your speech. Don't feel that this is too big, unlike yourself. Most actors start such exercises by overacting, then gradually refine their speech retaining only what is really effective.

PHRASING AND PAUSING

A phrase is a thought unit. Pauses serve as oral punctuation marks. Both are dependent upon the meaning of the lines, and each can contribute, not only to the intelligibility but also to the emotional impact of character and play. If we hurry in speaking a phrase, we subordinate it. By varying tones, we can alter moods and gain interest. Many different effects are gained by timing. But there is no correct or incorrect way to use timing. Only experience and instinct can guide you in knowing when to use it, for how long, and when to change. No substitutions of "ah's" or "I mean's" to begin speaking or fill pauses should ever be accepted as timing. When you have stage fright and gasp for air in the middle of a connected phrase, proper timing is destroyed. Therefore breath control is of the utmost importance.

EXERCISE 23. TIMING

Count 160 words in a newspaper or magazine article and place a pencil mark at that point. Now read aloud. If you reach the pencil mark in one minute you are reading at the rate at which most people can comprehend. If the article is simple, you may read up to 190 words per minute and still be able to convey meaning. At faster speeds, your articulation will need to be excellent. Also another element enters into the reading; faster speeds transmit an excitement or urgency. This device must be used sparingly or you may tire your listeners.

TONE AND RESONATION

Poor projection may also be the result of a thin, anemic tone which does not "carry." Production of sound, tone, or phonation is an extra duty superimposed on the human digestive tract and airway. The same muscles used for speech are also used when we cough, chew, and swallow.

Some musical instruments produce sound through the vibration of strings stretched over a sounding box or resonator. Other instruments produce sound when air is propelled through tubes. Human speech sounds are produced as the breath stream passes over the vocal bands and sets them in vibration, much as the lips of a trumpet player are set into vibration. Although the exact nature of these vibrations is not known, it is evident that they initiate disturbances or vibrations in the air column of the tracheobronchial tree, the larynx (Adam's apple), the pharynx (throat), the buccal cavity (mouth), the nose, and the nasopharynx, and possibly, but not probably, the sinuses. These disturbances produce sound waves in the outer air which are transmitted to the listener. The shape, size, texture, and firmness of the walls of these cavities, together with factors which are not as yet fully understood—such as movements of the epiglottis, soft palate, tongue, jaw, and lips—modify and amplify these tones, building up certain overtones and damping others, until there is produced the complex tone which we identify as voice.[2]

It is perhaps needless to mention that all these working parts of speech should be free of muscular tensions and obstructions. We are usually able to recognize a friend just by voice. If our friend is not feeling well or has a cold, we are apt to say, "You don't sound like yourself." The cold or illness has altered the tone emitted by the resonators.

[2]See G. W. Gray and C. M. Wise, *The Basis of Speech* (New York: Harper, 1946).

THE CREATIVE PROCESS

A good voice will be pitched at the level which is best for the particular individual.

> While seated at a piano, read aloud some written material. Try to identify a level of pitch which you most often use, and locate a note on the piano which approximates your level. This project is more effective when another person listens for your pitch and locates the note on the piano. After locating your *habitual level of pitch* you might continue with the piano to estimate your *optimum pitch*. Sing down to the lowest note you can produce with ease. From this, sing up the musical scale. Experiment until you have located the pitch which allows the greatest ease and richest tone. Should your habitual pitch and your optimum pitch levels be the same, you are to be congratulated; if not, then you should attempt to bring the pitch you use customarily closer to the pitch which will allow for the most effective use of your vocal instrument.

RANGE

An effective range gives variety and interest to speech. The difference between your lowest and highest notes might be said to be your range. Actors use variations in pitch to illustrate the temperament or personality of characters they portray. Such variations may also be used to transmit moods for certain words, phrases, or ideas. These variations from optimum pitch are called *melody*, a word most frequently associated by actors with Shakespearean playing. A simple change within a *single* phonation, either an upward or a downward glide, is called *inflection*. Try saying, "Where have you been?" with a rising inflection at the end, and then with a falling inflection, and note the change of meaning between the two. Changes in pitch within a *group* of phonations are known as *intonation*. When speakers repeat these changes so that they form a pattern and become monotonous, we say they are "intoning." *Always work for variety in your voice tones!*

ARTICULATION AND PRONUNCIATION

Most of us in America grow up learning "lazy language." As long as we are understood, we are content. We are satisfied with utility when we might have beauty of speech. The sad fact is that most people do not hear themselves accurately. We believe we are making one sound when in fact it is quite another. Also many do not realize that a word is not a single blur of a sound but is made up of a sequence of sounds. For instance, there are many different sounds in a word like "extinct." In pronouncing a word, a speaker may move so quickly from one sound to another that individual sounds are not easily detected.

> If you wish to improve your speech, you must first isolate each faulty sound and correct it. This is going to sound overprecise in the beginning, but it is the only way to improve. Later on you will find yourself speaking naturally and you will have lost the tendency to slovenly, lazy speech.

(PHOTO BY CLYDE HARE, COURTESY OF AMERICAN CONSERVATORY THEATRE.)

THE ACTOR'S VOICE AND SPEECH

Articulation has been defined as the process of forming meaningful oral symbols by manipulation of the tongue, lips, lower jaw, and palate. The phonated or nonphonated breath stream is interrupted or constricted, and with the aid of resonance, is formed into understandable sounds.[3] While articulation deals with proper manipulation of the articulars, pronunciation is the skill of producing acceptable sounds and correct accents. Included in this is the ability to form vowels and consonants properly and to divide words into syllables and accent them correctly. What is correct pronunciation? Is it the speech of the well bred in England and the educated in America? Such standards are unreliable. Neither can we depend upon the spelling of a word to know how it should be pronounced. In real life, the question might be answered by saying that correct pronunciation depends upon the occasion. But on the stage pronunciation must be appropriate to the character portrayed and the play being acted. It would certainly not be appropriate to use localized accents of American speech when acting in one of the great classical dramas. Such a mistake could destroy an otherwise perfect illusion of another time, another place. On the other hand, correct English will not do for other plays. In the United States there is no such thing as "standard English." Pronunciation differs in each locality, and even among individuals of each locality. The so-called "general American" dialect is divided into many headings and subheadings, and since no norm is to be found, the term is meaningless. No matter how an American tries to alter his pronunciation, it will be localized.

But for the actor, the problem is simpler. After a study of the play and the character he decides what is *the artistically correct pronunciation for the particular part and play.* "Stage English" is used only by the unoriginal and uncreative. When the sharecropper's daughter asks "Moth'ah wha's fah'thah?"—that's when most TV fans stop believing and switch to another station. An actor should not only look, think, and feel like the character, he must also *sound* like him. Don't feel that you are being affected when using unfamiliar speech on a stage. Like your costume and makeup, it is part of your characterization. Your objective should be to blend all the parts into a total concept so that no one part is isolated. Only then will the audience "believe."

HEARING

In the next few days, make it a point to study the manner in which your friends articulate. Do they:

> *Omit some sounds,* saying "pro'bly" for probably, "c'pany" for company, "lay'ees an' gen'l'mm" for ladies and gentlemen.
> *Make additions,* such as "athey'letic" for athletic, "naw" for no.
> *Substitute,* saying, "tinth" for tenth, "git" for get, "Toosday" for Tuesday, "as't" for asked.

[3]See Lyman Judson and Andrew Weaver, *Voice Science* (New York: Appleton-Century Crofts, 1942).

THE CREATIVE PROCESS

Run syllables together, making an uninterrupted string of gibberish such as "Wotchagotdare?" "howybin?" "wazzamatta?"

EXERCISE 25. SELF-ANALYSIS

Record your own speech by means of a tape recorder. In this way you will be able to make an impersonal self-analysis. As you play it back, be honestly critical. The only way you can improve is by isolating faults. Here are some words to practice; articulate all sounds and accent correct syllables:

monkey	February	door	potato	Wednesday
decision	deep	man	yell	egg
fat	yes	nose	sick	Pete
judged	cold	quiet	house	take
bait	can	Broadway	homage	task
bit	can't	sudden	Puck	water
bet	grandma	shrunken	daddy	loose
bat	and	God	punch	lose
Have you eaten?	that	guard	pseudo	anything
asked	clams	peace	photo	land
Didn't you?	calm	strength	piano	laugh
unanimity	clapped	pieced	folio	orange
psychology	tongue	the	fixed	Zsa Zsa
extinct	on	shoe	wing	ardvark
throw	light	shrink	shrub	vegetable

Here are a few words which Americans pronounce differently, depending upon locality. Compare your pronunciation with the dictionary preference:

appreciate	often	ammonia	status
conflict	ration	extraordinary	almond
interesting	hanger	hangar	protein
genuine	again	coupon	tedious

Now try recording some of your favorite long speeches from plays, as well as ordinary conversation. As you play it back check your speech against these faults:

1. *Lack of breath control:* Is your speech too fast, too slow? Do you take a breath and speak until that breath is exhausted? Are you frequently asked to repeat what you have said?
2. Obstructions in mouth, throat, and nasal passages: If the sound of your voice indicates obstruction, see a doctor and have the cause corrected.
3. *Muscular tension:* Do you sound tense, your voice strained or wavering?
4. *Other faults:*

   Harshness, resulting from prominence of overtones.
   Throatiness (or guttural sound), caused when tongue narrows the pharyngeal passage.

THE ACTOR'S VOICE AND SPEECH

Nasality, excess resonance in nasal passages.

Denasality, typical "adenoid" or "cold in the nose" speech.

Strident, hard, piercing, annoying speech (the "hard sell" voice).

Monotonous, lack of variety.

Weak, thin voice, faulty pitch, does not "carry;" and very undesirable.

Lack of volume, too loud, too soft, caused by lack of proper control.

After making such an analysis, talk over the results with your instructor. If he is of the opinion that you need more work on breath control or other phases of speech or voice, you will find additional aids in Appendix 2. In most colleges and universities, speech and voice studies are requirements for an acting class.

Whatever the thought, the actor is only able to express himself through the physical means of speech, gesture, and bodily movement. Through his voice, an actor brings images and impressions to his audience. If he has trained his voice into an instrument responsive to his thoughts he can also express colorations, silences, vibrations of force or gentleness which words alone could not express.

EXERCISE 26. INFLECTION

Here is a standard exercise which is not only helpful in training but also stimulates the imagination. It consists of just two words, "John" and "Marsha." Each time the names are pronounced they are given a different reading. It is best to plan no mood or story beforehand but allow meanings to be inspired accidentally through "the moment."

EXERCISE 27. STIMULATION OF TONE AND RESONATORS

The resonators are most important to an actor. To enrich vocal faculties, imitate different natural and mechanical sounds such as a foghorn, a coyote barking, an old man coughing, a motorcycle starting up, etc. Place these in the resonator most suitable to carry the sound:

a. Head
b. Mouth
c. Nasal
d. Occipital
e. Laryngeal
f. Abdominal

Speech is an integrated skill. Although each facet may be explored separately, the *entire* vocal process must be developed as a unit. If your breathing and phonation are poor, no amount of drilling will perfect your articulation. Your skill in using vowels and consonants depends upon phrasing and the quality of your voice as much as upon being able to hear and create sounds. To those who are convinced that an actor's voice is one of his chief means of communicating with an audience, this chapter will be all too brief and cursory. It has been necessary to limit material here in order to cover subjects not found in other acting books.

Speech is an exciting and rewarding study, for it is a social, physical, and physiological phenomenon. For those who wish more technical and detailed studies, a vast library has accumulated in the past twenty years. Here are just a few, in addition to those referred to in the text.

FURTHER READING: THE ACTOR'S VOICE AND SPEECH

Anderson, Virgil. *Training the Speaking Voice.* New York: Oxford University Press, 1961.

Brigance, William N., and Henderson, Florence. *A Drill Manual for Improving Speech.* New York: Lippincott, 1939. This book is a treasure of effective drills for improving speech.

Brodnitz, F. *Keep Your Voice Healthy.* New York: Harper, 1953. Especially good on care of voice; written by a medical doctor.

Eisenson, Jon. *The Improvement of Voice and Diction.* 2d ed. New York: Macmillan, 1965.

Fairbanks, Grant. *Voice and Articulation Drillbook.* New York: Harper, 1940-61. A standard.

Hahn, Elise, et al. *Basic Voice Training for Speech.* New York: McGraw-Hill, 1957. Recommended.

Machlin, Evangeline. *Speech for the Stage.* New York: Theatre Arts Books, 1970.

Schlauch, Margaret. *The Gift of Language.* New York: Dover, 1955.

Turner, J. Clifford with Foreword by British actress Peggy Ashcroft. *Voice and Speech for the Theatre.* London: Pitman, 1950.

4
Improvisation

Before I start work on a part, I read the script; but when shooting starts, I like improvisation right on the set. Even when I'm not consciously thinking about a part, I'm really thinking about it all the time.*

Sophia Loren
Academy Award Best Actress 1961
(for "Two Women")

*©1962 Lillian Ross. From *The Player, A Profile of an Art*, by Lillian Ross and Helen Ross, Simon and Schuster. Originally published in *The New Yorker*. (Photo by permission of Carlo Ponti)

In the theatre, improvisation is a means by which players can locate the authentic impulses of a scene or a play. The process is begun by discovering the established realities, as given by the playwright, or by supplying the given circumstances through the use of the "who-what-why" formula which is discussed later. Improvisation provides that the players supply words and actions while performing, and *without previous rehearsals.* Although pantomime may be improvised, the process is not the same.

Improvisation is not play writing—but play understanding; it should never be used as an end in itself. In the theatre, actors are taught to respect the authority of the play, the playwright, and the director. But improvisations provide release from such authority, allowing the actor to get in direct contact with the essence of a dramatic, or comic, situation and characterization. He is no longer concerned with memorizing and speaking lines written by an author. The actor's main concern here is to discover ideas and responses deep in his subconscious by realizing the character in a situation.

Most of the so-called improvisations we see on TV are previously rehearsed and performed again and again. In a strict sense, improvisation is a tool to be used for the training and study of actors, not for the commercialism of public performances. In fact, public performances of improvisations have been prohibited in England.

One of the purposes of improvisation is to familiarize actors with the significant moving parts of a play through an active reference or experience they can grasp. If the experience is to be meaningful, the player will need to know the structural qualities of a play and scene. He will need to learn how a scene relates to the entire play, the theme, plot, and characters.

There are other advantages to be acquired by performing improvisations. They teach an actor how to plan his work, how to respond imaginatively to the given circumstances, and how to develop a dramatic or comic, incident. Through these the actor gains confidence in his acting potential. In improvisation, the players relate closely with one another and it often happens that one of the actors will hit upon something entirely accidental, but nevertheless truthful, to which the other players can react in kind.

During rehearsals, improvising becomes invaluable in clarifying a scene, some business,[1] or the motivation, and it also discourages imitation and stereotype reactions, which too often plague an inexperienced player.

AS A LEARNING EXPERIENCE, IMPROVISATION:

- Encourages creation of fresh images.
- Provides experience in stepping into the world of illusion.
- Encourages careful preparation through the understanding of dramatic presentation.

[1]Business: silent action important to plot and illustrative of character.

THE ACE TRUCKING COMPANY USES IMPROVISA-
TIONAL TECHNIQUES TO DEVELOP SKITS FOR
THEIR PROFESSIONAL APPEARANCES ON MANY
TELEVISION SHOWS. (COURTESY THE WILLIAM
MORRIS AGENCY.)

— Provides a student with the means to extend himself from a limited natural environment into wider experiences.
— Teaches the value of flexibility, collaboration, and point of focus.
— Trains in concentration, observation, and communication.
— Gives training in creating "the illusion of the first time,"[2] and in following impulses.
— Provides experience in working from a plan, or overall artistic design.

THE GIVEN CIRCUMSTANCES

When you act in a play, the time, the place, the situation, and the character have been provided for you by the playwright. When you improvise, *you* must provide these factors. Although this form is impromptu, it is best done when there is first an overall plan or artistic design. Improvisation begins with some established realities, a problem stated, or a given circumstance. In order to develop this given premise, certain correlatives are usually needed, and should be supplied, before the improvisation can be considered ready for performing.

THE WHO-WHAT-WHY

WHO: are the characters?

WHAT: happens (situation)?

WHY: did it happen (motivation, theme)?

WHERE: does it happen?

WHEN: does it happen today, yesterday, tomorrow?

Rarely are all of these components stated in a given circumstance. Whatever point or points are missing must be supplied by the actors based upon what *has* been given or implied. When this is not possible, then the actors must create the missing elements imaginatively. When more than one student is involved in an improvisation, all members should discuss and agree on the who-what-why and, from the information they have, invent a plan which will dramatize their answers. Most plans will be improved by the addition of conflict (what happens and why), sequential development, and a conclusion.

As an illustration, let us take a given circumstance.

A and B have a heated argument in the home of C, who tries to make peace, but finds himself attacked by both.

[2]Illusion of the first time: giving the audience the impression that the lines and situation are impromptu.

THE CREATIVE PROCESS

CENTER THEATRE GROUP/MARK TAPER FORUM'S IMPROVISATIONAL THEATRE PROJECT WORK IS DIRECTED BY WALLACE CHAPPELL AT THE MARK TAPER FORUM OF THE MUSIC CENTER IN LOS ANGELES. (PHOTO BY STEVEN KEULL, COURTESY THE CENTER THEATRE GROUP.)

Now let us apply the formula to it—

WHO: *A and B...*

WHAT: are having a heated argument...

WHERE: in the home of *C*...

Here are characters, a situation, a conflict, and sequential development. The missing elements of WHEN and WHY will need to be supplied by us. "Don't stick your nose into other people's business" might, at this time, function as a kind of theme for us.

Now, in order to perform this scene as an improvisation, we must create a rough scenario by supplying characterizations, and we must break up the action into "beats," or small developing scenes, beginning with the premise—

A and B are having an argument . . .

Are they friends, relatives, strangers, business partners? How old are they? Suggest backgrounds through body postures, habits, etc. Are they in disagreement about money, wives, gossip, cars, business, ethics, politics, children, religion, or what (decide which will contribute most to your improvisation)? Will you build this scene from a quite innocuous remark to loud insults and threats? Or will you begin with high emotions? Which will be best dramatically? How will you vary tempo and audibility when C enters the scene?

In the home of C . . .

What brings them together? What sort of home has C? Is this meeting social or business? Does C enter from another part of the house

IMPROVISATION

or is he present when the argument begins? What is *C*'s relationship to *A* and/or *B*? Is he a friend to both? A stranger? What answers will contribute most to the improvisation? Trace all the possibilities.

Who tries to make peace . . .

Obviously this action constitutes a fresh development, a new scene, needed for dramatic interest because of what has happened in the first scene. It entails a physical change in positions—an encounter—as *C* takes central position. If *C* comes between *A* and *B* this would be understood by the audience as a visual symbol of intervention between opposing forces. The movement alone activates the theme, or point of focus, of this little scene. We must decide the reasons for *C*'s intervention. Will animosity between the men jeopardize some future plan of his? Or perhaps it is simply that he does not want the neighbors to hear, or the baby wakened. What points of argument does he make as he tries to stop the conflict? His statements could lead us into the next scene in which *A* and *B* turn on him.

But finds himself attacked by both.

Why do they object to his peace-making efforts? Do they attack him physically, or only verbally? How is it concluded? Do they knock him out, call the police, call others in, or walk away friends, leaving *C* their common enemy?)

SCENARIO—PLAN OF PROCEDURE

Decisive answers to questions such as these will constitute a plan sufficient to begin an improvisation, providing all performers understand it. You will note that no dialogue has been planned, merely sequential development and content for each "beat."

Before improvising, the three actors assigned the problem will have agreed on what is to happen, the order in which it will happen, and the characterizations they are to assume. Narrative, definitive characterization, and emotional reactions are left to be extemporized. The plan of procedure (or scenario) will be better remembered by all three if written down and not left to oral agreement.

Before performing, it is suggested that the players free themselves of all preconceptions and contact their specific material directly, allowing their sensory equipment and the characterizations to create fresh impulses. This direct contact is one of the main reasons for improvising. Long speeches or soliloquies should be discouraged; whatever narrative is necessary should be presented physically, in action, rather than by rhetoric. *Don't tell us, show us!*

After performing several improvisations, the importance of imaginative planning, of spontaneous responses, and of concentration upon the given circumstance, will become clear. Short improvisations are best; otherwise students may run low on inspiration.

Improvisations provide the highest level of independent study for individuals, being self-initiated and self-directed. They permit students

THE CREATIVE PROCESS

to make their minds work *as they want them to work*, independent of what a director wants them to do. This allows an actor individual incentive. Another value becomes obvious later. When rehearsing a play, the actor can improvise a scene not written by the author.

EVALUATIONS

After each exercise in improvising, there should be an evaluation, not only of what has actually been presented but also of the planning. Other students should decide how effective players have been in solving their problems. Unless one is watchful, improvisations can slip away from the problem as stated, ending up as a comfortable presentation of what the student feels he does best.

As in the physical exercises, the spirit of play must not be lost in doing "improvs." However, giggling and clowning should not be encouraged. Of course, there are times when something happens accidentally that is genuinely amusing; and a laugh at this time will relieve tension. However, *when the work of the players is being ridiculed, acting the fool should not be tolerated.*

When beginning improvisational work, it is best for students to choose roles near their own age and interests. Previous physical exercises should have loosened up any reticence, so that at this point, there should be no problem in forcing anyone to participate against his will.

Everyday conversations and casual movements do not make the points so necessary to improvisations. *Action and words must be distilled.* Tempo, suspense, and complication, should be built into the scenario. In each exercise, try for the physical as well as the spiritual sensations in the situation.

The who-what-why formula used to develop an improvisation is, in reality, a kind of prototype for dramatic composition. Another method, used sometimes, is similar to the who-what-why, except that different words are used:

SITUATION: What happened?

CHARACTERS: To whom did it happen?

LOCALE: Where did it happen?

MOTIVATION: Why did it happen?

ATMOSPHERE: When did it happen?

Whichever method you choose, always move simply from one objective and action to another.

ENRICHING AN IMPROVISATION BY ADDING ELEMENTS

EXERCISE 28. IMPROVISATION #1

Let us begin with an everyday nondramatic occurrence and add only one element at a time.

IMPROVISATION   37

Two people meet	Improvise "who?"
Two friends meet	Improvise. Now add the "when."
Two old friends meet	Improvise. Now add the "what."
Two old friends meet and fail to recognize each other.	Improvise (situation) Now add the "where."
As both are boarding a plane for Europe.	Improvise. Now add the "why."
One is a CIA agent who does not wish to be recognized and his old friend is a gregarious insurance salesman.	Improvise.

By inventing motivations (the "why") we have also helped in the characterizations and given a conflict-relationship between our two old friends. One is hiding, the other probing.

EXERCISE 29. IMPROVISATION #2 THE "WHY" ELEMENT

Begin by using only the "why" (motivation element).

Each student selects a mood such as anger, suspicion, fear, expectancy, happiness, etc.

Each is to improvise a scene consisting of one simple line, "I'll get it," in answer to a telephone or door bell ringing.

All else must be supplied by the player.

EXERCISE 30. IMPROVISATION #3. THE "WHERE" ELEMENT

Use only "where" (locale).

Statement of the problem: *A man is standing in line.*

Questions to be answered by players: What line? Where is this line? Who is the man? Why is he standing in this line?

NOTE: This is the starting point of one of the off-off Broadway plays. Its title? *Line* by Israel Horowitz.

EXERCISE 31. IMPROVISATION #4. THE "WHAT" ELEMENT

In this series of improvisations, the problems state one or two elements, others are to be supplied by the students when planning what they will do. Mostly these situations give the "what" element, the others must be added. Try to choose elements which relate to each other.

1. A robbery in a busy bank.
2. A suburban home catches fire.
3. Teacher returns to her classroom to find students in an uproar.
4. A job interviewer discovers that one of his idols is applying to him (or her) for a job.
5. A girl is temporarily blinded by seeing what she believes to be a UFO. A friend is with her.

EXERCISE 32. IMPROVISATION #5. THE "WHEN" ELEMENT.

Assign situations, characters, and season of the year; then improvise in the following periods:

1. Modern
2. Elizabethan
3. Eighteenth century
4. Victorian

EXERCISE 33. IMPROVISATION #6. THE "WHEN" ELEMENT.

Set up several improvisations in which people prepare to take a trip on a plane. Suggestions:

1. A girl learns her mother is seriously ill in another state and she makes arrangements to travel to her, including getting permission from her boss.
2. A Cuban exile has reasons to return to Cuba and plans to hijack the plane.
3. A TV comic, who is a "white knuckle flyer," must fly to fulfill an engagement.
4. A student is late for registration.
5. A bankrupt businessman looking for "greener fields."
6. A dignified matron impatient with delays.
7. A strike organizer.
8. An elderly foreign woman on her first flight.
9. A reporter for a national magazine on an assignment.
10. A couple on their honeymoon.
11. A rich, former cowboy star.

Once actors become facile at improvisation, they may wish to experiment further with the technique. Selected improvisational scenes may be combined into a collage, giving a total result which is somewhat different from the effect created by the parts. Perform each of the above improvisations singly and then do another in which all these people are waiting to board a jet at 4 A.M. Retain the characters and moods established in previous improvisations. The boarding gate will not be open for some time but the passengers cluster around the entrance hoping to have first choice of seats. As they wait they strike up conversations.

IMPROVISATION   39

1. Play an emotional scene without overt emotional display.
2. Create an improvisation which is in direct contrast to a soap-opera TV program. This will require two separate improvisations and casts. Play them in counterpoint.
3. A printing plant in which the actors improvise the noises and actions of machines. This may require a visit to an actual plant.
4. Choose a basically narrative description of some character from a famous novel. Reconstruct the narrative into an active or dramatic improvisation. Student should look, sound, and feel like the character. At a signal from the director, another actor takes over the characterization, then another, etc.

NOTE: Several actors should work on this problem so that all are prepared. They need not collaborate as in other improvisations.

5. *Character:* A tough, wounded Marine is being loaded into a helicopter.
6. Use banal dialogue, such as "Nice day," "What's doing?" "How'ya been?" etc., in—

   A. A dramatic situation.
   B. A comedy situation.
   C. A situation using characters which are recognizable, functional, predictable, or *one dimensional,* such as: Smokey the Bear, the Devil, St. Peter, Santa Claus, Pride, Sloth, etc.
   D. Now, use the same one-dimensional characters and give them some human attributes (*two dimensional*) in an improvisation which brings out such things as home life, disappointments, success, etc.
   E. Same characters in *three dimensions,* bringing out individual qualities, such as inner conflicts, background, psychological drives, all rooted in lifelike situations. Note how the posterlike simplicity of the one-dimensional characters disappears as they are complicated by individual human attributes. As a three-dimensional character, Santa Claus will seem unlike himself; proof enough that the charm of simple characters is in keeping with their simplicity.

7. A woman shoplifter being interrogated by a nearsighted desk sergeant.
8. An improvisation between Adam and the Creator, Noah and his sons, a girl and her alter ego, etc.
9. *Situation:* a freeway accident. Students create characters and improvise action and dialogue.
   Suggestions: argument, exchanging names and addresses and finding they know each other.
10. *Premise:* A series of mishaps caused by attempts to answer phone. May be used for different students portraying different characters. Begins in a bathtub. Phone rings, tries to reach towel— it falls in water. Phone continues ringing—decides to let it ring;

THE CREATIVE PROCESS

finally reaches for robe—slips on floor. Phone continues—wipes feet on bath mat which blocks door; struggles to force open door; while trying to dry self with robe, knocks over vase still trying to force door. Gets out, answers phone—and says "wrong number"—hangs up—gets back in tub and sighs with relief. Phone rings again.

11. Memorize the lines of a short scene from a play. Use the same inflections and tempo you would in speaking the author's lines but speak *gibberish* instead in the following characters:

  A. As two ghostly spirits (An amusing improvisation when done using two bed sheets).

  B. As two angels (use makeshift halos or wings).

  C. As two robots.

12. Adapt *colloquial speech* to a short scene from Shakespeare, using characters' names and situation.

SUGGESTIONS:

Nurse and Juliet from *Romeo and Juliet*, Act III, Scene ii.

Launce and dog from *Two Gentlemen of Verona*, Act II, Scene iii (use people as props and animals).

Hamlet and Polonius from *Hamlet*, Act II, Scene ii.

Taming of the Shrew, Introduction, Scene ii.

The most satisfactory way to create your own improvisations for special requirements, is to begin with *characters in a situation*. In this context we may define a *situation* as an incident or event in which characters are involved with each other or with outside forces. The types of characters which seem to work best in improvisations are those which relate to each other, to some object, or an idea, motivating them toward some goal or desire.

POINT OF FOCUS

Any object, event, or thought on which all players agree is the focal point of the improvisation. This point might be compared to the ball in a ball game on which all the players concentrate. People who improvise can never remind themselves too often, "Keep your eye on the point of focus." The established realities are stated in the problem, scene, or play—in other words, what is supplied to the actor by the author or idea. What is *not* stated must be supplied by the actor.

 NOTE: An improvisation should consist of a conflict and have *development*. It should never be planned so that it ends as it began. Some students have a proclivity for devising improvisations dealing with human suffering, frustration, and despair. Such experiences seem easier to remember than happier moments which we are more reluctant to share with others. But do so whenever possible, as they lift the spirit and encourage security in a player.

WALLY CHAPPELL'S IMPROVISATIONAL PROJECT FOR THE CENTER THEATRE GROUP OF LOS ANGELES PERFORMS FOR A SATURDAY MATINEE CROWD. (PHOTO BY STEVEN KEULL, COURTESY THE CENTER THEATRE GROUP.)

EXERCISE 35. IMPROVISATIONS #8

Suggestions for Characters

A person with a gambling problem
A person influenced by East Indian philosophy
An ambitious young music student
A brilliant but arrogant young student
A plain but wealthy young woman
A young married
A young mother
A bill collector

A person of ideals
A ranch hand
A perfume saleslady
A detective
A man hater
A teacher
A real estate agent
A sign painter

Suggestions for Situations

Select two of the above characters and involve them in one of the following situations:

—Undergo an experience that results in a change of viewpoint.
—Forsake cherished goals to carry out a moral duty.
—Seek a crafty way to avoid misfortune.
—Because annoyed by unwelcome attention from opposite sex, pretend to have a spouse.

THE CREATIVE PROCESS

—Become involved, through curiosity, in an unusual enterprise.

—Become implicated in an accident which has its bright side.

—Find an obligation at variance with pleasure or ambition.

—A threatening complication results from misjudgment.

—Seek revenge for a fancied wrong that proves baseless.

—Secretly hide another from danger.

—Happen upon an important secret which might endanger personal ambitions; a decision must be made.

—Become involved in a situation in which there seems no solution, but one is found accidentally.

—By involving himself in a risky situation, a shy young man proves heroic.

—Assume the personality of a criminal in a legitimate enterprise.

EXERCISE 36. IMPROVISATION #9. MORE SUGGESTIONS

Locations

A veterinary office	A boutique
A mental hospital	An elevator
A welfare office	A jewelry store
A drive-in movie	A gangster funeral
A Venetian ballroom	A pie bakery
in the 14th century	A free clinic
A weight-reducing gym	A fire
The Little Big Horn	A monkey house in a zoo

Characters

A bill collector	A cook
A photographer	A traveler
A dress designer	A police officer
A real estate agent	A travel agent
A teacher	A pilot

Situations

Shopping for a mattress

Making a date.

Pretending to be another.

Getting a license.

Being rescued or rescuing someone.

Becoming involved in a petty theft.

A jury attempting to reach a verdict.

Being late for an important appointment.

Informing a dying girl that no more can be done for her.

Talking to a hard-to-please lady at an employment agency.

Handling an irate customer.

IMPROVISATION

43

Apologizing for another you know to be wrong.
Becoming involved in a harmless act which could appear otherwise.
Two people trying to hide a fateful secret from the world.
Attempting to unravel mistaken identity without each other knowing.
Being impelled by unusual motives to engage in a crafty enterprise.
Undergoing an experience that results in character changes.
Applying for a job.
Conflicting personalities.
Experiencing love at first sight.

EXERCISE 37. IMPROVISATION #10

Perform an improvisation of:

1. A student is being teased about his girl by his pals.

Now make the following adaptations:

2. A young medieval boy in Italy is being teased about his girl by a group of boy friends.

EXERCISE 38. IMPROVISATION #11

Like the improvisation above, this one is in two parts:

1. A student-actress dresses for a dance.

Now make the following adaptations:

2. A fourteen-year-old girl in medieval Italy dresses for her first ball.

EXERCISE 39. IMPROVISATION #12. CHARACTERS

Several personalities are being interviewed on a talk show. After the moderator introduces each, he questions them about their work, their views on various topics, and asks about their future plans. Each student is to develop a complete character unlike himself. Suggestions:

1. A housewife who has invented something now on the market.
2. A European movie star
3. A black mayor
4. A student lawyer
5. A hillbilly who operates a still
6. A college professor who has just written a book on the feminist movement
7. A lady lobbyist from Washington
8. A housewife with a talking dog
9. An actress who has just opened in a play
10. An editor of a woman's magazine

THE CREATIVE PROCESS

IMPROVISATION AND PLAYWRITING

Improvisations are now used extensively in the creation of new plays for off-off Broadway production. In workshops, directors give "notions" to actors as a starting point. Later, these notions are solidified; the "author" uses paste pot and scissors to jigsaw them into plays. The results are not so much playtexts as pretexts for productions. Despite claims of originality, this technique for creating drama is not exactly fresh. Down through theatrical history, a great deal of drama has been created by actors using no scripts. Offhand, who can name the playwrights of the Commedia dell'Arte or, for that matter, the authors of the morality plays?

Several years before off-off Broadway, *A Hatful of Rain* was developed through improvisations. Joan Littlefield has been using improvisations for some time to produce such plays as *A Taste of Honey* and *Oh! What a Lovely War.* According to the "playwright," *Comings and Goings* was created by the actors as, "an enjoyment of technique, pure virtuosity on the part of the actors."

The Open Theatre, led by Joseph Chaikin, conducted improvisations on the book of Genesis and later performed these professionally under the title, *The Serpent.* Peter Brook's production of *US* and *Marat/Sade* owe much to improvisations.

There can be no doubt that, today, improvisations are the "in" thing. However, when improvisations are presented commercially as plays, there is the ever-present danger that actors will become involved with their own involvement, exposing a slipshod amateurism and self-indulgence. To hire a hall, to pay for the printing of tickets, to furnish lights and scenery, all require playing to more than a single audience and, therefore, repeating something that has been rehearsed, set, and completed — which is the exact opposite of improvisation.

FURTHER READING: IMPROVISATION

Hodgson, John and Richards, Ernest. *Improvisation, Discovery and Creativity in Drama.* London: Methuen. New York: Barnes & Noble, 1968.

Slade, Peter. *Experience of Spontaneity.* New York: Fernhill House Ltd., 1969.

Spolin, Viola. *Improvisation for the Theatre.* Evanston, Illinois: Northwestern University Press, 1963.

5 The Actor's Environment

The actor is the only man who goes onto a stage and knows he's lying. You go onstage to say something written by somebody else—and you may not believe him—but you transform these words into some strange kind of extraordinary truth. The actor never stops working. The painter doesn't, the writer doesn't, the artists don't. We're always watchful, always learning.*

Richard Burton

*From American Broadcasting Company television interview by ABC's Bob Young and Walter Wager, editor of Playbill. By permission.

DIFFERENT STAGES

A great majority of productions in high schools and colleges are mounted on proscenium stages. For nearly two hundred years plays have been written for and are most effectively staged upon it. These are the plays of realism; the audience is seated on one side of a raised platform and the actors and action are set within a frame. It is the theatre of curtains, borders, and wings. This was not always so. Early festivals and ceremonies in earlier cultures used a form much the same as the one we know today as open, arena, circus, environmental, theatre-in-the-round, space, circle, or center theatre. Another form now being used extensively is Shakespeare's thrust stage, in which the audience is seated on three sides of the stage.

Proscenium Staging

In this form, the actor is concerned with acting positions as indicated in the sketch.

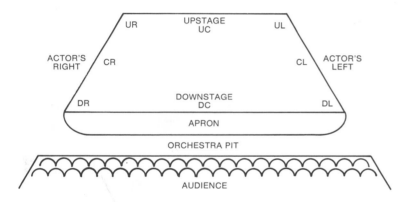

Study these positions until the terms are familiar to you: up left (UL), down center (DC), right center (RC), and a walk or cross (X). Up (U) stage and down (D) stage are so indicated because early stages were built on an incline to allow the audience an unblocked view of all actors, even those farthest away from them. And so we get the term "upstaging," which means to take unfair advantage of a fellow-player positioned downstage. Some such raked stages still exist, notably Piper's Opera House in Virginia City, Nevada. Directions such as *stage right* or *left* always indicate the actor's right or left as he faces the audience. *Onstage* means toward center while *offstage* indicates the periphery of the acting area.

EXERCISE 40. STAGE POSITIONS, PROSCENIUM

Acting is *doing*. You will remember these positions better if you get up on stage and take the following positions, keeping the placement of furniture in mind. Better yet, ask someone to read the directions as you walk them.

THE ACTOR'S ENVIRONMENT

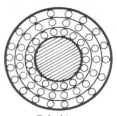

Primitive

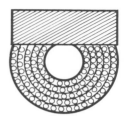

Greek

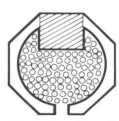

Elizabethan (Thrust)

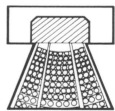

Proscenium

Circle or Arena

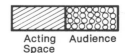

Acting Space   Audience

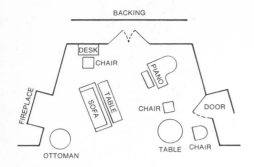

BACKING

DESK
CHAIR
PIANO
FIREPLACE
TABLE
SOFA
CHAIR
DOOR
OTTOMAN
TABLE
CHAIR

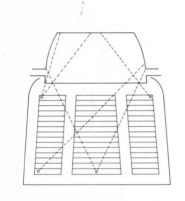

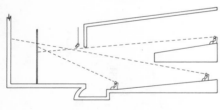

LINES OF SIGHT

Enter up right center (URC) from right (R).
Cross (X) down left (DL), open door and look out 3/4 left (L).
Cross (X) upstage center (USC) to piano and look in bench.
Cross (X) to desk up right (UR) to desk and search in it, full back.
Cross down right (CDR) to fireplace, stir fire.
Cross (X) below sofa to table at left (L).
Cross up right (XUR) to desk, pick up paper.
Turn up center (UC) to French windows.
Turn right (R) and left (L) to see offstage.
Cross down left (XDL) to small table down left (DL).
Sit upstage of table (T) looking at paper.
Cross downstage (XDS) of sofa to fireplace right (R).
Throw paper in fireplace.

Published plays catering to nonprofessionals frequently indicate stage directions in this code. More creative directors prefer to plan stage movements according to their interpretation of a play.

Lines of sight, Proscenium. Sight lines are imaginary lines indicating the audience's line of vision from different parts of the house. Scenery, props, and furniture are all arranged with these sight lines in mind, but the actors must also be conscious of them during preparatory rehearsals. Otherwise one actor can "cover" or "block" the audience's view of other actors or an important piece of business (usually some silent action important to the plot). Examples of stage business could be the opening of a letter, the lighting of a cigarette, or even a look. Stage business is frequently confused with stage movement. The latter is geographical whereas business is usually illustrative of a character. Following is an illustration of stage movement — when an actor's position is CL and he is playing a scene with someone at C, then his upstage (or right) foot should be a little before his left. This allows his body to be angled DS and gives the audience a good three-quarters view of his face and expression. Such positioning may not be important for modern plays, but for the classics it makes a considerable aesthetic difference.

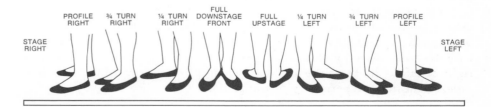

PROFILE RIGHT ¾ TURN RIGHT ¼ TURN RIGHT FULL DOWNSTAGE FRONT FULL UPSTAGE ¼ TURN LEFT ¾ TURN LEFT PROFILE LEFT

STAGE RIGHT
STAGE LEFT

Thrust Staging

Many acting positions for thrust staging remain the same as in proscenium except that visual dynamics are altered. The line parallel to the footlights is eliminated and players quite literally step out of the picture frame. On a thrust stage the actor is facing spectators on three sides, not one. Entrances and exits are often made by way of passages[1] from under the raised stage or seating area, in addition to proscenium entrances. Curtains or other scenic devices can be used at rear as scene dividers, however, a main curtain is seldom used on thrust stages. Lighting devices from the front are elaborate and are able to highlight certain scenes on various sections of the stage, leaving others in darkness in lieu of using curtains.

ARENA OR CENTER STAGING

In this type of theatre, actors are usually on a level with the audience or, as in the Arena Stage in Washington, D.C., the audience is seated on steeply banked rows of seats. In either case, the height of the acting area can be altered by the use of platforms. Actors can be "discovered at rise" less easily on the center than on the proscenium stage; but spotlights are often used for this purpose on center stages. The circular or four-sided arrangement must provide aisles which assume added duty as actor's entrances, exits, and sometimes even playing space. Lighting and support stands are not masked or concealed. They are accepted as part of the non-illusionary aspects of arena staging. It is necessary that scenery (usually only set pieces) and furniture be kept at a minimum because of the difficulty in making changes.

Actors find that more normal face-to-face positions are possible on this stage. Makeup and costumes must pass minute scrutiny and characterizations must be constantly maintained because of the proximity of the spectators. Stage positions and sight lines of the proscenium or thrust are useless on an arena stage. Positions for actors are usually designated as North, East, South, or West of center or are located by aisle numbers or numerals on a clock face. It might seem that more voice volume would be required on center stages but actors often find this is not so. Inactive characters are normally placed against set pieces or aisles where they will not block the view of the spectators. Actors working on an arena stage should consider their positions as part of a constantly changing series of movements, in which a dominant character moves to a central position, and supporting players to the periphery, of the circle. However, all moves should be the result of motivation; attitudes, moods, or reactions of the characters to what is happening in the play.

Formerly, arena and thrust stages were believed suitable only to the classics, the plays of Shakespeare, Molière, or the Greek poets, none of which were written to be played on a proscenium stage. But today all sorts of plays are produced on thrust or arena stages. These theatres are especially receptive to the new non-illusionary, more spectacular theatrical types, although plays by O'Neill and Pinter have also been given

[1]These passageways have the unattractive name, "Vomitoria."

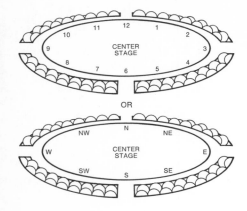

interesting arena productions. The actor's work on creating characters need not be affected by the technical adjustments he will want to make between performing on thrust, proscenium, or arena stages.

EXERCISE 41. EXPLORING ACTING SPACE

For groups contemplating the use of a center or thrust stage for the first time, it might be well to move now into the room which is to be used for performances. If at all possible, avoid rehearsing a space production on a proscenium stage.

1. Fill the acting area in geometrical patterns such as star, checkerboard, circle, etc. Move everyone into a tight circle at dead center, then spiral out in N.E.S.W. columns. Move out to periphery and back.
2. Try groups of three people just off center.
3. Walk everyone around the periphery clockwise; turn and reverse.
4. Play a scene which has previously been done on proscenium stage using exact movements.

Does it play as well in the new acting area?

What adjustments must be made for central or thrust staging?

STAGE ACTION

When actors are on stage they become part of an ever-changing, ever-moving stage picture. The objective is to convey the dramatic progression of a play *in movement*. Stage groupings are not still pictures but kinetic elements which flow from one to another. This action, however, must never seem mechanical, done just for the sake of motion, but must be properly motivated. *Invent for yourself some reason why your character moves to a particular position at a particular time, and be able to justify it should your director ask.*

Both director and actors must consider many reasons for moves to be made, and then select one that seems most expressive of the character and the play. The actor, then, is not moving out of a chair because he has been told to do so, or because the director thinks a scene has been static for too long. He is moving because he is so motivated. By justifying each move, the actor adds to his characterization and to the interrelationships between characters. Moving, speaking, reacting, are the results of a living response to continuous thought process and the use of improvisations.

In rehearsing isolated scenes, actors are not afforded an opportunity to experience the natural flow of an entire play. Nor are they able to test their ability to sustain the effort necessary when playing a long part. Instead, they become accustomed to concentrating and expending physical energies for only a short period.

Nevertheless, it is hardly possible that every rehearsal can be a complete run-through. Certain scenes will need more time and special attention than others. A rehearsal may include working on various scenes throughout the play *but you must always keep in mind the location of these scenes and how they fit into the development of the entire play,* for that is the way an audience will experience them and not as isolated scenes. An opening scene of narrative and character exploration will not require the speed, the intensity, of a scene near the climax. The playwright has made an effort to keep interest rising by disclosing situations in careful steps, one scene growing progressively out of the preceding one and in relation to it.

Audience Focus

The most important consideration for arrangements of characters on stage is to identify the proper focus for an audience. Principal characters in a play have a great deal more to say than others because they are the chief means of communicating the story to an audience. Obviously, such characters, with important scenes, should be placed in dominant positions because the audience has more interest in them.

Such positioning should never be made into old-fashioned groupings or "stage pictures." Actors should never be considered as solid mass but as unfettered action forces—stasis must become kinesis.

THE ACTOR'S ENVIRONMENT

Also, for an actor, it is much better to be in the right position on stage when delivering an important line, speech, or piece of business. If he isn't, he will need to use all his ingenuity to produce the same effect.

Entrances and Exits

The mechanics of getting into or out of a room should not be the primary concern of an actor playing a part. It is one of the few things we do onstage as we do offstage. Different characters enter and exit in different ways depending on "the moment" or the dramatic atmosphere of the scene. The mood of the character as he enters or leaves a stage is important, just as what has happened previously and what is about to happen to him are important.

Avoid long walks when leaving the stage. They are seldom dramatic. Something else should be happening to cover your exit. To break up a long walk, divide up your last speeches and take a few steps between, so that you are near the door for your final lines. There are times, however, when a long silent walk is effective, especially at the end of a scene or act.

Stage Balance

It is considered one of the actor's responsibilities to balance the stage, that is, he must be sure that he is neither covering others nor being blocked from the view of the audience by other actors. Also the clustering of too many characters on one side of the stage is very disturbing for the audience. The term "dressing" is used when this happens.

A director has every right to expect an advanced student to be aware of stage balance and be able to "dress" when other actors move. If you visualize the lines of sight as shown in the illustration on page 48, you are not apt to hear the director shouting from the house, "Dress the stage!" In this instance, the director means that the actor is to move out, break up the huddle—but always by inventing some proper motivation for so doing.

EXERCISE 42. STAGE BALANCE

a. Four people group in a half-circle, facing front. Student at center reads an interesting speech while others concentrate on the reader, except that one of the four has previously been instructed to hedge back on a certain word in the speech.

This demonstrates how an audience's attention can be lost by an apparently innocuous move.

b. Now place the reader downstage right (DSR) with the other four players upstage (USR) right. Note how the attention is lost by the imbalance.

c. Now place the reader at left upstage (USL) with the others downstage right (DSR).

Pauses

Pauses are a valuable tool for any actor. Perhaps "stillness" would be a more descriptive term, for it indicates that such moments are creative rather than just silent intervals. There are many such moments in that fine thriller, *Dial M for Murder,* but these stillnesses advance the plot with action, even though silently.

In Stanislavski's prompt book for his production of *The Lower Depths,* pauses are indicated by plus signs. He used these not only to indicate beats between speeches, but even between words of dialogue spoken by different characters. Such pauses are like rests in music. An actor may suggest where he feels pauses should be made but the final decision rests with the director who is out front and has an overall view of the entire production.

Silences are not necessarily dead pauses in which all dramatic action stops. They often indicate that characters are trying to remember something or trying to reach a decision. Such pauses really sustain the drama, add to the characterizations, and are often more effective than dialogue. This is especially true in plays by Harold Pinter, who has become known for them.

Even in films, the pause is important. Film star Glenn Ford has said, "I don't think a good director should get nervous when there's a bit of silence. Some directors think that there's nothing going on if you're not talking all the time. But many times the silences are more eloquent than talk. They are moments when the audience can do the acting. I'm not trying to get out of work, but in a good silent scene, all the talking can take place in the audience's heads."[2]

(PHOTO OF GLENN FORD COURTESY OF JMK PUBLIC RELATIONS.)

EXERCISE 43. PAUSES

Choose a speech from a favorite play, and mark a plus sign where you intend to pause, either for meaning or dramatic intent. Read it aloud or better yet memorize the speech and the pauses, and ask your class to listen to it.

Timing

When a ball is thrown toward you, there is an instant when you must gauge the distance and coordinate your muscles to catch it; you learn how to catch the ball by practice and instinct. It is the same with timing on stage, for timing represents a personal interpretation of deviations from a measured beat. It involves the actor's instinct for understanding the propitious moment to be silent or to speak. This instinctive reaction can be different at each performance because no two audiences are alike. The

[2]Digby Diehl, "The Western Today," *TV Guide,* April 1, 1972, p. 23. Reprinted with permission from *TV Guide*® Magazine. Copyright © 1972 by Triangle Publications, Inc. Radnor, Pennsylvania.

THE ACTOR'S ENVIRONMENT

ability to anticipate audience response is an instinct, especially in a completely inexperienced player. Some actors are born with a fine sense of timing; others must learn it by long exposure to different audiences. Comedians know that timing is instinctive, but some have learned it first mechanically, by counting beats. As an example, here are a few lines from Oscar Wilde's *The Importance of Being Earnest:*

EXERCISE 44. TIMING

LADY BRACKNELL	—are your parents still living?
JACK	I have lost both my parents.
LADY BRACKNELL	Both? [one-two-three] That seems like carelessness.

STAGE FRIGHT

Stage fright is the occupational disease of all speakers and actors. The better the actor, the more sensitive he is and the more susceptible to emotion. Callous actors are seldom very good actors; they lack the means to transmit emotion to an audience.

"Opening night jitters" are usually evidenced by poor eye contact, rapid heartbeat, constriction of muscles, a tremor in the voice and hands, a hollow feeling in the stomach, dry mouth, lack of coordination, and a marked loss of skill. We had best accept the malady as being common to all and try to work out some treatment.

First of all, remember that to be concerned, to care, is healthy. But if an actor cares too deeply, he develops fear and becomes insecure, tense, anxious, a condition in which he cannot function and certainly cannot create.

Some actors think of an opening night audience as a monster with a thousand heads. To help alleviate their fears, they might better think of the audience as human beings exactly like themselves who are willing, even eager, to communicate with the actors.

One of the most common causes of stage fright is lack of preparation. Self-confidence is dependent upon a sense of personal adequacy to meet the situation. Be positive that you are properly prepared, that you know your lines and your character. Focus on that character, never on yourself. Fear is the lack of knowledge. Walk into a strange dark room and you are apprehensive but if the room is your own dark room, you have no fear. You know the room even though you cannot see.

Stage fright can be diminished by narrowing your point of focus, blocking out all but your first words or the immediate scene to be played.

The sincere student will also seize every opportunity to appear before an audience no matter whether at an audition or at a lecture where he just asks a question from the floor. An actor must learn to be at ease before the public, and this can only be accomplished by practice.

THEATRE RELATIONSHIPS

The Actor and His Audience

Leslie Howard once said that acting was part audience and part actor, and that the combination was a "sublime communion." A play is not a play until it is played before an audience, and an actor is not acting until he is in contact with his audience: otherwise he is merely rehearsing. An audience is much more than a group of spectators. It is part of the team that makes theatre.

In order to better understand what makes up an audience, let us imagine a group of pedestrians walking along a street. They have no common interest at the moment, no focus of attention. Now suppose that a car stops at the curb; and it is a new and long-awaited model. All eyes focus on the car and everyone begins discussing it. From individual pedestrians, the group has now changed into an audience. Psychologists consider an audience an entity because of common interests.

A phenomenon of the actor-audience relationship, and a most important consideration for the actor, is the "feedback" or response. The actor communicates with the audience and, in turn, the audience responds by visible or audible means. This response, in turn, stimulates the actor to greater endeavor. It is a kind of circular game, and the ball is communication. An actor communicates with his audience in three ways: first, by gesture and movement of his body; then, audibly by his voice; and third, by emotion.

How does an actor create rapport with the audience? Most of all, he must convince the audience of his sincerity, but it is not so important *that the actor believes* what he is acting. The vital thing is that *the audience believes* everything the actor does on a stage.

An actor can learn a great deal about acting from an audience. It can show him where he has misjudged certain lines or scenes. It can even show him errors in his characterization and interpretation of the character. It can reveal entire vistas of development he never realized in his character and the play.

The highest-rated TV shows are now filmed when the cast is performing before a live audience, evidence of the vital importance of this actor-audience relationship.

The Actor and the Director

"There is something incomparably intimate and productive in the work with the actor entrusted to me," writes the great Polish director, Jerzy Grotowski. "He [the actor] must be attentive and confident and free, for our labor is to explore his possibilities to the utmost. His growth is attended by observation, astonishment, and desire to help; my growth is projected into him or, rather, is found in him and our common growth becomes a revelation—what is achieved is a total acceptance of one human being for another."[3]

Grotowski's point that the attitude between actors and director should be that of fellow-inquirers, is well taken. An introductory period of discovery is needed by both director and actors. The reason for this is to create a provocative, problematic climate in which the actor can understand his character by developing concepts and relationships within himself. This intuitive search into characterization often begins with only the smallest clue. Ideally, the director will stir the actor's imagination into an understanding of the character before any attempt is made to act it. Justification for a character's behavior is the responsibility of both director and actor. The director's further responsibility is to relate all characterizations to his visualization of the production as a whole. Imagination is creative only when controlled and directed toward some goal.

Both actors and the director should try to avoid stereotypes and stock responses. Beginning with a feeling of the play and its milieu, the actions and motivations of the characters are then reflected in a plausible and meaningful way. The search should be concentrated upon subtle and explicit reasons as given in the play for the behavior of characters. The problem of the actor-director relationship then becomes one of utilizing this knowledge in the actor's creation of a characterization. Different directors may use various methods of procedure:

The Physical Approach
Instinctive
Positive
Arrive at emotion and characterization by first reproducing physical acts.

The Emotional Approach
Memory recall
Comparison of similar experiences

Demonstration
This method is seldom used today. Great directors of the past used it—Molière, Reinhart, George M. Cohan—but they were also fine actors. Few directors are competent enough actors to demonstrate how to play a scene to an actor.

An actor who is fortunate enough to work with a director of sensitivity and experience is bound to improve, as many ideas generate from such a collaboration. A good director will not only serve the actor but will become a sounding board for ideas. He will be the actor's audience when there is no other. Stage and screen actor, Peter Falk, has a somewhat different idea of the director-actor relationship. "Actors make their own performances," he says. "The director can make a contribution.

(PHOTO OF PETER FALK COURTESY OF UNIVERSAL TV, PUBLICITY DEPARTMENT, AND ROBINSON ASSOCIATES.)

[3]Jerzy Grotowski, *Towards a Poor Theatre* (Denmark: Odin Teatrets Forlag, 1968), p 25. Copyright © 1968 Jerzy Grotowski and Odin Teatrets Forlag.

THE CREATIVE PROCESS

Certainly he's got to provide the right atmosphere—that's number one. You gotta get rid of tension. You gotta get rid of insecurity."[4]

The Actor and Other Actors

In the preparation of a play, there is usually a kind of camaraderie among those involved, and especially among cast members. Unfortunately, petty jealousies sometimes cause friction and should not be allowed to continue or the morale of the entire company will suffer.

Each member of the cast should be instilled with a pride in the company as a whole. There should be a spirit of cooperation and an eagerness to help each other. A "good trouper" has pride in the work of all his fellow-players.

Ensemble playing means playing together. Listen to another actor when he has most of the lines. Acting is reacting as much as acting. There are defensible current theories that it is *re-acting* which most interests an audience. Watch TV dramas; an actor speaks a line to another, and then quickly you see a close-up of the other actor, showing his reaction to what has been said.

In Louis Calvert's book, *Problems of an Actor,* he tells of a leading man who said to the villain of the play, "That was a good hand I got tonight, wasn't it?" The villain replied, "That was a good hand *we* got, yes." The hero bristled, "You had nothing to do with it, it's *my* scene!" At the next performance, the villain refused to react when the hero denounced him, and there was no response from the audience. The actor-hero was forced to admit that a denunciation scene is no good unless the one being denounced reacts.

No matter how childlike, egocentric, and mad actors may seem, there is always within them a consciousness of belonging to an ancient order. In order to join, a ritual of self-sacrifice has been followed, unspoken vows have been solemnized, even another language has been learned. True, the actor is often ambitious for himself and envious of another's success—but beyond this there is always a pride and an awareness that all actors are kin.

Over the years they worked together, Alfred Lunt and his actress-wife, Lynn Fontanne, developed an effect that sounded amazingly like extemporaneous conversation. "Cues," in the ordinary sense, were disregarded. They frequently spoke simultaneously but, always, important words or phrases were heard.

One of the values of ensemble was nicely put by the late Sir Tyrone Guthrie:

> *An interplay between two actors, by the exchange of looks and subtleties of vocal color and of rhythm can only occur when two imaginative actors react to suggestions of the other's performance, when they create and feel their scenes together.*[5]

[4]Dick Hobson, "America Discovers Columbo," *TV Guide,* March 25, 1972, p. 30.
[5]Tyrone Guthrie, *In Various Directions* (New York: Macmillan, 1965), p. 106.

EXERCISE 45. ENSEMBLE #1

A coiled rope is thrown into the air, high above the group. The shape it takes when landing on the floor is then used by the group as a pattern for freely inventing attitudes, or ideas. Each time the rope is thrown a new arrangement is created by the group.

What might these groupings convey to an audience?

EXERCISE 46. ENSEMBLE #2

Your entire group is in a subway car, jostling each other and swaying with the movement of the car. At intervals, the train stops, passengers get off and others get on. Some sit and stare, others listen or join in conversations—or resent them.

The object of this exercise is *physical human contact*. See what comes of it.

EXERCISE 47. ENSEMBLE #3

Here is another exercise Peter Brook uses to show the possibilities of ensemble playing and the results of sensitivity training.

Select a phrase of some ten or fifteen words from a well-known speech. One word is given to each actor. Standing in a circle with hands joined, they speak the words one after another until the entire speech flows and sounds like living speech.

EXERCISE 48. ENSEMBLE #4

In life, we are all affected by contacts with others and often such contact modifies our behavior, even our personalities. Characters in plays also often change through contact with other characters. Improvise:

1. A boy (or girl) in his father's office trying to get an increase in his allowance.
2. Outside, the boy meets a teacher or a boy friend and is negative about the increase.
3. Then, at a malt shop with his girl, he is positive and cheery about the increase.

How does each affect the boy? He acts—they re-act—and he re-acts from that. How?

Learning Lines

The task of memorizing lines seems of some concern to inexperienced actors. Under ideal conditions, lines should not be memorized before completely understanding the role. Many decisions, which must be made can alter the learning process. Lines may be changed or cut; if they have been learned, it becomes necessary to unlearn them and then to relearn the alterations, a difficult thing to do.

Here are some points or learning aids which might be considered in memorization.

1. The visual
2. The aural
3. The kinetic
4. The interpretive

It would be extremely difficult to learn lines by sight alone. The *sounds* of words and phrases must be *heard* to register in the memory. One might study by reading, only to find that when on stage the lines have vanished. Actors refer to this as "bedroom perfect." The kinetic component refers to learning lines by their relationship to action. The interpretive is often the means by which most actors stamp in the lines indelibly. But by whatever means the actor learns lines, once the memory is functioning, the method of doing so can then be eliminated, leaving the mind and emotions free to cope with more immediate problems.

A few misguided actors delay learning their lines, using the excuse that they must understand the play, the character, or the director's plans before doing so. Frequently this is just an excuse for lack of interest or just plain laziness. *Once the director orders that all lines are to be memorized by a certain time, there must be no procrastination on the part of actors.*

In film and TV production, the actor is required to memorize lines before he appears on the sound stage, perhaps without ever meeting the director or the other actors with whom he will be working. This kind of memorization is extremely difficult and the actor must develop some kind of system that enables him to remember the whole sequence. Sometimes he can find key words that form a pattern he can remember; at other times, he assigns a letter or a number to each thought and then remembers the thoughts in proper sequence by referring to this code. The associative method is not at all ideal and is used only when necessary. When lines are memorized in this way, it takes a great deal of ingenuity during shooting to make them seem natural.

EXERCISE 49. MEMORY

Choose one of the phrases below and explain to your group all of the details as you remember them.

1. A scent of perfume or cologne
2. A funny school photograph
3. An old familiar tune
4. Reminiscing with an old friend
5. New Year's Eve
6. Your first dance
7. Your first date
8. Your earliest remembrance as a child

Some Responsibilities of the Actor

There should never be any noise or horseplay backstage or in the dressing rooms. The theatre is an ancient and respected place. Show the same decorum here as you would in a library or church. Discipline is a very important word in the theatre. Self-discipline is equally important to the individual actor.

One of the rules of theatre is that an actor does not go into the audience section during performances. An actor in costume and makeup greeting friends in the lobby, during or after a performance, is the sure mark of the glory-seeking amateur. Get out of makeup and costume as quickly as possible and then wait backstage for your friends. Tell them beforehand, "Please come backstage to the dressing room after the performance."

Make it a habit to check the bulletin board (or as it is called in the profession, the callboard) before and after each performance or rehearsal. It is the company's newspaper and lawgiver.

The stage manager, or his assistant, calls out terms that let the actors know how much time there is before the curtain goes up. When any of the following are called out individually—"half-hour," "fifteen minutes," "five minutes," "places," or "beginners, first act"—you can gauge the time you have to spend with makeup and costume preparations. When the call boy knocks on your dressing-room door, calls your name, and gives you the time, answer him with a "thank you." Your response is the only way he can check whether or not you are present and getting ready. Some playhouses require that actors sign in before the half-hour. If an actor has not signed in or phoned by that time, then his understudy is made ready.

The Actor and His Costumes. Costumes should be thought of as clothes, not costumes. If you throw your clothes on the floor or crumple them on chairs, it is time you learned better. Always hang up your costumes. Remember, it is to your advantage that you look as well as possible while on stage. If your boots are dusty, polish them; if your costume blouse is soiled, ask that it be cleaned or get permission to clean it yourself. It is this kind of attention to detail that makes the difference between the ordinary and extraordinary actor.

The Actor and His Makeup. Many nonprofessionals do not realize that the purpose of makeup is to compensate for the washing-out effect of stage lighting on natural skin colors. Makeup should never *look* like makeup, except in nonrealistic stylized productions (where it serves a planned purpose). In most amateur and professional productions, it is the actor's responsibility to design and apply his own makeup. In films and TV, this job is done by professional makeup artists. When the actor is left to his own devices, he should study the subject of makeup carefully. There is not space in this book to cover this elaborate subject which could, and

RICHARD BURTON IN COSTUME.

THE CREATIVE PROCESS

has, been a book in itself. Usual errors in applying makeup are wrong color base, inexpert lining, and failure to apply crepe hair properly.

FURTHER READING: THE ACTOR'S ENVIRONMENT

Different Stages

Boyle, Walden. *Central and Flexible Staging.* Los Angeles: University of California Press, 1956.

Jones, Margo. *Theatre-in-the-Round.* New York: Harper, 1951.

Joseph, Steven. *New Theatre Forms.* New York: Theatre Arts Books, 1959.

Marshall, Norman. *The Producer and the Play,* rev. ed. London: Macdonald, 1962.

Southern, Richard. *Proscenium and Sight Lines.* London: Faber & Faber, 1939.

Stage Fright

Bergler, Edmund. "On Acting and Stage Fright," *Psychiatric Quarterly Suppl.* 23 (1949): 313-319.

Clevenger, T., Jr., "A Synthesis of Experimental Research in Stage Fright," *Quarterly Journal of Speech* 45 (1959): 134-145.

Defosses, Beatrice. *Your Voice and Speech: Self Training for Better Speaking.* New York: Hill & Wang, 1959. (Part I aims at developing confidence in the beginning speaker and overcoming stage fright.)

Audiences

Abernathy, Elton. *The Advocate, A Manual of Persuasion.* New York: David McKay, 1964. Chapter 6, pp. 118-125.

Smith, Raymond G. *Principles of Public Speaking.* New York: Ronald Press, 1958. Good section on audience analysis.

Memory

Filloux, Jean-Claude. *Memory and Forgetting.* New York: Walker & Co., 1949.

Young, Morris Walter Gibson. *How to Develop an Exceptional Memory.* Philadelphia: Chilton, 1962.

Costumes

Barton, Lucy. *Historic Costume for the Stage.* Boston: Walter H. Baker, 1940. Gives patterns made from authentic period clothes.

Brooke, Iris. *Costumes in Greek Classical Drama.* New York: Theatre Arts Books, 1962.

Corey, Irene. *The Mask of Reality, An Approach to Design for the Theatre.* Kentucky: Anchorage Press, 1968.

Dabney, Edith and Wise, Carl W. *A Book of Drama Costumes.* New York: Appleton-Century-Crofts, 1935.

Gorsline, Douglas. *What People Wore.* New York: Viking Press, 1952. Clothes of the American West.

Hansen, Henry Harald. *Costumes and Styles.* New York: Dutton, 1956.
"Motley." *Designing and Making Stage Costumes.* London: Studio Vista Ltd., 1964.

Makeup

Corson, Richard. *Stage Makeup.* New York: Appleton-Century Crofts, 1960.
Liszt, Rudolph. *The Last Word in Makeup.* New York: Dramatists Play Service, 1959.
Max Factor Studios, Hollywood, Calif., publishes nine booklets on makeup at 15¢ each. Write for list of subjects.

Building Your Own Acting Method

You are playing Othello, you give it all you've got. The author says to you, "You've given it all you've got? Good! You've done that? Fine. Now, more! More! M-O-R-E!" And your heart and your guts and your brain are pulp, and the part feeds on them. Acting great parts devours you. Great parts are cannibals.*

Laurence Olivier

*Interview with Laurence Olivier by Kenneth Harris, Los Angeles *Times*, Calendar, March 2, 1969. Reprinted by permission of the Observer Foreign News Service. (Photo shows Laurence Olivier in the film version of the National Theatre of Great Britain Production of *Othello*. Courtesy of British Home Entertainment, Ltd.)

It has already been said that, too often, students begin the study of acting by performing small scenes from plays when, in fact, they are ill-prepared to cope with the many problems which arise in creating a characterization. There is little growth in this. You've got to get down to the basics. Acting needs a planned and structured approach, a sequential study beginning with flexing acting muscles on exercises, getting to know the tools with which you will work and this begins by respecting yourself, the work done in class, and your fellow-students' attempts to improve. An actor lives on dedication to his work.

Assuming that you have benefited from the exercises given thus far, we can now approach other matters which are more complicated. In this chapter, we start using some tools with which you can eventually build your own acting method—concentration, observation, imagination, the creation of atmosphere, the use of gestures, mimicry, rhythm and self-discipline. And as we know, these will require beginning with a relaxed body and a free mind.

CONCENTRATION

Do you remember how, as a child, you used a magnifying glass to concentrate the sun's rays until they burned a hole in paper? An actor needs that sort of concentration. In today's world we live in an atmosphere of distractions: traffic noises, telephones, sirens, the news, and our own private jitters over the future. And as a result, many of us are simply losing our powers of concentration.

However, you cannot *will* yourself to concentrate any more than you can will yourself to relax. Concentration is like listening on a telephone. You must give it your undivided attention; any small distraction certainly destroys your point of focus. Think of boredom as the opposite of concentration. A toothache is an organism's signal for attention and concentration. Even such a simple everyday act as picking up a fork at dinner is a highly concentrated process, involving observation (sight and sound), stimuli (desire), and many muscles of the body. With proper concentration, an actor will always listen intently to what a fellow-player is saying and react to what has been said. With proper concentration, an actor develops what has been called "public meditation." It has been said that British star Paul Scofield concentrates so completely that he even asks for a prompt in character. The depth of absorption an actor needs is almost impossible to describe in words, but the following exercise may impress you with the sort of concentration you should give your work at rehearsals and performances.

EXERCISE 50. CONCENTRATION #1 (GROUP)

We need a chair placed in the center of the room, and six volunteers to help in the demonstration.

THE CREATIVE PROCESS

One person sits in the chair facing front, the other five stand in a semicircle around the chair. The seated player reads aloud some material, and it must be read intelligently.

Other players try to distract him in any way possible, except by physical contact. After one minute, the player standing at the reader's left takes the seat, and the former reader takes his place standing at right. This exercise continues until all players have had their minute in the "hot seat." The class will decide which player was best able to concentrate and read most intelligently.

EXERCISE 51. CONCENTRATION #2

1. Fix your eyes on some focal point such as the reflection of your own eyes when looking into a full-length mirror. Hold this concentration without blinking for as long as possible.
2. The game of Indian wrestling is also effective in developing eye-to-eye contact and concentration. Watching an adversary's eyes for signs of weakness makes a good Indian wrestler.

OBSERVATION

Human nature is one of the actor's most important studies. Experienced actors give it more attention than do beginners. "If there's unhappiness around you, you're likely to be observing it rather than feeling it directly," Sir John Gielgud says. "You constantly catch yourself trying to study how people really feel emotion. . . . If I see a bad accident, I watch the expressions on the faces of people. The dramatic side of every emotional experience seems to be always first with the actor. You jot it down. When you see somebody dead for the first time, you can't resist making notes of the way you yourself feel."[1]

As you study and observe character, use your imagination of course, but always build on what you have actually seen and felt.

(PHOTO OF JOHN GIELGUD COURTESY INTERNATIONAL FAMOUS ARTISTS.)

EXERCISE 52. OBSERVATION #1

As a beginning, describe orally to the class someone you know without giving names.

EXERCISE 53. OBSERVATION #2

Go to a park, an airport, or hotel lobby, anyplace where you can sit quietly and concentrate as you observe people. You may find that one particular person intrigues you more than others. Ask yourself questions about this individual and then answer them from your imagination. Ask yourself why this particular person caught your eye. Try to decide what makes this person tick. Why does he (or she) behave this way? What are his goals in life? What is he like

[1] © 1962 Lillian Ross. From *The Player, A Profile of an Art*, by Lillian Ross and Helen Ross, Simon and Schuster. Originally published in *The New Yorker*.

inside? When you return to class, don't describe what you have observed but act a character you have created from your observation and imagination.

Academy award nominee, Walter Matthau, often wanders about anonymously in large groups. He favors cafeterias. "I love the chance it gives me to browse around in people's external behavior. I can look around as much as I like. Not that you ever imitate people as such. But you get the feel and the smell and the taste of how they behave. I soak that up wherever I am. Then, when I'm onstage, I use it."[2]

EXERCISE 54. IN "SEEING"

Just how accurate is your ability to see—and remember? Most of us overestimate the efficiency of our imagery. In truth, our memory of what we have seen is sometimes vague, hazy, and often inaccurate. The actor must be scrupulously observant. He must be able to view a scene or see a fleeting gesture and remember it in every detail.

> Study the letters in the square. Take your time. Be sure you can see it in your mind's eye, that you have impressed each letter in your brain and left an impression there.

S J A O
H I N T
W T F P
G S O A

> Have you got it? All right, cover the figure, and don't uncover it. Now close your eyes and "read" the letters from that image in your mind. That's easy, isn't it? Close your eyes again and read the letters *diagonally*, first right to left, then left to right. That's another matter, isn't it? You have learned the letters by rote. You haven't really "seen" the entire square; if you had, the visual image would be complete and you would be able to read it from any direction with equal ease and speed.

IMAGINATION

Some students are blessed with vivid imaginations. In others this quality must be cultivated, *and it can be done.* Imagination is not something vague and mysterious; the dictionary tells us that it is "the picturing power or act of the mind; the constructive or creating faculty." Isn't everyone born with that? Even some animals demonstrate the faculty of imagining. Have you ever watched a cat playing with an imaginary mouse? That cat was creating something out of memory, instinct, and imagination.

Certainly all children possess imagination. They live in a world where the real is not separated from the imagined. A child doesn't lie; he is as innocent of deception as he is of truth. When she was four years old, actress Sandy Duncan had a friend she named Ann Puffenfuffer. The friend did not exist, except in Sandy's fantasy. She would walk and talk with Ann; when Sandy asked her mother for a glass of water, she wanted

[2]Ibid., p. 422.

THE CREATIVE PROCESS

another for Ann. One day her mother asked Sandy, "Whatever happened to Ann? You don't talk about her anymore." "She's dead," Sandy said flatly. "A car hit her."[3]

When a salesman plans what he will say to a customer he intends to visit, he is creating an imaginary conversation in an unreal time and place. Then why do we need to develop imagination? Because it interferes with our mature goals of reality and materialism. By adulthood, many of us have literally trained ourselves out of imagination. An actor needs to revive that childlike approach to pretending. The purpose of cultivating an active imagination in the actor is to give him a solid experience of living in a situation. Then, when he is called upon to create a character, he will feel the atmosphere of the play and become emotionally involved in it.

Creative talents need constant developing. Daydreams are imaginative but they are not creative. In order to transform wishes into creative activity, we need to concentrate, to remember clearly, to analyze, and then to visualize the new or to construct the new on the old.

EXERCISE 55. IMAGINATION #1

1. Perform some simple everyday function, first as you would do it as you are; then, pretend you are four inches smaller — taller — twenty pounds heavier — forty years older.
2. Tell a simple story; now add some physical infirmity — for example, you are crippled or have just been shot.

EXERCISE 56. IMAGINATION #2 PEOPLE PUPPETS

Puppets are built to perform certain bodily tasks. Each is an individual. A clown puppet is made loose jointed so that he can assume ridiculous postures, while a ballerina is made to move slowly and gracefully.

Design a puppet character for yourself and perform a short action. Remember to be constantly aware of the strings from above controlling you. A puppet walks by having his knee strings pulled up, gestures are made by moving strings on the wrist, while strings from the right and left shoulders carry most of the puppet's weight. At the back is one string that enables it to bend over and sit.

In the Motel scene of the award-winning *America Hurrah!* the cast of characters are all marionettes.)

EXERCISE 57. POINT OF FOCUS

There is a letter on a table. The table may be anywhere, any time, any place, but such details must be communicated. The character may be any person the student wishes, but must be shown *visually* because there is no speech, only pantomime.

[3]*Arnold Hano, "Funny Face," TV Guide,* September 18, 1971. Reprinted with permission of *TV Guide*® magazine. Copyright © 1971 by Triangle Publications, Inc. Radnor, Pennsylvania.

Each student performs solo, in character, while others serve as his or her audience. The only essential is that the letter be read and some reaction shown. It is a situation, a crisis, funny or sad. Concentrate upon that letter. It is the point of focus; then you must show a reaction. What is the size of the imaginary letter? Is it typed, handwritten, or what? Is it from a man or a woman? What does it say? Show us by your reaction.

It is an advantage to the student-actor if he learns quickly that there is a vast difference between what he *thinks he is showing an audience and what the audience actually sees and understands.* In the discussions afterwards, the observers explain what they understood and then the performer tells *what he intended to show.* In this exercise it is impossible to judge the effectiveness of the actor's work unless we know what he thought he was doing.

EXERCISE 58. IMAGINATION AND COMMUNICATION

Collect an assortment of objects from an attic or rummage sale. These should be items of clothing or accessories, *personal things* once owned and used by people. Each player examines the pack and selects an object that stimulates his imagination. The player imagines the sort of person who once used it—his intellectual, emotional, and physical attributes. He decides how this person thought, felt, and moved. As each player feels prepared, he assumes the fancied character, using improvised words or only silent action. The others should guess occupation, age, mentality, and emotional attitudes of the created character.

If you find that others have either not understood the character or misinterpreted it, figure out how you can improve your communication to clarify your meaning.

CREATION OF ATMOSPHERE OR MOOD

This important ingredient of theatre is the responsibility of both director and actor. An individual actor can create his own mood which can later be incorporated into the general atmosphere of the play, as the director desires. Let's try creating some without words.

EXERCISE 59. CREATING MOODS (GROUP)

A. (1) Class exercise. Improvise mood and action only. A crowd of mourners is returning from a funeral on a bright sunny day. (2) The same, but a dark rainy day.
B. Improvise mood and action only: A discouraged and weary woman tries to do her housework in her dreary walk-up flat located on the lower east side, New York City. Her son enters with news that he has a job.
C. Improvise the mood and action of a street scene on the Rialto in Venice, Italy, during the Middle Ages. Remember the costumes and the mores of that civilization.

THE CREATIVE PROCESS

D. Improvise mood and action only for a situation set on an isolated island in the South Seas. You are in a tin-roofed, general store and it has been raining for days. The heat is unbearable. Convey this to the class.

E. Improvise mood and action only: You are in the performer's tent of a small European circus. This is where the performers take a last minute check before "going on." Clowns are testing props, athletes are limbering up, and the owner and his wife are bustling about among equestrians, strong men, etc. Offstage, we hear the announcer and the circus band (use a recording). A stranger enters and stands silently at one side. Slowly, and one by one, they turn to him. After a moment of wonder, the owner walks to the stranger.

F. Improvise dialogue and action: A wife is being angrily harangued by her husband for something she has done, but behind this anger is the lifetime of unhappiness she has caused him. She sits quietly watching him, bristling with hate. The husband is in a wheelchair, a very sick man. His fury brings on one of his frequent heart attacks. He attempts to take medicine but spills it, and cries out for her to bring him another bottle from upstairs. She does not move; she actually wills him to die. He manages to crawl to the stairs crying out for help from the servants. Still she does not move. Create the atmosphere of the old South, the heat, the characters, and the inner conflicts.

G. Improvise dialogue and action: A family is leaving the home where they have spent most of their lives. The younger members and their friends look to the future. They gather luggage and clothing; their concern is to catch the train into the new life in the city. Their mother moves about the room where she leaves so many memories. The objects each remind her of the years she has lived among them. Finally, when everyone leaves, the old servant appears, having decided he will stay here with the past.

H. Improvise dialogue and action: An old janitor and his wife are no longer capable of facing the reality of their depressing lives, so they invent a reality based on their dreams. The couple act out a grand party where they are hosts to distinguished guests. The most important person in the world will address the gathering. They prepare the room for his speech, gathering chairs before greeting imaginary guests. When all is settled, the speaker arrives—but he is a mute.

Create your own dialogue first, then read what each playwright has written for the same dramatic situation.[4]

EXERCISE 60. ANIMATED INANIMATES

Choose some particular object or specimen from home or from nature— just some small insignificant object such as a discard, a flower, a rock, or

[4]C is from *The Merchant of Venice*; D, Somerset Maugham's *Rain*; E, Andreyev's *He Who Gets Slapped*; F, Lillian Hellman's *The Little Foxes*; G, Chekhov's *The Cherry Orchard*; H, Ionesco's *The Chairs*.

BUILDING YOUR OWN ACTING METHOD

a twig. Select something that you have seen so often that you take it for granted, even kick it out of your path because you are not really seeing it anymore.

1. Now take the object in your hand and *look at it as if for the first time.* Examine it for color. Is it a solid color? Multicolored? Is there some design or pattern to it? Look deeply. Is it flat or contoured? How many dimensions or planes has it? Now feel it; smell it; bring all your senses into the observation. Does this inanimate object suggest to you some animate object?

2. In answering the above questions, what word, mind picture, or emotional associations has it brought to mind? Does your specimen suggest an animal or human counterpart?

3. Translate into action your visual or emotional reactions to the object. Give a short pantomime of the thoughts or feelings evoked by the object. After you have performed for your group, produce the article and trace your thought or emotional construction from the inanimate to the animate.

NOTE: In this exercise you are beginning with reality—nature—and by observation and imagination you are creating your own object. In the play, *Joe Egg,*[5] the author describes one of the characters as a "vegetable." Can you get some inspiration for playing the character by studying a real vegetable?

GESTURES

An actor has many ways to communicate with an audience. Body and voice have always been considered most valuable tools, but there are others. A shrug, the lifting of an eyebrow, even a grunt—all may convey special meanings. Think of gesture as a vibration from thought, put lyrically. Beginners often make the mistake of believing that each spoken word should be accompanied by some movement of the arms or hands. All words are not of equal importance. Use gestures sparingly. *They should be used only to express something that you have not been able to express otherwise.* The type and the form gestures are to take will vary with different characters and play styles. Hands in pockets, flicks of the wrist, short, jerky, incompleted movements which we call gestures, may be all right for a Pinter play but would be unsuitable for Shakespeare. Classical drama requires that gestures be free, open, and completed—in keeping with the lyrical intentions.

Movement is as much correlated with gesture as it is with rhythm. Few gestures can be made without involving the entire body to some degree. When properly chosen and executed, a gesture can do a great deal to illustrate character, giving the audience an immediate image of a person. Some actors are inclined to use gestures on stage that are personal to themselves rather than those of their characters. Laurence Olivier has said:

LAURENCE OLIVIER AND MAGGIE SMITH IN *OTHELLO.* (BY PERMISSION OF THE NATIONAL THEATRE OF GREAT BRITAIN.)

[5]Peter Nichols, *Joe Egg* (New York: Grove Press, 1968).

70   THE CREATIVE PROCESS

Sometimes on the top of a bus I see a man. I begin to wonder about him. I see him do something, make a gesture. Why does he do it like that? Because he must be like this. And if he is like this, he would do (gesture) in a certain situation (gesture). Sometimes months later, when I am thinking about a bit of business, I hit on a gesture, or a movement, or a look which I feel instinctively is right. Perhaps not till later; perhaps weeks after I have been making that gesture I realize that it came from the man on top of the bus.[6]

Peter Brook defines a gesture as "a statement or wordless language" to be used only when emotion and words will not convey the meaning.

Popular TV character actor, John Dehner has said, "I've learned that the hardest thing for an actor to do is the simplest everyday gesture— opening a door, picking up a suitcase, sitting down on a chair."[7]

(PHOTO OF JOHN DEHNER COURTESY ARWIN PRO-DUCTIONS, CBS, AND THE WILLIAM MORRIS AGENCY.)

EXERCISE 61. SMALL GESTURES

   a. Decide the differences between the hands of an auto mechanic and those of a pianist.
   b. Perform some ordinary tasks as each might, such as, opening a can or packing a suitcase.

EXERCISE 62. HAND GESTURES

A boy and a girl are concealed behind a screen, leaving only their hands exposed at top. Work out a little action or story within a simple framework. An elaborate plot is beyond the needs of this exercise. Props such as flowers, boxes, or money might be used with good effect; in fact, anything could be used that can be recognized by sight and is small enough to be handled. The exercise is enhanced when a recording is used. Students are usually astounded at how much can be conveyed by so little.

EXERCISE 63. GESTURES

   1. Select a phrase from some dramatic work, or a poem, which, in your opinion, might be accompanied by gestures.

   Individually face the members of your group and, using gestures and emotions only, convey the meaning of the phrase without the use of speech or mouthing. When finished, indicate so by some gesture of finality; but remain in place for evaluation.

   NOTE: The test of how well the phrase has been chosen and how the gestures have conveyed the meaning will be indicated by how quickly others guess that meaning. Frequently, they will guess the actual phrase.

   2. The old game of charades is an excellent exercise in the use of gestures to transmit meaning.

[6]Interview with Laurence Olivier by Kenneth Harris, *Los Angeles Times*, Calendar section, March 2, 1969. Reprinted by permission of the Observer Foreign News Service.

[7]*TV Guide*, November 27, 1971.

Although pantomime employs gesture, it also requires action of the entire body rather than a part, which we are, at this time, interested in.

EXERCISE 64. GESTURE AND MOVEMENT #1 (GROUP)

One player reads from a short scene involving no more than four characters. Previously, actors have been assigned parts.

Players are to supply gestures as scene is read.

This exercise is more challenging when actors are hearing the lines for the first time and are reacting spontaneously.

EXERCISE 65. GESTURE AND MOVEMENT #2

You are in a phone booth making a call. We cannot hear your conversation but by your movement and gestures you are to convey to us which one of the following is on the other end of the line:

WOMEN	MEN
Your mother	Your wife
Your boy friend	Your boss
Your auto mechanic	Your girl friend
Your husband	Your tax accountant
Your dressmaker	Your dentist
Your doctor	Your florist
A bill collector	Your stockbroker

MIMICRY

Perhaps one reason why many community theatres prefer to produce Broadway or film plays is that, in this way, the local leading lady is afforded an opportunity to enact a role she has seen played by a stage or screen personality. It never occurs to the respectable local citizenry that they are encouraging a kind of dishonesty. From an artistic point of view to copy a famous actress is certainly not creative.

Few drama instructors would doubt that a mimetic sense is of value to a player. In learning any art, one goes through a period of imitation. However, we should not deceive ourselves. Imitation is not a creative process. It is reproducing an art already accomplished. It bears the same resemblance to acting as a photograph of a famous painting does to the original.

A beginning actor must take care that his admiration for a favorite star does not (consciously or unconsciously) lead him into an imitation of that celebrity's personal aura. He would be wasting valuable time in a study of the package without examining the product inside. Rather than working to achieve a cold reproduction of the outer evidences or technique of another actor, he would do better to study the inner motivating force—the cause as well as the results.

THE CREATIVE PROCESS

Some of your own individuality *should* be in every part you play. A character, as written, is only some black dots on paper. You must bring these marks to life. The playwright has gone as far as he can. He realizes, or should realize, that *his play is no play until it is acted by actors*. Authors are often amazed when they see what actors have been able to accomplish through their artistry. Don't mimic another actor. Be yourself and the character and determine that you are going to do more than lend your body and voice to the part.

It should be admitted at this point that there is a type of actor using mimicry who *is* creative — *the impressionist*. He does more than mimic celebrities; he selects their most individual traits, both inner and outer manifestations, distills these to an essence, and then holds them up for ridicule by the use of caricature. This requires not only careful selection of characteristic traits but also a vivid imagination; the result is a creative act in itself.

SELF-DISCIPLINE IN THE ACTOR

Art without discipline is exhibitionism. A baby assumes that the world exists just to meet its needs. The little ego is completely self-loving. At the age of three or four years (or sooner), the ego's demands are disturbed by the development of the superego as the child becomes aware of a world existing outside itself. When a child begins to wonder what is right and what is wrong, he is beginning to develop a conscience. This newcomer, or conscience, must come to terms with the resident ego; they must learn to live together in an inner balance. If the ego refuses to be superseded by superego, then we have such reactions as "I hate myself," "I don't feel like it," "Don't bother me." Ego is making a last ditch stand, fighting for unrestrained expression of instinct against conscience. The adolescent girl sometimes despises her femininity, the adolescent boy may reject responsibility. Normally, the superego wins and establishes certain standards for the self. The outside world looms larger and larger. The ego still exists, but it learns to satisfy itself by special skills and interests. But the battle is usually hard fought. Procrastination, postponement, hostility, and indolence are the weapons used by the ego in the struggle. While the struggle is *never* over, at least a certain balance is eventually reached within the individual.

Let us assume that a working arrangement has been reached between instinct and conscience. Let us also assume that the individual has his or her heart set on acting as a career. In training, he or she has been told to use and rely upon emotion, *to excite and release the very emotions which the student has only recently learned to control.* This may be just the straw to upset that delicate inner balance. The infantile ego may become free again to scream and storm for the world to serve its needs. No question about it, *this does happen!* We see it often when actors are apprehensive, anxious, mentally and physically exhausted from long, exacting rehearsals. At this time, when the usual controls are weakened, the leading lady suddenly "blows her top" and storms off the stage in a rage. G. K. Chesterton said, "The tragedy of the artistic temperament is that it cannot produce any art."

In becoming an actor, a most important and difficult task is to learn the use of the power of the will to its full capacity. Freedom may be sweet wine, but if you drink too much, its very sweetness can make you ill. An actor is popularly and mistakenly believed to be a free soul, living morally and physically as he pleases; a child of nature and a creature of instinct. This has never been true of actors worthy of the name. When an ambitious young actress travels to New York or Hollywood "to become a star," she suddenly finds herself free — of home town, parents, and parental expectations — only to find that what she expects of *herself* is much more demanding. She must assume responsibility for, and mastery of, herself. She must become her own disciplinarian, for no one is going to guard her interests but herself. She must fight her own indulgences, adopt a tough policy, and eventually acquire a pride in exerting her will power.

Freedom? The ambitious person is never free. He must compete. Ambition drives him on. He must be constantly learning. And learning means changing, giving up something he has for something he wants more. We all resent limits and boundaries. We confuse rational control of self with denial of the sweet things in life, and we have difficulty setting limits for ourselves. But the ability to live richly and rewardingly depends upon the integration of the ego and the superego.

RHYTHM

Architecture can be judged by its relationship to the space surrounding it. In the same way rhythm can only be appreciated when it is related to surrounding atmosphere and space, that is, to its silences and immobility. A rest in music is an interruption of sound, and yet is part of that music. No one would enjoy a symphony played at exactly the same tempo and volume. So it is with the performance of a play. It must also have stops, retards, syncopations, and structural emphasis.

Each actor in a play contributes a rhythm for his character, which is developed during rehearsals. The constant repetition of lines, movement, and silences serve to blend his rhythm with the rhythms of the other characters. There is a time during final rehearsals when the play takes on a music of its own. This imprinted behavior is a form of security which actors always depend upon during performances.

Rhythm is the impulse behind words and movement. It is time, pace, and meter all rolled into one. A regular step is a natural model of measure for a division of time into equal parts. Muscles are made for movement and movement is rhythm which involves time in space. It is impossible to conceive and convey a rhythm without thinking of a physical movement. It is not enough that an actor possesses natural rhythm, he must develop it into a precise tool by developing the muscles of his body. This informs the actor of the exact time to pause, to move or to be still and silent. If an actor comes on stage using a walk which is timed to an uneven rhythm, the audience will be immediately alerted to some disturbance in the natural flow of the play.

Tempo is often confused with meter and we should note that it most often involves the timing of a scene or entire play, the rate at which the unit of time is either increased or decreased and is more properly used as a director's term. But rhythm is more personal, generally describing an instrumentality of the actor.

EXERCISE 66. METER

Read lines from one of the great Greek tragedies to the accompaniment of a percussion instrument. Vary the rhythmic patterns and silences.

EXERCISE 67. MECHANICAL RHYTHM

Here is one Peter Brook uses. All members of the group are to memorize a soliloquy or verse of their choosing. Divide the piece into three sections; then, using no special expressive delivery, three individuals are to read the piece, in turn, but as a unit.

a. As quickly as possible.
b. Retard pace slowly.
c. Accent certain previously selected words using beats or silences for other words.

EXERCISE 68. RHYTHMIC MOVEMENT AND COORDINATION

OBJECTIVE: To develop feeling for time and rhythm. Use for all members of the workshop group. Use metronome or drum. Students should be trained to distinguish between various divisions of time and various accents within the divisions of time. For example, this exercise moves constantly in four-beat divisions (speaking as they walk will help).

1. Group begins by walking around the action circle in response to a regular beat.

   "Step—step—step—step.
   Step—step—step—step."

2. At a given signal and without breaking rhythm, CHANGE the first STEP to a STOMP.

   "STOMP —step—step—step.
   STOMP —step—step—step."

3. When all are accustomed to this rhythm, CHANGE the second STEP to a REST.

   "STOMP—REST— step—step.
   STOMP—REST— step—step."

4. Assorted variations of your own invention can continue the complication and concentration. Try clapping with each step on every other group of four beats.

"STOMP—REST—step—step.
Clap—clap—clap—clap.
STOMP—REST—step—step.
Clap—clap—clap—clap."

After constant repetition, muscular actions pass outside the control of the brain into automatism. You may want to combine or substitute speech or song with the already imprinted behavior. Exercise 68(#2) was used in double time for the army in the APA production of *Pantagleize*.

We have all noted the magic of combined and dissociated rhythms in nature, machinery, traffic, and in all life around us.

When asked if he had any "particular hobby horse" he rode in his work as actor-director, Laurence Olivier said:

*I rely greatly on rhythm. I think that it is the one thing I understand . . .
the exploitation of rhythm, change of expression, change of pace in crossing
the stage. Keep the audience surprised, shout when they're not expecting it,
keep them on their toes . . . change from minute to minute.*[8].

FURTHER READING: BUILDING YOUR OWN ACTING METHOD

Archer, William. *About the Theatre*. New York: Benjamin Blom, 1969.

Austell, Jan. *What's in a Play?* New York: Harcourt, 1968.

Bakshy, Alexander. *Theatre Unbound*. New York: Benjamin Blom, 1969.

Braun, Edward, ed. *Meyerhold on Theatre*. New York: Hill & Wang, 1969.

Cheney, Sheldon. *New Movement in Theatre*. New York: Benjamin Blom, 1969.

Fuchs, George. *Revolution in Theatre*. Ithaca: Cornell University Press, 1959.

Gassner, John and Allen, Ralph. *Theatre and Drama in the Making*. 2 vols. New York: Houghton Mifflin, 1967.

Kirby, E. T. *Total Theatre*. New York: Dutton, 1969.

May, R. *Theatremania*. New York: Heinman Imported Books, 1968.

Mitchell, Roy. *Creative Theatre*. New York: Benjamin Blom, 1969.

Rowe, Kenneth Thorpe. *A Theatre in Your Head, Analyzing the Play*. New York: Funk & Wagnalls, 1960.

Seltzer, Daniel, ed. *The Modern Theatre*. Boston: Little, Brown, 1967.

Weales, Gerald. *The Play and its Parts*. New York: Basic Books, 1964.

Weissman, Phillip. *Creativity in the Theatre*. New York: Dell, 1966.

[8]Interview with Laurence Olivier by Kenneth Harris, *Los Angeles Times*, Calendar section, March 2, 1969. Reprinted by permission of the Observer Foreign News Service.

Characterization 7

Half the actor's battle is won once a clear picture of the character is firmly engraved in his senses.*

Helen Hayes
Academy Award Best Actress
("The Sin of Madelin Claudet") 1931/32.
Best Supporting Actress ("Airport") 1971.

*From Morton Eustis, *Players at Work, Acting According to the Actors*, Theatre Arts Books, 1937, p. 18. (Photo by Marcus Blechman, courtesy Lucy Kroll Agency)

The fundamentals of acting remain forever constant: they are the same for Shakespeare or Chekhov. The actor first studies the play, including his character and its relationship to the play and the other characters, then determines what the character is inside, and finally develops the means to communicate this character to an audience. These are the fundamentals of an acting design.

But somewhere along the line you must be concerned with the needs of the play, the author, and the times for which the author wrote. All playwrights write out of the urgencies of their time. Each play reflects a certain civilization and a set of mores. Some actors find this difficult and out of frustration attempt to project themselves, with their alien values and standards, into another time. For Chekhov, you need a realistic approach, for Shakespeare an enlargement of reality. These needs are forever changing with the fashion in plays, but the artistic design in acting is perpetual.

Have you ever had the opportunity to watch an artist at work? I know a sculptor who starts with an idea or an inspiration. He makes a few pencil sketches—just doodling to others, but to him these scribbles represent the general mass or the overall movement of the piece he intends to create. Next he builds a strong armature to support the heavy clay with which he will be working. This will always remain inside the sculpture, never visible, but supporting all subsequent work.

Then he begins applying the clay, but only in a general way; "blocking in" he calls it. He is following the original idea or inspiration but only in mass and planes, with no detail yet. He is experimenting, trying to fit the physical object to his visual concept of it. As he models, he adds and takes away, and so continues on and on. This may take hours or days, but all during this time he is selecting, refining, and adding detail. He will have logical reasons for some decisions; others will simply "feel right" to him. The creative process in any art is both conscious and unconscious. When at last he decides that the work is a good representation of his original idea, then and only then, is he ready to show it to others.

When we look at his finished work, we may appreciate the original concept or we may admire his skill with the materials. But when a work of art is really successful, it takes on a life of its own, apart from method, materials, or idea, and becomes in itself a living thing.

Like the sculptor, the actor tries to do something like this when creating a part. He gets an idea from his study of the play and builds a strong support for the work he will be doing. He sketches, selects, refines, and finally adds detail. The actor has failed to create effectively if spectators say, "He had a great idea for the part," or "Didn't you love the way he swung that cape about?" If this is the reaction, he has shown his audience only the parts, not the whole. He must work to have them accept his characterization as an identity, aside from the idea, the technique, or the actor who created it. The character must seem a living, breathing, human being, whether horrible or wonderful. Acting, like any other art, must communicate something. Originality, skill, design, emotional and psychological interests, are the means, not the ends.

STUDY OF THE PLAY

Let us see how we can adapt the sculptor's creative process to our work. Where did that sculptor get his original idea or inspiration? How did he *begin*? A sculptor can create from his subconscious or from his experience. But before an actor can act, he must have a play or story. In our exercises, we have done many. A story can be very simple indeed, it can last two hours or one minute. The essentials are *characters in a situation and some sequential development*. It must also have something basically human at its center.

It is not necessary that a story be a written play. The actors of the Commedia dell'Arte used only a scenario. Marcel Marceau and Red Skelton are able to dispense with words entirely. On the other hand, Charles Laughton could read a passage from the Bible, doing so without movement, settings, or costumes, and thrill an audience with his imaginative powers. Indeed, acting can be deprived of much that we think of as theatre, and still be theatre. The indispensible elements seem to be — an audience, an actor with imagination, and a story. John Gassner has given a definition of a play: *A sequence of events in which characters express themselves through what happens to them, what they do, or fail to do.*

An actor, preparing to play a part in a play, must study the structure of the play, its genre, its language, and its characters. From this analysis, the overall objective, the facts, and the sequence of events, will become apparent. Then he will see how the attitudes of the characters motivate the play's objective, create its given circumstances, and provide the main drive.

Next, he must consider the incidents activating the objective, those sequential and accumulative organizations of physical actions that provide involvement and conflict in the lives of the characters. In general, a character is created by some or all of the following components.

1. A playwright's lines and descriptions of characters
2. The emphasis the director cares to give the character
3. The actor's contribution, mentally and physically
4. What other characters say about your character
5. What your character *does* in the play
6. Your character's ideas, ideals, goals, beliefs, and emotions
7. Your character's past, heredity, present environment and appearance
8. The general quality of imagination contributed by all those involved

The creation of character entails an analysis of drives of social, psychological, and physical factors, based on the play and the director's concept of the production. Read the play as a play; that is, imagine it up on a stage, see the people and the settings just as you envision it when it will be produced. Don't read words: try to experience the *feeling* of the words, what the author is trying to communicate.

What is the play's line of action? A good way to answer this is to ask yourself, "How does this play begin?" and, "How does it end?" What happens between those two points will be the line of action. Read the play again and again until there is no doubt in your mind about the super-objective. Study the incidents which actively relate to the main drive of the play. Background, moral issues, history, narrative, and theme are contributory and should be subordinated at this particular time. Strip the tree of its branches and leave only the trunk. No definition of a play's objective will apply equally to all plays, but a majority of plays are structured; that is, they have a sequential and accumulative organization of actions or situations, which provide involvement and conflict in the lives of the characters. Without characters and situation, there can be no drama.

Usually the dramatic pressure centers upon a protagonist. He is the one who wants something so sincerely that he is willing to fight, or even sacrifice his life for it. That something may be love, power, duty, money, politics, freedom, country, morality, honesty, ethics, revenge, or life itself. Hopefully, the audience will see something in this human, and his struggle which relates to them. So in a general way, *the particular becomes the universal.*

Along with the central character (or activist) there is, in most plays, a secondary character or characters almost as important to the plot as the protagonist. He, she, or they may be allies or antagonists. We would be unable to tell the story of Romeo and Juliet without mentioning their parents. Macbeth has Macduff and Lady Macbeth. The only reason these are secondary characters is that it is not their story. Taking another view, secondary characters might become leading characters; but the play as written makes them contributors to the protagonist's struggles, either by aiding or opposing him.

THE CHARACTER IN THE PLAY

An actor should not begin working on his characterization until he has a thorough knowledge of the complete play. Do not skim over the parts which do not concern your character. You may deprive yourself of information which could help you. Study the period for which the play was written. A girl of fourteen in a Shakespearian play is quite different from one in a farce by Oscar Wilde or one in a modern play such as *Marigolds*.

A playwright uses his characters as symbols through which he conveys his meanings. All artists deal in symbols—the playwright's symbols are endowed with human traits and drives which allow an audience to identify with them. Without characters, a play would simply be a series of events. We empathize with Romeo, or even with a villain like Richard III; good or bad, we recognize their humanity and associate with them.

Only events and actions relating to people are theatrically effective. A devastating flood or hurricane sweeps the Atlantic coast; this is an event, an action, but our interest is always in the effect of the event upon *people*, their lives and homes. We all remember Falstaff, Sherlock Holmes, Oliver Twist, Scarlett O'Hara, or Holden Caulfield. Most of us can close our eyes and see them. But how readily do we remember their stories?

The words of a playwright serve as an actor's blueprint for the creative job which lies ahead. Simply speaking lines committed to memory may be lecture or oratory, but certainly not acting. However, adding flesh and blood, strength and weakness, desire, mind and soul — this is the actor's art.

"Getting inside a character" means exactly that: the actor is lending his body, mind, and voice to be motivated, even possessed, by the character he represents. This almost religious attitude toward character creation has many precedents. Mythological tradition holds that images give power; the aboriginals, from ancient to modern times, have worshipped their hero-ancestors. And folklore gives the creator of images the role of sorcerer or magician — witness the festivals of Dionysus and later the miracle plays. Such convictions seem founded on two premises — the non-artist's awe of inspiration and the artist's skill at transposing vision into object. This synthesis of spiritual and visual sensibilities allows the created character to dominate, and this image is transmitted to an audience by means of symbols and impulses. Only training and discipline can perfect the actor in this art.

> The ability to regroup the fragments of experience mentally in new and significant combinations, to move backward and forward in thought, to go where we have not been, to be where we cannot go, and to re-create, even if imperfectly, another person's feelings, is the supreme gift of our responsive, uniquely personal human brain.[1]
>
> *Judith Groch*

From what the character says or does, how he looks, we can observe his physical actions. Richard III boasts of his ambitions and his villainy. He speaks directly to the audience — that is narrative — and then proceeds to do everything he has talked about. Lady Anne's loathing of him shows us that others consider him a villain. Later, although he is physically repulsive to her, she becomes his queen, and this shows us another side of Richard — his evil but irresistible magnetism. Here then are a few ways in which the actor might study his character: by what the character says and does, by what others say about him, by his ability to change others' opinions of him, and by his physical appearance.

Whenever we have a scene between two characters, we learn a great deal about each of them. In some plays there is often a contradiction between what the character says, and what he does. This adds another dimension.

---

[1]Judith Groch, *The Right to Create* (Boston: Little, Brown, 1969), p. 41.

CHARACTERIZATION   81

Read the play again and this time give all of your attention to your part. What is the objective of your particular character, in the overall play, and in each scene in which he appears? What is he thinking? What does he want from life? French actor-producer Jean-Louis Barrault[2] refers to this as the "What-am-I-doing-here?" step. Find your character's objectives: ask yourself all sorts of questions, and answer them using your imagination and what is given you by the playwright. You will recognize good answers by the way they validate, corroborate, and assimilate the character and the play. In this way you will be able to justify a logical and consecutive group of organic physical actions for the character, in the entire play and for each scene in which he appears. We might conclude from his physical actions that Petruchio has said, "I want to marry Katharine!"—that could serve as the character's main drive. But how Petruchio accomplishes this goal during each scene is another matter. To cure Katharine of her shrewishness, Petruchio pretends to be more hot tempered and irritable than she. Oedipus is driven to discover the circumstances of his birth. Yet in each scene he has individual goals, which may not immediately appear related to his main objective, but are, in fact, physical actions leading eventually to that objective.

UNDERSTANDING THE CHARACTER

We have been considering physical actions of characters and how they relate to objectives. But every character has both a physical and a spiritual life. From the exercises given earlier, you have learned how organic physical actions and definite objectives can lead to deep inner responses. "The body is biddable," Stanislavski has said. "Feelings are capricious; therefore, if you cannot create a human spirit in your part of its own accord, create the physical being in your role."[3]

You will know when you reach this moment of creation. But do not try to *will* yourself into the feelings of your character. Instead, perform his physical actions. Your instincts and your own experienced emotions will bring you to the creative moment when there is complete integration of the physical and spiritual being of a role.

Often an inexperienced actor or a professional lacking imagination will lean heavily upon the playwright, expecting him to carry them. In such circumstances, the play presents the actors instead of the actors presenting the play.

The director's task is to stimulate his actors into individual creativity, to suggest possibilities, to find relationships between the actor and his character, to encourage a sense of perception, and to serve as the actor's audience when he has none.

[2]Jean-Louis Barrault, *The Theatre of Jean-Louis Barrault* (New York: Hill & Wang, 1961), p. 34.

[3]Konstantin Stanislavski, *Creating a Role* (New York: Theatre Arts Books, 1961), p. 154.

THE CREATIVE PROCESS

However, it is the actor who makes the final contact with the audience. He is the relay team's anchor man. It is the actor who will finally win or lose the event. This alone should be sufficient reason for the actor to know his character better than the playwright who created the character, or the director who collaborated with the actor.

Understanding is the key to successful characterization. Some actors write biographies of their characters in order to get a more penetrating insight into their roles. Anthony Quinn is reported to have written 11,000 words on his part in the film *Flap.* His notes begin with "The character's character (very male), and his weight (139 pounds)"—and they continue for forty-five pages.[4]

When Rod Steiger was working on his characterization of Al Capone, he read the gangster's autobiography and all the newspapers of the time. Stieger asked himself, "What did this man *want*? I decided he wanted to be respected—he wanted recognition. I read the script and reread it, and somewhere inside me it clicks, and there's an 'Oh, Yes' in a secret place—I walk through a five-and-ten-cent store and associate objects with the part. Say I see a toothbrush. I'll think, How does he brush his teeth?—One thing I did for Al Capone was to take out all small gestures. I played it pretty big—I wore my coat draped over my shoulders, and my hat brim angled—because one thing I felt he wanted was to be big."[5]

In real life, we walk into a room filled with strangers and, after being introduced all around, find that one certain individual interests us more than all the others. We would like to know this person better, to ask about his background, his means of livelihood, his ambitions; but good manners do not encourage such direct interrogation. We must wait until such information is volunteered, bit by bit, and this may take years. Time alone can forge intimacy between people. Older married couples, after years of living together, become so well known to each other that they often come to look alike. This is the sort of intimacy the actor needs to develop between himself and his character. But the actor has not that luxury of time. The actor has only a short time, to *become* his character.

ACTOR INTO THE CHARACTER

Not only must an actor know his character, he must also *understand* him. He must know why the character does what he does in the play. When such a relationship is accomplished, and only then, will the actor be able to sense anything false to the character in his speech or movement. With the director's guidance he must reason out each problem in characterization. He must adjust to the events in the play and justify all lines and business in harmony with the author's concept. An actor will only be able

(COURTESY OF ANTHONY QUINN AND WARNER BROS.)

(COURTESY OF ROD STEIGER AND UNITED ARTISTS.)

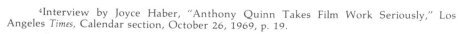

[4]Interview by Joyce Haber, "Anthony Quinn Takes Film Work Seriously," Los Angeles *Times,* Calendar section, October 26, 1969, p. 19.

[5]© 1962 Lillian Ross. From *The Player, A Profile of an Art,* by Lillian Ross and Helen Ross, Simon and Schuster. Originally published in *The New Yorker.*

CHARACTERIZATION

to create in direct proportion to his understanding of his fellow-man and through an ability to sympathize with him. How many girls anxious to play the part of Sadie Thompson[6] have ever lived through her exact set of experiences? If they were placed in that character's circumstances with the same mentality and background isn't it possible that they might behave exactly as Sadie did? Unless the actress is able to understand, even sympathize, with the character, she will not be able to bring her alive for an audience and move them emotionally. "The artist need not have experienced in actual life every emotion he can express," states philosopher Susanne Langer in her provocative *Feeling and Form*. "It may be through manipulation of his created elements that he discovers new possibilities of feeling strange moods, perhaps greater concentrations of passions than his own temperament could ever produce."[7]

When asked by a director to read a line or make a move that seems false, the genuinely creative actor never says, "I don't feel it that way." He relies upon his intimacy with the character to justify the line or move. In so doing, he is also ready with plausible answers should the director ask, "Why do you do that?" or "Why do you read the line that way?" But the hack, the unimaginative actor, never bothers much to create a character. He merely lends his voice, body, and personality to a part. He creates nothing; he is simply using what God and the playwright have given him, and does not deserve to be called an artist. An artist creates, using the materials available to compose, by selection, observation, research, experience, inspiration, and discipline, something which had no existence before he set his hand and heart to it.

Most actors do not study enough. Contrary to general opinion, acting is not a lazy man's pastime. A creative actor is never content to read lines written by an author and to be moved about the stage by a director like a pawn on a chessboard. Any actor worthy of the name does more than read a play once — or twice. It is not enough to be able to follow the story and to decide what he, as an actor, will do with the part he has been assigned. *Indeed, he does not view the work ahead from an actor's point of view at all, but from the character's.* He begins by *absorbing* the play and allowing it to seep through his pores until it becomes a living part of himself. He knows that his character cannot be pushed and jammed into the confines of an actor's ego. A character only begins to live after the actor knows him, understands him, and is on intimate terms with him. Even then, the character will come in his own time when he feels no longer a stranger and when the actor is at repose. This moment of revelation will be clear to the actor. He may note a different pitch in his voice, become conscious of an unfamiliar gesture or a strange way of thinking, as actor and character fuse into one. When this metamorphosis is complete, the actor will begin

[6]Sadie Thompson: the leading character in the play *Rain* by John Colton and Clemence Randolph from a short story, "Miss Thompson," by W. Somerset Maugham. — Editor.

[7]Susanne Langer, *Feeling and Form* (New York: Scribner's, 1953), p. 374.

THE CREATIVE PROCESS

to think, act, and even look like the character. Blind confidence will not accomplish this change. Logical steps must be taken. Development comes systematically, piece by piece, requiring intensive concentration, investigation and self-discipline from the actor, and systematic guidance by the director.

Here are four steps that the actor might use in working on characterizations.

CHARACTER DELINEATION

1. Orientation: Study the play, the milieu in which the character lives, and the character's relationships to others in the play. Find the individuality in the character. What makes him different from others in the play? Decide his mental and moral traits, his behavior, his dress. What is his importance to the play? To the plot? Who is he? What is he? When? Where? Why?
2. Motivational Period: What are his biological drives? What makes him do the things he does? What are his dominant characteristics? What does he say—or not say? What does he want? Find a sentence or speech in the part which illuminates the essence of the character.
3. Physical Aspects: All movements are motivated by thought (we decide to get up out of a chair before we do). Select the inner-dynamics of the character which can be shown physically and audibly. Select the rate and tension of his moves and what physical aspects can be adapted to the character. How does he fill space? Is he a small man, a fat one? What is the rhythm of his walk? The texture of his voice? Synthesize the character *in action*.
4. Spiritual Aspects: The character's ethics or morals are usually revealed during the play to the audience and, sometimes, to himself.

During the period of selection, logical thinking may become blocked. If this occurs, the actor may find some value in relaxing his conscious effort, allowing time for his unconscious to contribute. Metaphysical abstractions or inspirations may appear suddenly when the actor's thoughts are totally detached from the problem, seeming to arise from no apparent logic. On closer examination, these are usually found to be the result of conscious thinking previously accepted; by releasing pressure, you have allowed your unconscious to contribute. This does not imply that you should sit around waiting for inspiration to flutter over your head; it merely suggests that you relax if you come to an impasse. Should this fail, then get back to your studies. We have already concluded that the creative process is part conscious or logical, and part unconscious or intuitive, and that these should be combined with hard work. There is no substitute for sticking to the problem. It is the key to both logic and intuition.

EXERCISE 69. CREATING CHARACTERIZATION #1

Begin with some simple everyday duty, such as washing the face, reading a newspaper, threading a needle, etc.:

a. Pantomime the action as you might do it.
b. Now, do it as several different characters might.

This can become a very provocative and often rewarding exercise when a character from some well-known play is selected. Improvise a scene which is not in the play but using the character from it. For instance: How would Lady Macbeth wash her face? She had to, you know.

Unlike the elderly couple we considered before, the actor is not hampered by having to wait years to learn about his character. He can pry into his background and quickly learn a great deal about him. But to be valid, this search must *begin with the facts as stated in the play:* the author's description of the character, what is said by the character, what others say about him, and how he contributes to the play. In other words, an actor must work backwards—from what happens to the character during the action to the *reasons* for what happens. Whenever possible the facts in the play should be used to reach decisions on the intellectual or emotional motivations of characters. If none can be found in the play then these must be invented but based upon lines or incidents that *are* in the play.

All characters have an identity with a time and a place and this must always be considered. The social and educational backgrounds of all the characters must be decided upon; also the mental and moral attitudes, the drives, what action is taken to fulfill these drives, and the conflicts which inhibit them. An audience will not be able to see inside each character, but the externals must be shown because they reveal inner dynamic sources.

EXERCISE 70. CHARACTER CONCEPTS BY THOUGHT PROGRESSION

The objective in this exercise is to describe a character which an audience would believe capable of a given action. By use of logical thought patterns, we are to trace back and create a character whose background; age; mental, moral, emotional, and physical aspects; would cause the character to take the action he does. Put in another way, we are to give full justification for the action, by understanding the character himself.

This is not a physical exercise but one of thought progression and imagination. Students are not to mime or improvise but to *describe* the thoughts, feelings, and behavior of a character who would be believable to an audience, doing what he or she does.

1. A man (or woman) has walked to a parking lot two blocks away and finds that the keys to the car are in the office.
2. A girl slaps her mother in the face.

THE CREATIVE PROCESS

3. A mother slaps her daughter in the face, but for entirely different reasons from #2 above.

4. A young wife hears a noise during the night. She cannot arouse her sleeping husband and decides to investigate herself. When she enters the living room, she confronts a burglar.

5. A sensitive sixteen-year-old boy, a music student, is given his first summer job on a garbage disposal truck. After two days he quits, and attempts to explain it to his father.

6. Two office girls from Texas decide to spend their vacations together in New York. One is offered her plane fare by her employer, and she accepts. She explains why to her friend.

7. A freshman is dared by an upper-classman to call the White House and ask to speak to the President. He does, and the President comes to the phone.

8. A girl of humble circumstances has saved to buy a fashionable wardrobe in order to be admitted to a garden party of the socially prominent. At the party she overhears several guests ridiculing her clothes and awkward manner.

9. An overprotective mother objects to her daughter's dating. A very eligible young man calls and the mother either changes her attitude or not.

10. An old rancher, known as a teller of tall tales, tells a whopper—which comes true. Explain.

11. A young mother forces her eight year old son to attend a dancing class. He returns home with a black eye.

12. A young woman is separated from her hiking party and is saved from a rattlesnake by a boy she despises.

13. A protester sees a wounded policeman lying in the street, helps him to his feet and to an ambulance.

14. Trapped at a police barricade in an alley, a petty thief believes his world has come to an end.

Each member of the class is assigned one of the above problems. *He should describe the situation, filling in the cause and the effect, from the protagonist's viewpoint—in the first person.* At a following session, each student is to provide an improvisation using the circumstances as given. Students may use voice to express stream of consciousness, or monologue. Each should relate some personal experiences to the characterization, whether actual or vicarious. This exercise is to be judged on how well the student has shown:

The age of the character

The emotional aspects of the character

Was there an obvious difference between the actor and the character?

Were the thoughts, feelings, and actions explored in such a way that an audience would accept the character as doing what he or she would do in the given circumstances?

THE INNER MONOLOGUE

During a performance, much is often "said" by characters without lines written by the author. In an earlier theatre these thoughts were audible to the audience and known as asides or soliloquies. Today, words are not as important as they were once. Other means are used. The expression on an actor's face, his movements and gestures, his unspoken thoughts, can speak louder to an audience than would soliloquies or asides. And this also happens in everyday life. When we listen to someone who is talking, thoughts, impressions, and reactions are silently being created in our minds. It has often been said, and it is certainly true, that a good actor knows how to listen well. When required, or thought useful, the use of an unspoken subtext, or silent *inner monologue*, as Stanislavski called it, may help an audience to understand a character's private thoughts.

EXERCISE 71. INNER MONOLOGUE

> Choose a scene in which it is obvious that a character is not expressing his complete or honest thoughts in the lines as written. As you rehearse, try whispering these inner thoughts. Use two voice tones, and ask your fellow-players to disregard these whispered thoughts during the few rehearsals it will take to establish the inner monologue in your mind. *Understand that these thoughts will be audible only during rehearsals.* During performances, a solid imprint of thought processes will be operating and be evidenced to the audience not in words, but in expressions on the face, voice tones, movements, and gestures. In short, the mind will be transmitting character revelations even when you have nothing to say. Once mastered, this inner monologue will save you from standing on a stage looking lost in yourself as the actor, instead of being involved with your character and the others.

THE METAMORPHOSIS

Most present-day writers know that when they have studied their subject at length and collected stacks of notes, something more will be needed to give life to the material. This assimilated information is fed into the writer's own computer, his brain, and this knowledge along with his own experiences might stimulate and trigger the impetus which facilitates a fully realized characterization.

The intuitive search into characterization begins in discovery; some action of the mind produces a fresh insight or image. It might be done by examining the character's needs or goals, his pre-play history, physical traits, intellectual and emotional attributes, present mode of living; in fact, everything the author has not stated or made clear. Or the impetus can be a line, an action, or some sympathetic recall which sets off the creative mechanism. The role must then be divided into physical actions for each act, each scene, in which the character is involved. The physical movements must all grow organically out of "the moments"—the events taking place in the play—and in sympathetic actions with other players.

THE CREATIVE PROCESS

Suppose that Hamlet is to be your character, and that after a complete study of the play, the period, and whatever else you have been able to find on the subject, you have decided that Hamlet's outstanding characteristic is his indecision in carrying out his objective — to avenge his father's murder. Consider this in relation to the play and the way you might transmit this to an audience. Ask yourself dozens of questions, then answer them. How does this relate to the play's line of action — the super-objective? Are there lines in the play that justify his indecision? Does Hamlet know he is indecisive? In Act II Scene ii, he says:

> Yet I,
> A dull and muddy-mettled rascal, peak,
> Like John-a-dreams, unpregnant of my cause,
> And can say nothing: no not for a king,-

Let us suppose that after testing indecision as a piece of our puzzle we have decided that it might do. As we rehearse, the subconscious may suddenly recapitulate, select, refine, and arrange related material for our use. By consciously selecting an idea and experimenting with it, we will discover matters we knew only subconsciously. These ideas we put into action by improvisation and the use of our trained body and voice — our physical assets. Thus, the day-by-day work with technique during rehearsals leads us eventually to the emotional and spiritual Hamlet, and we are finally able to *enter into* the character, and live with him.

This process is used to some degree by all good actors. Experienced actors may no longer be aware that they use it. When assigned a part, all the cogs of the process mesh automatically. But a beginner must follow the creative process consciously at first, going from what is known to what is unknown, then allowing his imagination to create metaphors. Imagination will seek its own mode of expression, and intuition will constantly relate this information to his own personality, his own consciousness, and his own store of emotional memories, giving the concept the breath of life.

But in this process of metamorphosis, the concept will take on its own personality. It becomes no longer the actor. Hamlet will reveal his own voice, body, and character. And with this step in the creative process, we reach a realm that escapes logic. What happens is beyond explanation or reality. From a disciple of nature, the actor becomes nature's creator. The actor and the character are hidden behind a veil; when we see them again they will be fused into one being. This is the magic of acting, the same magic practiced by aboriginal man. The vision born in the artist's mind has now turned into a physical image. Its value does not depend upon its proximity to reality but upon its association with the artist's psychic existence.

It is obvious that all this study, selection, improvisation, and construction must be done in an atmosphere of peace and relaxation. It must be done when the actor studies and rehearses, alone or in the company of sympathetic fellow-artists. It cannot be done during performance when facing an audience. That would also seem obvious, and yet there are actors who wait until a performance to "feel" their parts.

All artists have ethics. No painter in his right mind paints in front of a client. Rembrandt once got so angry with a visitor to his studio that he barked, "Don't poke your nose into my pictures, the smell of paint will kill you!" Stanislavski placed certain emphasis on "feeling the part," but when he learned that some American disciples were placing undue emphasis upon "affective memory," he clarified the matter in an article written shortly before his death for the 1947 edition of the Encyclopedia Britannica:

> — this does not mean that the actor must surrender himself on the stage to some hallucination as that when playing he should lose the sense of reality around him, to take scenery for real trees, etc. On the contrary, some part of his senses must remain free from the grip of the play to control everything he attempts and achieves as the performer in his part.

STANISLAVSKI SHORTLY BEFORE HIS DEATH. (COURTESY OF THE MINISTRY OF CULTURE, USSR.)

During a performance, the actor assumes power of attorney over the prearranged image. This "phantasm," as Aristotle called it, is now under his control; it is not controlling him. And this overall metaphor will have, within it, just enough room for spontaneity and inspirational moments to keep the performance fresh. In a letter dated 1769, the great David Garrick speaks of this moment of spontaneity coming upon the actor during the warmth of the scene as if springing from a mine, and which, "—like an electric fire, shoots through the veins, marrow, bones and all, to every spectator."[8]

The ability to conceive, construct, and communicate an original portrayal to an audience is the standard of a good actor. The poor actor contents himself with being a copy of another actor who had this faculty.

ADDING TO CHARACTERIZATION BY USE OF NONTEXTUAL SCENES

Improvisations of offstage scenes, not written by the playwright but employing subliminal, or unconscious, involvement of the characters, can be a great asset to the actor in preparing his character. The audience is told what happens to Hamlet when he is sent to England. But if this action is dramatized by the actors in an improvisation, it will certainly deepen their understanding of the characters when Hamlet returns to Elsinore. The events on the voyage to England are going to make Hamlet a different person than when he left. By such offstage improvisations, an actor is afforded the opportunity to bring something on stage with him rather than simply making an entrance. The creation of a character might be likened to pieces in a mosaic, some pieces are best set in place tentatively and later adjusted to other pieces as the work on the complete design proceeds.

[8]David Garrick, *The Letters of David Garrick*, eds. Little and Kahrl (Cambridge, Mass.: The Belknap Press of Harvard University, 1963), vol. 2, p. 634, letter dated January 3, 1769.

CLICHÉS

In learning to act, almost as much can be accomplished by learning what not to do as in learning what to do. The paradox is that by studying negative aspects we reach positive values. In other times, apprentice actors were punished physically for mistakes. As a result, such lessons were learned quickly and not easily forgotten. But today it is common to see young actors persisting in poor habits which might have been eliminated early in their training.

Our stereotypes are so widely used that we are hardly aware of them. They are immediately understood by an audience and make the actor's work simpler, so why not use them? There are good reasons for *not* using them. If you are going to be like every other actor, where is that precious quality you have worked so hard to develop—your own individuality? When you use clichés, it isn't necessary to think creatively. The following are a few; you will be able to think of more you've seen used. Get to know them in order to avoid them. They are the killers of imagination.

> *Scratching head:* perplexity.
> *Looking up:* thinking.
> *Rubbing chin:* contemplation.
> *Fluttering hands:* Lack of poise, nervousness.
> *Raising eyebrows suddenly:* "Wasn't that funny?"
> *Playing with moustache:* lechery.
> *Open mouth:* surprise or stupidity.
> *Hitting head with palm of hand:* sudden idea, realization.
> *Biting lips:* anxiety.
> *Raising eyes up sadly:* "Heaven help us," or "He's sick."

Another frequently accepted cliché which most actors have not bothered to analyze is the old bromide, "There are no small parts, just small actors." This offends one of the primary laws of drama. There *are* small parts and they should remain small parts. Nothing disturbs the balance of a play so much as to see an actress, assigned a one-line maid part, attempting to give the audience a complete biography of her character. This destroys the author's carefully worked-out relationship between his characters and their relative positions in his story. An author needs, and writes, small parts. They are written to contribute to and not to dominate his play. Ensemble acting means all actors working toward a common interest, the presentation of the play; not six or eight individuals playing as many different stories.

ACTOR'S CHECKLIST

The following questions may help you during rehearsals to determine if you are on the right track in building your characterization and might even show you where you can improve.

1. Does my performance help elucidate the main objective of the play?
2. Am I effectively expressing my character's objective?
3. Is the relationship of my character to the play and to other characters correct?
4. Am I expressing ideas by both physical and mental means?
5. Is my voice quality effective for the part? Do I speak distinctly? Do I project properly?
6. Is everything I do clear and do I communicate to the audience? (This is very different from projection.)
7. Are any of my scenes dull? Do they have a tempo and rhythm? Do my important scenes build to a climax?
8. Is anything I do repetitive? Have I followed the director's instructions?
9. Does my performance have color and does it reflect the mores of the period? Does it have humanity?
10. Am I doing everything possible to cooperate with my fellow-players and our director?
11. Have I built my characterization from imagination and observation?
12. Am I completely relaxed at rehearsals?

FURTHER READING: CHARACTERIZATION

Carpenter, E., and McLuhan, M. *Explorations in Communications.* Boston: Beacon Press, 1968.

Cary, Joyce. *Communications.* Boston: Beacon Press, 1968.

Cherry, C. *On Human Communication.* New York: Science Edition Inc., 1961.

Dittman, A., et al. "Facial and Bodily Expression: A Study of Receptivity of Emotional Cues." *Psychiatry* 28 (1965).

Esslin, Martin. *Reflections, Essays on Modern Theatre.* New York: Doubleday, 1969.

Gassner, John & Allen, Ralph. *Theatre and Drama in the Making.* 2 vols. New York: Houghton Mifflin, 1967.

Gorchakov, Niklai A. *The Theatre in Soviet Russia.* Translated by Edgar Lehrman. New York: Columbia University Press, 1957.

Grosh, Judith. *The Right to Create.* Boston: Little, Brown, 1969.

Guthrie, Sir Tyrone. *Tyrone Guthrie on Acting.* New York: Viking Press, 1971.

———. *In Various Directions.* New York: Macmillan, 1965.

Haney, William V. *Communications and Organizational Behavior.* Homewood, Illinois: Richard D. Irwin, 1967.

International Theatre Institute. *Theatre 3, The American Theater 1969-1970.* New York: Scribner's, 1970.

Koffka, K. *Principles of Gestalt Psychology.* New York: Harcourt, 1935.

Mitchell, Roy. *Creative Theatre.* New York: Benjamin Blom, 1969.

Munk, Erica, ed. *Stanislavski and America.* New York:Hill & Wang, 1966.

Ortega y Gasset, J. *Man and People.* New York: W. W. Norton, 1957.

Osborn, Alex. *Achieving Characterization in Applied Imagination.* New York: Scribner's, 1963.

Parnes, Sydney and Harding, Harold F. *A Source Book for Creative Thinking.* New York: Scribner's, 1962.

Perls, F. S., et al. *Gestalt Therapy.* New York: Dell, 1964.

Stanislavski, Konstantin. *Building a Character.* New York: Theatre Arts Books, 1936.

Styan, J. L. *The Dramatic Experience.* New York: Cambridge University Press, 1964.

Vaughn, Stuart. *A Possible Theatre.* New York: McGraw-Hill, 1969.

8
Sensibility
and Emotion

. . . an actor can never let himself be
overcome by emotion. If he started to
cry during a scene, there wouldn't be
any play. Emotion can play a big part
in acting. Sometimes a role can tear
you to pieces. But it must always be
controlled emotion.*

Alfred Lunt

*From Morton Eustis, *Players At Work, Acting
According to the Actors,* Theatre Arts Books,
1937, p. 45. (Photo by permission of Alfred
Lunt)

The emphasis in the preceding chapters has been upon exercises. We began with relaxation and the use of the body and voice as pliable, effective acting instruments. From this base, we moved into other exercises dealing with pantomime, improvisation, concentration, imagination, play analysis, and characterization.

The exercises are not intended as an end in themselves. They are a means of uniting exterior physical actions with the actor's sensibilities: his interior impulses and feelings. Responses are never convincing if you attempt to *will* yourself to laugh or cry. Joy or sadness must come from within. Physical expressions for feelings are derived from analysis of the character and through the use of improvisation and emotional recall. These are immediate and direct means of "feeling the part."

Author Norman Mailer believes that

> . . . *actors, particularly stage actors, are very literal people. It's very important to them whether the salt shaker is here, or here. After all, a stage actor is a man or woman who is, if you will, the president of an emotional factory which has to produce the same product at the same minute every night. And so, they attach all sorts of conditioned reflexes in the gearing of their emotions to the placement of objects. They may pretend that they want motivation, a reason to pick up a salt shaker. But the fact of the matter is that the only way you can produce a certain emotion at a certain hour every night and do it without killing yourself is to set up a whole series of conditioned reflexes. Therefore, just as a dog salivates when he hears a bell ring, so the actor begins to weep when he reaches for the salt shaker.*[1]

There are machines today that store facts and reach decisions based on those facts. We have some machines that "think" and others with a built-in "will," but to date we have no machine that "feels." An actor who cannot feel is a machine. He will not move an audience because he lacks the human touch to interpret a character to an audience. This *Einfühlung*, or "feeling into," allows the actor an instant bond with the audience. He certainly cannot transmit emotion to others unless that emotion has actually been experienced by himself. How is this done? How can an actor convey the feelings of a murderer when he has never murdered? Thornton Wilder answers in this way:

> *We have all murdered, in our thoughts, or been murdered. We have all seen the ridiculous in estimable persons, and ourselves. We have all known terror, as well as enchantment.*[2]

CREATION AND RE-CREATION

Few laymen have any idea how a professional actor conditions himself for a character. While watching a play, the highest praise seems to be

[1]From Joseph Gelmis, *The Film Director as Superstar* (Garden City, New York: Doubleday, 1970, pp. 45-46.

[2]Preface to *Three Plays by Thornton Wilder* (New York: Harper and Row, 1957). By permission.

that an actor is "feeling the part"; otherwise they say he is "insincere." The fact is that if an actor feels the part at every performance, he will have no control over the elaborate and complicated machinery involved during the glandular and visceral changes brought on by instigating emotion. Once this machinery is set into motion, it is difficult to stop. Even in everyday life, after a siege of anger, grief, or fear, we need a cooling off interval, time again to gain control. On stage it is even more important that the actor have control, because others are also involved. If an entire cast on stage were feeling the part and doing nothing else, the result would be more madhouse than theatre. The paradox is that the actor cannot act unless he feels; but if he really feels, he cannot act.

Because this true paradox has been so controversial and remains confusing to many beginners and even to some professionals, I cannot say often enough that *the time for an actor to feel the part is when he studies and rehearses.* He can show raw emotion and be critical because when there is no pressure, raw emotion can then be adapted, designed, and *selected.* Only this process makes acting an art.

Emotion makes no sharp boundary between the true and the untrue. We all remember Pavlov's experiments with dogs. He rang a bell each time they were fed, and the dogs learned to associate the sound of the bell with food. When they were sufficiently conditioned, he rang the bell, and the dogs reacted automatically: saliva flowed, even though the food was not there. Were the dogs insincere?

In the creative acting process we must learn to use the three aspects of psychological life; thought, will, and emotion. We think out our problem, reach some decision, and, by force of will, re-excite emotion, and then we select that which is appropriate. *Later, before the audience, the previously arranged synthesis or conditioning will re-create the emotion.* It can even be made to appear spontaneous (which in fact it will be), and the entire process is sincere, controlled, and *artistically* true.

Clara Morris, one of America's first celebrated actresses, wrote:

> There are, when I am on stage, three separate currents of thought in my mind: one in which I am keenly alive to Clara Morris, to all the details of the play, and to the other actors and how they act, and to the audience; another about the play and the character I represent; and finally, the thought that really gives me stimulus for acting.[3]

To sum up our discussions thus far on emotion, we may conclude that the ability to summon emotion depends to a large extent upon the development of our imaginations: to be able to imagine a world of appearances as a real world, to see what is not before our eyes, to hear and feel sensations from past experiences as if they were in the present. If we can develop such an imagination, we can create emotion in ourselves and transmit it to others.

[3]Lewis C. Strang, *Plays and Players of the Last Quarter Century* (Boston: 1903), Vol. 2, p. 240.

EXERCISES IN EMOTION

Drills and exercises for the development of physical skills can be created much more confidently than exercises for developing emotion. Emotion eludes systematic inquiry. The intellect will submit to mechanical step-by-step methods, but the senses resist such mechanical props to produce or reproduce emotion. Each individual is apt to react differently to identical suggestions in dealing with emotions. Experience has taught me that the most rewarding method to cultivate sensory awareness in an inexperienced student is by development of an inner soliloquy. Emotion is a very private matter, and the teacher or drama coach is wise to admit at the start that he is an outsider. He must devise means of getting inside the private world and thoughts of his student. The following exercise in building emotion was constructed for a particular requirement and taken from a tape of my voice made during one of my classes. You may be able to adapt it to your special needs; if not, it will at least demonstrate one method of making the individual aware of his own conscience and how it may be used as a motivating instrument in building emotion.

EXERCISE 72. BUILDING EMOTION

Let's try a little exercise, not a difficult one when you are accustomed to it. In everyday life we try hard not to show our true feelings. In this exercise we are going to remove all such conditioned defenses. We'll need a volunteer, a man with a coat. All right, Frank, come up front please; turn your back to the class.

(Pause)

Now listen, but don't move until I tell you to. I want you to turn around easily and naturally. Remove your coat, just as you usually do—that's right—and place it on the chair; look front, now walk off left. Now what happened here? He completed a simple physical action. He was told precisely what to do and he did it. He had no need of initiative, he simply moved as instructed. All right, Frank, come back; put on your coat again please. Turn away, but listen.

(Pause. Voice here becomes more confidential)

Frank, this is Frank—the real one—speaking to you. Well, here we are back in our office again. Look around: same old desk, water cooler; yes, it's the same old dump. Let's go over to our desk. We were sure proud that first day when we got our own office, weren't we, Frank? Wow! Look at all that work piled up on that desk, and we have to finish it before we leave tonight. Well, get off the coat—yeah—and get to work. That's all we ever seem to do—work. I wish they'd fix this chair, put a little oil on it . . .

(Pause. Voice is normal)

Fine, Now, what was different? This time Frank motivated his own moves, or rather his conscience did. Now let's try something more difficult. Put on your coat, turn away, and concentrate. Relax, ease all tension. This won't work unless you're relaxed; you are going to allow your memory to take over. You are going to remember details which have been stored in your mind and long neglected. You'll remember even what indigestion *felt* like. Now, Frank, you work in this bank; this is your office, you have a key. You let yourself in. You are here tonight to fix the books. The examiners come tomorrow and they must not find that you have stolen six thousand dollars. You tried to get to the books today, but the boss got suspicious. Turn!

(The voice is confidential again)
Where's that watchman? He's got to think I'm working late, if he finds me here. All right, if he does I'll just act casual; you know, get a cup of water or something, ask about his kid—it'll be fine. That sandwich I bolted down is like a rock in my stomach. My mouth is dry; my hands are wet too. I'll rub them together. *Ah-oh,* here comes —that watchman. Steady, Frank, steady. I'll just take off my coat and smile at him. Is he coming in? No. He's smiling. Wave back, *wave back!* He's gone. I'm lucky. That was a close one. Now, where are the books . . .

(Normal voice)
That's all, thank you, Frank, very good.

An exercise of this kind is valuable not only in building characterization but also in exploring the feelings and actions of your character when he is not on stage. Obviously your character has not been standing waiting for his cue as you, the actor, have been. He has been somewhere, doing something, and this will affect what he does on stage. The Moscow Art Players developed *etudes,* as they call such invented scenes, to a fine degree. As the actor becomes accustomed to this technique, he will be able to use it without the aid of an instructor. He will invent words for his conscience himself and react to them.

In preparing a part, analyze each situation in the play with which you will be concerned, put it in simple terms as was done above, switch this information to your storehouse of memory, and allow it to motivate what the author requires of your character. In rehearsals, learn to select, refine, and control. Rely on getting help from inside. (Have you ever asked yourself, "Now, why did I do that?" Reasons can be found in that wonderful computer we call memory.) Learn to use messages from your memory. When you have no audience, ask your director what you have conveyed to him. Use him as your sounding board.

Each day we perform certain duties almost mechanically. Take one of your chores and add your imagination to it. Create a situation with your emotions. Relax. Transfer to automatic pilot and perform the duty.

EXERCISE 73. SOUNDS CAN STIMULATE EMOTIONS
1. Study of texture, pitch, volume, direction, and timing of human sounds such as those associated with fear, anger, grief, happiness, suspicion, and davening.[4]

[4]"Davening" is that rhythmic murmur or humming sound of repeated prayer or lament, such as old women make when in church or at funerals.

2. Make tapes of phrases of different mood sounds: a waltz, siren, merry-go-round, etc. The group should react physically to the moods presented in any way they feel moved.

EXERCISE 74. ANIMAL CHARACTERISTICS

Remember our animal exercises (#12) and how we worked to find attitudes of various animals? Now we extend this work to characterizations.

Using movement and speech, illustrate some animal characteristic *as it would apply to a human being.* As gentle as a lamb, roaring like a lion, strong as a bull, smart as a fox, etc.

EXERCISE 75. SENSE REACTIONS

Acting is one of the few art forms in which the creative moment is happening in the present, before the eyes and ears of the spectator. The actor must therefore be able to produce an efficacious moment at will, and spontaneously.

React to the following words by creating a sense stimulus for each:

SMELL: A bakery, a fish market, low tide, a perfume shop.
SIGHT: A miracle, maggots, a lake, an auto wreck, a tennis game.
HEARING: Tapping noises, birds, traffic, sirens.
TOUCH: Rain, velvet, thumb tacks, tree bark, marble, corrugated cardboard.
TASTE: Bitter medicine, ice cream, metal, honey, alum.

EXERCISE 76. EMOTIONAL RECALL

What counts in acting is what is done in preparation for an action. Consciousness must be associated with *the feeling of the action before that action is taken.* Muscular coordinations must be built up with corresponding sensory and emotional data. The actor's feelings control his bodily reactions. Rising from a chair is a physical habit. The actor needs to know the feelings that make him decide to get up.

Use the following words to revive feelings.

These words describe the effects to be created. The circumstances that produce the emotions are to be supplied by the actor.

Hate	Love	Fire	Water	Rejection
Joy	Fear	Flight	Cave	Heat
Pain	Cold	Surf	Blind	Threat

EXPRESSING CHARACTER AND EMOTION BY PHYSICAL MEANS

Let us suppose that one of your group has been assigned a part in a play. He has studied the play and his character, and discussed both with the director. The actor has decided that the essence of his character is craftiness and a distrust of others. Has anyone in the group ever seen or known

SENSIBILITY AND EMOTION   99

IN RICHARD MENNEN'S PRODUCTION OF EURIPIDES' *THE BACCHAE* (406 B.C.) FOR SWEET BRIAR COLLEGE, STRESS WAS PLACED ON THE FREE USE OF THE ACTOR'S PHYSICAL ATTRIBUTES, AS DEMONSTRATED BY THESE TWO SCENES OF THE ACTION. (COURTESY OF RICHARD MENNEN.)

a man who gave them such an impression? If so, the actor should describe his appearance and then, as he does, try to assume the character of the man *physically.* Perhaps someone has seen an animal that left him with such an impression of distrust and hostility.

IN GENERAL: In demonstrating physical aspects of characters, exercises are more effective if students are limited to the visual. You may have noted that all the simple exercises have certain limits that require you to isolate a particular aspect. In the following exercise, students should not speak or walk, but concentrate upon posture, stance, attitude, and facial expression. *In other words, they must limit themselves to a display of the visual symbol, the outer image of the character that will represent and reflect the inner character.*

Suppose the character is old. What happens physically in the aging process? Students should not begin their thinking with clichés for showing age: the bent back, the cane, or the piping voice. Instead, think of fading vision, faulty memory, unsteady balance, waning self-confidence, the stiffening joints of arthritis, how clothes hang, the weariness and despair all evidenced in the body and facial expression. Show the outer image of such a person. Perhaps our old man or old woman has lived a very active life. Perhaps he is an ex-wrestler or laborer and she a pioneer woman who has borne many children, driven teams of horses, chopped firewood. How might each look?

EXERCISE 77. CHARACTER ASSIGNMENTS

"Show us." The purpose of this exercise is to show physical attitudes. It should not be difficult if each player is fortified with study of the play and the character.

The instructor assigns one character from a well-known play to each student, who is to read and study the play out of class, with particular attention given to the role assigned. In a later session

100 THE CREATIVE PROCESS

each student will present to the group a *visual* characterization of that role. He may move about, perform short mimes, but he may not speak. Afterwards, he must be able to justify any movements he has made by quoting lines or actions from the play. (Notes are permissible when quoting lines or the author's description of the character.)

As an example, Sir Tyrone Guthrie directed *The Taming of the Shrew* with Petruchio as a shy, modest character. Are there lines in the play that might justify this concept?

Some characters from dramatic literature, novels, and life are suggested below. Additions might be supplied by the instructor.

MEN

FALSTAFF: Shakespeare tells us he is fat. What else is he? How will you show it?

A RETIRED ECONOMICS PROFESSOR: What is his age? How will his profession be indicated? His subject?

CHRIS: (in *Anna Christie*, by O'Neill)

MARCHBANKS:(in *Candida*, by Shaw)

FIRS: (in the *Cherry Orchard*, by Chekhov)

MOSCA: (in *Volpone*, by Ben Jonson)

ROSENCRANTZ:(in *Rosencrantz and Guildenstern Are Dead*, by Tom Stoppard)

WOMEN

AN OLD LIBRARIAN: Decide her age. Has she ever been married? Is she head librarian or an assistant? What are her hobbies? How does she dress and wear her hair? Is she a reader herself? What does she read?

LADY MACBETH: How does Shakespeare describe her? What do other characters in the play say about her? Do her actions in the play tell you what sort of woman she is? How will you show that? Translate Shakespeare's words into visual concepts.

MILLAMANT: in *The Way of the World* by Congreve. For further descriptions, refer to J. L. Styan's *The Dramatic Experience*, pages 8-9 (New York: Cambridge University Press, 1965).

Emotions are more vividly created by tangible motor sources than by intellectualizing and filtering the experience through words and abstractions. Your imagination responds much more readily to the shock of physical experience, to the sensations of body, weight, energy, and motion. The recurrence of physical sensations—such as the smell of a flower or the hearing of a sound—can revive unconscious memories of long-forgotten emotional experiences.

EXERCISE 78. EMOTIONAL CONTRASTS

A group stands around a single player, shouting personal insults at him. While they are in every way disagreeable, he answers them politely and with dignity. All players should allow their bodies to "feel out" private expressions. Definite objectives such as these take the actor out of himself and into another reality. Characterizations created by emotional means are dominated by a state of mind (or a mood) and by the alignment of the character's thoughts with the dramatic moment. Each player in this group should invent private circumstances for his wrath, just as the single player will have his reasons for his reaction.

EXERCISE 79. TRANSFERRING EMOTION BY THOUGHT

You are walking to class. You have just been awarded the lead in the new school play. The midterm C you had expected turned out to be an A. The world is a beautiful place. Be calm. Relax into these warm thoughts. Allow your emotions to reflect your contentment and happiness. Now a stranger is coming from another direction and your eyes meet. Transfer your emotion *by thought*. Don't use any mechanical tricks but allow your feelings to direct whatever you do. If the stranger reflects your joy, you have communicated your feelings to another.

In the beginning, a varying amount of stamping-in is required, depending upon the individual's aptitude. Once mastered, the re-exciting of emotion becomes autonomous or instinctive. Only *you* can develop this individual skill.

EXERCISE 80. CREATING AND SUSTAINING EMOTIONS

Improvise action and sound, but no dialogue. It is New Year's Eve, midnight. Place: a country club dance. Everyone is on the dance floor, noisy and uninhibited; the band is playing as the crowd celebrates. A woman enters. Her little son has just been run over. Her husband is a waiter here, and she must reach him through the crowd.

EXERCISE 81. CREATING CONTRASTING EMOTIONS

Improvise action and sound, but no dialogue. Two weary old guards stand in the foyer of a big city museum. The atmosphere is austere in deference to the museum's treasures. From outside, a tide of childish giggles and screechings can be heard; then an entire class of seventh-graders sweeps into the foyer, like surf hitting a beach. The guards move to restrain the youngsters, but the teacher anticipates them and controls the situation. Dignity regained, the class proceeds on its tour. The old men react to the near catastrophe, then in relief settle back into routine.

EXERCISE 82. CREATING EMOTIONAL REACTIONS

Improvise action, sound, and dialogue. Actual news item: A girl is murdered on a New York street in full view of a number of people. The two assailants escape unchallenged. A policeman finally arrives and questions every individual in the crowd. Each must explain why he or she did not interfere.

EXERCISE 83. SENSE IMPRESSIONS

Before the class meets, each student is to prepare himself by experiencing a sensory emotion, using the tongue, the nose, or the ear. A student might take a taste of hot pepper, or lemon. He might go to the beach at low tide or visit a candy factory to sense different smells, or listen to disturbing or calming sounds. This exercise deals with the *senses only*. These suggestions are given to stimulate your own thinking. Undergo the *actual experience!* (Not memory, at this time.) Later, in class, these experiences are to be translated into acting terms. *Memory* will then be used in class—*without the benefit of the stimuli.* The process is something like this:

1. Actual sensory experience *with* stimulus (taste the lemon).
2. Observation of emotional and physical reactions. (How did you feel when you tasted the lemon? How did the experience affect you physically? emotionally?)
3. Rehearse by recreating your reaction from memory; select, refine, and clarify, *then* present the learned behavior to the class; at that time, the actual experience should be relived.

Caution: In attempting to reproduce an emotion, a common fault of beginners is in forcing and straining, "willing" to feel. Sheer effort only defeats the purpose. The mind and body become tense and restricted. *Begin with relaxation.* "Seek hard, find not. Seek not, and find."

EXERCISE 84. MEMORY RECALL

Each student is to concentrate on a sensation, such as anxiety, pain, cold, heat, fatigue, pleasure, boredom, anticipation, hunger, or fear. Begin by recalling some time in your life when you actually experienced this emotion. Sit relaxed in a chair and begin telling the class about it, describe the time and place, the clothes you wore and how they felt, your mental state, the color of the room. No detail should be left out, no matter how insignificant it may seem. As you begin seeing it all again in your mind's eye, allow your relaxed body to feel the emotions again just as it happened before. You have begun with narration; now allow the emotion to take over, and gradually shift *from past to present tense.* It is happening now! Allow this to activate what you are now bringing out of your memory storehouse. Body involvement may be only slight, but *go through the motions;* that's the important thing. As the memory and the body begin to work together, you should actually be re-experiencing the emotion by a kind of subliminal guidance.

EXERCISE 85. EMOTIONAL REACTIONS

Improvise physical actions only:

Imagine you are spending the night in a haunted house. You do not believe in the supernatural but you are aroused by a knocking sound,

SENSIBILITY AND EMOTION 103

faint at first but becoming louder. Next, you hear footsteps approaching and feel a chill in the air. Show your reactions, being very careful not to use any cliches.

EXERCISE 86. TEARS

A child's tears may be the result of actual pain, or the means of getting what he wants. Tears can also be the result of some disappointment, such as *not* getting what the child wants. Some stimuli causing tears are: pain, desire, loss, sorrow, offense, injustice, anger, jealousy, hatred, and envy. Search back in your memory. Remember when you once cried? *Recall all the details of the circumstance.* Follow carefully the points as outlined in the exercise on memory recall and try producing tears.

A difficulty often encountered is the inability to release ourselves from the self-restraint conditioned since childhood. Parents often shame youngsters when they cry, telling them it is not "grown up." When the children do grow up, there is a firmly established association in their minds between tears and shame.

To produce the feeling for tears, remove that taint of shame from your mind and don't be concerned with how you look. Put yourself into the position of your character and the circumstances of the play. Call upon your emotional memory and your observation of people in similar situations. Think of what once made you cry. Then relax, concentrate, and give those emotions deep within you a chance to rise to the surface.

Maureen Stapleton quotes director Bobby Lewis as saying, "If crying were acting, my Aunt Rifke would be Duse." But Maureen feels that, "All you have to do to cry is set up the stimulus that will trigger the mechanism, and off you go. Laughing is much more difficult. On the whole, it's very hard to do a true laugh—a real laugh is so real you have no control over it."[5]

LAUGHTER

Max Eastman holds that "the mechanism of comic laughter may never be explained." Others have said that we laugh because we don't want to cry. There is extensive literature on the subject, but there are no solutions as to how to produce laughter at will, because it cannot be self-willed and still ring true. We cannot dissect it, and there are no mechanical formulas for producing it. We must be content to know what it is, what causes it, and where it starts. Josh Billings said, "Laughing is feeling good all over but showing it in one spot." Although laughter is exclusive with man, Eastman tells us, "Dogs can laugh—but only with their tails."

Psychologists see laughter as a defensive weapon, as if giving proof that the great are not so great, or a means of forestalling the other fellow's ridicule of us. Laughter is not an inborn instinct. We must learn to laugh

"I can't decide whether to go in for acting first and then politics, or go in for politics first and then switch to acting."

(FROM *THE WALL STREET JOURNAL.*)

[5]©1962 Lillian Ross. From *The Player, A Profile of an Art,* by Lillian Ross and Helen Ross, Simon and Schuster. Originally published in *The New Yorker.*

just as we learn to walk and talk. But it becomes a personal part of us. No police state can ever suppress laughter.

According to Aristotle, the ludicrous is "some defect or ugliness which is not painful or destructive." To understand this, we have only to remember that a baby's first laugh is apt to be stimulated by a momentary fear, then joy at the removal of that fear. A jack-in-the-box, the hunchback Punch of Punch and Judy, false faces, and lovable monsters, all follow Aristotle's theory.

Laughter cannot be accepted automatically as a sign of amusement alone. It may synthesize wonder, embarrassment, or discomfiture. It can be used as a weapon. We laugh at anything new. It can be used as an instrument for debunking. And when we laugh at a teacher's poor jokes, we do so for reasons other than amusement. It has been said that laughter can kill, and perhaps it can. One thing is certain; laughter likes society. Performers know that laughs are better when the house is full. We are not apt to laugh when we overhear a joke in a restaurant because we do not belong to the particular group enjoying it.

In summary, laughing expresses the emotions of joy or happiness, or it conceals other emotions: anger, shyness, derision, or contempt. We can conclude that *laughter and tears both begin in emotion coming from within.* If you can re-create emotion, you can laugh.

CHARACTERIZATION IN THE NEWER PLAYS

In the so-called Absurd plays coming from Europe and in today's non-structured plays being written for Off- and off-off Broadway, many innovations in playwriting have been made. Typical is the lack of a sequential build in a play; scenes are seldom accumulative. Whatever thread of story there is will often be shown in isolated, unrelated incidents and then left for the audience to develop as it will. Explanations of what has happened to the characters prior to the play are disregarded. Changing elements of time and place are introduced, as well as scenes of ritual, camp, or vaudeville.

In the Absurd plays, characters are more or less abstract and expressionistic; little or no personal development occurs within them. Frequently, they exist in an Orwellian void, as in the plays by Beckett and Ionesco.

Characters in a typical off-off Broadway play are often one dimensional, as in *America Hurrah!* or *Gorilla Queen*. In speaking of Jules Feiffer's plays, critic John Lahr says: "Characters have an immense intellectual resonance, but not necessarily a theatrical one. Performers find his plays difficult because they must perform in a strict and often ambigious circumference of gestures and emotions. The characters do not offer the actors a chance for emotional self-revelation. Feiffer's people, like Jonson's Lovewits and Congreve's Witwoulds, become an articulate amalgam of general attitudes focused in a particular man."[6]

[6]John Lahr, *Up Against the Fourth Wall* (New York: Grove Press, 1968), p. 81.

SENSIBILITY AND EMOTION   105

TRANSFORMATIONS

Off-off Broadway uses the term "transformations" to describe shifting characterizations. Each character has many different facets of character within him one being dominant and the most obvious. This dominant image, or face, we present to the world, but underneath are other faces that may burst through the skin of the main identity at any time, revealing contradictions or complexities. Advocates are careful to point out that this process is unlike the dual roles in hundreds of plays from Shakespeare to Brecht to Genet, in which one character pretends to be another. In the experimental plays, split personalities attempt to explore *the many different personalities within one personality.* The stated objective is that a continuity of progression will occur because the same actor plays the various facets of a character.

To make transformations convincing becomes a very difficult acting job. Not only is the actor required to assume several characters without previously preparing the audience, but he must be convincing in each. Actors are instructed not to attempt any Stanislavskian psychological motivations but to make these transformations only through physical manifestations. The changes must be made abruptly; the number of characters within a character that each actor must create is hardly conducive to penetration into any single role. By the time an actor has switched from being a condemned prisoner, to being his mother, and then to General Custer, the audience can be completely baffled.

EXERCISE 87. TRANSFORMATIONS #1

Explore a many-faceted character by first performing a single character improvisation, using established realities (given circumstances). Next devise another improvisation in which several different aspects of that same character are shown simultaneously. (See *Interview* by Jean-Claude Van Itallie, excerpt on p. 000.)

EXERCISE 88. TRANSFORMATIONS #2 (GROUP)

This exercise is for several actors. One student begins a narrative (such as where he was and what he was doing when the astronauts landed on the moon) using *first person narrative.* At a signal from the instructor another actor takes over, who must remember all the details established but must elaborate on the story—and keep the first person narrative.

FURTHER READING: SENSIBILITY AND EMOTION

Chekhov, Michael. *To the Actor.* New York: Harper, 1953.

Crile, W. G. *The Origin and Nature of Emotions.* Philadelphia: W. B. Saunders, 1929.

Gassner, John, ed. *Producing the Play.* New York: Holt, Rinehart, & Winston, 1953.

Geldard, F. A. *The Human Senses.* New York: John Wiley, 1959.

Ghiselin, Brewster, ed. *The Creative Process.* Berkeley: University of California Press, 1954; Mentor Books, 1955.

Gorchakov, Nikolai M. *Stanislavski Directs.* New York: Funk & Wagnalls, 1954.

Lund, F. H. *Emotions, Their Psychological, Physiological and Educative Implications.* New York: Ronald Press, 1939.

McClelland, D. *Studies in Motivation.* New York: Appleton-Century Crofts, 1955.

Marowitz, Charles. *Stanislavski and the Method.* New York: Citadel Press, 1964.

Milne, L. J. *The Senses of Animals and Men.* New York: Atheneum, 1962.

Pavlov, I. P. *Conditioned Reflexes.* New York: Dover, 1927.

Redgrave, Michael. *The Actor's Ways and Means.* London: William Heinemann Ltd., 1953.

Stanislavski, Konstantin. *An Actor Prepares.* New York: Theatre Arts Books, 1936.

———. *Creating a Role.* New York: Theatre Arts Books, 1961.

Wilson, Garff B. "Emotionalism in Acting." *Quarterly Journal of Speech* (Feb. 1956) pp. 45-54.

Woodbury, Lael J. "The Externalization of Emotion." *Educational Theatre Journal* (Oct. 1960) pp. 177-183.

Young, P. T. *Emotions in Men and Animals.* London: S. Wiley and Sons, 1943.

Young, Stark. *Theatre Practice.* New York: Scribner's, 1926.

9 Progression of Characters

"You study the character by living with him. When you rehearse, what the character is saying and how he is saying it begin to work in you. Even when you're sleeping, you're developing the character. It's solidifying in your unconscious. An actor shouldn't think on the stage. He must only do."*

Walter Matthau

*©1962 Lillian Ross. From *The Player, A Profile of an Art*, by Lillian Ross and Helen Ross, Simon and Schuster. Originally published in *The New Yorker*. (Photo courtesy of the William Morris Agency; by permission of Walter Matthau)

In the traditionally structured play there is a progression in the story; that is, the play does not end the way it began. There is also a progression in characters. They are introduced, we learn something of their past and what they want, and then they are confronted with a situation or crisis. In the resulting conflict, they are victorious or destroyed. Thus, progression keeps an audience interested in what is happening on stage.

As we have noted, some modern plays disregard progression, which may be one reason for their limited audience appeal. The function of mounting dramatic scenes is to reveal the constantly shifting psychic lives of the characters. In the great dramatic classics, such as *Romeo and Juliet*, transitions in the leading characters can be traced scene by scene. Physical actions are motivated by different drives but all eventually combine making the total goal of the character. For instance, in the opening of *Romeo and Juliet*, Romeo is brooding over a sentimental infatuation with a disdainful mistress. After seeing Juliet, he slips away from his friends and lingers in Capulet's garden, where he overhears Juliet's confession to the stars that she loves him. From this time on their *main goal* is to live happily as man and wife. But in each scene which follows, obstacles are put in the way.

Each action from then on has an individual motivation—but all will contribute to the main objective. In Act II, the drive of both is to be married, and so they are, in Friar Laurence's cell. But in Act III, Romeo is challenged by Juliet's cousin. Motivated by the thought that he is now Tybalt's kinsman, Romeo refuses to fight. But Mercutio, who does not understand Romeo's reluctance, takes the quarrel upon himself and is slain by Tybalt. Romeo then throws aside his leniency as he now has motivation to kill Tybalt—and for this he is banished. However, Juliet's parents, knowing nothing of her marriage to Romeo, believe that her grief is for her cousin Tybalt's death and try to alleviate her sorrow by insisting that she marry Paris. In this scene, Juliet's motivation is to avoid the union with Paris at any cost. *An actor must analyze each physical action for separate motivations which will lead also to the main goal.*

In a production, this character progression happens before the eyes of the spectators and yet the basic inner dynamism of the character is never lost. In any aspect of vital experience there is progression, some sequential development. Each living thing reacts to the outside world by constantly changing its total condition. When it ceases to do so, it is dead.

EXERCISE 89. CHARACTER PROGRESSION

1. Improvise a few lines of everyday dialogue such as, "Good Morning," "How are you?," "Nice day," etc.

2. Create characters and improvise the same as above.

3. Now, decide upon some experience these characters have just undergone. Show how they have changed—progressed or regressed, because of the experience, but use the same dialogue.

Sometimes it happens that an actor will be assigned a part which is only sketchily written by the playwright, or which is written so that it is abstract, or basically unsound. In such a case, imagination must be used to provide the concept of his character. The actor will need to fill in what the author has neglected to supply by using logical thought patterns as he would in planning an improvisation.

CHARACTER DEVELOPMENT

Unfortunately, many acting classes make a habit of working with short, isolated scenes or speeches and in this way students are never afforded the opportunity to study the relationship of that scene with others in the play. Also, the student is deprived of the experience of developing character, so important in acting. At best, students only have a chance to scan through the play and therefore fail to grasp the many dimensions of a character which might otherwise be revealed.

To provide students with more detailed experience, we are going to work on three scenes from Shakespeare's *Romeo and Juliet*. Each of these scenes requires a different approach to the characters, and yet all fit into the author's master objective for the entire play. In the work we are about to do you will benefit from work done previously in improvisations, play atmosphere, and characterizations.

PREPARATION FOR ROMEO AND JULIET

This play radiates a buoyant spirit of youth. It could only have been written by a young author; Shakespeare had just turned thirty. Although it has been thought of as Shakespeare's first tragedy, this word seems a morose label to place upon the most rapturous and joyful portrayal of young love in all dramatic literature.

The play begins in excitement and continues with a mounting, headlong speed. The theme, the sweetness and the bitterness of love, is of universal interest. The parent-child relationship is explored with significance and wisdom. The atmosphere is drenched in the subtropical climate of Verona and recalls odors of newly plowed spring earth. The sun burns hot to warm the blood of Shakespeare's lovers.

> *I pray thee, good Mercutio, let's retire,*
> *The day is hot, the Capulets abroad.*

At night, the moonlight streaks through medieval trees to caress them. One imagines that this play flowed easily from the poet's pen with one rapturous lyrical impulse. Some of the most moving emotions in all literature are found in this classic. Neither Romeo nor Juliet have the tragic flaws of character that Shakespeare gave to Lear and Macbeth; they are victims of a fate over which they have no control. There is also a great deal of humor in the play. Shakespeare might not have written it in this way had he waited until he was older.

THE CREATIVE PROCESS

Directions for a play cannot be written. This task must rest with the individual director and his particular actors. As Ingmar Bergman, the great Swedish director, has said:

> Written dialogue is like a musical score, almost incomprehensible to the average person. Its interpretation demands a technical knack plus a certain kind of imagination and feeling. One can write dialogue, but how it should be delivered, its rhythm, and tempo, what is to take place between the lines . . . all must be omitted for practical reasons. Such a detailed script would be unreadable. [1]

After a thorough study of this play, each student-actor should write a scene-by-scene description of what he imagines should be seen on the stage. This should be as brief as possible, say 250 words. Describe the setting as *you imagine* it; the lights, the color, the pace, the *feeling* you get from Shakespeare's play. Consider the progression of the story, the interweaving of elements, and the sequence of events that build surely and swiftly to the end. You will note how each scene serves a purpose, expresses a particular mood, and provides a development to carry the play along. Make it brief; remember that this entire story unfolds in four days' time. *Your condensation will show you the complete picture we must have in mind, even when we rehearse short, isolated scenes.* This procedure should be followed for all the excerpts in this book.

WHAT ARE WE TO CONVEY?

All of us have memories of love. As children, love fed and nurtured us. Actors should revive every sensation and action of love and recall these moments in their creative thinking. Do not think in the abstract, but remember where the loved one was, what he or she wore, what was said. As you rehearse, you will find Shakespeare's rich, mellifluous poetry a strong incentive. You must fashion a dream of old-world grace and poetry for your audience. You must transport them out of this century. An aura of fate permeates every scene, yet death and tragedy should not be emphasized for these are only the means by which our lovers attain their goal. They are victorious in death because in death they are together.

CHARACTERIZATION OF JULIET

Juliet's *objective* is to achieve life and love; her *antagonist* is her own mores. She is a fourteen-year-old girl (see Act I, Scene iii), living in the Middle Ages. A modern-day girl playing Juliet will need to know the position of women of that day, for only in the last century have women won their present position in society. Juliet, in the beginning of the play, is sheltered—her father calls her "green"; she is subservient, obedient, dutiful, and completely dependent upon her parents to make decisions. The

[1]Preface to *Four Screenplays by Ingmar Bergman,* translated by Lars Malmstrom and David Kushner (New York: Simon and Schuster, 1960). By permission of the publisher.

audience must never feel that the parents are cruel martinets. It was the accepted custom of the time that children obeyed without question. When Juliet decides to defy the authority of her mother, father, and nurse, we should appreciate her great courage in doing so.

Yet even in her happy moments, Juliet has premonitions of her death. She tells Romeo:

> Methinks I see thee now that thou art below
> As one dead in the bottom of a tomb.

The contrived and physical ideas of love held by the nurse contrast with Juliet's innocence and purity. However, Juliet is not all virginal innocence; her emotions are mixed with secret longings. Reread her speech in Act III, Scene ii, beginning with "Gallop apace you fiery-footed steeds . . ." You will realize that she is no cardboard doll.

When Romeo first sees her he says:

> What lady's that which doth enrich the hand
> Of yonder knight?
> O, she doth teach the torches to burn bright!
> Her beauty hangs upon the cheek of night,
> Like a rich jewel in an Ethiop's ear.

Juliet's youth and grace are noted by the Friar in his lines:

> Here comes the lady. Oh so light of foot
> Will ne'er wear out the everlasting flint;
> A lover may bestride the gossamer
> That idles in the wanton summer air
> And yet not fall, so light is vanity.

CHARACTERIZATION OF ROMEO

Romeo's *objective* is to bring reality to his dream world. His *antagonist* is fate. Hazlitt calls him "another Hamlet"—an impractical dreamer living not in this world but in one of his own making. He is a sentimentalist and less mature than Juliet. Shakespeare has given him many lines about dreaming as a key to his character. Some such lines are the cause of Mercutio's bantering "Queen Mab" speech. Juliet is his only reality. He scarcely hears what others say to him. Only after he kills Paris does he remember what has been said to him:

> What said my man when my betossed soul
> Did not attend him as we rode? I think
> He told me Paris should have married Juliet,
> Said he not so? or did I dream it so?

Montague describes his son in this way:

> But he, his own affections counselor
> Is to himself so secret and so close,
> So far from sounding and discovery,
> As is the bud bit with an envious worm,
> Ere he can spred his sweet leaves to the air
> Or dedicate his beauty to the sun.

SIMON WARD, WHO PLAYED THE TITLE ROLE IN THE FILM *YOUNG WINSTON*, APPEARS HERE AS ROMEO WITH SINEAD CUSACK AS JULIET IN SHAKESPEARE'S *ROMEO AND JULIET*. (COURTESY OF HER BRITANNIC MAJESTY'S CONSULATE-GENERAL.)

THE CREATIVE PROCESS

In the beginning of the play, Romeo is little more than an eager boy, but when he is forced by circumstances into responsibility and reality, he must learn to become a man. The audience must see this growth.

REHEARSAL

ROMEO AND JULIET

ACT II, SCENE ii

CAST: ROMEO
      JULIET

SCENE: *Exterior. The Capulet orchard directly beneath Juliet's balcony.*

Romeo has eluded his friends, Mercutio and Benvolio, and leapt the garden wall. As he appears from UR he looks back and overhears them making sport of his infatuation with Juliet.

(Enter Romeo)

ROMEO: He jests at scars that never felt a wound.[1]

But soft! What light through yonder window breaks?[2]

It is the East, and Juliet is the sun![3]

Arise, fair sun, and kill the envious moon,

Who is already sick and pale with grief,

[That thou her maid are far more fair than she.

Be not her maid, since she is envious;

Her vestal livery is but sick and green,

And none but fools do wear it; cast if off.][4]

[5]It is my lady; O, it is my love!

O that she knew she were![6]

She speaks, yet she says nothing. What of that?

Her eye discourses; I will answer it.[7]

I am too bold; 'tis not to me she speaks.

[Two of the fairest stars in all the heaven,

Having some business, do entreat her eyes

To twinkle in their spheres till they return.

What if her eyes were there, they in her head?

The brightness of her cheek would shame those stars

As daylight doth a lamp; her eyes in heaven

Would through the airy region stream so bright

That birds would sing and think it were not night.][8]

[9]See how she leans her cheek upon her hand!

O that I were a glove upon that hand,

That I might touch that cheek!

1. Romeo comments to himself about his friends' remarks. He stands almost hidden in the moonlight.

2. He turns as a light appears in Juliet's window.

3. Juliet walks out on the balcony looking at the beautiful, warm night. Seeing her is a breathtaking experience for Romeo.

4. These lines (within brackets) are frequently cut as they slow the action.

5. Juliet breathes in the beauty of the night. Just to see her gracious movements excites Romeo.

6. Her lips form the name "Romeo." She relishes each syllable but there is no sound.

7. She looks back into her room. Romeo dares one step out of the shadows, then steps back.

8. Lines within brackets are suggested cuts.

9. Juliet sits, leans her cheek upon her hand.

PROGRESSION OF CHARACTERS

10. She fills her lungs, enjoying the warm night air, pauses, then as she exhales, she voices a long sigh of pleasure.

11. Suggested cut.

12. Juliet stands. *Wherefore:* Why? for what reason?

13. He speaks out almost subconsciously.

14. Juliet pauses only a beat to allow Romeo to speak his line. Not conscious of his presence, she continues as if maintaining the original thought.

15. *Owes:* owns.

16. This speech makes Romeo bold enough to step into the light.

17. Not expecting Romeo, she is frightened.

18. *Counsel:* privacy.

19. She recognizes Romeo's voice.

20. *Dislike:* displeases.

21. *Wherefore:* why? for what reason?

JULIET: [10]Ay me!
ROMEO: She speaks.
  O, speak again, bright angel![11] [for thou art
  As glorious to this night, being o'er my head,
  As is a winged messenger of heaven
  Unto the white-upturned wond'ring eyes
  Of mortals that fall back to gaze on him
  When he bestrides the lazy-pacing clouds
  And sails upon the bosom of the air.]
JULIET: O Romeo, Romeo! wherefore[12] art thou Romeo?
  Deny that father and refuse thy name!
  Or, if thou wilt not, be but sworn my love,
  And I'll no longer be a Capulet.
ROMEO: [13]Shall I hear more, or shall I speak at this?
JULIET: [14]'Tis but thy name that is my enemy.
  Thou art thyself, though not a Montague.
  What's Montague? It is nor hand, nor foot,
  Nor arm, nor face, nor any other part
  Belonging to a man. O, be some other name!
  What's in a name? That which we call a rose
  By any other name would smell as sweet.
  So Romeo would, were he not Romeo called,
  Retain that dear perfection which he owes[15]
  Without that title. Romeo, doff thy name;
  And for that name, which is no part of thee,
  Take all myself.[16]
ROMEO: I take thee at thy word.
  Call me but love, and I'll be new baptized;
  Henceforth I never will be Romeo.
JULIET: [17]What man art thou that, thus bescreened in
    night,
  [18]So stumblest on my counsel?
ROMEO: By a name
  I know not how to tell thee who I am.
  My name, dear saint, is hateful to myself,
  Because it is an enemy to thee.
  Had I it written, I would tear the word.[19]
JULIET: My ears have yet not drunk a hundred words
  Of that tongue's utterance, yet I know the sound.
  Art thou not Romeo, and a Montague?
ROMEO: Neither, fair saint, if either thee dislike.[20]
JULIET: How camest thou hither, tell me, and wherefore?[21]
  The orchard walls are high and hard to climb,
  And the place death, considering who thou art,

If any of my kinsmen find thee here.

ROMEO: With love's light wings did I o'erperch[22] these
    walls;

For stony limits[23] cannot hold love out,

And what love can do, that dares love attempt.

Therefore thy kinsmen are no let[24] to me.

JULIET: If they do see thee,[25] they will murder thee.

ROMEO: Alack, there lies more peril in thine eye

Than twenty of their swords! Look thou but sweet,

And I am proof[26] against their enmity.

JULIET: I would not for the world they saw thee here.

ROMEO: I have night's cloak to hide me from their sight;

And but thou love me,[27] let them find me here.

My life were better ended by their hate

Than death prorogued,[28] wanting of thy love.

JULIET: By whose direction foundst thou out this place?

ROMEO: By love, that first did prompt me to enquire.

He[29] lent me counsel, and I lent him eyes.

I am no pilot, yet, wert thou as far

As that vast shore washed with the farthest sea,

I would adventure for such merchandise.

JULIET: Thou knowest the mask of night is on my face;[30]

Else would a maiden blush bepaint my cheek

For that which thou hast heard me speak tonight.

Fain would I dwell on form—fain, fain deny

What I have spoke; but farewell compliment![31]

[32]Does thou love me? I know thou wilt say "Ay";

And I will take thy word. Yet if thou swearest,

Thou mayst prove false. At lovers' perjuries,

They say Jove laughs. O gentle Romeo,

If thou dost love, pronounce it faithfully.

[33]Or if thou thinkst I am too quickly won,

I'll frown, and be perverse, and say thee nay,

So thou wilt woo; but else, not for the world.

In truth, fair Montague, I am too fond,

And therefore thou mayst think my 'havior light;[34]

But trust me, gentleman, I'll prove more true

Than those that have more cunning to be strange.[35]

I should have been more strange, I must confess,

But that thou overheardst, ere I was ware,[36]

My true love's passion. Therefore pardon me,

And not impute this yielding to light love,

Which the dark night hath so discovered.

ROMEO: [37]Lady, by yonder blessed moon I swear,

22. *O'erperch:* fly over.

23. *Stony limits:* stone wall.

24. *Let:* hindrance.

25. A sudden fear for Romeo's safety.

26. *Proof:* protected.

27. *But thou love me:* unless you love me. Once the lovers admit their love, they alternate between a lyrical joy and fear, as though that which they have discovered is too good to be true.

28. *Prorogued:* prolonged.

29. *He:* Cupid, God of Love.

30. Here Juliet is conscious of her upbringing, the etiquette and manners she has been taught.

31. *Compliment:* formality, politeness.

32. Discarding her inhibitions, she decides to be bold.

33. Again conscious that she may seem unladylike.

34. Common, unchaste.

35. *Strange:* aloof.

36. *Ware:* aware.

37. This is a sincere and solemn oath.

38. And Juliet takes it seriously. Like the child she is, Juliet expresses a tenderness, a wonder and longing, but she is ever conscious that this meeting is forbidden. Therefore, she is always aware of the house behind her. It represents a bondage to her background and to the sheltered way she has been raised. In contrast, Romeo standing in the garden, represents life and love. Juliet must convey her struggle between loyalty and desire.

39. *Idolatry:* all she idolizes.

40. *Contract:* understanding. Again she feels a kind of foreboding.

41. *Unadvised:* hasty.

42. She sits, leans over to say good night.

43. Romeo's boldness embarrasses her. Trying not to show it, she giggles like a child.

44. She rises.

45. *Frank:* liberal.

46. *Bounty:* my desire to give.

47. Nurse moves about offstage.

48. Nurse calls, "Juliet."

49. *Anon:* in a little.

50. She whispers hurriedly to Romeo, then goes inside. Tempo accelerates due to Juliet's fear of being discovered by the nurse. Physically and mentally she is being drawn first one way, then another.

51. Romeo moves about ecstatically, his soul sings as he seems to walk on air.

52. These lines should be spoken clearly, unemotionally. They should indicate for us what sort of practical and efficient woman this child could become. Juliet should speak these lines as one speech.

53. *Bent:* intentions.

That tips with silver all these fruit-tree tops—
JULIET: [38]O, swear not by the moon, the inconstant moon,
That monthly changes in her circled orb,
Lest that thy love prove likewise variable.
ROMEO: What shall I swear by?
JULIET: Do not swear at all;
Or if thou wilt, swear by thy gracious self,
Which is the god of my idolatry,[39]
And I'll believe thee.
ROMEO: If my heart's dear love—
JULIET: Well, do not swear. Although I joy in thee,
I have no joy of this contract[40] tonight.
It is too rash, too unadvised,[41] too sudden;
Too like the lightning, which doth cease to be
Ere one can say, "It lightens." Sweet, good night![42]
This bud of love, by summer's ripening breath,
May prove a beauteous flow'r when next we meet.
Good night, good night! As sweet repose and rest
Come to thy heart as that within my breast!
ROMEO: O, wilt thou leave me so unsatisfied?
JULIET: [43]What satisfaction canst thou have tonight?
ROMEO: The exchange of thy love's faithful vow for mine.
JULIET: I gave thee mine before thou didst request it;
And yet I would it were to give again.[44]
ROMEO: Wouldst thou withdraw it? For what purpose, love?
JULIET: But to be frank[45] and give it thee again.
And yet I wish but for the thing I have.
My bounty[46] is as boundless as the sea,
My love as deep; the more I give to thee,
The more I have, for both are infinite.[47]
I hear some noise within. Dear love, adieu![48]
Anon,[49] good nurse! Sweet Montague, be true.
[50]Stay but a little, I will come again.
ROMEO: O blessed, blessed night![51] I am afeard,
Being in night, all this is but a dream,
Too flattering sweet to be substantial.
                              (Re-enter Juliet above)
JULIET: [52]Three words, dear Romeo, and good night indeed.
If that thy bent[53] of love be honorable,
Thy purpose marriage, send me word tomorrow,
By one that I'll procure[54] to come to thee,
Where and what time thou wilt perform the rite;

And all my fortunes at thy foot I'll lay[55]
And follow thee my lord throughout the world.
NURSE: *(Within)* Madam![56]
JULIET: I come, anon.—But if thou meanst not well,
    I do beseech thee—
NURSE: *(Within)* Madam!
JULIET: By-and-by I come.—
    To cease thy suit[57] and leave me to my grief.
    Tomorrow will I send.
ROMEO: So thrive my soul—
JULIET: A thousand times good night![58]
ROMEO: A thousand times the worse, to want thy light!
    Love goes toward love as schoolboys from their books;
    But love from love, towards school with heavy looks.[59]

                        (Enter Juliet again)

JULIET: Hist! Romeo, hist! O for a falc'ner's[60] voice
    To lure this tassel-gentle[61] back again!
    Bondage[62] is hoarse and may not speak aloud;
    Else would I tear the cave where Echo lies,
    And make her airy tongue more hoarse than mine
    With repetition of my Romeo's name.[63]
    Romeo!
ROMEO: It is my soul[64] that calls upon my name.
    How silver-sweet sound lovers' tongues by night,
    Like softest music to attending ears!
JULIET: [65]Romeo!
ROMEO: My sweet?
JULIET: What o'clock tomorrow
    Shall I send to thee?
ROMEO: By the hour of nine.
JULIET: I will not fail. 'Tis twenty years till then.
    [66]I have forgot why I did call thee back.
ROMEO: Let me stand here till thou remember it.
JULIET: I shall forget, to have thee still stand there,
    Remem'bring how I love thy company.
ROMEO: And I'll still stay, to have thee still forget,
    Forgetting any other home but this.
JULIET: 'Tis almost morning. I would have thee gone—
    And yet no farther than a wanton's bird,[67]
    That lets it hop a little from her hand,
    Like a poor prisoner in his twisted gyves,[68]
    And with a silk thread plucks it back again,
    So loving-jealous of his liberty.
ROMEO: I would I were thy bird.

PROGRESSION OF CHARACTERS

54. *Procure:* arrange.
55. Like a triumphant army.
56. Each off-stage call gets louder.
57. *Cease thy suit:* stop courting her.
58. She throws him a kiss and exits.
59. Romeo walks slowly into the shadows.
60. *Falc'ner:* one who hunts with falcon.
61. *Tassel-gentle:* a male falcon.
62. *Bondage:* Here she refers to her subservient position in her father's house.
63. A full stop as he walks back into the light. Then as she devours him with her eyes, she repeats his name as if addressing a god.
64. Juliet is his soul mate.
65. Evidently Juliet has satisfied the nurse inside. She is calmer, fixing her eyes adoringly upon Romeo.
66. Another pause. Again embarrassed, she giggles, then speaks, "I have forgot."
67. *Wanton's bird:* a playful child's bird.
68. *Gyves:* bonds.

117

70. *Ghostly father:* spiritual adviser (friar).

71. *Dear hap:* good fortune. Slowly Romeo walks off stage, hardly believing what he has seen or heard.

JULIET: Sweet, so would I.
   Yet I should kill thee with much cherishing.
   Good night, good night! Parting is such sweet sorrow,
   That I shall say good night till it be morrow.
ROMEO: Sleep dwell upon thine eyes, peace in thy breast![69]
   Would I were sleep and peace, so sweet to rest!
   Hence will I to my ghostly father's cell,[70]
   His help to crave and my dear hap to tell.[71]

PREPARATION FOR ACT III, SCENE v

The permanent stage of the Elizabethan theatre was adaptable enough to allow the first lines of this scene between Romeo and Juliet to be played above on the balcony. Then, for the remainder of the scene, Juliet descended to the lower stage by means of the tiring house[3] stairs. According to Quarto I ("She goeth from the window"), this descent was covered by the Nurse's lines until after Romeo had made his exit.

However, for purposes of the proscenium theatre, the confusion is usually settled by representing the interior rather than the exterior of Juliet's bedroom. DL is a door to the hall, at R a large window showing the balcony and garden outside. UR is a chair (or bed).

The character of Juliet reaches a climax in this scene. She must make a decision. Either she obeys her father and mother as she has always done, or she must renounce everything she has ever known and follow the dictates of her love—even if it means death. "If all else fail myself have power to die." Juliet's inner struggle is conveyed in many lines dealing with fate and prophecy.

Just as the Elizabethan common man believed that fate was controlled by the heavens, he was also convinced that his future could be read in the stars. In the prologue, Shakespeare refers to Romeo and Juliet as a "pair of star-crossed lovers." In Act I, Scene iv, Romeo speaks of those stars:

> *My mind misgives*
> *Some consequences, yet hanging in the stars,*
> *Shall bitterly begin this fearful date*
> *With this night's revels and expire the term*
> *Of a despised life, closed in my breast,*
> *But he that hath the steerage of my course*
> *Direct my sail!*

Later, when hearing of Juliet's death, Romeo says, "Then I defy you stars." Did Shakespeare himself believe this? Probably not, for in *Julius Caesar* Cassius says:

[3]Tiring house: attiring house, now dressing rooms or backstage.

> Men at sometime are masters of their fates;
> The fault dear Brutus, is not in our stars
> But in ourselves.

The point is that he was so great a man of the theatre that he makes us believe it by artfully reflecting the climate of opinion in which he lived. This belief in stars is used throughout the entire play to give the feeling that fate is pressing in, consuming the lovers. The important scene we are going to consider next deals not only with Juliet's moment of decision but with the beginning of her courageous fight against destiny.

ROMEO AND JULIET

ACT III, SCENE v

CAST: ROMEO JULIET
       CAPULET NURSE
       LADY CAPULET

SCENE: *Interior. Juliet's bedroom.*

The scene begins with Romeo and Juliet in an embrace, standing before the interior of her balcony window (now at UR). Gently and reluctantly he takes his lips from hers. As if to return them, she pleads,

JULIET: Wilt thou be gone? It is not yet near day.
    It was the nightingale, and not the lark,
    That pierced the fearful hollow[1] of thine ear.
    Nightly she sings on yon pomegranate tree.[2]
    Believe me, love, it was the nightingale.
ROMEO: It was the lark, the herald of the morn;
    No nightingale.[3] Look, love, what envious streaks
    Do lace[4] the severing clouds in yonder East.
    Night's candles[5] are burnt out, and jocund day
    Stands tiptoe on the misty mountain tops.
    [6]I must be gone and live, or stay and die.
JULIET: Yon light is not daylight;[7] I know it, I.
    It is some meteor[8] that the sun exhales
    To be to thee this night a torchbearer
    and light thee on thy way to Mantua.
    Therefore stay yet; thou needst not to be gone.
ROMEO:[9] Let me be ta'en, let me be put to death.
    I am content, so thou wilt have it so.
    I'll say yon grey is not the morning's eye,[10]
    'Tis but the pale reflex of Cynthia's[11] brow;

1. *Fearful hollow:* apprehensive.

2. Romeo knows she is trying to reassure him and corrects her gently with a smile as he shakes his head, "No."

3. He turns his head, looks out the window. *Envious:* Malicious.

4. *Lace:* streak. *Severing:* scattering.

5. *Night's candles:* stars.

6. Turns from her and tenderly states a fact.

7. Trying harder to convince him.

8. *Meteor:* Elizabethans believed that a meteor was a sign from one of the Heavenly bodies.

9. He steps back, his gesture conveying that he willingly offers his person as a sacrifice.

10. Might be restated as, "This beginning light is not from the sun."

11. *Cynthia:* moon goddess. *Reflex:* reflection.

12. *Vaulty:* arched.

13. *Care:* desire. He sees the dread in her face and tries to comfort her.

14. A sincere vow. This with his reference to death frightens Juliet.

15. But her fears burst out.

16. Some actresses cut these bracketed lines of description as they tend to break the emotion of terror they are trying to sustain. You might try the lines as Shakespeare wrote them and determine if you can hold the mood.

17. The nurse has been outside on guard. Now she enters DL.

18. *Be wary, look about:* be careful, watch out for yourself.

18a. Method of determining days by counting up every unit.

19. *Much in years:* aged. Juliet's sense of foreboding is again coming to the surface.

20. He climbs over the balustrade and disappears.

21. Again the prophecy, as she looks down at Romeo, standing in the orchard.

22. Grief was thought to consume blood.

23. She speaks to the unseen fates around her.

Nor that is not the lark whose notes do beat
The vaulty[12] heaven so high above our heads.
I have more care[13] to stay than will to go.
Come, death, and welcome![14] Juliet wills it so.
How is't, my soul? Let's talk; it is not day.
JULIET:[15] It is, it is! Hie hence, be gone, away!
It is the lark that sings so out of tune,
Straining harsh discords and unpleasing sharps.
[16][Some say the lark makes sweet division;
This doth not so, for she divideth us.
Some say the lark and loathed toad changed eyes;
O, now I would they had changed voices too,
Since arm from arm that voice doth us affray,
Hunting thee hence with hunt's-up to the day!]
O, now be gone! More light and light it grows.
ROMEO: More light and light—more dark and dark our
    woes!

(Enter Nurse hastily)[17]

NURSE: Madam?
JULIET: Nurse?
NURSE: Your lady mother is coming to your chamber.
The day is broke; be wary, look about.[18]

(Nurse exits)

JULIET: Then, window, let day in, and let life out.
ROMEO: Farewell, farewell! One kiss, and I'll descend.
JULIET: Art thou gone so, my lord, my love, my friend?
I must hear from thee every day in the hour,
For in a minute there are many days.[18a]
O, by this count I shall be much in years[19]
Ere I again behold my Romeo!
ROMEO: Farewell!
I will omit no opportunity
That may convey my greetings, love, to thee.
JULIET: O, thinkst thou we shall ever meet again?
ROMEO: I doubt it not; and all these woes shall serve
For sweet discourses in our time to come.[20]
JULIET: O God, I have an ill-divining soul![21]
Methinks I see thee, now thou art below,
As one dead in the bottom of a tomb.
Either my eyesight fails, or thou lookst pale.
ROMEO: And trust me, love, in my eye so do you.
Dry sorrow drinks our blood.[22] Adieu! Adieu!

(He exits)

JULIET: O Fortune, Fortune![23] all men call thee fickle.

　　　　　　　THE CREATIVE PROCESS

If thou art fickle, what doest thou with him
That is renowned for faith? Be fickle, Fortune,
For then I hope thou wilt not keep him long
But send him back.

LADY CAPULET: *(Within)* Ho, daughter! are you up?

JULIET: Who is't that calls?[24] It is my lady mother.
Is she not down so late,[25] or up so early?
What unaccustomed cause procures[26] her hither?

(Enter Lady Capulet)

LADY CAPULET: Why, how now,[27] Juliet?

JULIET: Madam, I am not well.

LADY CAPULET: Evermore weeping for your cousin's
death?[28]
What, wilt thou wash him from his grave with tears?
An if thou couldst, thou couldst not make him live.
Therefore have done. Some grief shows much of love;
But much of grief shows still some want of wit.

JULIET: Yet let me weep for such a feeling[29] loss.

LADY CAPULET: So shall you feel the loss, but not the
friend
Which you weep for.

JULIET: Feeling so the loss,[30]
I cannot choose but ever weep the friend.

LADY CAPULET: Well, girl, thou weepst not so much for
his death
As that the villain lives which[31] slaughtered him.

JULIET: What villain, madam?

LADY CAPULET: That same villain, Romeo.

JULIET: *(Aside)* Villain and he be many miles asunder.
God pardon him! I do, with all my heart;
And yet no man like[32] he doth grieve my heart.

LADY CAPULET: That is because the traitor murderer lives.

JULIET: Ay, madam, from the reach of these my hands.
Would none but I might venge my cousin's death!

LADY CAPULET: We will have vengeance for it, fear thou
not.
Then weep no more. I'll send to one in Mantua,
Where that same banished runagate[33] doth live,
[34]Shall give him such an unaccustomed dram
That he shall soon keep Tybalt company;
And then I hope thou wilt be satisfied.

JULIET: Indeed I never shall be satisfied
With Romeo till I behold him—dead—[35]
Is my poor heart so for a kinsman vexed.

24. "Who is't that calls" is spoken loudly, giving her time to look about herself, the room, and to voice her inner thoughts ("It is my lady mother", etc.)

25. *Down so late:* in bed.

26. *Procures:* brings.

27. "How now" is not a challenge or a suspicion, but a warm greeting. Juliet's mother is a lady of breeding and authority. She is accustomed to respect and shows that she expects it. She is not a witch, and Capulet is not a villain. They are devoted to their daughter and nothing is too much trouble where Juliet is concerned. Lady Capulet enters from the door DL, takes her daughter's hands, holding her fondly at arm's length in order to study her face. Juliet is embarrassed at her mother's concern (like any teenager) and walks a little UC on her line, "I am not well."

28. Lady C assumes that her daughter is grieving over the death of her cousin Tybalt. She goes to Juliet to comfort her.

29. *Feeling:* Heartfelt.

30. Lady C crosses Juliet to R near window.

31. *Which:* who.

32. *Like:* as much as.

33. *Runagate:* renegade, fugitive.

34. *Shall:* who shall.

35. Juliet starts this line truthfully, then realizes she is speaking to her mother and adds "dead."

36. *Temper:* adulterate. This would satisfy her mother because it might be assumed she means to mix poisons.

37. Lady C has finished this subject and puts a full stop to it by walking upstage and sitting. She smiles in anticipation as she begins a fresh topic.

38. Juliet kneels beside her mother.

39. *Careful:* provident.

40. *Sorted out:* chosen.

41. *In happy time:* opportune.

42. Lady C believes she is the bearer of joyful news; therefore she enjoys "starring" each important word.

43. This line is the high point of Lady C's speech. On it Juliet rises.

44. Juliet paces in anger, ends at DLC.

45. Realizes her rashness and quickly corrects it. She is in tears.

46. Lady C moves DL level with Juliet.

47. Capulet also believes Juliet grieves for her cousin's death. *Conduit:* a water pipe or more politely, a fountain, but the former is more like Capulet's earthy style. He crosses in front of his wife to Juliet.

48. Suggested cuts.

49. *Counterfeitst:* copy.

50. Nurse remains before door DL. At this point Juliet is at window (DR) her father L of her, and Lady C is at UR.

Madam, if you could find out but a man
To bear a poison, I would temper[36] it;
That Romeo should, upon receipt thereof,
Soon sleep in quiet. O, how my heart abhors
To hear him named and cannot come to him,
To wreak the love I bore my cousin Tybalt
Upon his body that hath slaughtered him!
LADY CAPULET: Find thou the means, and I'll find such a
    man.[37]
But now I'll tell thee joyful tidings, girl.
JULIET: And joy comes well in such a needy time.[38]
    What are they, I beseech your ladyship?
LADY CAPULET: Well, well, thou hast a careful[39] father,
    child;
One who, to put thee from thy heaviness,
Hath sorted out[40] a sudden day of joy.
That thou expects not nor I looked not for.
JULIET: Madam, in happy time![41] What day is that?
LADY CAPULET: Marry, my child, early next Thursday morn
    The gallant, young, and noble gentleman,[42]
    The County Paris, at Saint Peter's Church,
    Shall happily make thee there a joyful bride.[43]
JULIET: Now by Saint Peter's Church,[44] and Peter too,
He shall not make me there a joyful bride!
I wonder at this haste, that I must wed
Ere he that should be husband comes to woo.
I pray you tell my lord and father, madam,
I will not marry yet; and when I do, I swear
It shall be Romeo,[45] whom you know I hate,
Rather than Paris. These are news indeed!
LADY CAPULET: Here comes your father.[46] Tell him so your-
    self.
And see how he will take it at your hands
                                    (*Enter Capulet and Nurse*)
CAPULET: When the sun sets the air doth drizzle dew,
    But for the sunset of my brother's son
    It rains downright.
    How now? a conduit,[47] girl? What, still in tears?
    Evermore show'ring?[48] [In one little body
    Thou counterfeitst[49] a bark, a sea, a wind:
    For still thy eyes, which I may call the sea,[50]
    Do ebb and flow with tears; the bark thy body is,
    Sailing in this salt flood; the winds, thy sighs,
    Who, raging with thy tears and they with them,

Without a sudden calm will overset
Thy tempest-tossed body.][48] How now, wife?
Have you delivered to her our decree?

LADY CAPULET: Ay, sir; but she will none, she gives you
    thanks.[51]
I would the fool were married to her grave!

CAPULET: [52]Soft! Take me with you, take me with you,[53]
    wife.
Is she not proud? Doth she not count her blest,
Unworthy as she is, that we have wrought[54]
So worthy a gentleman to be her bridegroom?

JULIET: Not proud you have, but thankful that you have.
Proud can I never be of what I hate,
But thankful even for hate, that is meant love.

CAPULET: How now, how now, choplogic?[55] What is this?
"Proud"—and "I thank you"—and "I thank you not"—
And yet "not proud"? Mistress minion you,[56]
Thank me no thankings, nor proud me no prouds,
But fettle[57] your fine joints 'gainst Thursday next
To go with Paris to Saint Peter's Church,
Or I will drag thee on a[58] hurdle thither.
Out, you green-sickness[59] carrion! out, you baggage!
You tallow-face![60]

LADY CAPULET: Fie, fie, what, are you mad?[61]

JULIET: Good father, I beseech you on my knees.
                        (She kneels)
Hear me with patience but to[62] speak a word.

CAPULET: Hang thee, young baggage![63] disobedient
    wretch!
I tell thee what—get thee to church a Thursday
Or never after look me in the face.
Speak not, reply not, do not answer me!
My fingers itch.[64] Wife, we scarce thought us blest
That God had lent us but this only child;
But now I see this one is one too much,
And that we have a curse in having her.
Out on her, hilding![65]

NURSE: [66]God in heaven bless her!
You are to blame, my lord, to rate[67] her so.

CAPULET: And why, my Lady Wisdom? Hold your tongue,
Good Prudence. Smatter[68] with your gossips, go!

NURSE: I speak no treason.

CAPULET: O, God-i-god-en![69]

NURSE: May not one speak?

51. *She gives you thanks:* no thank you. Lady C moves down on a level with the others.

52. Now Capulet begins a long tirade, starting with a kind of disbelief that his plans have not been happily received. During the speech he convinces himself of his injuries. Later when he delivers his ultimatum, he is at "the top of his bent."

53. *Take me with you:* let me understand you.

54. *Wrought:* managed.

55. *Choplogic:* pedantic nonsense.

56. *Mistress minion:* spoiled hussy.

57. *Fettle:* make ready.

58. *Hurdle:* sledge used to drag criminals to execution.

59. *Green sickness:* anemia affecting adolescent girls. *Carrion:* flesh.

60. *Tallow:* yellow-white.

61. Lady C berates her husband for losing his temper as she goes to him at center.

62. *But to:* just long enough to.

63. *Baggage:* burden.

64. *Itch:* that is, he confesses an impulse to throttle his daughter. *Scarce:* little.

65. *Hilding:* wretch. In anguish, Lady C moves to UL.

66. Nurse steps up level with Capulet. Her remarks tend to sober his anger. She is more annoying to him than irritating.

67. *Rate:* scold. Now begins an ensemble "build" of excitement and temper in which each character contributes.

68. *Smatter:* idle chatter.

69. *God-i-god-en:* God give you a good evening. Usually spoken as one word, Godyegoden.

71. Lady C moves from UL to UR as this fishwife quarreling offends her.

72. *God's bread:* consecrated bread. Capulet is relating what pains he has been to, to serve his daughter well. It is his justification for his former tirade, but what was begun as an apology ends in an angry threat as he becomes caught up in his emotions. In other words, Capulet has *two* "builds," the first starting low and building to a climax. Annoyance with the Nurse quiets him, and he begins again in control of himself, but builds to a greater climax than previously.

73. *Demesnes:* domains, property.

74. *Parts:* qualities.

75. Capulet is at center, Juliet at his R, Lady C at UR, and Nurse, DL. *Puling:* whining.

76. *Mammet:* marionette. *In her fortunes tender:* a fine opportunity.

77. *Pardon you:* quibble on "Excuse me."

78. *I do not use to:* Not accustomed to joke.

79. *Advise:* consider.

80. *Trust to't:* be assured of it. *I'll not be forsworn:* I'll not break my oath.

81. Juliet moves a step toward door where he left, as if to plead with him, but stops, looking about for other help. There is none.

82. *Monument:* burial vault.

83. Lady C is cold, resigned that her husband must be obeyed. She crosses Juliet to DL near door, speaking her final line just before leaving.

84. Her pledge on earth and heaven—how can she marry twice?

CAPULET: Peace, you mumbling fool!
  Utter your gravity o'er a gossip's bowl,[70]
  For here we need it not.
LADY CAPULET:[71] You are too hot.
CAPULET: God's bread![72] it makes me mad. Day, night, late, early,
  At home, abroad, alone, in company,
  Walking or sleeping, still my care hath been
  To have her matched; and having now provided
  A gentleman of princely parentage,
  Of fair demesnes,[73] youthful, and nobly trained,
  Stuffed, as they say, with honorable parts,[74]
  Proportioned as one's thought would wish a man—
  And then to have a wretched puling fool,[75]
  A whining mammet,[76] in her fortune's tender,
  To answer, "I'll not wed, I cannot love;
  I am too young, I pray you pardon me!"
  But, an you will not wed, I'll pardon you.[77]
  Graze where you will, you shall not house with me.
  Look to't, think on't; I do not use to jest.[78]
  Thursday is near; lay hand on heart, advise;[79]
  An you be mine, I'll give you to my friend;
  An you be not, hang, beg, starve, die in the streets,
  For, by my soul, I'll ne'er acknowledge thee,
  Nor what is mine shall never do thee good.
  Trust to't.[80] Bethink you. I'll not be forsworn.
                    (*He exits*)[81]

JULIET: Is there no pity sitting in the clouds
  That sees into the bottom of my grief?
  O sweet my mother, cast me not away!
  Delay this marriage for a month, a week;
  Or, if you do not, make the bridal bed
  In that dim monument[82] where Tybalt lies.
LADY CAPULET: Talk not to me, for I'll not speak a word.[83]
  Do as thou wilt, for I have done with thee.
                    (*Exit*)

JULIET: O God!—O nurse, how shall this be prevented?
  My husband is on earth, my faith in heaven.[84]
  How shall that faith return again to earth
  Unless that husband send it me from heaven
  By leaving earth? Comfort me, counsel me.
  Alack, alack, that heaven should practice stratagems[85]
  Upon so soft a subject as myself!

What sayst thou? Hast thou not a word of joy?
Some comfort, nurse.
NURSE: Faith, here it is.[86]
Romeo is banisht; and all the world to nothing[87]
That he dares ne'er come back to challenge[88] you;
Or if he do, it needs must be by stealth.
Then, since the case so stands as now it doth,
I think it best you married with the County[89]
O, he's a lovely gentlemen!
Romeo's a dishclout to him.[90] An eagle, madam,
Hath not so green, so quick, so fair an eye[91]
As Paris hath. Beshrew[92] my very heart,
I think you are happy in this second match,[93]
For it excels your first; or if it did not,
Your first is dead—or 'twere as good he were
As living here[94] and you no use of him.
JULIET: [95]Speakest thou this from thy heart?
NURSE: [96]And from my soul too; else beshrew them both.
JULIET: [97]Amen!
NURSE: [98]What?
JULIET: Well,[99] thou hast comforted me marvelous much.
Go in; and tell my lady I am gone,
Having displeased my father, to Laurence' cell,
To make confession and to be absolved.
NURSE: Marry, I will;[100] and this is wisely done.
                              (Exit)[101]
JULIET: Ancient damnation! O most wicket fiend!
Is it more sin to wish me thus forsworn,
Or to dispraise my lord with that same tongue
Which she has praised him with above compare
So many thousand times? Go; counselor!
Thou and my bosom henceforth shall be twain.[102]
I'll to the friar to know his remedy.
If all else fail,[103] myself have power to die.
                              (Exit)

85. *Stratagems:* dreadful deeds. *Upon:* attempt to trap.

86. Nurse chuckles with self-satisfaction as she crosses to chair UR and sits.

87. *All the world to nothing:* odds are all to nothing. Juliet walks up to her in disbelief. She might kneel beside her.

88. *Challenge:* claim.

89. *The County:* Paris. Noticing Juliet's shocked expression, she reassures her.

90. *To:* compared with. *Dishclout:* rag.

91. *Green:* color much admired in eyes. *Quick:* lively.

92. *Beshrew:* may I be cursed.

93. Nurse is positive she has solved the problem.

94. *Here:* in this world.

95. Heretofore, Juliet has always had sympathy and understanding from her old Nurse; now even this is denied her.

96. Nurse repeats her oath firmly.

97. And Juliet puts a final benediction on the oath. Her tone is far from reverent.

98. Nurse rises.

99. Each word is sarcastic.

100. But the Nurse is satisfied, walks to door DR and speaks "This is wisely done," just before she exits.

101. A long pause. Then *Ancient Damnation:* damned old woman.

102. *Thou and my bosom henceforth shall be twain:* I'll never confide in you again.

103. This is Juliet's lowest point in the play. Never again, not even in the tomb, will she be so defeated and alone. She can think of only one hope, the Friar. She takes up a cape, throws it over her shoulders, and starts to leave.
Now that she has chosen this path to follow, she never wavers from this point on.

ROMEO AND JULIET

ACT V, SCENE iii

CAST: ROMEO JULIET PARIS

SCENE: *Interior of the Capulet tomb illuminated by candles. Juliet is lying on a bier at C. UR is a door or an arch. Paris is kneeling in prayer near the bier. He hears Romeo approaching and backs into the shadows. Paris knows who is coming. Romeo enters, having come almost by instinct alone. He is not able to think or plan logically; in fact, he has many of the characteristics of a person in shock. He looks about. In so doing he must convey to us the dank and dark and smell of a tomb as well as his mental and emotional state.*

ROMEO: Thou detestable maw,[1] thou womb of death,[2]
   Gorged with the dearest morsel of the earth.

PARIS:[3] This is that banisht haughty Montague
   That murdered my love's cousin—with which grief
   It is supposed the fair creature died—
   And here is come to so dome villainous shame
   To the dead bodies. I will apprehend him.[4]
   Stop thy unhallowed toil, vile Montague!
   Can vengeance be pursued further than death?
   Condemned villain, I do apprehend thee,[5]
   Obey, and go with me; for thou must die.[6]

ROMEO: I must indeed; and therefore came I hither.
   Good gentle youth, tempt not a desp'rate man.
   Fly hence and leave me. Think upon these gone;[7]
   Let them affright thee. I beseech thee, youth,
   Put not another sin upon my head
   By urging me to fury.[8] O, be gone!
   By heaven, I love thee better than myself,
   For I come here armed against myself.
   Stay not, be gone. Live,[9] and hereafter say
   A madman's mercy bid thee run away.

PARIS: I do defy that conjuration.[10]
   And apprehend thee for a felon here.[11]

ROMEO: Wilt thou provoke me?[12] Then have at thee, boy.

                (They fight)

                (Paris is hit)

PARIS: O, I am slain! *(Falls)* If thou be merciful,
   Lay with me Juliet. *(Dies)*

---

1. *Maw:* stomach.

2. On the word "death," some Romeos pick out the form of Juliet at this point with a kind of blurred vision, then on the next line walk unsteadily toward the bier.

3. Paris appears DL out of the shadows. While visible to the audience, Romeo cannot see him. Romeo stands in dumb grief over Juliet.

4. Paris steps into Romeo's view.

5. He threatens Romeo.

6. Paris draws his sword. The line to Paris, "Good gentle youth," shows Romeo's maturity. Actually they are about the same age.

7. Paris is wary. He knows Romeo has already killed one man and is a formidable adversary.

8. Paris puts his sword to Romeo's throat. Romeo pushes it aside with his hand.

9. Romeo is too distraught to be angry, rather he entreats.

10. *Conjuration:* the magic spell that is supposedly around a man-killer.

11. Paris makes jabbing movements taunting Romeo.

12. In a flash of desperation, Romeo draws his sword. This fight should be carefully planned and drilled. If possible, get the help of an expert fencer. Use rapiers, not broad swords.

                THE CREATIVE PROCESS

ROMEO: In faith, I will. Let me peruse this face.[13]

Mercutio's kinsman, noble County Paris!
What said my man[14] when my betossed soul
Did not attend him as we rode? I think
He told me Paris should have married Juliet.
Said he not so? Or did I dream it so?
Or am I mad, hearing him talk of Juliet,
To think it was so? O, give me thy hand,
One writ with me in sour misfortune's book!
I'll bury thee in a triumphant grave.
A grave? O, no, a lantern,[15] slaughtered youth,
[16]For here lies Juliet, and her beauty makes
This vault a feasting presence[17] full of light.
Death,[18] lie thou there, by a dead man interred.
How oft when men are near the point of death
Have they become merry! which their keepers[19] call
A lightning[20] before death. O, how may I
Call this a lightning? O my love! my wife!
Death, that hath sucked the honey of thy breath,
Hath had no power yet upon thy beauty,
Thou art not conquered. Beauty's ensign[21] yet
Is crimson in thy lips and in thy cheeks,
And death's pale flag is not advanced there.
[22]Tybalt, liest thou there in thy bloody sheet?
O, what more favor can I do to thee
Than with that hand that cut thy youth in twain
To sunder his that was thine enemy?
Forgive me, cousin![23] Ah, dear Juliet,
Why art thou yet so fair? Shall I believe
That unsubstantial Death is amorous,
And that the lean abhorred monster keeps
Thee here in dark to be his paramour?[24]
For fear of that I still will stay with thee
And never from this palace of dim night
Depart again. Here, here will I remain[25]
With worms that are thy chambermaids. O, here
Will I set up my everlasting rest[26]
And shake the yoke of inauspicious stars
From this world-wearied flesh. Eyes, look your last!
Arms, take your last embrace! and, lips, O you
The doors of breath, seal with a righteous kiss
A dateless[27] bargain to engrossing death!
Come, bitter conduct;[28] come, unsavory guide!

13. More unsteady than ever now that his fury is spent, Romeo kneels beside Paris.

14. *My man:* Romeo's servant.

15. *Lantern:* lantern or a light in a tower.

16. This is Shakespeare's first indication that Romeo has seen Juliet, but most actors prefer to make her the the focal point of the entire scene, and I agree.

17. *Feasting:* festive. *Presence:* presence chamber where one awaits the pleasure of a king.

18. *Death:* in this instance, he is referring to the dead Paris.   19. *Keepers:* nurses.

20. *Lightning:* a lifting of the spirits. Romeo is now standing over Juliet in tears as he gently caresses her folded hands.

21. *Ensign:* a banner.

22. Shouts off into the shadows where Tybalt is interred.

23. *Cousin:* Tybalt. Romeo kneels putting his arm over Juliet and kissing her cheek.

24. *Paramour:* mistress.

25. A celebrated Romeo picked up a flower from the bier at this point, crumbled it in his palm, and allowed the petals to fall over Juliet as he gently sobbed.

26. *Set up my everlasting rest:* take my eternal repose.

27. *Dateless:* endless. *Engrossing:* monopolizing.

28. *Conduct:* guide.

29. He pours the poison from the vial into a stirrup cup attached to his belt.
Thou desperate pilot: poison.

30. Still holding the cup, Romeo with his head on the bier beside Juliet, is upstage.

31. In this exercise the Friar's lines do not appear. For a full production, refer to complete play.

32. As Juliet rises slowly, she does not notice Romeo's head beside her.

33. Now as she turns, she first sees the stirrup cup in in his hand; his face is hidden by his other arm.

34. *Churl:* miser.

35. *Restorative:* love and life can be hers even in death by kissing him.

36. *Sheath:* a case for a sword or dagger.
This is thy sheath: her body.

Thou desperate pilot,[29] now at once run on
The dashing rocks thy seasick weary bark!
Here's to my love! (*Drinks*) O true apothecary![30]
Thy drugs are quick. Thus with a kiss I die.

> (*Falls*)
> [31]
> (*Juliet rises*)

JULIET: I do remember well where I should be,[32]
 And there I am. Where is my Romeo?[33]
 What's here? A cup, closed in my true love's hand?
 Poison, I see, hath been his timeless end.
 O churl![34] drunk all, and left no friendly drop
 To help me after? I will kiss thy lips
 Haply some poison yet doth hang on them
 To make me die with a restorative.[35]

> (*Kisses him*)

Thy lips are warm!

> O happy dagger!
> (*Snatches Romeo's dagger*)

This is thy sheath;[36] there rest, and let me die.

> (*She stabs herself and falls*)

10
The Character and His World

I think that classical plays require more imagination and more general training to be able to do. That's why I like playing Shakespeare better than anything else; because I think he wrote the greatest plays for people, and I think they require more to be brought to them. And I think one learns more through acting in classical plays than one does in anything else.*

Vivien Leigh
Academy Award Best Actress, 1939
(For "Gone with the Wind")

*From Lewis Funke and John E. Booth, *Actors Talk About Acting*, Random House, 1961, p. 239. Reprinted by permission of Random House.

Thornton Wilder has said, "Every masterpiece was created this morning." There are plays dealing with elements so eternally human that they transcend their own time. Such a play is called a classic, and it deserves to be placed with a Beethoven symphony, a Rembrandt painting, a Gothic cathedral, and a Michelangelo sculpture. Such great art brings an entire age into sharp focus. Contrast the austere simplicity of Greek architecture with the elaborate and lacy detail of Gothic churches. We learn much about a civilization when we see its art.

When we experience the theatre of a people, we become involved in their emotional, spiritual, and physical concerns. An Elizabethan play, staged with its original excitement, makes us almost taste Falstaff's "pint of sack," feel the cobblestones underfoot, smell the streets and the marketplaces, and hear the pipes and the hautboys. When we see a Sheridan play, we get a sense of the eighteenth-century man; we almost share his love of brocade and silk on the skin; we hear the harpsichord and keep time to the stately minuet. In short, a play reaches us through our senses as well as our intellect and can express more of an age than a dozen history books. The ever-present question is not whether theatre is contemporary or traditional but whether it will be absorbing to an audience.

IMPORTANCE OF GREAT PLAYS

It has been said that the purpose of drama is to show man struggling with the problems of being alive. Most great plays do indeed deal with conflict between man and himself, his god, or other men. Hidden beneath these conflicts are specifics which must be explored by the actor. To him it matters a great deal who this man is who grapples with life. He may be a king of Thebes, a drug addict, or a perfumed elegant. Into what sort of world has the king been placed? Is the drug addict in America or in an oriental civilization which tolerates rather than censures his addiction? The perfumed elegant could blend easily into the eighteenth century, but in Russia during the revolution he would be completely out of place. When we act in the plays of another time, we must understand how the people thought and felt.

Sir Michael Redgrave has said there is a style for Shakespeare and a style for Chekhov. A play is created out of a need of a people, and reflects the hopes, the desires, and the attitudes of that people. This need is ever changing, ever in a state of flux, as people themselves change. A dramatic masterpiece isolated from its time is not easily understood by present-day audiences unless those responsible for its production have prepared themselves with a knowledge of the period and style in which it originated. Only in this way will the urgency and force of first life be restored to it. It is not enough to imitate physical components, such as an Elizabethan stage or Greek costumes. We must understand the people of that time, their social and economic goals. We should also be aware of the conditions under which the actors worked and the standards of acting they set for themselves. Knowledge of this kind can but add richness and texture to a performance.

AT LEFT, *TROJAN WOMEN*, AND AT RIGHT, *THE TAMING OF THE SHREW*, INDIANA THEATRE COMPANY. (COURTESY OF RICHARD MENNEN.)

AN ACTING METHOD FOR EACH PLAY

If we transplant a play from its native earth, we must take some of that earth with it, or the play will never flower. And each play has a climate in which it lives, part of which is the style for acting it. If the play is to be properly presented, this climate or atmosphere must be transmitted to the audience.

If theatregoers fail to support a particular type of play, then it is replaced by plays they will support. *By selecting the plays, audiences also determine the style in which those plays are to be acted.* When it became obvious that audiences wanted plays of realism, then actors found a method to suit. The heroic method of the Greek actor is wrong for Chekhov, just as the realist style of acting is wrong for *Medea*. Suppose an actress is called upon to play Shakespeare's *Cleopatra*; she would approach this part in an entirely different way than she would Shaw's *Cleopatra*. Why? Both are Cleopatra. Let us also suppose that our actress is interested in history and believes she knows the "real" Cleopatra. If she tries to get this into her portrayal, she only adds inconsequentials. It would make no sense artistically. *But to create a Cleopatra within the context of the given play and act it in the style of that play makes for harmony and a complete artistic design.*

TODAY'S FASHIONS IN ACTING

Forty years ago, an acting student was taught according to his individual teacher's interpretation of the Stanislavski system. In time, such students became teachers themselves—of *their* version of "the Method." This resulted in an overproduction of assembly-line actors stamped with psychological realism and truth. *Then, came the revolution!* A young and imaginative generation of directors and playwrights no longer submit to the confinements of realism, with its box sets and kitchen sinks.

THE CHARACTER AND HIS WORLD 131

The new plays are no longer exclusively realistic. Some are not even tightly structured as plays but are inspired by improvisations and theatre games. Language is less authentic than it is imaginative. In addition to plays of the existential-absurdist school, there is a definite interest in the production of classical and semiclassical dramas.

The dilemma of the actor trained exclusively in psychological realism is that his body and speech are not sufficiently developed to cope with the sheer physical challenges of today's theatre. And so, most of the old guard "methodists" now find themselves in films, where the confinement of the camera and the proximity of the mike make unnecessary any voice skills or physical coordination.

England's most esteemed actress, Dame Edith Evans has observed:

> . . . There are too many actors today and they don't speak up. They won't take advice either . . . there is no discipline today. Kids are snapped up for the telly and films as soon as they learn to stand up straight. They have no training and many of them go to psychiatrists. . . . its over here [in America] that you do that sort of thing, where you have so many Method actors. There are a frightful lot of chi-chi classes in the Method, but it's such bunk. To me there is only good acting and bad acting.[1]

Acting instructors are now coming face to face with the fundamental problems of working with the body and voice. There is now a concerted effort to find means of training young actors who will be capable of playing the outsized roles found in the classics and in the imaginative dramas being presented for a new generation. This methodology must include the training of supple, receptive bodies and voices of power and range. These are the chief tools with which an actor works, and have been so considered by all great actors since Aeschylus.

IMPORTANCE OF DIFFERENT STYLES IN ACTING

Today an actor is required to know many different styles of acting. Theatre has become decentralized. All over the United States there are permanent and successful companies that have developed their own discriminating audiences, which demand a more varied theatrical fare than when New York audiences alone called the tune. A beginner's first job may be in Florida playing Genet or in Minneapolis playing Shakespeare. And he cannot approach work on either of these as he would approach Ibsen. A recent check of theatres, even in New York, revealed that current productions included plays by Van Itallie, Ibsen, Moliere, Shaw, Genet, Albee, Chekhov, Shakespeare, Euripides, and O'Neill — a sampling of twenty-five centuries of theatrical history.

You are going to become familiar with various acting styles: first by learning something of the times in which they flourished, why they are

---

[1]Rex Reed, *Do You Sleep in the Nude?* (New York: New American Library, 1968), interview with Dame Edith Evans, p. 139. Appeared in Chicago-Tribune Syndicate. Reprinted by permission of the author.

what they are; and then by working in actual classics from different periods, to acquire personal experience in a variety of styles. The great historical plays contain universal human experiences, illusions, myths, and truths, which make them just as valid today as they were in previous generations. But there is always a disparity between truth and form; these we must leave for the actor to homogenize.

Six-time Oscar nominee Arthur Kennedy has said—

> To me, when they speak of the range of an actor, it doesn't mean to play a Mexican peasant or an older or a younger man. It means to play different STYLES. The problem facing American actors today is the lack of experience to play these styles. This kind of training, with few exceptions, does not exist.[2]

Let me add that "style" when applied to an individual actor is an entirely different matter. When we speak of Gielgud's style we are referring to a distinctive quality he possesses, which enables him to project his particular personality to an audience. There is also a difference between the exploitation of a personality and an individual style. Olivier has style but it is always *in the part*. Style is form and finish in an actor, a kind of precision, ease, and confidence, along with that quality which Walter Huston called "intention." It is manner without mannerisms. It is a quality always admired—in a thoroughbred horse, an Olympic champion, or in an actor.

But a *style of acting* entails an approach to a play through study of the particular period which gave it birth. It refers to any device or process which creatively reflects the mode of a play's particular genesis. It can supply depth, authority, and authenticity to portrayals and production—a sense of being in the right time and the right place. Martin Esslin has said "Every age has a common aspect which makes the most divergent elements of the epoch instantly recognizable as stemming from it: A baroque Jesuit may have been at daggers drawn against a baroque Protestant or a baroque freethinker; yet their style, their mode of thinking, their whole attitude, will be instantly recognizable to us as having a common basis."[3]

When he is performing, an actor's attitude and state of mind is always obvious to an audience. It is a part of the created empathy. In our context, style is a means for the actor to become imbued in the atmosphere and mood of a particular play so that he can provide a framework for his creative ideas and concepts. A spectator can "tune in" to a style remote from his own time exactly as he can tune in to a painting that represents a life style or period different from his own.

Ever since a Polish author named Jan Kott wrote *Shakespeare Our Contemporary*, we have been deluged with productions ostensibly dedicated

(PHOTO OF ARTHUR KENNEDY COURTESY PHIL GERSH AGENCY.)

[2]By permission of Arthur Kennedy.

[3]Marin Esslin, *Brief Chronicles, Essays on Modern Theatre* (London: Temple Smith, 1970), p. 238.

THE CHARACTER AND HIS WORLD

to bringing Shakespeare "closer to the people" by making his plays "relevant." Poor Shakespeare, who has been bowdlerized, vulgarized, and bastardized for three centuries. Shades of Naham Tate![4] I will describe only one of the latest adaptations inspired by Mr. Kott, who cannot read Shakespeare in English. The play is Shakespeare's *Henry V* and this production erected considerable obstacles between the play and the audience. The stage was a jungle gym, cluttered with jump ropes, pipes, and swings. The players were literally players; clapping, shouting, and chasing each other through the pipes. Canterbury and Ely were rag-doll clowns. The avowed intent was, of course, to open up the play to a contemporary audience. Instead, the lines were muffled between shenanigans and were completely lost. Such concepts seem to be a flat denial of the original intent, and appear to be an apology for attempting Shakespeare at all. I once described one of these gimmick-ridden productions of *Hamlet* to my old friend B. Iden Payne.[5] When I had finished Iden sighed and quietly remarked, "What a pity . . . it's such a *good* play."

Another serious fault is to force the classics, and especially Shakespeare, into our modern speech idiom. Attempts to sound natural by breaking up the formal style only muddle the clarity of the language. One does not think of a speech such as "The ages of man . . . ," on the spur of the moment.

To reorient himself, to become saturated in the intellectual and psychological attitudes of a day far different from his own, is not easy for a contemporary actor. He must, like Alice, step through the looking glass into an entirely different world. But it is a rewarding venture. Those who can act in the classics find that great dramatic literature feeds and nourishes them. They give an actor fluidity, grace, and variety, and redouble his faith in himself.

To be a competent and desirable actor today requires variety. Working in the classics offers this training to a student. An amateur might "walk on" in a play like *Blue Denim* and give a satisfactory account of himself, but for *Macbeth* he will need study and training.

Since this book is about acting, we consider the history of the theatre only as it affects our particular subject. In order to concentrate upon one particular style of acting at a time, we apply ourselves to periods of history which have stamped their own characteristics upon acting. But different acting styles did frequently coexist in the same period. The popular and accepted style of the eighteenth century was romantic, flamboyant, and recitative; but pioneers such as Garrick, Talma, and "the Siddons" were calling attention to themselves by a more naturalistic method. Today, when realism has grown old and tired, we find interest being aroused in the acting school of the avant-garde, and in Brecht's alienation theories of acting. There is also a revived demand for the style of acting required

[4]Naham Tate (1652-1715): English Poet Laureate, whose name is connected with a long series of mangled versions of Shakespeare's plays.
[5]Ben Iden Payne will be remembered as an eminent director of Shakespeare.

THE CREATIVE PROCESS

for the classics. We shall consider all these acting methods in chronological order, beginning with civilization's first acting style—that of the Greeks.

USE OF SHORT SCENES

Educators frequently deplore the fact that available acting books include exercise scenes chosen from Broadway hits, so that students are oriented away from educational objectives and channeled into commercialism. As a result, our rich legacy of classical dramatic literature is neglected. Should that word "classical" bring to mind visions of marble statues and museums, let me hasten to add that such plays are just the opposite, being the very foundation of living and perpetual theatre.

In this book you will find excerpts from plays which have outlived the authors who wrote them, the public for which they were written, and will most probably survive all of us. By relegating these great works to "required reading" in schools, we turn what might have been a pleasure into a duty. Classical drama cannot be appreciated by merely reading the printed page, any more than a symphony can be appreciated by reading its score. The missing and elementary factor is the interpretative, creative magic of the actor, which turns words into humanity. *Oedipus, Macbeth,* and *Tartuffe* were not written to be read, but to be acted as living theatre.

Whenever possible, I have chosen the "obligatory scene" (as it was once called); that is, the moment when the conflicting forces of the play clash—the climax or turning point of the entire drama. There can be no pretense that a short scene is a substitute for the complete play. However, by actual physical involvement with a scene, the student will, to some extent, experience the taste and feeling of the whole play. These excerpts are offered merely as samples to encourage the student into further exploration of dramatic literature. If only a minority of young people using this book are so stimulated, then the inclusion of these plays will have served a worthy purpose.

Criteria used in the selection of these scenes are that they (1) be suitable for young student-actors, (2) illustrate points about acting and style, (3) stimulate further exploration into our wealth of the classics, and (4) be effective and rewarding—that is, they are to give the student a sense of accomplishment, so he will feel he has exerted time and effort on worthwhile material which will become part of his cultural education.

STAGING THE SCENES

All of these scenes can be performed in an ordinary room. It would be preferable to have a stage or platform, if possible, but even this is not necessary. There are only four vital elements—actors, a play, a director, and an audience (in this case, the class).

You do not need lights, curtains, scenery, furniture, or props. You will need some chairs, a table, and a few wooden boxes to represent steps, rocks, and boundaries. The boundaries of the working space should be defined (either by chalk or tape) so that the actors may learn how best to use their playing space. By use of these makeshift materials you will actually be duplicating the appurtenances of a professional rehearsal. When props are indicated but are not available (for example, the tea service in *The Importance of Being Earnest*, or the double door in *Tartuffe*) an interesting problem in pantomime may result for the students. It will be their task to convey the identities of such objects to the spectators, by use of their imaginations.

Before an entrance is indicated, a character should not be visible. If this is impossible because of the confinements of the room, the actor should stand with his back to the audience until he is required in the scene.

Costumes are unnecessary, but the instructor should be satisfied that carriage, movement, and manners coincide with play and period.

These rehearsals will give the student practice in the interpretation, characterization, and creation of atmosphere necessary to portray people in dramatic situations. It is only when we understand the psychology of a character and the aesthetics of each type of play that we can, with intelligence and emotion, be prepared for acting problems. The preliminary study and notes for each exercise are planned to make the acting more satisfying and enjoyable. Whatever of thought, research, and study you put into a characterization will be revealed in your performance. If you put little or nothing in, that's exactly what will come out.

The marginal notations are suggestions as to movements and motivations. They should be accepted as merely one way to stage the scene, and by no means the only way. You will have your own ideas, of course. Perhaps the notes will help stimulate your thinking into creative channels, even if only to disagree.

On the pages devoted to *Preparation* we will explore some particulars of each play: the locale, the time, the economic, social, and cultural status of the characters. The "atmosphere" is created in part by director, set designer, and electrician, but, most importantly, it must be imbedded into each characterization. Before speaking a word, an actor must know what constitutes the emotional tone, or spirit, the individual aura, of each play he performs. Where does the province of the director end and the work of the actor begin? It is the relationship between the two we must explore along with the play. All directors should know the language and problems of the actor, and the actor must become familiar with the jurisdictions of the director.

FURTHER READING: THE CHARACTER AND HIS WORLD

Burton, Hal. *Great Acting*. New York: Hill & Wang, 1967. (Interviews and photos of Olivier, Richardson, Redgrave, Gielgud, Coward, etc.)

Chapman, R. A. *The Spirit of Molière, An Interpretation*. New Jersey: Princeton University Press, 1940.

Clurman, Harold. "Actors in Style—and Style in Actors." *New York Times Magazine* Dec. 7, 1952: pp. 26-38.

————. *Lies Like Truth.* New York: Grove Press, 1958.

Cunningham, J. V. *In Shakespeare's Day.* Connecticut: Fawcett, 1970.

Gardner, R. H. *The Splintered Stage.* New York: Macmillan, 1965.

Guthrie, Tyrone. *In Various Directions.* New York: Macmillan, 1965.

————. *Tyrone Guthrie on Acting.* New York: Viking Press, 1971.

Hunt, Hugh. *Old Vic Prefaces: Shakespeare and the Producer.* London: Routledge & Kegan Paul, 1954.

Kernodle, George R. "Style, Stylization, and Styles of Acting." *Educational Theatre Journal* Dec. 1960: pp. 251-261.

Marshall, Norman. *The Producer and the Play.* London: Macdonald, 1962.

Nicoll, A. *A History of Early Eighteenth Century Drama 1700-1750.* New York: Cambridge University Press, 1925.

Parrott, T. M., & Ball, R. H. *A Short View of Elizabethan Drama Together with Some Account of its Principle Playwrights. Conditions under which it was Produced.* New York: Scribner's, 1958.

Reinhardt, Paul D. "Movement in Period Plays." *Educational Theatre Journal* March 1962: pp. 50-55.

Saint-Denis, Michel. *Theatre, A Rediscovery of Style.* New York: Theatre Arts Books, 1960.

Vaughn, Stuart. *A Possible Theatre.* New York: McGraw-Hill, 1969.

Wilson, Garff B. "What is Style in Acting?" *Quarterly Journal of Speech* April, 1955: pp. 127-132.

11
Greek Drama

We have less information on the Greek theatre than we have on any other. One indispensable document is Aristotle's *Poetics*, but this deals mostly with the theory of drama and literary criticism. Fortunately, we can learn from the paintings and sculpture of the time; some works of art even depict actors at work. We have also some Greek plays—thirty-three tragedies, eleven comedies—out of at least two thousand plays of superior quality that we know were written and produced in Athens between 480 and 380 B.C., when the population was no more than forty thousand citizens.

We also have the ruins of their theatres to convince us that only the broadest gestures and the fullest voices would have been practical. When working on the proscenium stage, gestures and movements may be intimate. However, anyone who has worked "in the round" knows that here larger actions are required. This gives us some idea at least, of the great freedom and style practiced by the Greek actor.

The tradition of the actor-playwright-director began with the Greeks. Of the three immortals—Aeschylus, Sophocles, and Euripides—only Euripides did not act, but he did direct. It is interesting that all three were at one time associated with the priesthood, for that is where the profession of acting began.

ORIGINS

Even before the Greeks, primitive man depended upon the actor-priest to create a sympathetic association between man and nature, by assuming the spirits of gods, animals, and natural forces. By acting out a visit of the rain god to a tribe, he caused them to believe that a visit from the real god

DURING THE ANNUAL FESTIVAL OF EPIDAURUS, THIS ANCIENT GREEK AMPI-THEATRE IS USED TO REVIVE THE GREAT CLASSICS. (COURTESY THE GREEK NATIONAL TOURIST OFFICE.)

would take place. The actor-priest or medicine man subsequently began enlarging his repertory of characters. By assuming the spirit of a dead patriarch or ancestor of the tribe, he created the first hero and enacted the life struggles of that hero and his dramatic encounter with death. *Oedipus* and *Medea* are related to such commemorations. Animal and human sacrifices are part of the transference of life or the magical spirit from one individual to another. From its beginnings, acting has always been associated with *spirit transference, magic, ritual,* and *mystery.*

ACTORS OF ANCIENT GREECE

Greek actors began as amateurs but gradually developed into highly trained professionals. At the height of their glory they had their own Actor's Equity, with set rules controlling wages and conditions. They were exempt from military duty. One of the leading actors, Polus, received the equivalent of twelve hundred dollars for two days' performances — that's a professional! Even today our theatre is not subsidized by the state, as was theirs. Nor are our actors held in such respect; with an almost religious deference. We must remember that in those times religion and theatre were very near. We can get some impression of the Greek theatre by attending a Christmas or Easter ceremony of the high church, with its chants, choir, processions, costumes, symbolism, and stylized actions.

Greek audiences had high standards for acting. They considered the actor Aeschines so bad that they actually stoned him out of the business. Like Shakespeare's audience, the Greeks appreciated great plays as well as good acting. People from all walks of life were devoted to theatre. Their great plays were rich in drama, conflict, and profound characterizations.

Greek actors are known to have developed an almost unbelievable range in voice. They had special instructors in mime, dance, and gesture. During performances, the Greek actor was weighted down with heavy trappings, but because of his exhaustive training he moved with grace and ease.

Women did not act. Even if they had been accepted as socially equal to men, they would not have had the physical strength necessary, and their voices could certainly not have filled the great amphitheatres.

In our day of the confidential actor, it is difficult for us to realize that all through the history of acting the voice was considered the actor's greatest asset. The Greek actor trained constantly with voice specialists. Supporting actors were also expected to sing as well as dance. In the course of a regular performance, an actor was required to be efficient in three types of voice production:

1. *Iambic trimeter:* declamatory style with particular emphasis upon enunciation
2. *Recitative:* intoned with a musical accompaniment
3. *Lyrical:* the song proper, written as a solo, duet, trio, or chorus.

MODERN REVIVAL OF GREEK CLASSIC IN ANCIENT AMPI-THEATRE. (COURTESY THE GREEK NATIONAL TOURIST OFFICE.)

STYLES IN ACTING

In addition, the actor was obliged to have at his command an entire catalogue of conventionalized movements—a complete repertoire of coordinations in body, voice, and gesture.

This was a theatre of the star system. The leading part was played by the chief actor, often the director and manager also. A play was said to be "done by" him. Oedipus, Electra, Medea, Antigone, male or female, he played them all. Another actor played the chief supporting roles. A utility actor (with a bass voice) would play passionate heralds, dignified kings, etc. All three might interchange parts having a complete knowledge of the entire play, the verses, the dances, and the formalized gestures.

The sincerity of these actors is demonstrated by an incident involving the actor Polus. In his portrayal of Electra, he used the actual ashes of his own dead son, so that he might express the character's grief over "her" dead brother's ashes. Here we have an actor in a period before Christ using the association method.

The acting style of the Greeks was great in scope, larger than life, formal in speech and gesture. The Greek actor was never required to play a Willy Loman.[1] Such a suggestion would have been contemptible to him. He played hero-kings, even gods. Greek actors were esteemed not only as artists, but as leaders of the community. With the decline of Greek civilization, the status of the actor sank to the level of a vagabond, and was not restored until much later. Even today it is questionable if actors have the venerated status of the ancient actors, in spite of the knighting of many English actors.

EXERCISE 90

Study the art books in your library or, if possible, visit your museum and study the statues.

Try to find the particular emotion the sculptor sought to express. Was it dignity, fear, grief? Study how these artists gave grace to the human figure by the balance of weight, by the drape of a costume. You can learn much from these art masterpieces.

COSTUMES

Unlike the ordinary Athenian citizen, who did not cover his arms in the day-to-day business of life, the tragic actor wore an ornamented costume with long sleeves to give grace and flow to his gestures. This garment was usually striped or embroidered perpendicularly, and brilliantly colored. Think of this vivid coloring as you consider the statuesque image of the Greek actor. He was imposing, graceful, and beautiful, but not colorless like a marble statue. There was *nothing* cold about the Greek actor. Over-garments of saffron and purple often completed a wardrobe.

Members of the chorus were uniformly dressed, according to the characters they represented, whether old men, maidens, or women of the

[1]Willy Loman: chief character in Arthur Miller's *Death of a Salesman*—Ed.

city. They wore sandals or were barefooted, as they had a great deal of dancing to do. Leading actors wore thick-soled boots (*cothurni*). This footgear was very much like the boots worn by Chinese actors in ancient times and today. The high headdress (*onkus*) worn above the mask also added to the illusion of height. The long lines of the costumes, the ornaments, the mask, body padding, cothurnus, and onkus, made the Greek heroic actor a truly awesome and commanding figure.

MASKS

Often made of wood or cork, Greek masks were not made to fit the face, but were placed over the head. Domed at the crown, they were in all details made to further the impression of height. The open mouth served to amplify the voice. To the Greeks, these masks were the symbol, the essence of a character. When manipulated by the actor, light played upon the sculptured planes, giving the illusion of changing expressions. In using a mask, an actor cannot depend upon facial expression to reveal his inner feelings. He must know the art of mime. The mask is not a hindrance but an aid to expressing emotions if the body is used as a controlled instrument. No mincing or half-executed movements will do. The actor must be precise and calm in execution, using only the simplest actions. A mask changes an actor from a creature of flesh and blood into a crystallized image of the character. Nuances of expression must be managed by manipulation of the mask and entire body. By use of the mask, these actors were able to play many characters in quick succession ("doubling").

Several masks might be worn for the same character, for example, Oedipus. When he becomes convinced of his guilt, Oedipus leaves the stage, returning later with eyes gouged out and blood streaming from them. Gruesome? Not the way the Greeks performed it. The emotion was there, but by the use of the mask, violence and horror were eliminated. It was *artistically* true, but an aesthetic distance was maintained.

The stylized lines of the mask transmitted emotion. In the great amphitheatres, human expression could not have been seen. This audience would not have accepted ordinary facial expression, which they considered vulgar on the stage. We must remember the Greek ideal of art. They were interested in experiencing an emotion, but only in terms of art. They expected an artistic arrangement of emotion, never the emotion itself.

SOPHOCLES (495-406 B.C.)

PREPARATION FOR OEDIPUS THE KING

Before attempting the scene from *Oedipus the King* which follows, it is assumed that you have studied the entire play. *Oedipus* has been called

the world's greatest tragedy of fate and one of the most solidly constructed dramas ever written. You might test your knowledge of the play
by answering the following questions:

1. What did the Delphic Oracle tell Oedipus' father?
2. Who was Jocasta?
3. Trace the events in the life of Oedipus from the time the Messenger brought him to Corinth until the opening of the play.
4. How much time passes between the beginning and end of this
   play?
5. What motivates Oedipus to search so relentlessly for his identity?
6. Describe the character of Oedipus. What sort of man is he?
   What is the tragic fault in his character?
7. Does Oedipus fit Aristotle's definition of a tragic hero as set
   down in *Poetics* XIII?
8. Are there any points of similarity between this story and a
   modern detective story? How is Oedipus different from a common murderer?
9. How does Oedipus change during the course of this play?
10. What reason does the author give that the murder of Laius was
    not investigated at the time of his death?
11. How can a modern actor identify himself with Oedipus?
12. Check the phrase that most nearly describes the theme of this
    play:
    A struggle for knowledge
    Success does not bring happiness
    The struggle of a free man to avoid fate
    A critique of rationalism
    The uncertainty of human life
    The irony of fate
13. In a few descriptive words, indicate the style of acting that
    should be used for this play.
14. Give several reasons why this play has lived 2000 years and is
    still being produced.

If you find these questions difficult to answer, read *Oedipus* again—the
entire play—before attempting to rehearse the scene. You must know
where the pieces fit.

The scene given here has been chosen because it is the climax of a
long series of investigations Oedipus makes to reveal the truth. During
this scene, he learns the most damning truth of all. It is the turning point,
the end of the hero's use of his free will against fate. Although he has
felt the truth instinctively, he must go searching on and on, no matter
what the cost. The revelation in this scene is the beginning of Oedipus'
destruction.

The character of Oedipus is a prototype of the hero in quest of himself. This play demonstrates what Ibsen, centuries later, was to set down

as a rule for characters he created—that they must reveal past mistakes by retrospection. So skillfully is this play constructed that *the audience always knows more than the hero.* In his *Poetics,* Aristotle used the play *Oedipus* as a prime example of tragedy. What is the appeal of tragedy? It proves that man is a creature capable of heroic dignity and significance. By means of Sophocles' mastery of drama, we are able to witness a hero with a tragic flaw in a story that builds scene by scene to a towering climax. In this scene, just one old man, the Shepherd, can give the proof which will destroy Oedipus. He not only fears for his life; he also has pity for the king. He cannot face his master, and it requires force to get the truth from the meek old slave.

At first, the group should read the scene aloud, slowly and for sense, not emotion. As the sense and meter are experienced, try to add not only the feeling of the characters but the larger-than-life style in which it was played. Feel the weight of the costumes. Remember that voices must fill an amphitheatre, and keep in mind the prestige and dignity enjoyed by the Greek actors.

REHEARSAL

OEDIPUS THE KING*

An Excerpt

CAST: OEDIPUS   SERVANTS
       MESSENGER
       SHEPHERD

SCENE: *On the steps before the great palace of Thebes, Oedipus waits impatiently as the Messenger comes from L forcing the old Shepherd before him into the presence of the King. The Shepherd falls to his knees in fright and awe before Oedipus. There is a recognition of this between Oedipus and the Messenger. Oedipus takes a step to them, touches the Shepherd on the head. Throughout the scene, the Shepherd avoids any direct eye contact with the King. Positions are as follows: Oedipus at C, Shepherd to his L, and the Messenger DL of him. Up back to R there is a group of three servants to balance the group DL.*

MESSENGER: This is the man.
OEDIPUS: Well then old man! Look at me!
   Tell me—you served Laius?
SHEPHERD: I was his slave.
   Not bought by him, but reared in his house.
OEDIPUS: Doing what work? What was your way of life?[1]

1. A pause as he looks to the Messenger, who strikes him on the shoulder, then pulls him to his feet. Then he speaks.

*Excerpt from translation of *Oedipus the King* by John Gassner, in *A Treasury of the Theatre* published by Simon & Schuster, New York, 1951. By permission of John Gassner.

                              STYLES IN ACTING

SHEPHERD: For the best part of my life I tended flocks.

OEDIPUS: Where did they graze?

SHEPHERD: Sometimes on—[2] Citheron, sometimes *near* the mountain.

OEDIPUS: (*Pointing out the Messenger*) This man—do you recall having ever met him there?

SHEPHERD: Not to say off-hand, from memory.[3]

MESSENGER: And no wonder, master![4]

But he will, when I remind him. We kept
  pasture there three half-years,
    he with his two flocks, I with one.
They grazed together from springtime to the rise
  of Arcturus[5] in the fall.
Then I drove my sheep to our fold at home
And he brought his back to Laius.

(To the Shepherd)

Was this so as I tell it or not?[6]

SHEPHERD: It was[7]—but it was a long time ago.

MESSENGER: And tell me now, do you remember giving me a boy,[8]

an infant then, to rear as my own?

SHEPHERD: (*Frightened*) What do you mean?[9]
Why do you ask me that?

MESSENGER: (*Pointing to Oedipus*) Here is the
man, my friend, who was then the child.

SHEPHERD: (*Violently*) The plague take you! Hold your
tongue![10]

OEDIPUS: How now? You have no right to blame
him.
The words that offend are yours.

SHEPHERD: Offend? How have I offended, master?[11]

OEDIPUS: In not telling us about the child.

SHEPHERD: He busies himself with no business of[12]
his own. He speaks without knowing.

OEDIPUS: Herdsman! If you will not speak to
please me, you shall be forced.

SHEPHERD: For God's love, master,[13] do not harm
an old man!

OEDIPUS: (*To his servants*) Hold him fast; twist
his arms behind him![14]

SHEPHERD: Wretch that I am![15] What do you want
to know?

OEDIPUS: You gave him a child?[16] The child he asks
about?

SHEPHERD: I gave it. Would I had died before!

2. Well aware that the name of the mountain is a dangerous word to utter.

3. Speaks quickly, trying to end the matter.

4. Messenger is angry at not being remembered, but decides to try kindness with the old man. He smiles, walks in front of the Shepherd, facing the King. He speaks in a friendly tone.

5. Arcturus: a star behind the dipper.

6. Puts his hand on the Shepherd's right shoulder.

7. Shepherd shrugs off the Messenger's hand with irritation.

8. Messenger is now between the two men.

9. Shepherd turns away, pretending not to have heard. Messenger seizes him, turning him back to face them.

10. In rage, Shepherd swings the Messenger to his left, but is arrested by the voice of the king.

11. Innocently.

12. Turns left to Messenger, snarling at him.

13. Falls to his knees, pleading as he sees the Servants UR moving back of king to threaten him.

14. Servants act to Oedipus' orders.

15. A loud cry.

16. Oedipus bombards him with questions like a district attorney pressing for a point. The following four lines of dialogue are spoken in fast tempo.

KING OEDIPUS AND THE MESSENGER FORCE THE TRUTH FROM THE OLD SHEPHERD, AS PERFORMED AT THE BURGTHEATRE, VIENNA. (PHOTO COPYRIGHT HAUSMANN.)

17. A change in tone and tempo. Oedipus speaks almost to himself and obviously is somewhat discouraged. Shepherd has turned away, avoiding the king's eyes. One Servant turns his head to face Oedipus, who indicates that the others apply pressure to the arm.

18. Another and louder cry.

19. Louder still as he threatens the old man.

20. Staccato (same as before): fast crossfire of questions and answers.

OEDIPUS: You will now, if you do not speak the truth!
SHEPHERD: And it will be worse with me if I
    speak it.
OEDIPUS: The fellow trifles with us still[17]—evades
    the question.
SHEPHERD: (*As the servants twist his arms*) No,
    no![18] I have told you that I gave him the child.
OEDIPUS: From whom did you have it?[19]
    Did someone give it to you,
    or was it your own?
SHEPHERD: It was not mine.
    Another gave it to me.
OEDIPUS: Which of these citizens?[20] From whose home?
SHEPHERD: Master, I beg of you—
    I beg you, do not ask it.
OEDIPUS: You are a dead man if I ask again.
SHEPHERD: It was a child, then—of the house of Laius.
OEDIPUS: A slave's child? Or born of the King's own
    family?

SHEPHERD: I stand on the knife-edge of dreadful
    words;[21] I fear to speak.
OEDIPUS: And I, to hear.[22] Yet I must!
SHEPHERD: The child was called his son;[23]
    but she within, your lady, could best say how it was.
OEDIPUS: Did she then give it to you?[24]
SHEPHERD: So it was,[25] my King.
OEDIPUS: For what purpose? Speak!
SHEPHERD: That I should do away with it.
OEDIPUS: Wretched woman! Her own child?
SHEPHERD: Yes, from fear of the evil prophecies.
OEDIPUS: What prophecies?
SHEPHERD: That he should kill his parents, it was said.
OEDIPUS: Why, then,[26] did you give him to this old man?
SHEPHERD: Through pity,[27] master.
    I gave him the child,
    thinking he would take it to another land, his own.
    He did so but, alas, he saved it for the worst of
    sorrows.
    For, if you are the man he says you are,[28]
    then surely you were born to great misery!
OEDIPUS: (*Uttering the cry of a wounded animal*)[29]
    Oh—Oh—Oh!
    Everything is proved true—everything has come
    to pass!
    Light of the sun,
    Never shall I look on you again,
    I who am revealed
    damned by the light I saw at birth,
    damned by my marriage,
    damned by the blood I shed.

(*Oedipus rushes into the palace*)

21. A pause; he glances hopelessly about as if about to be pushed over a cliff.

22. Prophetically, Oedipus dreads what the man might say, but he must hear. This line is the key to Oedipus in this scene, and perhaps in the entire play.

23. These are the words he must say and he knows what they will mean to everyone when he says them. This is a high dramatic moment of the scene. He is resigned, defeated, speaking as a doomed man.

24. With only a slight hope that the previous six words he has uttered will not seem so awful.

25. This interchange is not so fast, more labored and grim. These are questions that must be asked and answered.

26. Meaning the other old man, the Messenger.

27. Almost sobbing in grief. Very moved.

28. In awe.

29. This wellspring of emotion must be started by the actor playing Oedipus *before* this point is reached. *Then it bursts:* man crying out in anguish to the fates. Suggestion: Recall the cry of a trapped or dying animal or a woman's wail at hearing her husband has been killed.

ARISTOPHANES (446-380 B.C.)

If your work on Oedipus has left you with the impression that the ancient Greeks were a baleful lot, remember that they enjoyed tragedy. They liked seeing their great heroes struggling against a remorseless and inevitable destiny, living courageously even though, like themselves, they knew the futility of escape. They came away from the play exalted and inspired by the potentialities of their own natures for they measured the stature of a man by how he withstood the buffeting of fate. Life was not all tragedy, because a man could laugh; the Greeks believed that this was a part of a man's courage.

THE BEGINNINGS OF COMEDY

During the great festivals of Dionysus, young men dressed as satyrs (half-men, half-goats) paraded through the streets amusing the spectators with derisive remarks. Today we have night club comics who still carry on this tradition of the amusing insult. From this early custom grew the satyr play. Later, these bits of nonsense were presented as after-pieces to the great tragedies. Some time around 486 B.C., they were officially recognized, and comic poets were asked to submit comedies in competition for prizes. These satires retained the taunting, irreverent quality of the original satyrs. Gilbert and Sullivan followed this style, as do our own topical revues which ridicule public figures and customs.

PREPARATION FOR THE BIRDS

In our next rehearsal you will see that the Greeks had a highly developed sense of humor, wild as it was. Aristophanes manages his satire with irony and a vivid imagination. He lampoons man's perennial discontent with his lot, his desire to escape, and create "the great society." Here we meet two defectors from the great city of Athens who retreat to the mountains to establish a utopia. Their scheme is a delightful madness: they propose that the King of the Birds establish a cloud cuckooland and support it by levying a tariff between men and gods. Even in naming his two con men, Aristophanes is satirical: Euelpides means hopeful and Pithetaerus means plausible.

Suggestions for Characterizations

In this scene, a great deal depends upon the performer playing Epops. He must develop dances and a weird bird-like screech and have great vitality. The sounds and dances need to be as carefully developed as were the sounds for the Woody Woodpecker cartoons or the comic dance routines of Ben Blue.

The character Epops is obviously the great-granddaddy of the Mad Hatter and every other kooky character written since his time.

Definite characterizations should also be created for the old men. As a suggestion, Euelpides might be a crafty, pompous, but blundering fool, who imagines himself as a leader of men. Pithetaerus, then, in contrast might be slow-witted, shy, depending upon his blustering partner to speak for him. However, once he achieves confidence in himself, he is irrepressible — and still a fool.

THE BIRDS*

An Excerpt

CAST: EUELPIDES   TWO OLD TRAVELERS
       PITHETAERUS   KING OF THE BIRDS
       EPOPS

SCENE: *Exterior. Several platforms or steps of different heights. These can be masked by cardboard cutouts and painted to resemble jagged rocks.*

Discovered, Euelpides and Pithetaerus. They turn as they hear a blood-curdling screech from up and off.

EPOPS: (*Off*) Open the thicket that I may go out!
                         (*Enters, above*)
EUELPIDES: Heracles save us! What creature is this? What plumage! (*Grasps Pithetaerus*) What means this triple crest?

EPOPS: Who wants me?[1]
EUELPIDES: [2]The twelve gods have done you ill.
EPOPS: You twit me about my feathers? I—Epops,— who was once a man like you?
EUELPIDES: We laugh not at you—
EPOPS: At what then?
EUELPIDES: At your beak. It seems so strange to us.[3]

    Excerpt from adaptation made by author.

1. They venture closer to inspect the bird-man.

2. Epops struts proudly.

3. Epops runs to a high place, screeches, jumps, and ends by doing his peacock-strut dance before them.

GREEK DRAMA

4. Epops will not be pinned down to specifics.

5. Again he screeches and does his dance.

6. Inspecting Epops' short skirt.

7. Epops slaps his hand away indignantly, then struts away with great pomp and circumstance.

8. He struts back menacingly.

9. Turns away, then jumps back to the attack, accusing them.

10. Pokes his finger at Euelpides' chest, accenting each word.

11. These next few lines are spoken very fast.

12. Euelpides holds up his hand as if to ask patience that he may continue and come to a conclusion with his prepared oratory.

13. Sarcastically, with overdone sympathy.

14. This also is sarcastic, as Pithetaerus has been standing in silence and looking quite stupid.

15. Has trouble finding his voice as it has been in disuse so long. Trys different pitches on "my."

16. Unseen by Epops, Euelpides nudges Pithetaerus, clears throat, and speaks directly to Epops.

EPOPS: I am a bird!
EUELPIDES: A peacock?
EPOPS: [4]A bird.[5]
EUELPIDES: Then where are your feathers?[6]
   I see none.
EPOPS: [7]They have fallen off
   All birds moult their feathers,[8] every winter
   And fresh ones grow in their place[9]
   But tell me—[10] W-w-what-are-you?
EUELPIDES: [11]We—? Mortals.
EPOPS: What brings you here?
EUELPIDES: To speak with you.
EPOPS: Yes, yes? What for—?
EUELPIDES: Because once you were a man like us
   Because you once had debts—like us
   And had no desire to pay them—
EPOPS: As you do not now.[12]
EUELPIDES: And then you changed into a bird,
   And flew over land and sea. You know what men feel
   And how birds feel too. That's why we've come to you
   And ask you to direct us to some cozy town,
   Where we can snuggle down, and live, all soft and warm.
EPOPS: You're looking for a greater city than Athens?
EUELPIDES: One more pleasant to live in.
EPOPS: An aristocratic country—?
EUELPIDES: Not at all.
EPOPS: Then what sort of city would suit you best?
EUELPIDES: Why, one where our greatest care would be
   Some friend knocking on our door at break of day
   And saying "By Olympian Zeus, bathe early today,
   Come to a wedding banquet at my house,
   And bring the children too. I give a nuptial feast,
   And must not be disappointed by my friends."
EPOPS: [13]I see you are fond of suffering
   And—[14] noisy one, what say you?
PITHETAERUS: [15]My tastes are similar.
EPOPS: There is a city of delights such as you want.
   It's on the Red Sea.
EUELPIDES: Oh no! Not a seaport
   Where some galley can appear carrying
   a process-server.
   This[16]—this bird life here—

STYLES IN ACTING

You should know full well,
What it's like to live with the birds—
EPOPS: It's not altogether disagreeable,
Not disagreeable at all.
In the first place one has no need of a purse.
EUELPIDES: See there! That does away with roguery!
EPOPS: For food the gardens yield white sesame,
Myrtle-berries, poppy, cress and mint.
EUELPIDES: By Zeus, you live a bridegroom's life![17]
PITHETAERUS: Oh![18] Oh, O-O-O-h!
I have just been hit with the most incredible idea[19]
A plan to transfer supreme power to the birds.
Will you hear my advice?
EPOPS: Your advice? What advice?
PITHETAERUS: Do not fly in all directions with open beaks.
It is not dignified.
Among us when we see a
thoughtless man, we ask,[20] "What sort of bird is this?"
A man with no brain is a bird, for he never remains
in one place.
EPOPS: [21]This is your "advice?"
PITHETAERUS: Hear me out. Stay in one place.
Found a city.
EPOPS: We birds—? What sort of city should we found?[22]
PITHETAERUS: That's done it.
You have just made the most idiotic remark.
Look down there—[23]
EPOPS: [24]What?
PITHETAERUS: Now—look up!
EPOPS: All right—I'm looking.[25]
PITHETAERUS: Now[26]—twirl your head around![27]
Again!
EPOPS: What? And wring my head off my neck?
PITHETAERUS: Now tell me friend,[28]
What did you see?
EPOPS: I saw the clouds and sky.
PITHETAERUS: And is this not the property of the birds?
EPOPS: Property? The air—?
PITHETAERUS: Eggessactly!
The air between earth and heaven
Is the property of the birds.
When we mortals go to Delphi,
The Boeotians make us pay to pass over their land
In this way—when men pray to the Gods,

17. Poppyseed was used by Greeks on wedding cakes, myrtle berries for bridal wreaths; hence, "bridegroom's life."

18. Holding his head, he jumps up and down as if in pain.

19. Grasps Epops.

20. Although there is sense here, it must seem to be nonsense as it is spoken.

21. Complete disgust.

22. Pithetaerus throws up his hands in despair, walks away, thinks better of it, and returns to the attack.

23. Pointing to the floor.

24. Epops does not understand, but complies anyhow.

25. Still puzzled but receptive.

26. As he winks to Euelpides.

27. He gestures a circle in the air. Epops jerks his head around until he becomes unsteady.

28. Calms Epops by putting his hands on his shoulders. Here we have a standard comic situation, where the fool or clown is smarter than the smart men.

You must make the Gods pay tribute.
You but exercise the right of every nation toward
  strangers,
And forbid the smoke of sacrifice to pass the
skies over your property.

29. Epops leaps into the air with a screech.

EPOPS: By Earth! By snares and traps and cages![29]
  Never have I heard of anything so neatly conceived
  If the other birds approve,
  I'll build your city on our property.
PITHETAERUS: Who will explain the plan to them?
EPOPS: None but you. Before I came they were ignorant
  And knew not how to speak. I have amended that.
PITHETAERUS: How can we gather them together?
EPOPS: Easily. I will arouse my messenger from the thicket.
  The Nightingale will bring them on hot wings.

30. The screech.
31. He flies about calling to the north, east, south, and west.

PITHETAERUS: Dear bird, lose no time.
EPOPS: Epopopoi, popoi, popopopoi, popoi,[30] here, here,
  quick, quick, my comrades of the air[31]
  All you who pillage the fertile lands,
  You numberless tribes who gather barley,
  Whose gentle twitter resounds through the fields,
  Tiotiotiotiotiotiotiotiotio![32]

32. He uses the entire stage until he really seems to be flying. The last of his call should be off-stage and seem to come from a distance.

VASE PAINTING OF ACTORS DRESSED AS BIRDS. ARTIST MIGHT HAVE WITNESSED A PERFORMANCE OF ARISTOPHANES' *THE BIRDS*. (COURTESY OF THE TRUSTEES OF THE BRITISH MUSEUM.)

STYLES IN ACTING

And you who hop about the branches of the ivy
You mountain birds who feed on wild-olive berries,
Trito, trito, totobrix—
                          Hurry to my call!
You who snap the sharp-stinging gnats in the marshes
You who dwell on the plain of Marathon all damp with
  dew,
Come hither.
Let all the tribes of long-necked birds assemble here
And know what a clever old man has brought to us
In inspiration and reforms. Come—here, here, here![33]
Torotorotorotorotix, kikkabau, kikkabau,
torotorotorolililix!
PITHETAERUS: What a throat that bird possesses!
He has filled the thicket with honey-sweet melody!

Here is a little scene from the same author's great antiwar play.

REHEARSAL

LYSISTRATA*

ACT I

2 FEMALES

LYSISTRATA: Kalonika, I tell you if Greece is to be
  saved, it is the *women* who must do it.
KALONIKA: The women? Why, then,[1]
  Greece will be a long time being saved.
LYSISTRATA: It will be saved by us—or be forever
  ruined.
KALONIKA: But, Lysistrata, even so, what makes you
  think that women can do what our great
  statesmen have failed to do? They always
  try for peace.
LYSISTRATA: They *say* they try.[2]
KALONIKA: They are men with great minds. They think
  of everything.
LYSISTRATA: They make us believe they do.
KALONIKA: And when their great peace conferences fail,
  they can go to war. But we, Lysistrata, we

33. The air is filled with the sounds of birds. If loudspeaker is available, recordings of bird sounds are available. (See list under *Recordings.*) Otherwise, rehearse the class to make sounds with human voices and mechanical bird calls. The noise must be deafening at the end of the scene.

1. Not at all impressed.

2. Sardonically.

*From pp. 1477–1478 of *Lysistrata*, trans. by Gilbert Seldes, in *A Treasury of the Theatre*, by John Gassner, ed. © 1935, 1940, 1950, 1951, 1953 by Simon and Schuster, Inc.

know nothing about great affairs. We sit
here waiting for the men to come to tell
what they have done, dressed in transparent
gowns of yellow silk, flowing about so that
we can hardly walk, with flowers in our hair
and embroidered slippers on our feet.

LYSISTRATA: You have just recited the catalogue of our
most powerful weapons.

KALONIKA: Weapons?

LYSISTRATA: [3]The filmy yellow tunic. Yes.
The intoxicating perfume and
your dainty slippers.
Yes. Your lotions and your
rouge and your provocative,
flowing robe.

KALONIKA: What about them?

LYSISTRATA: These are the weapons by which every woman
can make the men of Greece lay down their arms.

KALONIKA: If that were true I'd get myself a dress so
thin I'd be embarrassed even before my husband.

LYSISTRATA: I ask you now, if we have such power, should
we not use it?

KALONIKA: We should, indeed. Why Lysistrata, you've
hit upon a really grand idea. Each one of
us will buy new clothes and jewels and lovely
perfumes and seduce our husbands—and the war
will end. Why, who'd have thought of it?

LYSISTRATA: There's more than that to do, but to commence
with—that is enough. I tell you, Kalonika,
we can do it—just as I say—and ought not
every honest Grecian woman come to help us?

3. As she speaks, Kalonika touches her own clothes as if not quite understanding the argument but merely verifying the fact that these things exist.

AN AMERICAN PRODUCTION OF *TROJAN WOMEN* PERFORMED AT SMITH COLLEGE, DIRECTED BY RICHARD MENNEN, WITH COSTUMES BY PETER BOYDEN. (COURTESY RICHARD MENNEN.)

FURTHER READING: GREEK DRAMA

Aristotle. *Poetics.* Edited by A. Gudemen. Translated by Lane Cooper. New Jersey: Cornell University Press, 1928.

Arnott, Peter D. *An Introduction to Greek Theatre.* London: St. Martin's, 1956. A study of the background against which the plays were written.

Bacon, Helen H. *Barbarians in Greek Tragedy.* New Haven: Yale University Press, 1961.

Bates, William. *Euripides, A Student of Human Nature.* New York: A. S. Barnes, 1961.

Bieber, Margarete. *The History of Greek and Roman Theatre.* New Jersey: Princeton University Press, 1961. Many beautiful illustrations.

Butcher, S. H. *Aristotle's Theory of Poetry and Fine Art,* with an essay by John Gassner. New York: Dover, 1951.

Casson, Lionel, ed. *Masters of Ancient Comedy.* Translated by Lionel Casson. New York: Macmillan, 1960.

Cornford, Francis MacDonald. *The Origins of Attic Comedy.* New York: Doubleday, 1961.

Dickinson, G. Lowes. *The Greek View of Life.* New York: Collier, 1961. Greek attitude toward life and the individual.

Hogan, Robert Goode. *Drama, the Major Genres.* New York: Dodd, Mead, 1962.

Kitto, H. D. F. *The Greeks.* Baltimore: Penguin, 1964.

————. *Greek Tragedy.* New York: Doubleday, 1960.

Lattimore, Richmond. *The Poetry of Greek Tragedy.* Baltimore: Johns Hopkins Press, 1958.

Letters, F. J. H. *The Life and Works of Sophocles.* New York: Sheed and Ward, 1946.

Lever, Kathrine. *The Art of Greek Comedy.* London: Methuen, 1956.

Lind, L. R. *The Greek Plays in Contemporary Translations.* New York: Houghton Mifflin, 1957.

Lucas, D. N. *The Greek Tragic Poets.* 2d ed. London: Cohen & West, 1959.

McGowan, Kenneth, and Melnitz, William. *The Living Stage.* New Jersey: Prentice-Hall, 1964. Excellent chapters on early theatre, with illustrations.

Mantzius, Karl. *History of Theatre Art in Ancient and Modern Times.* 6 vols. London: Duckworth, 1903-1921. The good old standard.

Steiner, George. *The Death of Tragedy.* New York: Hill & Wang, 1961.

Sophocles

Bates, W. N., *Sophocles: Poet and Dramatist.* New York: A. S. Barnes, 1961.

Aristophanes

Aristophanes. *The Birds,* translated by William Arrowsmith. Ann Arbor: University of Michigan Press, 1961.

Corrigan, R. W. ed. *Greek Comedy.* New York: Dell, 1965. Contains Walter Kerr's translation of *The Birds.*

Ehrenberg, Victor. *The people of Aristophanes.* New York: Schocken Books, 1962.

RECORDINGS

American Bird Sounds. Cornell University. Folk 6115.

Bird's World of Song (4-61). Cornell University. Folk 6115.

THE LIVING PLAYS OF SOPHOCLES

Antigone (441 B.C.)	*Electra* (410 B.C.)
Oedipus the King (441-430 B.C.)	*Oedipus at Colonus* (405 B.C.)

THE LIVING PLAYS OF ARISTOPHANES

The Knights (424 B.C.)

The Clouds (423 B.C.)

The Birds (414 B.C.)

Lysistrata (411 B.C.)

The Frogs (405 B.C.)

After the premature death of Alexander the Great, Greek drama declined along with the civilization that created it. To the west, Rome was rising and by A.D. 180, it controlled England and western Europe as well as the Balkans, Asia Minor, Babylon, Egypt, and the entire coast of west Africa.

In their drama, however, the Romans were not leaders but followers. Italian dramatic forms, no doubt, existed before 240 B.C. We have surviving evidences in art of some characters of these dramas such as Maccus the stupid clown, Bucco the glutton or braggart, and others. These dramas were performed during festivals, triumphs, or dedications of temples, on a temporary structure of wood with no seating arrangements for the spectators. The authors of such plays were frequently slaves and usually they enacted the chief roles. This gives us some idea of the esteem, or lack of it, in which these dramas were held.

Later, Italian writers began to translate and adapt the great Greek poets, especially Euripides and Menander. The most representative of these Roman playwrights were Plautus, Caecilius, and Terence. Unlike the Athenians, who wrote for an exclusive and sophisticated audience, these native Italians competed for the attention of a bawdy, earthy group of spectators accustomed to such diversions as boxing, wrestling, and gladiatorial combats.

TITUS MACCIUS PLAUTUS (CA 255-184 B.C.)

Foremost of these authors was Plautus, whose works bridge the gap between ancient Greece and the Renaissance dramaturgy. Over a hundred comedies are ascribed to him, some existing only in fragmentary condition, but at least twenty are accepted as being of his authorship. Plautus was not merely a translator. In *Miles Gloriosus*, he was facile enough to amalgamate plots of two different Greek originals. He is considered a master in the use of the vigorous, colloquial language of the Augustan age. His dialogue denies the platitude that Latin is a dry and uninteresting language and, indeed, for his time he demonstrated a consummate knowledge of stagecraft. His influence on subsequent dramaturgy is obvious. Molière, Corneille, Racine, Marlowe, Ben Jonson, and Shakespeare, all owe Plautus a debt of gratitude. The first known English comedy, *Ralph Royster Doyster* (acted before 1551), was undoubtedly founded on Plautus' *Miles Gloriosus*. The lost play, *The Historie of Error* (acted in 1577), was probably based upon Plautus' *Amphitruo*. Shakespeare's *Comedy of Errors*, (about 1591) is an adaptation of *The Menaechini*, by Plautus. In writing *The Taming of the Shrew*, Shakespeare was certainly influenced by Plautus in several respects; he lifted the names "Tranio" and "Grumio." Thomas Heywood adapted the *Amphitruo* for his *Silver Age*; Dryden's *Amphitryon* (1690) is based partly on Plautus' *Amphitruo*, and Molière's adaptation of it. In our contemporary theatre, we have an adaptation of this play by Jean Giraudoux, *Amphitryon 38*, produced successfully on Broadway with Alfred Lunt and Lynn Fontanne playing the leading roles. Because of these many adaptations, Plautus' *Amphitruo* has become *Amphitryon*.

PREPARATION FOR AMPHITRUO BY PLAUTUS

The actual date of the first production of this play is not known but has been conjectured to have been around 186 B.C. It is considered to be one of Plautus' most successful comedies.

Background

The mythological Jupiter, enamored of the soldierly Amphitryon's beautiful wife, Alcmena, assumes the mortal Amphitryon's physical being in order to seduce her. The god Mercury disguises himself as Sosia, Amphitryon's servant, so that he might better supervise Jupiter's little game. In the scene which follows, the real Amphitryon returns; not realizing that both he and his wife are victims of the god's jest, he suspects her of infidelity. Alcmena is not only a devoted and faithful wife but also a woman of dignity and honor.

REHEARSAL

AMPHITRUO*

An Excerpt

AMPHITRYON: ¹D'ye say we came here yesterday?   1. He speaks directly
ALCMENA: I do.   to Alcmena.
  And coming you saluted me, I you,
  And kissed you.
SOSIA: That kiss does not quite please.
AMPHITRYON: I will pursue my enquiries.
ALCMENA: Then you bathed.
AMPHITRYON: What then?
ALCMENA: You came to supper.
SOSIA: Excellent!
  Enquire about that.
AMPHITRYON: Don't interrupt.²   Go on.   2. He gestures Sosia to be
ALCMENA: Dinner was served; we sat together there.   quiet, then faces Alcmena.
AMPHITRYON: On the same couch?
ALCMENA: The same.

*From pp. 41–43 of *Amphitryon*, by Plautus, trans. by Sir Robert Allison from *Complete Roman Drama*, edited by George B. Duckworth, © 1942 by Random House. Reprinted by permission.

SOSIA: He does not like
   The dinner.
AMPHITRYON: Let her state her arguments.
   What after we had dined?
ALCMENA: You said that you
   Were sleepy; so the table was removed.
   We went to bed.
AMPHITRYON: Where did you sleep, I pray?
ALCMENA: In the same bed with you.

3. A pause as he walks away from her.
AMPHITRYON: O God![3]
SOSIA: How now?
AMPHITRYON: She's good as killed me.

4. She moves to him.
ALCMENA: Why, what is it, dear?[4]

5. But he moves away.
AMPHITRYON: Don't speak to me![5]
SOSIA: What is it?
AMPHITRYON: I'm undone!
   To all the troubles of my absence this
   Is added that the honour of my wife
   Is lost.
ALCMENA: And why, my lord, do I hear you say so?
AMPHITRYON: What! I your lord? Nay, do not use that name!

6. To audience.
SOSIA: [6]The matter is at a deadlock indeed
   If she has changed him now from lord to lady.
ALCMENA: What have I done you should address me so?
AMPHITRYON: You tell the tale, yet ask how you have sinned?
ALCMENA: It was with you I married, where's the sin?

7. With disbelief.
AMPHITRYON: You were with me? A more audacious lie[7]
   Was never told; and even if you have
   No modesty, you might assume a little.

8. This does it. She draws herself up to her full dignity.
ALCMENA: Such conduct as you hint does not become[8]
   My race; and if you try to prove a charge
   Against me of immodesty you'll fail.
AMPHITRYON: Now, Sosia, by the gods, at least you know me!
SOSIA: Why, rather!
AMPHITRYON: Yesterday I dined on board?
SOSIA: We've many witnesses to speak to that.
   I know not what to say unless there be
   Amphitryon the second who looks after
   Your business in your absence, and can fill
   Your place; to have another Sosia
   Was strange; but it was stranger still to find
   A new Amphitryon standing in your shoes.
AMPHITRYON: Some witch, I think, this lady does befool.

ALCMENA: By the high heaven, by Juno too, herself,
    Whom most of all I reverence and regard,
    I swear that no one else has ever come
    Near me to wreck my modesty.

AMPHITRYON: I wish[9]
    Indeed 'twere so.

ALCMENA: I speak the truth, but you
    Will not believe.

AMPHITRYON: You are a woman still,
    And swear audaciously.

9. The next few lines are spoken quickly.

ALFRED LUNT AND LYNN FONTANNE IN *AMPHITRYON 38*. (PHOTO FROM BROWN BROTHERS; PERMISSION BY ALFRED LUNT AND LYNN FONTANNE.)

ALCMENA: Who has not sinned
    Must needs be bold, and speak with confidence,
    Aye, ev'n and forwardness, in her defence.

AMPHITRYON: Boldly enough, I grant.

ALCMENA: As one who is
    Quite innocent.

AMPHITRYON: Yes, you are so in word.

ALCMENA: [10]A dowry, sir, is not what people deem;

10. She now speaks deliberately and with dignity.

ROMAN DRAMA   163

But love and modesty, and all desires
Controlled in fitting bounds, the fear of Heaven,
Respect of parents, good will to my friends,
Conforming in my likings to your own,
Bounteous in kindly service for your good,
These things I had, and these my dowry were.

SOSIA: If she speaks true she's innocence itself.

AMPHITRYON: I am bewitched; I know not who I am.

SOSIA: You are Amphitryon surely; see that you
Don't let another man your name usurp
And take it to himself (men change so much),
Now that we have at last arrived at home.

AMPHITRYON: I'll probe this matter to the very bottom.

FURTHER READING: ROMAN DRAMA

Beare, W. *The Roman Stage: A Short History of Latin Drama in the Time of the Republic.* 3rd. ed. New York: Barnes & Noble, 1968.

Bond, R. W. *Early Plays from the Italian.* New York: Oxford University Press, 1911.

Casson, Lionel, ed. *Amphitryon, and Two Other Plays.* New York: W. W. Norton, 1971.

Copley, Frank O., transl. *The Comedies of Terence.* New York: Bobbs-Merrill, 1967. Contains *Women of Andros, The Brothers, Phormio, The Mother-in-Law,* and *The Eunich.*

Corrigan, Robert W. *Roman Drama.* New York: Dell, 1966.

Duckworth, George E., ed. *The Complete Roman Drama.* 2 vols. New York: Random House, 1942.

————. *The Nature of Roman Comedy: A Study in Popular Entertainment.* 4th ed. New Jersey: Princeton University Press, 1967.

Eastman, Max. *The Sense of Humor.* New York: Octagon, 1971.

————. *Enjoyment of Laughter.* New York: Johnson, 1971.

Frank, Tenney. *The Status of Actors at Rome.* New York: Russell, 1933.

Gassner, John. *Masters of the Drama.* 3d ed. New York: Dover, 1953.

Hamilton, E. *The Roman Way.* New York: W. W. Norton, 1932.

Harsh, A. *A Handbook of Classical Drama.* California: Stanford University Press, 1944.

Highet, G. *The Classical Tradition.* New York: Oxford University Press, 1949.

Matthews, Brander, ed. *The Chief European Dramatists.* New York: Houghton Mifflin. Contains *The Captives* by Plautus and *Phornio* by Terence.

Nicoll, Allardyce. *Masks, Mimes and Miracles: Studies in Popular Theatre.* New York: Cooper Square Publications, 1931.

Norwood, Gilbert. ed. *The Art of Terence.* New York: Russell, 1965.

————. *Plautus and Terence, Our Debt to Greece and Rome.* New York: Cooper Square Publications, 1932.

————. *Greek Comedy*. New York: Hill & Wang, 1963.

Perry, H. T. *Masters of Dramatic Comedy and Their Social Themes*. Dallas, Texas: Kennikat, 1968.

Roby, Robert C., and Ulanov, Barry. *Introduction to Drama*. New York: McGraw-Hill, 1962. Contains *Miles Gloriosus* by Plautus.

Rose, H. J. *Gods and Heroes of the Greeks,* Gloucester, Massachusetts: Peter Smith, 1934.

Segal, Erich W. *Roman Laughter, The Comedy of Plautus*. Boston: Harvard University Press, 1968.

Wright, Frederick A. and Rogers, Lionel. *Three Plays by Plautus*. New York: St. Martin's, 1925.

The Living Plays of Plautus

Miles Gloriosus (The Braggart Soldier)   *The Slipknot*
The Menaechini (The Twins)   *Pseudolus, or The Trickster*
The Captives   *Amphitruo*
Rudens   *The Two Bacchides*

13
Medieval Drama

As the great Roman civilization began to decay, the art of acting in formal comedies and tragedies also declined; by the fifth and sixth centuries acting was almost a lost art. Roman theatres were demolished by invading armies, and only the church remained, which was openly hostile to drama. In the Dark Ages, only the transient and ephemeral mime with his comedy routines and gymnastics kept the art alive. Although such performers were professional, theirs was a sorry life indeed, wandering from town to town all over Europe, acting in the streets or at festivals, and occasionally living high while performing at some castle for a feudal lord.

Oddly enough, it was the church, which had been so antagonistic toward the theatre, that eventually served as an instrument in reviving it, and the art of acting. It was the priests themselves, not the itinerant performers, who were the first actors of the Middle Ages. At the Christian feasts of Easter, they chanted and sang in Latin a liturgical drama of the discovery of Christ's resurrection on Easter morning. In time, the monks wrote and acted original dramas about Bible events. The church altar represented the empty tomb of Jesus; sections of the church were transformed into the Garden of Gethsemane, Pilate's palace or Calvary, by temporary structures of wood and cloth. These enactments became so popular that they could not accommodate the crowds and were eventually moved into the church yards and streets. Being human, sensual attitudes of the people began creeping into these plays along with occasional irreverences and parodies of sacred religious rituals. This caused some of the church hierarchy to become disillusioned, feeling that these plays had grown too far away from their original religious intentions.

It was then that lay associations and craft guilds took over. What began as religious spectacles, devised by ecclesiastics for the edification of the laity, came to appeal to the deep-seated instincts of the people, and was, to them, an inexhaustible source of wonder and delight. This deeply felt instinct for the magic of drama comes naturally to man and he is not complete without it.

Although this lay activity in religious drama thrived all over middle Europe during the fourteenth and fifteenth centuries, a prosperous England had its full share in the early development of popular, more secular dramas, supported mainly by the workers' guilds or municipal governments. Shakespeare's portrayal of Bottom and his fellow craftsmen in *Midsummer Night's Dream* no doubt reflected a professional's scorn of these earlier rustic amateurs.

These honest little plays were translated from the Latin into the vernaculars and assumed some elements of characterization (although not comparable to modern standards). Actually, their crudeness and naïveté enhanced their effectiveness and proved entertaining to the public as well as fortifying to religious faith and vision. As John Gassner has said, medieval drama "affords the spectacle of an entire people growing and displaying its dramatic art as an act of communion."

THE PLAYS

The plays are generally grouped into several different genres.

The Mystery plays dealt with scriptural events, such as, the Nativity, the Passion, and the Resurrection.

The Miracle plays were concerned with the legends of the saints, St. George, St. Nicholas, etc.

The Morality plays were abstract, illustrating and teaching moral truths allegorically, such as *Everyman, Mankind,* etc. Characters were personified virtues or qualities.

THE ACTORS

In England, trade companies or guilds performed the above plays, especially the moralities and the assignments were amusingly literal. The guild of bakers might choose a play having something to do with food, the guild of goldsmiths might enact the presentation of the gifts by the Magi, and the fisher's guild chose either the parable of loaves and fishes or Noah's flood. Generally a prologue was spoken by a herald or narrator and frequently the actors performed upon movable stages. The mouth of hell might be shown (with or without fire), and with demons wearing hideous head masks.

The Devil had an attendant fool called Vice, Shift, or Fraud, whose job it was to tease the Devil, to the amusement of the crowd. Later, this domestic fool survived in regular drama and is accepted as a prototype of the clowns found in Elizabethan dramas. The Moralities and the Mysteries were performed until, and often into, the Renaissance, when more traditional drama began. But these medieval plays found such favor with the public that some of the guild players left their crafts to wander into the hinterlands, writing and performing their own plays; and in England, some moved into, and substantially influenced, the rich Elizabethan theatre. Very few details can be gathered from the existing records, but one is a direction note in the Cornish plays. When a character first entered, it was customary for him to be introduced, whereupon he would strut about the stage in a circle before taking his place in the scene. In some English halls, this custom still exists. Evidently, the Prompter was a functionary of some importance, often whispering the player's lines to him in a resounding stage whisper.

PREPARATION FOR THE NOAH REHEARSAL
(14th TO 15th CENTURIES)

In rehearsing this little play, keep in mind the sincere dedication and the unsophistication of these people. In his *Medieval Stage,* E. K. Chambers writes that *Noah* was an activity of the guild of ship-wrights at York, and of the watermen's guild at Beverley, Newcastle, and York (p. 118).

STYLES IN ACTING

NOAH, A MORALITY PLAY*

An Adaptation

4 FEMALES, 4 MALES

NARRATOR: At first in some high place
   Or in the clouds it may be
   God speaketh unto Noah:-

   "I God, that all the world have wrought,
   Heaven and Earth, and all of nought,
   I see my people, in deed and thought,
   all set foully in sin.

   Man that I made I will destroy,
   Beast, worm, and fowl that fly.

   Therefore, Noah, my servant free,[1]   1. Noah stands
   That righteous man art, I see,

   *An original of this play is in the British Museum, Harleian Manuscript M.S. 2124, as printed in *The Chester Plays*, Part 1, edited for the Early English Text Society by H. Deimling, 1892. I have modernized the spelling for better interpretation, and have added stage directions.

MEDIEVAL DRAMA   169

A ship soon that shalt make thee,
Three hundred cubits it shall be long,
And fifty of breadth, to make it strong.

With water I shall overflow,
Man that I did make.
Destroyed all the world shall be,

2. Noah's wife stands   Save thou; thy wife,[2]

3. Shem, Ham & Japheth   Thy sons three[3]
stand.   And all their wives also with thee[4]

4. The wives stand, each   Shall be saved, for thy sake."
on individual cue.
NOAH: Thy bidding, Lord, I shall fulfill,
And never more grieve nor grill,
That such Grace has sent me till
Among all mankind.

5. To his family   To work this ship, chamber and hall,[5]
As God hath bidden us do.
SHEM: Father, I am all ready bound:
An axe I have, by my crown,
As sharp as any in this town.
HAM: I have a hatchet wondrous keen,
To bite well, as may be seen.
JAPHETH: And I can make a pin,
And with this hammer knock it in.
SHEM'S WIFE: Here is a good hack stock;
On this you may hew and knock.

6. Slitch, viscous clay.   HAM'S WIFE: And I will gather slitch,[6]

7. They all pantomime   [7]The ship to caulk and pitch.
working.   JAPHETH'S WIFE: And I will gather chips here,
To make a fire for you here,
And for to make your dinner,
Against you come in.
NARRATOR: And so, all of Noah's family set to work,-
All but Noah's wife who saw no need.
NOAH: Good wife, do now as I bid thee.
NOAH'S WIFE: Not I, not ere I see more need.
Though thou stand all the day and stare.
NOAH: Lord, that woman be crabbed, ay,
And never is meek, that I dare say.
NARRATOR: Again was heard the voice of God,-
"Of clean beasts with thee thou take
Seven and seven, ere thou slake;
He and she, mate to mate,
Quickly do thou bring

⁸Of beasts unclean two and two,
 Male and female, and no more;
 Of clean fowls seven also,
 The he and she together:
 Of fowls unclean two and no more,
 As I of beasts said before
 These shall be saved through my love,
 Against I send the weather.
 This world is filled full of sin,
 And that is now well seen."
NOAH: Sir, here are lions, leopards in.
 Horses, mares, oxen and swine,
 Goats, calves, sheep and kine
 Here sitten,-thou may see.
NOAH'S WIFE: I will not out of this town,
 If I have not my gossips every one.
 They shall not drown by St. John,
 If I may save their lives.
 They loved me full well, I attest,
 Unless thou let them in thy chest;
 Row forth, Noah, wither thou list,
 And get thee a new wife.
NOAH: Shem, son, lo! thy mother is wroth!⁹
SHEM: I shall fetch her in, by my troth,
 Without any fail.

 Mother, my father after thee sent,¹⁰
 And bids thee into yonder ship wend.
NOAH'S WIFE: Son, go again to him, and say
 I will not come therein today.
HAM: Shall we all fetch her in?
NOAH: Yea, sons, in Christ's blessing and mine.
NOAH'S WIFE: That I will not, for all you call,
 But I have my gossips all.
SHEM: In faith, mother, yet you shall,
 Whether you will or nought.¹¹
NARRATOR: Then Noah shutteth the windows of the ark.

12

NOAH: Now forty days are fully gone,
 Send a raven I will anon,
 This betokenth God has done us some Grace,
 And is a sign of peace.
NARRATOR: And God spoketh again to his servant,-
 "Noah, take thy wife anon,

8. Shem & wife, Ham & wife, Japheth & wife, pantomime different beasts in pairs.

9. wroth, angry.

10. Shem goes to his mother.

11. They carry her in.

12. Blackout. Thunder strikes.
Lights flash on and off revealing actors swaying and clutching each other. Screams, rain effect, thunder and lightning. Ham and Shem roll a long length of blue-green cloth between them simulating great waves. Then, all is calm. Noah pantomimes reopening windows.

And thy children every one;
Out of the ship thou shalt be gone,
And they all with thee,
Beasts and all that fly
Out anon they shall hie
On earth to grow and multiply."

NOTE ON INCIDENTAL MUSIC

Noye's Fludde, based on the Noah play in the Chester Cycle, by one of England's leading composers, Benjamin Britten, is played every four years at Lancing College in Sussex, England. See also André Obey's play *Noah.*

FURTHER READING: MEDIEVAL DRAMA

Adams, Joseph Quincy. *Chief Pre-Shakespearian Drama.* New York: Houghton Mifflin, 1952. Contains versions of Roister Doyster, Gorbuduc, Creation of Eve, Gammer Gurton's Needle, etc.

Brooke, Iris. *Medieval Theatre Costumes.* New York: Theatre Arts Books, 1963.

Cawley, Arthur Clare, ed. *Everyman and Medieval Miracle Plays.* 2d ed. London: Dent, 1958.

Chambers, E. K. *The Medieval Stage.* 2 vols. New York: Oxford University Press, 1963.

Cheney, Sheldon. *The Theatre: Three Thousand Years of Drama, Acting, and Stagecraft.* New York: Longmans, 1930.

Clarke, Sidney M. *Miracle Plays in England.* New York: Gordon Publications. 1941.

Craig, Hardin. *English Religious Drama of the Middle Ages.* London: Oxford University Press, 1955.

Gassner, John. *A Treasury of the Theatre.* New York: Simon and Schuster, 1963. Vol. 1, pp. 186-204, Medieval Drama.

MacDonald, J. W. and Saxton, J. C. W. *Four Stages.* New York: St. Martin's, 1963.

Malcolmson, Anne B. *Miracle Plays.* New York: Houghton Mifflin, 1959. Contains illustrations.

Meade, Anna McClymonds. "The Actor in the Middle Ages." Master's Thesis, Columbia University, May 1927.

Nicoll, Allardyce. *British Drama: A Historical Survey from the Beginning to the Present Time.* London: Harrap, 1947.

Prosser, Eleanor. *Drama and Religion in the English Mystery Plays.* California: Stanford University Press, 1961.

Rhys, Ernest. *Everyman and Other Interludes.* New York: Dutton, 1970.

Rossiter, A. P. *English Drama from Early Times to the Elizabethans.* New York: Barnes & Noble, 1960.

Salter, F. M. *Medieval Drama in Chester*. Canada: University of Toronto, 1955. Assembled from guild and church wardens' account books and municipal documents.

Smith, Lucy Tonlmin, ed. *York Plays*. New York: Russell, 1963. Illustrations.

Thorndike, Ashley H. *English Comedy*. New York: Macmillan, 1930. From medieval times to 1900.

Wickham, Glynne. *Early English Stages, 1300 to 1660*. New York: Columbia University Press, 1959. Vol. 1, 1300 to 1576.

Williams, Arnold. *The Characterization of Pilate in the Townley Plays*. Michigan: Michigan State University Press, 1950.

Young, Karl. *The Drama of the Medieval Church*. 2 vols. London: Oxford University Press, 1962.

14
The Commedia
dell'Arte

It was not until some time in the latter part of the sixteenth century that a new and vital style of theatre became evident. The Commedia dell'Arte was so totally different in concept that its influence exists even to this day.

Various Italian troupes of itinerate actors began the style which eventually spread all over the continent where it reigned as the popular theatre for at least two hundred years. It was not until the eighteenth century that the style came to be known as the Commedia dell'Arte. It was old and it was new. It was new in its use of improvisation, but old in its use of masks and plots. Actual speeches were not written, but left to the actor's impromptu wit and intelligence. Only the characters were known beforehand. A scenario describing the main developments in the story line were written and posted backstage where actors might refer to it. This was known as "the plot" and it is interesting that later prompt books were also called "plots."

PLOTS AND ACTORS

Using stock characters, performances were a striking mixture of the grotesque, bitter irony, and boisterous, bawdy farce. In general, plots dealt with some variation of mistaken identity or love and intrigue: a young wife (the Amorosa) married to an old husband (Pantaloon), a clever but dishonest servant (Zanni or Harlequin) or a bragging warrior (Capitano) who usually proved cowardly during a crisis. Frequently an actor would choose one of these stock characters, design his own costume, add his own personality or special abilities, and become so famous that he continued to play the part for the rest of his life.

These actors were expected to supply not only set comedy routines—called *lazzi*—but juggling and acrobatics while the actresses did the ballet or musical interludes. Some actors were accomplished gymnasts. One at eighty-three years of age could box another actor's ears with his foot. Another convulsed his audiences by doing a complete somersault while holding a glass of wine in his hand. Particular athletic skills often became the specialty of an actor.

For the first time, women assumed an important part in theatrical history, performing female roles. In the beginning women's parts served mostly to further the plot by adding romance. Heroines were a sheltered lot of young things, disciplined by parents but ripe for love. Usually the heroine had a confidante, equally doll-like. Later, this confidante developed certain traits, thanks to the actresses who played her. She might be saucy, brazen, sly, but certainly more experienced in the ways of the world than the innocent heroine.

Free from the confinements of a written play and dialogue, these actors took full advantage of the opportunity and made it, in every sense, an actor's theatre. The playwright and director were shadowed figures in this theatre, if they existed at all. Leading actors had their own set speeches for love scenes or situations common to most plots, such as denunciations, farcical panic, etc. They were expert with a device known

PANTALOON

CAPITANO

THE COMMEDIA DELL' ARTE

175

THE WORKS OF CARLO GOLDONI ARE FREQUENTLY STAGED USING COMMEDIA DELL'ARTE CHARACTERS, AS WAS DONE IN THIS PRODUCTION BY THE TYRONE GUTHRIE THEATRE IN MINNESOTA (COURTESY THE MINNESOTA THEATRE COMPANY.)

CHARLIE CHAPLIN—THE INDIVIDUAL *VS.* THE MACHINE—IN *MODERN TIMES*.

as *tirata della giostra*—or the use of gibberish, which modern actors are convinced they invented. Topical jokes were favored by both actors and audiences. These masters of farce could always be counted upon to make use of incidents occurring in the audience or in the news of the day. Troupes of four or five actors would take to the road, playing on makeshift stages during fairs or celebrations. Other, more elite companies were often the favorites of royalty, playing at court where they were held in great esteem.

For three hundred years these actors reigned supreme over the entire European theatre. They left their mark on the Shakespearean clowns, on Molière's plots and characters, and on our own vaudeville and nightclub comedians.

Although the style of acting of the Commedia contained some elements of what went before, these actors added enough of themselves so that the total effect was fresh and distinctive. They wrote the rules for playing farce. If possible, they were even more physical actors than the Greeks. Not content with graceful dances and pageantry alone, they developed skills in tumbling, juggling, and dangerous, involved horseplay. Released from the responsibilities of enacting great plays, their goal was to please the common man, and in so doing they found they had also pleased some intellectuals. Several hundred years later, Charlie Chaplin, working with a new medium, had the same experience as his professional ancestors.

ACTING TECHNIQUE

The word *comedy* is a generic term. As used by the Greeks, it denoted the form that was not tragedy. In France all actors, comedians or tragedians, were referred to as *comédiens*. Over the years, many types of comedy have developed, each with its own specific technique. There is satire, comedy-romance, farce-comedy, high and low comedy, etc. *The Birds*, written as social criticism, is most effectively played as farce. *Comedy, pure comedy, as we know it today, is intellectual.* It consists of the play on words, the witty remark, an amusing situation, even the lift of an eyebrow; for acting, it requires a bright mind and a feather touch.

Farce, on the other hand is physical. In farce we use the sock on the head, the chase, the ridiculous fight, elaborate mechanical gadgets, all physical devices. In *Modern Times*, Chaplin was pitted against the towering machines of mass production; circus clowns have their machines which turn giants into dwarfs, or dogs into sausages. The makeup and costumes of farce are outlandish and absurd. The slapstick of our early "comedy" movies was, in reality, farce. Also the "comedy" of the Commedia dell'Arte is really farce. Characterizations are not symbolic, meaningful, or significant. They are one dimensional, existing for their own sake. Situations may be normal, but reactions are off center and improbable. Thought or reason is seldom used in farce. One of its chief characteristics is the accumulation of incredible events. Mack Sennett once said that farce must always have "a touch of madness" in it. It is only fitting that both actors and comedians recognize their debt to this first great actor's theatre—the Commedia dell'Arte.

Clown vs. Comedian

"To be Othello," William Hazlitt wrote, "a man should be all passion, abstraction, imagination: to be Harlequin, he should have all his wits in his heels and in his fingers end."[1] It is important that the student-actor know the differences between acting comedy and acting farce. The comedian always reacts normally. He is indignant or angry when he has a reason, happy at the same things we are; indeed, he is motivated very much as we are ourselves, except that he is more incisive, more observant and acute in his feelings. He takes an ordinary situation and underlines its ridiculousness. His comments are all part of his viewpoint, his special way of thinking.

But the clown's reactions are untypical, improbable, often the complete antithesis of ours. He jostles a harmless table and jumps back, nervous and frightened. He is menaced by the inanimate. When a gun is pointed in his face, he is calm. He may cry when another clown takes his balloon, but laugh when it bursts in his face. His innocence causes us to love him. His responses are not justified either physically or psychologically. Neither are his emotions predictable. He might pick flowers on a railroad track and remain undisturbed by the approach of a train. Clowns are mentally undeveloped. They do not reason and are more childish than children, so children feel superior and protective, and therefore identify immediately with them. The clown reacts slowly, but when he does, he cries louder and runs faster than any of us. Anger is seldom shown in the clown, although he is often frustrated. A clown is never a "real" person, but he must always be theatrically true to what he is inside, naïve as it may be. The sadness of Emmett Kelly, the circus hobo, is a mockery of sadness, he is so sad that he is funny. The wonderful bicycle clown, Joe Jackson, Sr., was constantly frustrated by his inability to master his machine, but he never got angry.[2] He bore his frustration with a sweet, almost silly, "Oh well, that's life" attitude. Watching Jackson perform told me more about man's fumbling through life than all three acts of *Waiting for Godot*.

Let me illustrate the difference between the comedian and clown by naming two personalities. Alan King is considered our foremost monologuist today, and is the author of several books on humor. Let us assume that both Joe Jackson and Alan King start with the theme of frustration. The clown, Jackson, reacts to it physically, whereas King, the comedian, reacts mentally.

HARLEQUIN

[1]William Archer, ed., *Hazlitt on Theatre* (New York: Hill & Wang, 1958), p. 188.
[2]Joe Jackson, Jr., is now doing his father's act and has frequently appeared on television.

JOE JACKSON, SR. (LEFT) AND JOE JACKSON, JR. (RIGHT). (FROM THE NEW YORK PUBLIC LIBRARY THEATRE COLLECTION.)

EXERCISE 91

Name your favorite funny man and after considering his method of working, decide if he is a clown or a comedian.

In the following Commedia dell'Arte scenario, we are going to act the parts of clowns. Later, when we have our first comedy, we will take up the study of comedy, which is a more complicated and subtle art to learn. This should not be taken to mean that both are not high art forms.

PREPARATION FOR THE TWINS

Around 200 B.C., Plautus wrote a simple and even primitive little farce called *The Twin Menaechmi*. In it, identical twin boys from Syracuse are separated by a shipwreck, then set together years later in the same town. By means of a series of mistakes in identity, they are once again united. Plautus was concerned not with exploring character but with an accumulation of comic incidents.

In the sixteenth and seventeenth centuries, actors of the Commedia dell'Arte borrowed this plot and added to it with their own special skills. They discarded the dialogue Plautus had written, preferring to speak extempore. Their own favorite characters were used, notably Pantalone, the eccentric quack Dottore, the nagging wife, and the zany servant. No doubt, this story of the twins was one of their favorite scenarios.

Later Shakespeare profited by the Plautus original in writing *The Comedy of Errors* (1591), even naming some characters by the names Plautus had given them. But Shakespeare added more dimension to characters, and more significance to the plot. Undoubtedly, the Commedia actors achieved somewhat the same end by adding personalities and acting skills to the entertainment.

STYLES IN ACTING

THE TWINS

4 males, 1 female

NARRATOR: A Captain arrives in Parma in search of his long lost twin. Before his brother, Silvio, is found, the Captain is several times mistaken for him. Because Silvio has been drinking and associating with women other than his wife, Flavia, she has sent for her father, Pantaloon, in the hope that he can straighten out her husband.

Pantaloon mistakes the Captain for Silvio, curses him for his loose living and drinking. The Captain denies all, even knowing the old man. Pantaloon reluctantly informs his daughter that her husband is "possessed by demons" and leaves her to search for a physician.

Improvise the following Scenario:

The Captain enters, and is followed on stage by an angry, shouting Flavia. She accuses him of being a poor provider, a philanderer, and a drunk. At first, the Captain tries to explain that she has mistaken him for someone else, but she begins striking him. Now convinced that she is a mad woman, he restrains her but each time he does she releases herself and bursts with more invective. When he denies that he ever saw her before, she tells him that she sees through his pretense and that he is trying to shed his legal responsibilities as a husband and threatens him with the law. Pantaloon enters with the Physician, who is a little strange himself. Disregarding the Captain's violent protests, they try to take him into Silvio's house where they can examine him. Believing that they are trying to murder him, the Captain tries to escape. The only way they can subdue him is by sitting on him and then the Doctor examines him. After several comic pieces of business with implements, the Doctor pronounces his opinion, "The man is mad!" He must be given a physic, bled, and confined. The Captain kicks and fights shouting that they are thieves and murderers. At this point, Silvio enters. All turn to discover him. At first they believe they are seeing a ghost but the Doctor, who is a specialist in this sort of thing, convinces them that what they are seeing is a supernatural phenomenon—and begins strange incantations. The Captain pushes them back and asks if Silvio ever had a twin. After several questions and answers, they decide that they are brothers and embrace. The old men cannot tell which is which, but Flavia assures them that she can tell. After ceremoniously kissing both she picks Silvio as her husband, saying a wife certainly knows her husband's kiss. Silvio simpers in pride, but she tells him not to be a fool, that he never kissed her like the Captain.

SILVIO

FURTHER READING: THE COMMEDIA DELL'ARTE

Beaumont, Cyril V. *The History of Harlequin* 1926. Reprint. New York: Benjamin Blom, 1967.

Disher, Maurice Willson. *Clowns and Pantomimes*. New York: Benjamin Blom, 1968.

DuChartre, Pierre Louis. *The Italian Comedy: The Improvisations, Scenarios, Lives, Attributes, Portraits and Masks of the Illustrious Characters of The Commedia dell'Arte*. Translated by Randolph Weaver. New York: John Day, 1929.

Herrick, Marvin M. *Italian Comedy in the Renaissance*. Chicago: University of Illinois, 1960.

Kennard, Joseph Spencer. *Masks and Marionettes*. New York: Cooper Square Publications, 1968.

————. *The Italian Theatre*. 2 vols. New York: Rudge, 1931.

Lea, Kathleen M. *Italian Popular Comedy: A Study of the Commedia dell'Arte (1560-1620) with Special Reference to the English Stage*. 2 vols. 1924. Reprint. New York: Russell, 1962.

Mantzius, Karl. *A History of Theatrical Art in Ancient and Modern Times*. 6 vols. Massachusetts: Peter Smith, 1937. Commedia in vols. 1 and 2.

Nicoll, Allardyce. *Masks, Mimes, and Miracles: Studies in Popular Theatre*. New York: Cooper Square Publications, 1931.

————. *The Development of the Theatre*. New York: Harcourt, 1937. See "Dialogues on Stage Affairs" by Leone Di Somi.

————. *The World of Harlequin*. New York: Cambridge University Press, 1963.

Niklaus, Thelma. *Harlequin, or the Rise and Fall of the Bergamask Rogue*. New York: George Braziller, 1958.

Oreglia, Giacomo. *The Commedia dell'Arte*. New York: Hill & Wang, 1968.

Riccoboni, Lugi. *An Historical Account of the Theatres of Europe, Together with an Essay on Acting*. 1738. Reprint. New York: Benjamin Blom, 1969. One of the first writers on acting.

Sand, Maurice. *The History of the Harlequin*. 2 vols. 1915. Reprint. New York: Benjamin Blom, 1968.

Smith, Winifred. *The Commedia dell'Arte: A Study in Italian Popular Comedy*. New York: Benjamin Blom, 1965.

15
Shakespeare
(1564-1616)

In Tudor and Elizabethan England, groups of strolling players wandered from town to town, detached from the protection of their guilds and ekeing out a precarious living. In the opinion of the townspeople, such players were considered no better than beggars or thieves, for whom laws were implacable—flogging was mandatory. In order to avoid such treatment, the players often sought the protection of some titled Englishman.

James Burbage, an actor in one of these troupes, and a former carpenter, became weary of his transient and precarious life. In 1576, he built a permanent structure for production of plays. Not surprisingly, this "plaiehowse" was called, *The Theatre*, and Burbage fashioned it after the inn yards in which he and his "fellowes" had been playing. Soon there were many other theatres, literally setting the stage for the luxuriant Elizabethan dramas.

After several years, the landlord refused to renew the ground lease on which the Theatre was built. James Burbage, his actor son Richard, and several actor-shareholders, tore it down under cover of darkness and carried it piece by piece—literally on their backs—to a new location. This was done while the company was giving performances at court during the day. When they were finished, they could no longer call it the Theatre as there were too many liens against that name. In honor of their Herculean task they called their little world *The Globe.*

THE ACTORS OF THE GLOBE

To illustrate the physical condition of these actors, we know that Will Kemp, the much-loved comedian of the Globe Company, once wagered

MOVING THE THEATRE

STYLES IN ACTING

he could dance all the way from London to Norwich, over one hundred miles. He did this in nine days, accompanied by pipe and tabor, to the great delight of country people along the way. Is it any wonder that modern actors performing Shakespeare for the first time are amazed at the sheer physical stamina it requires?

For the Elizabethan actors, there was always the problem of having sufficient breath to maintain the sustained tone and then be ready for bursts of passion beyond that. It is interesting that eyewitnesses describing the acting of that time always allude first to the voice. Most of Shakespeare's characters are representative of royalty or nobility or are heroes of grandeur and spirit, not characters met in everyday life. The actors of the King's Company certainly realized that they were not speaking the words, phrases, or thoughts of ordinary people in everyday conversation.

These actors might very well play thirty or more parts per season. Some were in new plays, which required more effort than plays already in the repertory. Usually they performed a different play each time. Actors who could not read had to learn parts by ear, and those who could read were supplied little rolls on which were written their cues and speeches. This roll could be worked through the fingers of one hand, leaving the other free for sword play or "business" as they rehearsed. One such part is still in existence at Dulwich College in England.

Until 1608 it was the rule that vacancies in the company left by the death of some senior member could only be filled by their own graduate apprentices. Twelve- or thirteen-year-old boys began by playing pages and children, while working under the tutelage of a senior shareholder. A Globe apprentice was little more than a slave: "He must do all servile offices about the house," Ben Jonson has recorded, "and be obedient to all his master's commandments and suffer such correction as his master shall meet . . . being bound only to . . . teach him his occupation."[1]

When these apprentices were thought to be qualified, they were advanced to feminine roles and, as they matured, were made regular members of the company. Thus each replacement was already a seasoned performer, familiar with the repertory, and in possession of impressive physical and vocal skills. We can assume from the way apprentices were trained that this was an excellent group of players. Many foreign visitors coming to London were struck by the quality of acting they saw. One traveler wrote, "Nothing quite like them has been known in Europe."

At first it might seem impossible to compare Shakespeare's friend and business partner, Richard Burbage, with the great actors who followed him. Their fame rests mainly on the excellence they displayed in one or two particular characters. But what an enormous range of acting talent Burbage must have had in order to create many if not all of Shakespeare's tragic heroes — Hamlet, King Lear, Macbeth, Richard III, and Othello — all most likely under the direction of Shakespeare himself. There can be

KEMP'S "NINE DAIES WONDER," DANCING FROM LONDON TO NORWICH.

[1]Marchette Chute, *Ben Jonson of Westminister.* (London: Penguin, 1960), p. 37.

SHAKESPEARE

little doubt that these two men created the standards for playwriting and acting as we know them today.

During the time it takes to perform a Shakespearean play, the hero might experience more exceptional and dramatic events than do a dozen men in real life. Shakespeare gives no literal imitation of life. On occasion, he uses a lifelike gravedigger or a porter who serve to establish recognizable fact with the larger-than-life protagonists. The complex characters of his heroes gain existence only through the use of poetry which is studied, formal, and "true" insofar as it resembles actual speech. Perhaps you have been told that "people talked like that in those days." Not true; Shakespeare wrote poetry—words chosen for their beautiful sounds and their expressiveness, and then arranged these into melodic patterns to best elucidate meaning.

In everyday conversation we change pitch, hesitate, even make unpleasant sounds. We improvise. But poetry is planned. When speaking poetry the actor must use a sustained tone without resorting to chant. The trouble that Americans encounter in acting Shakespeare is due in great part to a disregard of these rules. We approach his plays as though they were realistic dramas. There is much proof of the error in this sort of thinking. As far back as the beginning of the twentieth century, André Antoine, the French leader of naturalism, tried unsuccessfully to produce Shakespeare using this approach at his Théâtre Libre. Stanislavski also tried it, and in despair wrote:

> Yet why can I express my perceptions of Chekhov but cannot express my perceptions of Shakespeare? . . . Apparently it is not the inner feeling itself, but the technique of its expression that prevents us from doing that in the plays of Shakespeare which we are able to do to a certain degree in the plays of Chekhov. That is the only solution. We have created a technique and methods for the artistic interpretation of Chekhov, but we do not possess a technique for the saying of the artistic truth in the plays of Shakespeare.[2]

IMPORTANCE OF SHAKESPEARE

After four hundred years, Shakespeare's plays are produced more than those of any other playwright, living or dead. In nineteen years, he wrote thirty-seven plays; an amazing number of these "smash hits." If he could collect his royalties for current productions, they would exceed those of all present-day playwrights combined. As a "master-sharer" (one of the business partners) in the Globe playhouse, he had the responsibility of keeping the company busy acting in plays which the public would pay to see. If a play was not "doing good business," another had to be ready.

[2]From *My Life in Art* by Constantin Stanislavski, p. 350. Copyright 1924 by Little, Brown and Co., and 1948 by Elizabeth Reynolds Hapgood. Reprinted by permission of Theatre Arts Books, New York.

Some Elizabethan scholars have tended to depreciate Shakespeare the
actor in favor of Shakespeare the poet. The impression has been given
that he was no more than a small part actor, never entrusted with a part
more important than the Ghost in *Hamlet*. Unfortunately, we have no pro-
grams and no critical reviews showing the parts he did actually play; but
there are many legal documents in existence, such as grants, licenses,
and royal commands for court performances, listing Shakespeare as one
of the three most important actors of his company. The name of a mere
"bit" player would hardly be listed immediately after the name of the
leading actor of the Globe, Richard Burbage. When Ben Jonson supervised
the printing of his play, *Every Man in His Humour*, he listed the actors who
first acted in this play in 1598. The name "Will. Shakespeare" heads
the list at left and "Ric Burbage [sic]" the list at right. In publishing
Sejanus, His Fall, Jonson listed actors Shakespeare and Richard Burbage as
equally important. Several years after Shakespeare's death the two oldest
"sharers" in the King's Company, who had been his colleagues for nearly
twenty years, in a dedication emphasizing that the plays are vehicles for
actors, placed Shakespeare's name first in a list of "the names of the
principall actors in all these playes."

However, the most convincing proof of Shakespeare's importance
as an actor is so obvious that it seems to have been overlooked. The company to which he was so devoted, the Lord Chamberlain's Men (after 1603,
the King's Men), had three levels of personnel. First there were the senior
actors, or "fellowes," who contributed capital and as "sharers" received
the profits or took the losses. They were responsible for the management,
and were the "housekeepers," as well as playing all leading parts. The
second group were the "hired actors." They received a salary and were
employed as needed with no responsibilities other than acting. From this
group the subordinate parts were cast. The third group were younger
members who played pages, children, and women. When we remember
that there were no managers, producers, directors, playwrights, or lawyers
sharing in the company, Shakespeare's position as a principal "sharer"
is also strong testimony to his importance as an actor.

When Shakespeare was thirty-two, all of his worldly possessions
were appraised at the equivalent of twenty-five dollars; when he retired
at fifty, he was considered the Elizabethan equivalent of a millionaire.
Was this sizable fortune accumulated by acting? Other Elizabethan
actors had done so.[3] Certainly Shakespeare's fortune was not made from
royalties from the immortal plays—there were no royalties. The plays
were sold outright to the company. Shakespeare started his fortune as an
actor, a "sharer," and by subsequent wise investments accumulated

---

[3]At his death Burbage left £300 yearly in lands, and a rival actor, Ned Alleyn, bought
a manor and endowed Dulwich College, which exists to this day.

enough to retire to his beloved Stratford-upon-Avon and live his final years as the most distinguished and perhaps wealthiest gentleman in that community.

SHAKESPEARE THE DRAMATIST

Shakespeare began writing for the stage around the middle of 1591, a few years before the Globe was built. Eventually he wrote historical plays, tragedies, satires, light comedies, and farces, in fact, almost everything except a play dealing realistically with the London scene of his day.

No other playwright has ever surpassed him in characterization. He always managed to create his portraits, not in descriptive words, but in the dialogue itself, and the characters express themselves with accuracy, brilliance, and deep emotion. They are written with careful regard for the play and the relationships to other characters in that play, so that the ultimate in character exploration is achieved by means of conflict. As an example, Hamlet, the thinker who cannot act, is juxtaposed with Laertes, who acts without thinking.

Because Shakespeare began as an actor and continued to act, he knew much better how to create drama than the better educated "university wits" of his time. His was the output of a professional man of the theatre. This is evident in each of his plays. No other writer in Elizabethan England wrote this way.

THE ELIZABETHAN AUDIENCE

Since he was a commercial playwright, we should know the audience he tried to please. This will also give us some insight into the times and be useful when acting his plays.

During Shakespeare's early years in London, Elizabeth sat on the throne. It was an extremely creative period in the theatre. Most people could not read or write, but they had been awakened to developments in the sciences, the arts, and indeed to all things cultural. Entranced by the Italian Renaissance, which reached England by way of France, and by the invention of the printing press, they were eager for any sort of knowledge and devoured it eagerly. A "plaiehowse" was a club, a social hall, and a school, in addition to being a place where one could be thrilled and entertained.

A typical audience might include nobles from Elizabeth's court, lowly apprentices, poets from the universities, and sailors just returned from the New World. It was an uninhibited, mixed crowd, drinking, eating, and smoking, very much like the people we see today at baseball games. If they showed a preference for history and kings, Shakespeare provided such plays. Whatever they wanted, comedy, tragedy, or romance, Shakespeare obliged. He never tried to give them what he thought they

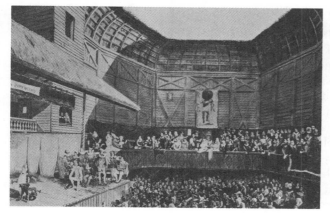

ARTISTS' RECONSTRUCTIONS OF THE GLOBE PLAYHOUSE, BOTH INTE-
RIOR AND EXTERIOR (INTERIOR, FROM THE BETTMANN ARCHIVE; EXTER-
IOR, COURTESY THE BRITISH TOURIST AUTHORITY.)

should have or what others thought would be good for them; and he never
preached or tried to reform.

He knew that the average man liked a plot, some sort of story he
could follow. Shakespeare thought so little of plots himself that he wasted
no time inventing them. Instead he borrowed from history, from folklore,
even from other plays. But he borrowed only when he could add other
levels of interest. The Elizabethan man cared nothing about the seed when
he was admiring a flower. For the spectators in the pit (the "groundlings"),
Shakespeare had puns, coarse jokes, and plays on words, but even those
were used with a professional's sure touch; he knew when and how much
to use them.

To his contemporaries, Shakespeare was no towering immortal.
No biography of him was published during his lifetime nor for nearly one
hundred years after his death. He was just one of a company of players
and these players worked with almost superhuman strength, playing in
broad daylight to a noisy, unruly mob standing in the open air. Shakespeare's players had to compete with animal noises coming from the bull-
baiting pits nearby. It required stamina and a big voice to capture and hold
the attention of that audience. How many of our Academy winners of
today could do that?

SHAKESPEARE

THE MUSIC OF SHAKESPEARE

While American children are taught to *read* Shakespeare, English children are taught to *speak* it. They learn to form the sounds of speech, to enunciate clearly and crisply, and to give melody to human communication by the use of Shakespeare's lines. Shakespeare's characterizations are so imbedded in the iambic and alliterative constructions that they seem to elude the American actor; while the Englishman, with Shakespeare such a part of him, accepts the unreality of blank verse, realizing that such eloquence is impossible for real people in real life situations.

While some playwrights preferred to use rhymes for their plays, Shakespeare chose blank verse. But by deviating from the metrical pattern, he could obtain startling dramatic effects in sound, imagery, and emotion. His blank verse is, by definition, unrhymed iambic pentameter — "blank" because the listener can anticipate rhymes when the rhythmical pattern is at all regular. It also allows the actor to emphasize sounds he feels are essential for the revelation of character and emotion.

An iambus is a foot of two syllables, a short, or unaccented one followed by a long, or accented one. The human heart, for example, beats iambs; two recurring strokes — brief, long; brief, long — and this is the fundamental rhythm of English poetry. Our breathing is also done in the iambic foot, out-breathing, in-breathing, which stress on the in-breathing because it takes longer and is more consciously done, whereas out-breathing is more automatic.

EXERCISE 92

Imagine that you are listening to a metronome ticking at about the usual heartbeat rate. Indicate these beats by saying aloud, "tick," each time the pendulum swings right or left:

$$\text{Tick} - \text{tick} - \text{tick} - \text{tick} - \text{tick}$$
$$1 \quad\quad 2 \quad\quad 3 \quad\quad 4 \quad\quad 5$$

The sound and movement of the metronome is measured, the rhythm never changing. Let us call each basic unit, each "tick," a *foot*. Now instead of the one word "tick," say two words, "to be," in the same time it took to say "tick." Ready?

$$\text{To be} - \text{to be} - \text{to be} - \text{to be} - \text{to be}$$
$$1 \quad\quad 2 \quad\quad 3 \quad\quad 4 \quad\quad 5$$

Now let us stress or accent the second syllable, the "be."

$$\text{To bē} - \text{tó bē} - \text{tó bē} - \text{tó bē} - \text{tó bē}$$
$$1 \quad\quad 2 \quad\quad 3 \quad\quad 4 \quad\quad 5$$

Note: The mark (ʹ) indicates the short syllable or nonstress. The mark (–) is the long or accented syllable. When we speak words arranged so as to make sense using *meter* and *stress* (or accent), we *scan*. The stresses should reveal not only meaning and feeling of the words, but also in many cases, proper pronunciation. Now instead of saying, "to be," say

To be—or not—to be—that is—the quest(ion)
   1   2   3   4   5

(The final syllable of the word "question" is unaccented, or slurred.)

Now let us review the terms. We have been working with a line consisting of five feet (or iambs), with accent on the second syllable of each foot. Each line should take from two to four seconds to speak. Such formalized lines taken together are called iambic pentameter. Shakespeare accustomed his listeners to this overall design, but he delighted in deviating from it for dramatic effects. So in the reading of blank verse the actor must be allowed liberty, but not license. The rhythm must remain underneath, no matter how the actor interprets.

Let us try another line.

The qual i ty of mer cy is not strain(ed)
   1   2   3   4   5

Obviously, this language is very different from everyday speech in which we use trite images, repetitions, hesitations, and substitutions. Its only purpose is to convey meaning, and we don't care how that is accomplished. If we need to use grunts, gestures, or facial contortions, we do so. But the poet designs and selects; each word must be the right word to express his meaning or emotion. He plans formally, using meter and managing an intensity of expression.

As an example, let's have a look at these lines from *Richard III,* Act III, Scene v.

> *Come, bustle, bustle. Caparison my horse.*
> *Call up Lord Stanley, bid him bring his power.*
> *I will lead forth my soldiers to the plain,*
> *And thus my battle shall be ordered.*
> *My forward shall be drawn out in length,*
> *Consisting equally of horse and foot.*

Note how the *sounds* themselves express the excitement of the coming battle. Observe how the repetition of the word "horse" in the first and last lines prepares for the famous line to come, "A horse! A horse! My kingdom for a horse!" Note how the repetitions are designed and appropriate to the dramatic situation. Shakespeare was very clever about using surprises, using pauses in the lines, and in reversing the iambic beat now and then, especially in the third foot, to give an effect. This freedom to alter the pattern keeps his lines from ever sounding monotonous, and discourages an actor who would intone the lines like an old-time preacher. Declamatory delivery, while austere and dignified, is not dramatic, and must be avoided in speaking Shakespeare's lines.

SHAKESPEARE

Another device that Shakespeare frequently uses to make his dialogue active is the *half-line*. A speaker will end his speech in the middle of a metrical line and another will take it up and complete it. As an example:

MACDUFF: How does my wife?
ROSS: Why, well.
MACDUFF: And all my children?
ROSS: Well too.

(*Macbeth*, Act IV, Scene iii)

Read Shakespeare aloud, and many reasons for the effects he uses will become obvious to you.

EXERCISE 93

Here is one Peter Brook uses. All class members memorize a soliloquy or stanza of their choice, and divide the piece into three sections. Then, using no special expressive delivery, three individuals read the material aloud as a unit —

1. First, reading as quickly as possible;
2. Then, retarding the pace slowly;
3. And finally, accenting certain previously selected words using beats or silences for other words.

NOTE: When speaking verse, there are mechanical beats which must be found. The difference between "intoning" and speaking verse properly is in *adjusting the emphasis in accordance with the meaning.* The three main faults of the amateur in speaking verse are: (1) melodious or "stagey" reading; (2) academic singsong; (3) colloquialism which chops up the verse and is unforgivable. SEARCH OUT THE MEANING AND THE VERSE WILL APPEAR AUTOMATICALLY. REALITY CAN BE ACHIEVED ONLY THROUGH THE VERSE.

ATMOSPHERE

Previously we discussed the importance of atmosphere, which might be defined as the emotional tone created for a play or a scene. When the curtain rises on a proscenium stage, the setting has the first word. It sets the mood by its design and coloring. Next the audience notes the characters, how they are grouped; if they are in symmetry and simply arranged, the audience will feel an atmosphere of serenity. But Shakespeare could not depend upon settings or lighting. On his "unworthy scaffold," as he called his stage, actors could be revealed (or "discovered") only at the rear of the stage. His characters had to walk on. In order to create atmosphere he had to use sheer dramaturgy. Leaf through the first few pages of any of his plays and note how he establishes the mood for the play to follow. The lone soldier standing guard in *Hamlet*, his startled "Who's there?" The unexplained fears of "Nay, answer me. Stand and unfold yourself."

And the bitter cold evidenced in the lines, the ghostly visitation, all these cause the audience to *feel* that sense of fate which permeates the play to come. Evil fills the air above the Witches in the opening scene of *Macbeth*. After this scene, the audience is receptive to the deep penetrations into human existence which follow.

Illusion, then, is one of the keys to Shakespeare's plays. He was not beyond criticism as a man, nor was he always a great artist, but one fact is irrefutable—at his best he is the most exciting creator of imaginative theatre who ever lived.

COLOR

Shakespeare always selected words or phrases which, when spoken by the actor, would produce calculated emotional reactions in an audience. Read aloud the following lines:

> *The devil damn thee black, thou cream-faced loon;*
> *Where gott'st thou that goose look?*

Note how the lines actually duplicate the sound of rage. In these two lines, we can feel the anger of the trapped Macbeth as his trembling "whey-faced" servant comes to report that the English soldiers are advancing. The sensual experience of that dramatic moment has been captured for us in the lines. Read some of Shakespeare's love scenes and note the soft syllables and liquid sounds. Find some scenes of mystery; and note the breathy sounds. Shakespeare was very skillful at finding the sounds that expressed the mood or emotion he wished to convey.

RHYTHM AND RESTS

The word "rhythm" is often used by actors when they are really referring to meter. As we have learned, meter deals with feet and stresses (as in iambic pentameter) but each line may have its own rhythm. Meter is set, *mechanical*; rhythm is *organic*, depending not upon regularity but upon irregularity. It gives color, variety, and meaning to a line, and when so used it is called *cadence*.

No other playwright is so aware of actors as is Shakespeare. He has generously provided proper breathing pauses and moments of rest for the actor before he has to continue. Such rests usually last the time it takes to speak ten syllables—plenty of time to catch a breath. Such pauses are called *caesuras*.

PROSE AND POETRY

Shakespeare wrote not only poetry but also prose. As actors, let us examine the difference between poetry and prose. Will you agree that there is a kind of music in the lines of certain more modern playwrights? Think of the New York-Jewish cadences in the works of Odets and

Miller.[4] What is the difference between this "music" and Shakespeare's? You simply cannot fool around with Shakespeare's words. His lines will not tolerate any insertions of "ah's" or incoherent mumblings to make the thoughts seem a sudden invention by the actor. Shakespeare, as an actor, was well aware of actors' devices; he wrote these devices into his lines. They must be spoken as written. You have no leeway in this, you are either right or wrong.

Let us examine the difference between poetry and prose by use of an example. Following is a passage from one of Shakespeare's sources: Plutarch's *Life of Marcus Antonius*, as translated by North. In its rich Elizabethan prose it describes Cleopatra's retinue:

> —her barge in the river Cyndus, the poop whereof was of gold, the sails of purple, and the oars of silver, which kept stroke in rowing after the sound of the music of flutes, hautboys, cithers, viols, and such other instruments as they played upon in the barge. And now for the person of herself: she was laid under a pavillion of cloth-of-gold of tissue, apparelled and attired like the goddess Venus commonly drawn in picture . . .

Now here is what flowed from Shakespeare's pen:

> The barge she sat in, like a burnish'd throne,
> Burnt on the water: the poop was beaten gold;
> Purple the sails, and so perfumed that
> The winds were love-sick with them: the oars were silver,
> Which to the tune of flutes kept stroke, and made
>
> The water, which they beat, to follow faster,
> As amorous of their strokes. For her own person,
> It beggar'd all description: she did lie
> In her pavillion—cloth-of-gold of tissue—
> O'er-picturing that Venus, where we see
> The fancy outwork nature . . .

From *Antony and Cleopatra*, Act II, Scene ii

The source is prose, Shakespeare's lines are poetry.

SHAKESPEARE AND YOU

All actors are judged by their ability to play Shakespeare. It would be difficult to imagine this world without Shakespeare. As long as humans live, so also will "the Bard." If you continue acting, one day you will surely act in one of his plays. Shakespeare is the best possible training for actors just beginning. He is also the standard used to judge a master actor.

Hamlet, Lear, Lady Macbeth, Juliet—these remain the summit of achievement in the art of acting. Actors also find that a sense of pride comes when they are associated with Shakespeare. It is not just that he also was an actor. To be a Shakespearean actor gives self-esteem to a

---

[4]Clifford Odets, a playwright of the 1930's, author of *Golden Boy, Awake and Sing, The Big Knife, The Country Girl,* and others; Arthur Miller, author of *Death of a Salesman, The Crucible, After the Fall,* and others.—Ed.

performer. It is as though some of the great man's genius rubs off. He lifted the "profession" to dignity by his art. When we forget or neglect him, as we did for a while after his death, actors and actresses sink back into the gutter where he found them — as mountebanks, fools, and bawds. With him, we gain the respect of our fellow-man and ourselves — after all, are we not business associates of the great Shakespeare? As his Players, we are extraordinary beings. Just to know his lines is an education, and we don scholarly robes with the confidence that we can — at least — speak some of the wisest words ever written.

ACTING STYLE FOR SHAKESPEARE

Shakespeare guides actors in the what, why, and how of his plays without stooping to condescending directions; these are in his lines. If an actor understands the lines, he understands the character, the time, the place, and the dramatic situation of the play.

"Fine speaking is of the most crucial importance to the interpretation of Shakespeare in the theatre. A sense of style is almost equally essential." These are the words of Margaret Webster[5] written for her excellent book, *Shakespeare without Tears*. Miss Webster continues:

> It has become the fashion to belittle the need for this much misinterpreted quality. "Style" is supposed to consist of a lot of outworn flourishes and mannerisms indicative of some dead and forgotten period when men wore long, curled hair and women encased their digestive apparatus in steel and whalebone . . . this is a misconception. Style, to begin with, is much more than a harmonious visual effect. . . . You wear your sword so because otherwise the scabbard will get between your legs and you will fall over it; you take the weight of your cloak over the elbow and fling it thus around your shoulder because in this way it will keep you warm without tying you up in a cocoon; you swing your farthingale like this because otherwise, when you sit down, it will bounce up in front of you. You hold your shoulders back because they must carry the weight of armor; you keep your knees straight because, in tights, you would look knock-kneed if you didn't.
>
> But rightly used they will acquire rhythm and dignity. More than that, they will begin to belong to you and you will gain a feeling of reality. They will cease to be "costume" and become clothes.

Miss Webster then draws a parallel between the character and the actor:

> You cannot put his hands in your pockets, because he had none. Neither can you put your thoughts in his head. You cannot claim that this or that feels false or unreal to you because you yourself would feel it or say it differently. There is a style in thought as there is in speech or dress, a kind of inner breeding, and acting is the perfect fusion of these things.

[5]I traced the Websters back to 1797 and Benjamin Nottingham Webster, but when I found he was of theatrical parentage, I stopped, willing to accept the fact that there is a long association between the London Theatre and the Websters.

Shakespeare's characters, the major ones, are likely to be bigger in mental stature than the average modern actor, more perceptive in imagination, bolder and freer in action, sharper in wit, swifter in words. We have plenty of acting talent in America today. But they completely lack practice in their craft. They do not know, because they have never seen "stature" and "manner" in acting Shakespeare. They think of it as something exaggerated and "ham" and believe that the slip-shod speech and lazy, commonplace attitudes of the present day are, in some obscure way, more "real."[6]

PREPARATION FOR HAMLET

This play, written around 1600, is the product of a rich period in Shakespeare's writing. During a five-year span he wrote not only *Hamlet*, but *Julius Caesar*, *Othello*, *Macbeth*, and *King Lear*. *Hamlet* remains the supreme acting drama in the English language. Its history as a play is also the history of great actors and acting.

Before attempting to stage this short scene you should read the play in its entirety. If you have studied well, you should have no difficulty answering the following questions:

EXERCISE 94

1. There are various opinions as to Hamlet's sanity — to which do you subscribe?
   a. That he is neither mad nor pretends to be so.
   b. That he pretends madness.
   c. That he is mad at times and at other times pretends madness.
   d. That he is really mad.
   Can you give lines from the play to prove your conviction?
2. The enactment of the play before the court has been called the turning point of this play. Do you agree? If not, what in your opinion is the turning point?
3. What secret does Shakespeare share with just his audience and Hamlet?
4. What basic similarity has this play to Greek classical tragedy?
5. Give examples of Hamlet's procrastination and irresolution. Give examples of Hamlet's immediate action.
6. It has been said that in this play Shakespeare wrote of two worlds, the real and imaginary. Give examples of each. What are the consequences of the death of Polonius?
7. What do you understand to be Hamlet's inner conflict?
8. Do you think Hamlet ever loved Ophelia?
9. Do you see any evidence in the play that Hamlet is a Christian?
10. Why is Claudius able to enlist Laertes in his schemes?

[6]Margaret Webster, *Shakespeare without Tears* (Greenwich, Conn.: Fawcett, 1942; paperback edition, 1955), pp. 296-297.

STYLES IN ACTING

11. Of what purpose is the Osric scene?

12. Hamlet finds the King alone in Act III, Scene iii, and has an opportunity to kill him but he does not. In the closet scene, however, he does kill Polonius. What are Hamlet's motivations for each seemingly opposing action?

13. Does Hamlet ever become a man of supreme action?

Character Portrayals

Hamlet. The drive of the famous "closet scene" which follows is supplied by the play's protagonist, Hamlet. One element separates this play from a vulgar tale of brutal violence: Hamlet is a thinking man. He has a sense of justice, which is often mistaken for a lack of will, although Shakespeare gives much proof to the contrary. Hamlet does not lack will when he leaves the security of his friends to follow the Ghost. He is prompt in action when he kills Rosencrantz and Guildenstern, who planned to kill him. If Hamlet were merely a creature of blind and furious emotion, the play would be deprived of its deep insight into humanity. Hamlet *is* emotional, but he has within him a kind of self-restraint counseling him, as does every other man of intellect. Hamlet's instincts and impulses are tempered with justice, prudence, and conscience. This human vs. animal struggle is within all of us, and it is this that gives the play its universal appeal. All of us hope we are human, but we are constantly being reminded that we are also animals. This is Hamlet's terrible dilemma—as it is ours.

RICHARD BURTON AS HAMLET. (COURTESY OF ZODIAC.)

Polonius. A careless reader might envision Polonius as a doddering old clown, but as we consider the fatherly devotion he gives Laertes and Ophelia, we begin to appreciate admirable qualities in the old man. Once a shrewd and effective politician, he still maintains some knowledge and wisdom, but both are now in the process of atrophying. Samuel Johnson described Polonius in a single notable phrase, "dotage encroaching upon wisdom." Polonius has loved the past and chooses to live in it still. He does, however, realize that he is not as effective as he was and therefore overcompensates with frantic effort. This results in making him appear a meddlesome, pedantic bore.

Queen. Shakespeare's genius for deep character exploration is obvious in his portrayal of Gertrude. As he unfolds the many layers of her character, we realize her many dimensions. We cannot overlook her sins as a wife, but this does not lessen our respect for her as a woman of stature and gentleness. But it is in her tenderness toward Ophelia and her son that we find identification. We see her more as the victim of a horrible chain of consequences than as a direct accomplice in murder. Indeed, we cannot find that she had any suspicion of the fratricide. As Shakespeare reveals his Queen, we find her to be warm and vibrant, a gentlewoman buffeted by chance.

The Ghost. Shakespeare uses this symbolic figure to personify the emotional undercurrent of the play. He limits the Ghost to a slow, stately walk, to measured speech in unearthly tones, and gives him a majestic solemnity. In this way, Shakespeare deprives him of the physical in order that we become more conscious of the emotional. It is through the Ghost that we feel the preternatural, the grandeur of the events, the accentuation of conscience as an active force. And it is no mistake that Shakespeare starts his play with the appearance of the Ghost, for by this means he creates early and efficiently the atmosphere for the entire play which follows. One of the most moving touches in the portrayal is the Ghost's tender solicitude toward his former Queen. We can well believe that Shakespeare loved this character. It is one of the few parts we know certainly that he acted himself.

Background

You will remember from your study of the entire play that at this point Hamlet has been interviewed by the King's sycophants, Rosencrantz and Guildenstern. Realizing that anything he says will be immediately relayed to his enemy, Hamlet does not disguise his aversion to their efforts or to them personally. Subsequently, on his way to obey a summons from his mother, he encounters the King at prayers. He is tempted to kill him, but then decides to await a more auspicious time. Hamlet feels that he could "drink hot blood" and could do "such bitter business as the day would quake to look upon." With his mother he decides "to be cruel—to speak daggers to her but use none." In this wild and defiant mood, he enters the next scene. (Hamlet should convey all this background as he comes before her.)

REHEARSAL

HAMLET

ACT III, SCENE iv

CAST: HAMLET
        POLONIUS
        QUEEN GERTRUDE

SCENE: *The Queen's room. A chair ULC.*

1. The Queen is discovered at LC. She paces in anxiety, rubbing her hands together. As she returns to LC, Polonius tiptoes into view UR. He speaks in a husky whisper without moving from a point where he can still view the hall.

2. *Screened . . . and him:* she has protected Hamlet from the King's anger.

3. *I'll silence me:* I'll hide behind the curtain and be quiet.

3a. *Be round with him:* speak sharply to Hamlet.

                                        (*Polonius enters to Queen*[1])
POLONIUS: He will come straight. Look you lay home to
   him.
   Tell him his pranks have been too broad to bear with,
   And that your Grace hath screened and stood between
   Much heat and him.[2] I'll silence me[3] even here.
   Pray you be round with him.[3a]
HAMLET: (*Within*) Mother, mother, mother!

                                                  STYLES IN ACTING

QUEEN: I'll warrant you; fear me not. Withdraw; I hear
  him coming.

                  (*Polonius hides U, behind a curtain.*
                  Hamlet enters.[4])

HAMLET: Now, mother, what's the matter?[5]
QUEEN: Hamlet, thou hast thy father much offended.
HAMLET: Mother, you have my father much offended.
QUEEN: Come, come, you answer with an idle tongue.
HAMLET: Go, go, you question with a wicked tongue.
QUEEN: Why, how now, Hamlet?[6]
HAMLET: What's the matter now?
QUEEN: Have you forgot me?[7]
HAMLET: No, by the rood,[8] not so!
  You are the Queen, your husband's[9] brother's wife,
  And—would it were not so—you are my mother.
QUEEN: Nay,[10] then I'll set those to you that can speak.
HAMELT: Come, come, and sit you down, you shall not
    budge!
  You go not till I set you up a glass
  Where you may see the inmost part of you.
QUEEN: What wilt thou do? Thou wilt not murder[11] me?
  Help, help, ho!
POLONIUS: (*Behind*) What, ho! help, help, help!
HAMLET: [12](*Draws*) How now? a rat? Dead for a ducat,
    dead!

          (*Stabs through the arras and kills Polonius*)

POLONIUS: (*Behind*) O, I am slain!
QUEEN: O me,[13] what hast thou done?
HAMLET: Nay, I know not.[14] Is it the King?
QUEEN: O, what a rash and bloody deed is this!
HAMLET: A bloody deed—[15] almost as bad, good mother,
  As kill a king, and marry with his brother.
QUEEN: As[16] kill a king?
HAMLET: Ay, lady, 'twas my word.
      (*Pulls aside curtain and sees Polonius*)
  Thou wretched,[17] rash, intruding fool, farewell!
  I took thee for thy better. Take thy fortune.
  Thou find'st to be too busy is some danger.—
  [18]Leave wringing of your hands. Peace! sit you down
  And let me wring your heart; for so I shall
  If it be made of penetrable stuff;
  If damned custom have not brazed[19] it so

SHAKESPEARE   197

4. Hamlet is excited, expecting anything. As he realizes his mother is alone, he stands defiantly with feet planted solidly far apart, grasping his sword in readiness. He speaks in a rude, challenging voice.

5. These four lines are snapped back and forth in anger.

6. The Queen is hurt and surprised at her son's manner, but it does not change.

7. Have you forgotten that I am the Queen and your mother?

8. *By the rood:* by the cross of Christianity.

9. He speaks these words with venom, but softens some on the last line.

10. She is indignant and starts UR, but he grabs her hand and forces her back into the chair at UL. He is at her R and still holds her.

11. Charlotte Cushman reportedly spoke this line "Thou wilt not kill me?" not only destroying the meter but substituting a weak word for a strong.

12. Hamlet springs impetuously to action, drawing his sword, and in a flash plunges it into the curtain. French actor-producer Jean Louis Barrault has the theory that Hamlet could not draw a sword to kill a man. Therefore, his emotional reaction is to cry out, "a rat?"

13. The Queen stands in terror.

14. Almost hopefully.

15. Accusing her.

16. She separates the words, trying to understand.

17. Hamlet was fond of the old man who was to be his father-in-law, therefore he is sad. The Queen rubs her hands together, trying to dry the cold sweat.

EDMUND KEAN AS HAMLET. (COURTESY OF THE HENRY E. HUNTINGTON LIBRARY AND ART GALLERY.)

18. He speaks and handles her harshly.

19. *Brazed:* like bronze metal.

20. Crying out in bewilderment.

21. Kneels at her R.

22. *Blister:* prostitutes were branded on the forehead.

23. *Contraction:* marriage contract.

24. Actors have interpreted these lines in different ways. Edwin Booth wore a medallion of his father around his neck. He handled the cameo of his uncle worn around the neck of the Queen. Salvini and Irving represented the pictures in the "mind's eye." Notice that the lines describe a full figure, not a portrait bust or cameo. Other actors have used the medallion of the father and the uncle on a string around Hamlet's neck. In this way Hamlet compares the two.
(See "Shakespearian Studies" by Matthews and Thorndike. Col. U.Pr., 1916.)

25. *Hyperion:* the standard of male beauty like our Apollo.

26. *Station:* posture.

That it is proof and bulwark against sense.

QUEEN: What have I done[20] that thou dar'st wag thy tongue
In noise so rude against me?

HAMLET: [21]Such an act
That blurs the grace and blush of modesty;
Calls virtue hypocrite; takes off the rose
From the fair forehead of an innocent love,
And sets a blister[22] there; makes marriage vows
As false as dicers' oaths. O, such a deed
As from the body of contraction[23] plucks
The very soul, and sweet religion makes
A rhapsody of words! [Heaven's face doth glow;
Yea, this solidity and compound mass,
With tristful visage, as against the doom,
Is thought-sick at the act.]

QUEEN: Ay me, what act,
That roars so loud and thunders in the index?

HAMLET: Look here upon this picture, and on this,
The counterfeit presentment of two brothers.[24]
See what a grace was seated on this brow;
Hyperion's[25] curls; the front of Jove himself;
An eye like Mars, to threaten and command;
A station[26] like the herald Mercury,
New lighted on a heaven-kissing hill:

STYLES IN ACTING

A combination and a form indeed[27]
Where every god did seem to set his seal
To give the world assurance of a man.
This was your husband. Look you now what follows.
Here is your husband, like a mildew'd ear[28]
Blasting his wholesome brother. Have you eyes?
Could you on this fair mountain leave to feed,
And batten[29] on this moor?[30] Ha! have you eyes?
You cannot call it love; for at your age
The heyday[31] in the blood is tame, it's humble,
And waits upon the judgment; and what judgment
Would step from this to this? [Sense sure you have,
Else could you not have motion; but sure that sense
Is apoplexed: for madness would not err;
Nor sense to ecstasy was ne'er so thralled
But it reserved some quantity of choice
To serve in such a difference. What devil was't
That thus hath cozened you at hoodman-blind?
Eyes without feeling, feeling without sight,
Ears without hands or eyes, smelling sans all,
Or but a sickly part of one true sense
Could not so mope.]
O shame! where is thy blush? Rebellious hell,[32]
If thou canst mutiny[33] in a matron's bones,
To flaming youth let virtue be as wax
And melt in her own fire.[34] [Proclaim no shame
When the compulsive ardor gives the charge,
Since frost itself as actively doth burn,
And reason panders will.]
QUEEN: O Hamlet, speak no more!
Thou turn'st mine eyes into my very soul,
And there I see such black and grained[35] spots
As will not leave their tinct.[36]
HAMLET: [37]Nay, but to live
In the rank sweat of an enseamed bed
Stewed in corruption, honeying and making love
Over the nasty sty!
QUEEN: O speak to me no more!
These words like daggers enter in mine ears.
No more, sweet Hamlet!
HAMLET: A murderer and a villain![38]
A slave,[39] that is not twentieth part the tithe[40]
Of your precedent lord; a vice of kings;[41]

27. Reverently.

28. *Mildew'd ear:* an ear of wheat that is rotten and worthless.

29. *Batten:* fatten.

30. *Moor:* barren upland.

31. *Heyday:* youthful high spirit.

32. *Rebellious hell:* Hamlet refers to the evil impulses rebelling against the good in humans.

33. *Mutiny:* Verb does not occur again in Shakespeare. Meaning here is "rebels."

34. Queen claps her hands over her ears. She is very moved by the attack.

35. *Grained:* ingrained.

36. *As will not leave their tinct:* lose color.

37. Undaunted and in order to better press his attack, Hamlet now stands. *Enseamed:* greasy.

38. A piteous cry from Gertrude.

39. His attack is savage now. He "speaks daggers" to her.

40. *Tithe:* one tenth, not one two-hundredth.

41. *Vice of kings:* roguish clown in old plays, usually wore torn clothes, hence "shreds and patches" also.

42. *Cutpurse:* a pick pocket.

43. Hamlet has now reached the top of his savagery and hate, but all breath leaves him as he sees the Ghost, drops to his knees and crosses himself, eyes transfixed upon the apparition. Note: In an effort to intensify this moment of shock for the audience, Garrick is supposed to have used a mechanical device which shattered the Queen's chair.

44. Sadly the Queen must admit to herself that her son is mad as all have been saying.

45. Possessed by the apparition, he whispers to it. *Lapsed in time and passion:* wasted time and impulse.

46. Gently, lovingly, the Ghost refers to the pathetic, terror struck creature he once called his Queen.

47. *Conceit:* A word often used by Shakespeare meaning imagination.

48. Now softened by the Ghost's reference to the Queen, Hamlet reaches back for her without taking his eyes from the Ghost.

49. She takes the outstretched hand and kneels beside him as she strokes the hand, then caresses it.

50. Crying now, she touches him with a motherly tenderness. Remember, she does not see anything but her son, and she is sure he is now experiencing the manic state.

51. *Incorporal:* bodiless.

52. *Conjoined:* united.

53. Hamlet fears that the "piteous action" of the Ghost will soften his resolve to deal in revenge and blood. Queen rises slowly, hand on his shoulder.

A cutpurse[42] of the empire and the rule,
That from a shelf the precious diadem stole
And put it in his pocket!
QUEEN: No more!
                    (*Ghost appears*)
HAMLET: A king of shreds and patches!—[43]
Save me and hover o'er me with your wings,
You heavenly guards! What would your gracious figure?
QUEEN: Alas,[44] he's mad!
HAMLET: [45]Do you not come your tardy son to chide,
That, lapsed in time and passion, lets go by
The important acting of your dread command?
O, say!
GHOST: Do not forget. This visitation
Is but to whet thy almost blunted purpose.
But look,[46] amazement on thy mother sits.
O, step between her and her fighting soul!
Conceit[47] in weakest bodies strongest works.
Speak to her, Hamlet.

HAMLET: [48]How is it with you, lady?
QUEEN: [49]Alas, how is't with you,
That you do bend your eye on vacancy,[50]
And with the incorporal air[51] do hold discourse?
[Forth at your eyes your spirits wildly peep;
And, as sleeping soldiers in the alarm,
Your bedded hairs, like life in excrements,
Start up and stand on end.] O gentle son,
Upon the heat and flame of thy distemper
Sprinkle cool patience! Whereon do you look?
HAMLET: On him! on him!—Look you how pale he glares!
His form and cause conjoined,[52] preaching to stones,[53]
Would make them capable.—Do not look upon me,
Lest with this piteous action you convert
My stern effects. Then what I have to do
Will want true color—tears perchance for blood.
QUEEN: To whom do you speak this?
HAMLET: Do you see nothing[54]
there?
QUEEN: Nothing at all;[55] yet all that is I see.
HAMLET: Nor did you nothing[56] hear?
QUEEN: No,[57] nothing but ourselves.
                    (*Ghost moves*)

STYLES IN ACTING

HAMLET: [58]Why, look you there! Look how it steals away!
My father, in his habit as he lived!
Look where he goes even now out at the portal![59]

(*Exit Ghost*)

QUEEN: [60]This is the very coinage of your brain.
This bodiless creation ecstasy[61]
Is very cunning in.

HAMLET: [62]Ecstasy?
My pulse, as yours, doth temperately keep time
And makes as healthful music. It is not madness
That I have utt'red. Bring me to the test,
And I the matter will reword;[63] which madness
Would gambol from. Mother, for love of grace,[64]
Lay not that flattering unction[65] to your soul,
That not your trespass but my madness speaks.
[It will but skin and film the ulcerous place,
Whilst rank corruption, mining all within,
Infects unseen.] Confess yourself to heaven;
Repent what's past; avoid what is to come;
[And do not spread compost on the weeds
To make them ranker. Forgive me this my virtue;
For in the fatness of these pursy times
Virtue itself of vice must pardon beg—
Yea, curb and woo for leave to do him good.]

54. For the first time since the appearance of the Ghost, Hamlet ventures a quick glance back at his mother, then back to the vision as he asks, "Do you see nothing there?" pointing to the Ghost.

55. Attempting to comfort her poor, mad son.

56. Accents "hear."

57. Warm tones, soothing, comforting, like a lullaby.

58. Springs to his feet with a cry as he points to the moving "illusion" and turns to follow it, holding the pose.

59. Hamlet stands frozen looking after the Ghost. Gertrude steps back in amazement. After the outbreak of emotion, this silence should be thrilling.

60. Sadly, as she tries to reassure him.

61. *Ecstasy:* madness.

62. Impetuously he turns, repeating the word in contempt, as if it were preposterous. He then steps to her to make points to prove his sanity.

63. *Reword:* repeat.

64. Again returning to the deep shame he feels because of her conduct.

65. *Unction:* salve, soothing.

RICHARD BURTON AS HAMLET SPEAKING THE LINES. . . "BUT GO NOT TO MY UNCLE'S BED."
(COURTESY FRIEDMAN-ABELES, INC., PHOTOGRAPHERS, NEW YORK CITY.)

SHAKESPEARE

66. The anguish she is feeling inside makes her shriek.

67. He makes a move to kiss her, but is repelled as he remembers her intimacy with his uncle, the "bloated king." At this point, Sarah Bernhardt (who played Hamlet with great success) is said to have taken a strand of the Queen's long hair, and bent to kiss it.

68. Unlike his previous accusing tone, Hamlet now speaks to her with pity and compassion for her frailty.

69. Suggested cuts.

70. Hamlet means that when he finds his mother praying for absolution, he will kneel and ask her forgiveness.

71. He feels that he is Heaven's instrument of punishment for all their sins.

72. He starts to lift the body, then turns up to speak to her.

73. Remains behind: a prophecy that more is to come and that it will be worse. ·

QUEEN: O Hamlet,[66] thou hast cleft my heart in twain.
HAMLET: O, throw away[67] the worser part of it,
And live the purer with the other half.
[68]Good night—but go not to my uncle's bed.
Assume a virtue, if you have it not.
[69][That monster, custom, who all sense doth eat
Of habits evil, is angel yet in this
That to the use of actions fair and good
He likewise gives a frock or livery,
That aptly is put on.] Refrain tonight,
And that shall lend a kind of easiness
To the next abstinence; the next more easy;
For use almost can change the stamp of nature,
And master thus the devil, or throw him out
With wondrous potency. Once more, good night;
And when you are desirous to be blest,[70]
I'll blessing beg of you.—For this same lord,
I do repent; but heaven hath pleased it so,
To punish me with this, and this with me,
That I[71] must be their scourge and minister.
I will bestow him, and will answer well
The death I gave him.[72] So again, good night.
I must be cruel, only to be kind;
Thus bad begins, and worse remains behind.[73]

THE LIVING PLAYS OF SHAKESPEARE

(Dates are educated guesses.)

COMEDIES
The Comedy of Errors (1585)
Two Gentlemen of Verona (1592)
Love's Labor Lost (1593)

HISTORICAL
Henry VI Parts I, II, III (1593)
Richard II (1592)
Richard III (1593-94)
King John (1594-96)
Henry IV Parts I, II (1597-98)
Henry V (1598-99)
Antony and Cleopatra (1606-7)

EARLY TRAGEDIES
Romeo and Juliet (1596-97)
Julius Caesar (1598-99)

ROMANCES
A Midsummer Night's Dream (1595)
The Merchant of Venice (1595)

FARCES
The Taming of the Shrew (1594)
The Merry Wives of Windsor (1599)

COMEDY-ROMANCES
Much Ado about Nothing (1599-1600)
As You Like It (1599)
Twelfth Night (1599-1600)

PROBLEM PLAYS
All's Well that Ends Well (1600-1603)
Measure for Measure (1603-4)

TRAGICOMEDIES
The Tempest (1611-12)

LATE TRAGEDIES
Hamlet (1600)
Othello (1604-5)
King Lear (1605-6)
Macbeth (1605-6)

STYLES IN ACTING

Every page in this book might be filled listing the thousands of books on the various aspects of Shakespeare. We have space for only a few. For aspects other than acting, consult Bibliographies, concordances, and indexes.

Jaggard, William. *Shakespeare Bibliography.* New York: Ungar, 1959. Lists 36,000 entries. Both this and the following are expensive; consult your librarian.

Smith, Gordon Ross. *A Classified Shakespeare Bibliography.* University Park: Pennsylvania State University Press, 1963. Lists some 20,000 books on Shakespeare.

Elizabethan Background

There are many books that will give you the look and feel of Elizabethan times. The first listing below is good, the second is more complete.

Chute, Marchette. *Shakespeare of London.* New York: Dutton, 1949. Now in paperback.

Raleigh, Walter et al., eds. *Shakespeare's England: An Account of the Life and Manner of His Age.* London and Oxford: Clarendon Press, 1916-1962. *Vol. I,* religion, court, army, navy, travel, education, handwork, law, commerce, medicine, sciences, etc.; *Vol. II,* fine arts, heraldry, costume, home, London, books, actors and acting, playhouses, masques, court entertainment, sports, Shakespeare's English, ballads, games, and index of passages cited from Shakespeare.

Dictionaries

Abbott, E. A. *A Shakespearian Grammar.* London: Macmillan, 1874. Old, but none quite like it; studies differences between Elizabethan and modern English.

Bartlett, John. *A Complete Concordance of Shakespeare.* London: St. Martin's, 1960. Index of words, phrases, and passages.

Irvine, Theodora. *A Pronouncing Dictionary of Shakespearian Proper Names.* New York: Barnes and Noble, 1947.

Variorums

Granville-Barker, Harley. *Prefaces to Shakespeare.* Princeton, N.J.: Princeton University Press, 1947. The famous variorums in 4 vols.

Hazlitt, William. *The Characters of Shakespeare's Plays.* New York: Dutton, 1929. Essays of 1817.

General Information

Bentley, Gerald E. *Shakespeare, A Biographical Handbook.* New Haven, Conn.: Yale University Press, 1961. A good buy in paperback.

Chambers, E. K. *The Elizabethan Stage.* Oxford and London: Clarendon Press, 1923. Expensive, in 4 volumes, but it is *the* generally accepted authority. Consult library.

Chambers, E. K. *William Shakespeare.* London: Oxford University Press, 1930. The most authoritative book of facts on the life of Shakespeare.

Craig, Hardin. *An Interpretation of Shakespeare.* New York: Dryden Press, 1937.

Eliot, T. S. *Selected Essays.* London: Faber, 1934.

Harbage, Alfred. *Shakespeare's Audience.* New York: Columbia University Press, 1961. Paperback.

————. *As They Liked It.* New York: Macmillan, 1947. A study of Shakespeare and his audience.

Thorndike, Ashley. *Shakespeare's Theatre.* New York: Macmillan, 1960. Paperback.

Van Doren, Mark. *Shakespeare.* New York: Holt, Rinehart, and Winston, 1939.

Acting Style for Shakespeare

Barrault, Jean-Louis. *The Theatre of Jean-Louis Barrault.* New York: Hill & Wang, 1959.

Clurman, Harold. "Actors in Style and Style in Actors." *New York Times Magazine,* Dec. 7, 1952. An excellent article that should be reprinted.

Munk, Erica, ed. *Stanislavski and America.* New York: Hill & Wang, 1966. See "Stanislavski and Shakespeare" by Michel St. Denis.

Saint-Denis, Michel. *Theatre—A Rediscovery of Style.* New York: Theatre Arts Books, 1960.

Webster, Margaret. *Shakespeare without Tears.* Greenwich, Conn.: Fawcett, 1955. Paperback.

Elizabethan Actors and Acting

Baldwin, T. W. *The Organization and Personnel of the Shakespearean Company.* New York: Russell, 1961.

Hodges, Walter C. *Shakespeare and the Players.* New York: Coward McCann, 1963. Aimed at teenagers; has charming drawings.

Leech, Clifford. *When Writing Becomes Absurd.* London: Ridgeway, 1963. Includes acting of Shakespeare and Marlowe.

Sprague, Arthur Colby. *Shakespeare and the Actors.* Cambridge, Massachusetts: Harvard University Press, 1945.

RECORDINGS

See list in *Theatre Books in Print.* New York: Drama Book Shop, 1963.

FILMSTRIPS

Full list of Shakespearian films and filmstrips in *Educational Theatre Journal* XIV:3 (Oct. 1963), Northwestern University, Evanston, Ill.

16
Molière
(1622-1673)

To the French, Molière is the best loved of all French authors and is to them what Shakespeare is to us. A strange comparison? Until the nineteenth century the French considered Shakespeare a barbarian who mixed cruelty, comedy, and tragedy into a single play. But Molière had that gay, debonair French touch. Unlike Shakespeare, he was neither a philosopher nor a dramatic poet. But there are interesting similarities between the two playwrights. Molière was born six years after Shakespeare's death and both died in their fifties. Both began and continued as actors, attached to a permanent company of players. Both borrowed plots from other sources to revolutionize the drama of their day. Shakespeare wrote thirty-seven plays to Molière's thirty—and both are immortals.

We need not theorize or assume anything in adopting an acting style for Molière's plays. We could have no better instructor than Molière himself, for he was also a great teacher of acting. One of his contemporaries, de Vise, felt that Molière could teach a stick to act, and this was probably because Molière himself had to work hard to acquire his skill as an actor. He understood how "all the pieces fit."

MOLIÈRE AS ACTOR

In France during the seventeenth century, an obscure young actor and more obscure author was playing in barns, racquet courts, inn yards— anywhere his little company could find an audience. Molière learned the job of utility actor, then supporting player, and finally how to "carry a show" himself, taking the leading parts. To this task, he added the job of management and authorship. He had been well educated at a Jesuit school. A good part of his fourteen-year apprenticeship was spent under the tutelage of several great Commedia dell'Arte players. This was to make an indelible impression on all his future work as both actor and playwright.

Nature did not fashion Molière in the accepted mold of the actor. He was not tall, did not have a fine voice, and never had that romantic look.[1] All his life he tried to cure himself of a habit of speaking too quickly. When he tried to overcome it, he was seized by uncontrollable hiccoughs. He also had difficulty in making his eyebrows behave; they were thick, black, and kept darting all over his forehead. But he studied the actors of the Commedia dell'Arte troupe which he had joined. In this troupe were at least three performers who were the best of their time.

APPRENTICESHIP

He watched these men acting behind their masks, saw them getting effects by the use of gesture, posture, and bodily movement alone. He

---

[1]Talma had the romantic look, as did Molière's pupil, Baron. Edwin and J. W. Booth, Mounet Sully—all had it—and in the last generation, John Barrymore.

practiced tirelessly. There was time; he was still in his twenties. He tried to act by use of his square, unresponsive body, to make none but the most necessary and telling gestures. He decided to turn to his advantage the shortcomings nature had given him: the wide-set eyes, short legs, and peasant face were all displayed proudly to his audiences. Always alert to the audience, he studied what they wanted. He began to try different ideas; some were not good and came to nothing; but others got response.

When he found himself slipping into his old habit of rushing his speeches, he stopped dead, then changed the tone and tempo of his voice. This, he found, created a comic effect in itself and so he developed it. One of the actors he worked with wrote later that Molière "seemed to have several voices." The wandering eyebrows, which had given him such concern at first, were saved until they could be used to make a point. "No one has ever been so good at rearranging his face," a Parisian was to write when Molière had become recognized as a virtuoso of mime.

There is an object lesson for all young actors in the career of Molière. It is plain that he took inventory of himself, developed what was effective with audiences, then studied to turn his liabilities into assets. Obviously, to work and study as he did meant that Molière wanted to entertain. The critic Sarcey[2] quotes Molière as saying, "There is no other rule of the theatre than that of pleasing the public."

MOLIÈRE'S STYLE

When Molière finally did reach Paris, he seemed to hold up a mirror in which Frenchmen could see themselves. He showed how extravagant and effete they had become. He laughed at their clothes, their manners and society; ridiculed their politics, speech, religion—and even French "amour." But it was a gentlemanly and cultured laughter, more like an indulgent smile. It never stung, but always was "of gay disposition."

Molière calls the individuals he writes "types"; Chekhov wrote "characters." The miser, the invalid, the hypocrite, the noble, the pedant, the bore, the coquette, are types. Molière depended upon the actor to supply the personality and flesh and blood, to make the types into people. Tartuffe is sketched in broad outlines. I have seen the part developed as an unctuous little con man, and I have seen him portrayed as a threatening cadaver with hypnotic eyes; each interpretation was interesting.

Authorities seem amazed by evidence that Molière, as an actor, relied so much upon his body in the interpretations of his characters— his use of posture or silhouette to express a point—when he could have written lines to accomplish it. Having been trained in the great Commedia school, *Molière knew that such a moment would be more memorable if shown by action rather than words.* And so we must remember that in a play

---

[2]Francisque Sarcey (1827-1899), the most important French dramatic critic of his time. Author of *Comediens et Comediennes*.

by the great Frenchman *there are places where the author expects the actor to enrich the moment by the acting skill Molière presupposed as part of every actor.*

It was Molière—not Aristophanes or Shakespeare—who first used such comedy techniques as the cumulative repetition (of lines or business), the malaprop, the echo-reply, the comic business of peeling off layer after layer of clothing, the double take, the fast transition of speech or action, pomposity's pratfall, and others you will find if you study his plays. When these are used most effectively, they should seem natural, but *we can be sure that Molière devised them, worked on them over and over, until they had the neatness and precision needed in playing farce-comedy.*

Precision of movement, speech, gesture—so necessary to the successful playing of comedy—can also be seen in the sweep of a brush across a canvas, the painter leaving his deft, sure mark for all time. It can be seen during those measured seconds as the Olympic champion prepares for his try. Great dancers have precision, and indeed it can be seen in many fields of endeavor. Wherever you find the expert you find precision.

THE STAMP OF THE COMMEDIA

The lessons Molière learned from the Commedia are sealed forever in his plays: the precision of the Italian performers, the clear-cut *substance* of a comedy moment. In *Precious Damsels,* some characters wear Commedia masks while others are in clown white. In *The Would-Be Gentleman,* two girls chase two boys around the room; then, at a given signal, the chase reverses, and the boys chase the girls—pure Commedia dell'Arte!

In most of Molière's great comedies, the skillful execution of comedy routines seems more important than plot. Like Shakespeare, he seems to have considered plot as merely the cord tying the parts together to make a package. And what attractive packages they made! Molière's special gift was in adding refinement to the wonderfully theatrical Commedia technique; he did so with his wit, his light satiric touch, his love and understanding of all the human frailties. The Commedia actors took a comedy situation and crystallized it into one hilarious moment by means of a "piece of business" (or as they called it, a *lazzi*). Molière gave these isolated bits an order, a design—and a quality of literature. Each comedy unit he made dependent upon previous units, these in turn contributing to those to come. Then all were set into a pattern, which contributed to the overall comedic effect.

ZEST IN PLAYING FARCE-COMEDY

When an audience becomes convinced that the actors themselves are enjoying playing in a comedy, then the audience's enjoyment is increased. This contagious quality, which is so essential in comedy or farce, has been described in various ways. Some refer to it as enthusiasm. It is a

THE WORLD-RENOWNED ACTOR COQUELIN BECAME SO FOR HIS INTERPRETATION OF CYRANO DE BERGERAC, BUT FOR MANY YEARS HE MADE A SPECIALTY OF THE COMIC HEROES OF MOLIERE. HERE HE IS PICTURED AS SGANARELLE IN *LES PRECIEUSES RIDICULES.* (COURTESY OF THE HENRY E. HUNTINGTON LIBRARY AND ART GALLERY.)

STYLES IN ACTING

kind of "bubbling over," the display of a zest for life. This joyous spirit comes down to us directly from the Commedia dell'Arte; it is the essence of their style. A Molière play produced without this quality becomes only an interesting museum piece. It was a foregone conclusion with Molière that actors and directors would supply life for his plays so that they could sparkle with brilliance and wit. However, in planning your approach to his plays, always remember that he refined and gave sophistication to the uninhibited farcical antics of the Commedia clowns.

MOLIÈRE AS DIRECTOR

In directing the members of his company, Molière was often accused of being a martinet. On the subject of the proper accentuation of a line, he would tolerate no difference of opinion. The verse he wrote was the Alexandrine[3] iambic hexameter—a line of twelve syllables, sometimes divided in the middle and with a rhyme at the end. The Alexandrine is the traditional line of French poetry (so named because early romances about Alexander the Great were written in this form). His justly celebrated prose was also devised so that the proper meaning of the line is best expressed when correctly accented. *It is no wonder he was so determined that actors spoke his lines correctly!*

PREPARATION FOR GEORGE DANDIN

Read the full play carefully before attempting this excerpt. It has some of the typical characteristics of farce; the jealous husband who locks out his erring wife from their home, the importance of some physical prop (in this case, a door), and lines spoken directly to the audience.

A rich peasant, George Dandin, has married the daughter of a noble but impoverished family. Dandin learns that a young neighbor has been making love to his wife and complains to his wife's parents. They confront the young lovers and both deny the accusations. The parents then reprove Dandin for his jealousy. Each time he sees the lovers together he complains to the noble family but the daughter is clever enough to convince her parents that Dandin is wrong. The situation is made difficult because the parents believe that the exchange of Dandin's money for their noble strain was to his advantage. The third time his wife is with her lover, Dandin locks her out of the house and sends for her parents so they will be convinced of her ways by seeing for themselves. As with all farce, the following scene must be played with spirit and speed. Note the short, repetitive words for comic effect, the "clipped" speeches, and the "build" to a comic line.

[3]There is an adaptation of *Tartuffe* by Richard Wilbur which attempts the almost hopeless task of putting the Alexandrine into similar English verse, still retaining the sense of the play.

PHOTO IS OF LUDWIG BREKMANN AS GEORGE DANDIN, IN AN AMUSING PRODUCTION OF THIS PLAY, AT THE MUNICIPAL THEATRE, HAMBURG, GERMANY. DIRECTOR ERNEST MATRAY CONCEIVED AND STAGED THE FARCE IN THE STYLE OF THE COMMEDIA DELL' ARTE. (PHOTO BY ROSEMARIE CLAUSEN, HAMBURG. FROM *THE THEATRE IN GERMANY*. REPRINTED BY PERMISSION OF F. BRUCKMANN VERLAG.)

1. As he appears at the window.
2. Again she tries the door.
3. Mocking her.
4. An accusation.
5. Hard, firm delivery.

6. Genuinely shocked.

7. He claps his hands together.

8. Smugly.

9. Sincerely.

GEORGE DANDIN

An Adaptation

ACT III, SCENE viii

CAST: GEORGE DANDIN *"Dandin" means "Ninny" (Rabelais was the first to use the word as a proper name.)*
ANGÉLIQUE *Young wife of Dandin and daughter of M. de Sotenville.*

SCENE: *In front of George Dandin's house.*

TIME: *After midnight. Moonlight bathes the stage in half-light.*

AT RISE: *Angélique enters and moves surreptitiously to the house, looking from side to side. She wears a cape. George Dandin is in a long, red, striped night-gown and stocking cap. Angélique carefully tries to open the door and is surprised that it is bolted from inside.*

GEORGE DANDIN: [1]*Ah ha!* So, I've caught you playing your pranks because you think me sound asleep. Well, wife, I'm glad to see you out there at this time of night.

ANGÉLIQUE: There's no harm in my going out for a breath of cool night air.[2]

GEORGE DANDIN: [3]"There's no harm in my going out for a breath of cool night air." No, No! After midnight is the proper time to be getting fresh air. You must think I'm stupid.[4] I know all about your rendezvous with that—that—Don Juan! I saw you! I overheard everything you said.[5] This time your mother and father can't help being convinced of how right I was. This time they'll believe that I've been right about you all along. I've sent for them. They'll be here any minute now!

ANGÉLIQUE: [6]Oh heavens—

GEORGE DANDIN: Now comes my triumph![7] Yes, Yes! Until now you have denied everything, fooled your parents and whitewashed your evil ways. No matter what I said I saw you were very clever in the way you twisted my facts, and put me in the wrong. Yes, yes! But now the truth is going to be plain—

ANGÉLIQUE: Oh, please—open the door.

GEORGE DANDIN: Ah, no! We'll just quietly wait for your parents. What a delight it's going to be when they see you outside at this time of night.[8] While you're waiting why don't you think up some clever way of getting out of this!

ANGÉLIQUE: [9]What could I possibly say—

210   STYLES IN ACTING

GEORGE DANDIN: *Nothing!* There's nothing you can invent this time that I can't prove false.

ANGÉLIQUE: [10]All right, it's true! I've been wrong and you have good reason to complain. But I ask you, please, don't let my parents see me standing out here. Please? Open the door?

GEORGE DANDIN: No.

ANGÉLIQUE: [11]Oh, my poo-o-r little husband—

GEORGE DANDIN: Yes, I'm a "poor little husband" because you are caught.[12] Never once have you ever said such a sweet thing to me before.

ANGÉLIQUE: I promise you, I'll never, never—

GEORGE DANDIN: Your promises have nothing to do with it. I want your parents to know once and for all what your behavior has been—

ANGÉLIQUE: You have every right to be angry.[13] But you ought to forgive a young girl of my age who has seen nothing of the world she has just entered; who has used her liberty without thinking of the harm she might be doing to others. I won't try to excuse myself for the wrong I've done you. I only ask you to forget and spare me the angry reproaches of my father and mother. I give you my word that in the future you will find me the best of wives and I'll show you such love and devotion that you'll never have cause to mistrust me again.

GEORGE DANDIN: No.

ANGÉLIQUE: Be generous.[14]

GEORGE DANDIN: No.

ANGÉLIQUE: Please, please—

GEORGE DANDIN: *Never!* I am determined that your mother and father see you for what you are, a shameful—

ANGÉLIQUE: All right then![15]
I warn you that a woman in my situation might do anything! I'll do something to make you sorry—

GEORGE DANDIN: [16]What will you do?

ANGÉLIQUE: See this knife?[17] *I'll kill myself!*

GEORGE DANDIN: Good, good— Ha, ha—

ANGÉLIQUE: Not so good—*for you!* Everyone knows how we quarrel, how you shout at me. When I'm found dead, no one will have any doubt but that you killed me and my parents will see that you're punished for for murder. You'll pay the full penalty—the guillotine!

GEORGE DANDIN: Nonsense, you can't fool me with that—

ANGÉLIQUE: George Dandin, if you don't open this door at once you'll find out what a woman will do when she's desperate!

GEORGE DANDIN: [18]You're only trying to frighten me.

ANGÉLIQUE: Oh, I am, am I?[19]
Since I must, this will end it and show if I am deceiving you or not—[20]

10. This is a true confession.

11. A pause. She decides upon a change of attitude, almost "baby talk".

12. His conciliatory tone gives her hope, but this is changed with his next speech. From a blubbering self-pity he changes quickly to an austere firmness on "Your promises—"

13. Acting out the innocent.

14. The next four lines should be spoken quickly and with "build" to "All right then—"

15. A pause. Then she quietly threatens him.

16. Laughing derisively.

17. She holds it high like a heroine in a melodrama.

18. His laughter is a little hollow now.

19. Weakening.

20. Now that she realizes she can convince him, she drives on.

MOLIÈRE

Margin notes:

21. Again the melodramatic heroine. Pretends to stab herself.

22. He cannot believe it has happened—but it may be true.

23. Thinking only of the effect of her death upon him. Spoken directly to the audience.

24. Door must open *on* stage.

25. Holding candle high and peering into the darkness R and L.

26. She speaks sweetly at first then as she pretends to recognize her husband, she barks with a shrewish rage.

27. Completely subdued. Pleads.

28. As he glances offstage, he becomes frantic and returns to beating on the door. Angélique shouts over the noise.

---

[21]I hope they punish you in full, George Dandin for my death—and—and—your cruelty—ah-h-h—

GEORGE DANDIN: [22]Oh, my goodness!

[23]Can she be so malicious as to kill herself just to get me hanged? I'll take a light and see.

(*He unbolts door, then opens it furtively.*[24] *He holds the candle high and looks about, but she is not in sight. As he opens the door, ANGÉLIQUE slips quietly behind it.*)

GEORGE DANDIN: [25]No one here! Or here! I thought so. She's run off. She's run off. She couldn't get anywhere with me with her tears and threats. Well, that makes it worse for her. Her parents will now be *convinced* that she runs around at night!

(*He tries the door.*)

It's locked! It must have blown shut.

(*He beats on the door.*)

Hey! Someone—! The door is locked.

I'll wake the servants. You in there—hear me?

The door—open it—open up—

(*He beats furiously*)

Open this door at once—!

(*ANGÉLIQUE appears at the window, all smiles and pretending she was asleep.*)

ANGÉLIQUE: [26]W-w-hat? Who is it? Who's there? Oh, it's you. You dirty old drunkard, out all night in your nightshirt! Is this a proper hour to be coming home? Why, it's nearly daylight. Is this the sort of life a decent man leads?

GEORGE DANDIN: Let me in.[27]

Open up—pl-e-e-a-se?[28]

Your father and mother are coming!

Quick! Let me in!

ANGÉLIQUE: Ah, no. I'm tired of you staying out all night. I want them to see just what I've been putting up with—!

PREPARATION FOR TARTUFFE

Read the entire play carefully so that you are able to answer the following questions.

EXERCISE 95

1. Can you give some reasons why *Tartuffe* is the most often produced of all Moliere plays?
2. In as few words as possible, describe what this play is about.
3. Does the theme of this 300-year-old play apply to today's society?
4. Name the conflicting forces in *Tartuffe*.

5. In *Tartuffe*, which group is Molière writing about: (1) St. Eustache peasants, (2) the French bourgeoisie, (3) nobility of Louis XIV's Court.

6. Molière is considered to be the champion of which form of play-writing: (1) comedy-drama, (2) farce, (3) tragedy, (4) romance?

7. Describe Mariane, Dorine, Orgon, and Tartuffe from lines in the play.

8. In your opinion, which author has most influenced present-day comedy: (1) Aristophanes, (2) Molière, (3) Shakespeare?

9. It has been said that Molière's solutions to his plays do not follow the lines of comedy. Can you think of other endings more in keeping with the comic spirit of this play?

10. Molière hides Orgon under a table while a scene is played that otherwise might not be comic. Is this device one that might be used by the Commedia actors?

11. Molière acted the part of Orgon. Do you see any evidence in the play that the author knew acting and actors? Give examples.

12. What was Molière's outstanding contribution to the theatre?
    a. His use of stock Commedia characters
    b. The construction of his plays
    c. Adaptation of old Roman plots
    d. Memorable characterizations
    e. The follies and absurdities of mankind

13. A rule of old-time comedians was to "rehearse slow — play fast." Why would this advice be valuable in preparing our scene from *Tartuffe?*

14. This scene has been called "brilliant." Check the qualities you believe essential to a successful performance of this scene:
    a. The pert, irrepressible characterization of Dorine
    b. The pompous but futile exasperation of Orgon when bantered by Dorine
    c. The running comic threat of a slap

TARTUFFE

ACT II, SCENE ii

*Adaptation by Robert Bruce Wallace**

CAST: ORGON

DORINE

MARIANE

1. As Dorine staggers head first past Orgon and Mariane, Orgon shouts victoriously, "Ah hah!"

2. Orgon runs to Dorine.

3. He takes her ear with one hand and with his upstage hand indicates that she has a bump on her head. Positions: Dorine DR, Orgon to her L, and Mariane on stool.

4. In an attempt to cover her embarrassment, she assumes an officious manner.

5. Orgon nods, forcing a smile, pretending to agree.

6. The strained smile fades quickly. He has had enough and is suddenly serious.

7. Spoken as a dictate.

8. She has been shaking her head "no," shrugging and chuckling steadily.

9. Addressing Mariane.

10. Positions at this point: Mariane on stool C, Dorine to her R, Orgon to Dorine's R. Dorine shakes her head, "no." Her body should express self-confidence and sureness—feet apart, planted firmly, arms folded.

11. Soothing him as she places her hand on his chest, gently patting him. On his speech, he pushes her hand away.

SETTING: *Required: a stool at C, a double door L. At rise, Mariane is DC seated on a high stool. Her father, Orgon, has evidently been lecturing her—he is stopped in the middle of a gesture to listen. He puts his finger to his lips, motioning her to be silent, points to the door DL, tiptoes to it, and opens it suddenly. Dorine, who has been leaning against the door, stumbles into the room, trying to regain her balance as she screams loudly and fearfully.*

ORGON: Ah hah![1] What were you doing?[2] Spying? [3]That must be a big bump of curiosity you have there—to make you eavesdrop on us this way.

DORINE: I heard some gossip[4]—guesswork—a lie, I'm sure, about a marriage. But I didn't believe it.

ORGON: Indeed?[5] Is it so far beyond belief?

DORINE: I wouldn't believe a word of it, sir, even if it came from you!

ORGON: I know how to make you believe it, though—[6]

DORINE: Of course! You'll concoct some clever explanation—

ORGON: I'm telling you[7] exactly what will happen—very soon.

DORINE: Nonsense![8]

ORGON: What I am speaking of, my girl, is not a subject to be joked about.

DORINE: (*Crossing to Mariane*) Go on—! [9]Don't believe a word your father says— He's only joking.

ORGON: I'm telling you—[10]

DORINE: No, no, no,—no—no—. No matter what you say, no one would believe you.

ORGON: I'm—getting—angry—!

DORINE: All right.[11] You are believed—! So much the worse for you. I don't understand—you *look* like an intelligent man with that beard and all. Then how can you be idiot enough to want—

ORGON: *What?* Now you listen to me, young woman,—you have taken certain liberties in this house which I don't like—

*This adaptation by Robert Bruce Wallace makes no attempt to reproduce the Alexandrine in English, but rather to keep Molière's characterizations and comedy rhythms intact.

STYLES IN ACTING

DORINE: Please, Monsieur,[12] let's talk without getting angry. You must be fooling with this scheme of yours. Your daughter[13] has nothing in common with that bigot! He has other things to think about, besides— how would you benefit by the match? You have all the money you need so why take on a beggar as a son-in-law?

ORGON: You are far too free with that tongue of yours—[14]far too free —for anyone in your position! If he has nothing—all the more reason to respect him. His poverty is noble. It raises him beyond desire for worldly goods. He lost his fortune because he cared nothing for earthly things while he was striving for the blessings of eternity. My help may be the means of getting him out of trouble and restoring his property to him. His vast estates were well known in his own district where he is still regarded as a gentleman.

MARIANE PLEADS WITH ORGON IN THIS PRODUCTION OF MOLIÈRE'S *TARTUFFE* AT THE REPERTORY THEATRE OF LINCOLN CENTER (NEW YORK). (PHOTO BY BARRY HYAMS.)

DORINE: [15]So he says. But, sir, such pride is not compatible with piety. If he embraces the simplicity of a holy life, he shouldn't boast of his fine and noble birth. Why such pride? But this discussion is offending you.[16] Let's talk about him as a person and forget his noble state. Can you have the heart to give a girl like this to a man like him? Shouldn't you, in all decency, forsee the outcome of such a marriage? It's hard enough to be a faithful wife, but he who gives his daughter to a man she hates must someday answer to heaven for her missteps. Think, sir, of the chances you take![17]

ORGON: You presume to tell me how to live— You—you a servant girl?

DORINE: You could do worse than follow my advice.

ORGON: Daughter, we'll waste no more time on this nonsense. I know what's best for you. I'm your father! [18]Oh, I know I once promised

12. Again patting his chest. Same business for Orgon on her line, "this scheme of yours."

13. Dorine turns to Mariane and puts a protecting arm on her.

14. On her last line, Dorine begins the patting business, but Orgon sees it coming and brushes her away with his line ending "in your position." Dorine steps menacingly to him, eyes narrowing, chin jutting out. Orgon grabs her and thrusts her easily to his right.
Positions: Dorine R, Mariane at C, Orgon between them.

15. On "So he says," she again strides threateningly to him. Orgon starts for her, and she ducks in front of both to L of Mariane.

16. Positions at this point: Mariane at C, Orgon at her R, Dorine ranging freely up and down LC, during this speech. One minute she is bold and shouting at him, the next darting about, avoiding his mounting anger.

17. As they snarl at each other, Mariane becomes a shield to protect Dorine and an obstacle preventing Orgon from getting to Dorine. Marine's head goes from right to left—as if at a tennis match. Note: This must be carefully drilled—a certain word, a certain movement.

18. The quarrel is getting more heated and louder.

19. On "anything else," Orgon takes a pinch of snuff. He has become so angry and nervous he hopes this will conceal his frustration, but we can see his hands tremble. He then paints a beautiful romantic picture and uses honey tones.

20. This is too much for the practical little Dorine—she can stand no more and tries to jump in, but Orgon anticipates her and raises his fervor and his voice.

21. Dorine tries again, and again same business by Orgon.

22. Now meek and sweet, she steps in front of Mariane to face Orgon.

23. Almost automatically, he passes Dorine to his right, facing his daughter again. Orgon speaks quickly and quietly, but we see he is trying to control his feelings. Dorine is using her charm, but she is throwing darts at him. Neither are showing anger at this point, but it begins to build from here on.

24. Stamps his foot in frustration on "Will you shut up," then hunts for some horrible name to call her.

25. Still not angry, she shames him for his outburst as if he were a six-year-old.

26. Shrugging. Cheerfully resigned.

27. Passes his left hand back at her as if shooing a pesky fly. Note: It may help Orgon to get the feeling of this scene if he imagines he is intent on some work and a persistent fly is bothering him.

28. He wags his finger at her with a harsh, threatening tone. Then in sudden contrast, turns to Mariane again with his soft, warm tones.

you to Valère, but he's a gambler and I suspect him of being a free thinker. And I never see him in church.

DORINE: You expect him to be there at certain times when you are—to make sure you see him?

ORGON: Who asked your advice on this matter? Are you the family lawyer or a maid? Tartuffe is on the best of terms with heaven and that means more than anything else.[19] This marriage will fulfill all your hopes and dreams. It will be full of pleasure and joy. You will live tohether in faithful love like two young children, like two turtle doves. There will never be a harsh word between you—.[20] Don't interrupt! Hold your tongue![21] Don't stick your nose into what doesn't concern you!

DORINE: [22]I only speak for your own good, Monsieur—

ORGON: [23]Very nice of you. Now be quiet!

DORINE: If I didn't like you—

ORGON: Spare me that, please. I don't need your affection—

DORINE: All right then, I'll like you—in spite of yourself—

ORGON: Damn!

DORINE: Your good name means a great deal to me. I don't want people making fun of you.

ORGON: Silence—silence—silence!

DORINE: It would be a crime to permit such a marriage.

ORGON: [24]Will you shut up? You—you—*serpent with a poisonous tongue!*

DORINE: What?[25] You—a religious man, losing his temper?

ORGON: Yes, I must get better control of myself—but you infuriate me with your talk. Once more, will you be quiet?

DORINE: Very well.[26] But if I can't speak, I'll go on thinking all the more.

ORGON: Think all you like,[27] just don't let us hear what you're thinking. Or!
(*To his daughter*) Now, child.[28] I'm not a stupid man and I've looked carefully into every angle of—

DORINE: (*Aside*) It drives me wild when I can't talk!

ORGON: [29]I admit that Tartuffe isn't handsome, still his looks are—

DORINE: Like a bulldog's![30]

ORGON: Even if one cannot appreciate his other qualities—

DORINE: She's getting a bargain, all right. (*Orgon turns to Dorine, crossing his arms and staring at her*) If I were in her place, no man would marry me without risking the consequences. He'd soon learn that a woman always has a way to get even.

ORGON: So—(*To Dorine*) No matter what I say, it makes no difference?[31]

DORINE: [32]Who said anything to you?

ORGON: What were you doing then?

DORINE: Just talking to myself.

STYLES IN ACTING

ORGON: [33]That does it! (*To Mariane*) I'll just give her the back of my hand for such insolence—Daughter, you should approve of my plans and accept the husband I have chosen for you—(*Looks to Dorine*) Well—? Aren't you going to say something to yourself?

DORINE: I have nothing to tell myself.

ORGON: Just—one—more—word[34]

DORINE: I don't feel like it!

ORGON: Oh, come now—I'm waiting—

DORINE: I'm not such a fool! (*Now satisfied, he faces Mariane and speaks firmly*)

ORGON: Daughter! This is final.[35] You will obey my wishes and accept my choice.

DORINE: I wouldn't accept him if he were the last man on earth![36]

ORGON: Child, that maid of yours is a pestilent little hussy. She made me forget myself—[37] Just look—how I'm trembling![38] I can't continue the discussion—[39] I must calm down—Yes—some fresh air—a walk—a walk—some fresh air[40]

MARIANE: (*Titters*)[41]

THE LIVING PLAYS OF MOLIÈRE

The School for Husbands (1661)	*George Dandin* (1668)
The School for Wives (1662)	*The Would-Be-Gentleman* (1669)
Tartuffe (1664-69)	*The Learned Ladies* (1672)
The Misanthrope (1666)	*The Imaginary Invalid* (1672)

FURTHER READING: MOLIÈRE

Bishop, Morris, ed. *Eight Plays by Molière.* New York: Modern Library, 1957. For Molière's opinions on acting, read "The Versailles Impromptu," pp. 124-150.

Fellow, Otis, E. *French Opinion of Molière.* Providence, R.I.: Brown University Press, 1937.

Fernandez, Ramon. *Molière, The Man Seen Through the Plays.* New York: Hill & Wang, 1958. Paperback.

Gassner, John. *Masters of the Drama.* New York: Dover, 1954. pp. 286-314.

Moore, Will G. *Molière: A New Criticism.* New York: Doubleday, 1962. Plays examined in relation to theatre of that day; paperback.

Palmer, John. *Molière.* New York: Brewer and Warren, 1930. Biography; also insight into theatre and people of the time.

Verneil, Louis. *The Fabulous Life of Sarah Bernhardt.* New York: Harper, 1942. Description of Sarah Bernhardt as Dorine in *Tartuffe.*

RECORDINGS

Recordings for *Tartuffe* and other Moliere plays are listed in Schwann Record Catalogue, 137 Newbury Street, Boston, Mass. 02116.

29. Orgon darts a quick murderous glance to Dorine; she cringes, then shrugs it off with a mischievous smile. Orgon resumes his pompous lecture to Mariane.

30. Straight front.

31. From a high perch of outraged dignity.

32. Looks at him with wide-eyed innocence.

33. Now suddenly all his control vanishes—he storms at her. Orgon starts a gesture to slap her, but she sees it coming and slaps the hand back. The force of his turned body sends it on its way again. This time she bends slightly, the blow barely missing her. She smiles with satisfaction. This must be rehearsed in slow motion and allowed to increase in speed as it becomes automatic. In performance it must be fast to be funny.

34. Raises his right hand to threaten her and with his left coaxes her to speak.

35. This is an order!

36. He dashes to her with hand raised, all control gone now. She avoids him, they circle once around Mariane. Then Dorine runs off R, screaming with laughter.

37. He looks fearfully at his outstretched hands.

38. Looking at his shaking fingers—they even frighten him.

39. Orgon starts walking to L.

40. He is off by now.

41. Mariane, who has sat without uttering a sound during the entire scene, now begins to titter to herself; it grows louder and louder. If this is done imaginatively, it can be almost startling to an audience who has become accustomed to Mariane's silence.

17
The Restoration and the Eighteenth Century

The magnificent repertory of drama identified with the Elizabethan (or Renaissance) period declined into a period of decay and disintegration. The decline was slow, taking almost a quarter of a century, but the doom of the theatre was irrevocable. The Puritans had opposed the stage since Elizabeth's day. Year by year they gathered support. The civil war began in 1642, and soon all London theatres were officially closed. Authorities were instructed to treat stage players as rogues and pull down all stage galleries, seats, and boxes. Nevertheless, not all public interest in theatre disappeared. Actors scattered to the provinces or performed surreptitiously in London. There are numerous records of recurrent raids and the seizure of actor's property. Evidently these actors were a tenacious group; they survived floggings, jailings, and social ostracism.

In 1660, with the return of Charles II from exile in France, the Restoration period began. Soon two theatrical companies were active in London. Enchanted by what he had seen on French stages, the new king sponsored the theatre. He remembered the lovely female charms he had seen displayed by the French actresses—charms which no boy actor could provide. In addition, boy actors had grown mature, and a new generation had not been trained to take their places. Therefore, the first actresses began appearing on the London stage. Paradoxically, they were most popular as boys, in "breeches parts." They must have been light, airy, and saucy to attract the royal patrons as they did.

All entertainments were aimed at pleasing the aristocracy, unlike Shakespeare's theatre, which had been an institution for all classes of people. Few of the plays written during the Restoration are performed today. The small leisure-class audience found pleasure in the comedies of Etherege, Wycherley, Farquhar, Vanbrugh, Dryden, Otway, and later in the more brilliant work of Congreve. These plays have been called comedies of manners. In the writing of Dryden and Congreve, "manners" had a different connotation than we give it today. When Lady Froth in Congreve's *Double Dealer* is asked what "manner" is, she replies, "Some distinguishing quality . . . something . . . a little *jene-scay-quoysh*." These comedies show the influence of Molière, the Commedia, and especially Ben Jonson.[1] But instead of the earthy Jonsonian flavor, they had a more intellectual quality, a style and a grace totally lacking in Jonson's more brutal, "realistic" plays. Elements of the comedy of manners are, as Allardyce Nicoll phrases them, "At least one pair of witty lovers, the woman as emancipated as the man, their dialogue free and graceful, an air of refined cynicism over the whole production, the plot of less consequence than the wit."[2]

NOTICE DATED 1647 ORDERING ABOLISHMENT OF ALL STAGE PLAYS.

---

[1]During the years 1660-1700, Jonson was a more admired playwright than Shakespeare; at least it was said that his work needed no "improvements." In contrast, *Romeo* was given a happy ending, and the *Macbeth* witches were suspended on strings; even songs and dances were added to Shakespeare.

[2]*History of the English Drama*, 1660-1900 (London: Cambridge University Press, 1961). p. 197.

THE RESTORATION AND THE EIGHTEENTH CENTURY

DAVID GARRICK (RIGHT) GREETS HIS FRIEND WILLIAM HOGARTH (LEFT). HOGARTH WAS THE BRILLIANT CARICATURIST OF THE EIGHTEENTH CENTURY AND GARRICK THE GREATEST ACTOR OF HIS DAY. (FROM A CONTEMPORARY SILHOUETTE OWNED BY THE HENRY E. HUNTINGTON LIBRARY AND ART GALLERY AND REPRINTED WITH THEIR PERMISSION.)

Audiences enjoying such plays were mostly court followers and aristocrats. They sat (often on stage) in their elegant silks and brocades under the glow of a hundred candles and were more vociferous than the actors whom they applauded, cursed, interrupted, and judged. They argued, fought, drank stout, ate fruit bought from orange girls who wandered at their peril among the benches (there were no aisles). (See end papers at front and back of this text.) One of these orange girls later became a popular actress, "Mrs." Nell Gwyn.[3] It is obvious what sort of plays this rakish audience demanded. Some of the titles are revealing: *She Wou'd If She Cou'd, The Lady of Pleasure, Love in a Tub,* and *Virtue Betrayed.* Plays had low moral standards, as did most actors of the time. Although plays dealt with illicit love and intrigue, playwrights zealously avoided indelicacy and coarseness in dialogue, as if saying, "We do as we please, but hide it."

SOME CHARACTERISTICS OF RESTORATION COMEDY

Playwrights of this time catered to libertine audiences made up mostly of the upper classes. Manners of the time were conventionalized on the stage as a social game with self-conscious gestures in which each movement was observed. Characters were types, serving much the same purpose as the symbolic face-painting of the Chinese actors. Restoration types might be classified—the gallant reluctant to marry, the testy duchess, the plain citizen, the philandering wife, the gossip, the rich husband or uncle, the country maid, and the cuckold. Such characters were placed in painted settings and framed inside a proscenium arch. Plays were full of bustling actions and intrigue, and the dialogue was spiced with a lively wit.

FIRST ENGLISH BOOKS ON ACTING

Early in 1700 there appeared the first two books in English on the subject of acting. Previously there had been instruction books printed on oratory and declamation. The earliest book was attributed to a celebrated actor of the Restoration, Thomas Betterton.[4] A writer, Charles Gildon (1665-1724), collected the actor's thoughts and published these posthumously. Some of these thoughts are worthy of note. Betterton held that the actor:

> must be Master of Nature in all its appearances which can only be drawn from Observation.

And that:

> in all good speech there is a sort of Music with Respect to its Measure, Time and Tune.

[3]Single girls did not use the "Miss" prefix as it had unsavory connotations. "Mrs." was pronounced "Mistress," and Nell Gwyn surely became mistress of Charles II, bearing him several children to whom he gave titles.

[4]Charles Gildon, *The Life of Mr. Thomas Betterton, The Late Eminent Tragedian. Wherein the Action and Utterances of the Stage, Bar and Pulpit Are Distinctly Consider'd* (London: printed for Robert Gosling, 1710). See also T. Cole and H. K. Chinoy, eds. *Actors on Acting,* (New York: Crown, 1949), pp. 97-102.

STYLES IN ACTING

Other advice is reminiscent of preceding books on oratory and later books on Victorian elocution:

> When you speak of yourself, the Right not the Left hand must be apply'd to the Bosom.

A few years later there appeared another acting book authored solely by an actor. Luigi Riccoboni, a former Commedia player, was an actor of experience and intelligence. For those who believe that creative acting is the exclusive knowledge of our century, read what Riccoboni wrote in 1728.

> The actor must show nature, yes; but in an Elevated and Noble form, the Trivial being reserved for the streets.

He gave a timely warning:

> There are Some who say that on a Stage we should Imitate Real Life — they are Fools who do not Seek, and who Deny, that there is any thing Further or Better.
>
> If a man enters Strongly into a proper Enthusiasm and Speaks in the Accents of the Soul, his Features will naturally form themselves into an agreement.
>
> The great business of the Stage is to Enchant the Spectators into a Persuasion that the Tragedy they are beholding is no Fiction, and that they who speak and act are not Players but real Heroes.[5]

The great Garrick, prodded no doubt by James Boswell, planned to write a book on acting. What a treasure that would have been to us! He mentions it in a letter to William Powell, dated 1766.[6] If he did write it, it was never found and never published. But "Little Davy"[7] was a very busy man in the theatre. Not only was he manager-actor-author-director, but also an inventor of stage devices, lighting, costume designer, a socialite, and rake. Garrick is thought to be the acting model described by his friend, Denis Diderot, in *The Paradox of Acting* (1830).[8] The "paradox," according to Diderot, was that an actor should move an audience, never himself — not much of an innovation. James Boswell accepts this in his *On the Profession of a Player* (1770), calling it "a kind of double feeling,"[9] a duality in which the actor's own character is placed into the recesses of his mind as he allows the character to take possession. Diderot's "paradox" was later to cause a tempest in a teapot between Coquelin and Irving.

(HENRY E. HUNTINGTON LIBRARY AND ART GALLERY.)

[5]*Riccoboni's Advice to Actors* translated and paraphrased from dell'Arte representative (1728) by Pierre Rames. Florence, Italy: *Mask Magazine*, Volume III, April, 1911, pp. 175-180. See also *Actors on Acting*, pp. 59-63.

[6]David M. Little, *et al.*, eds., *Letters of David Garrick* (Cambridge, Mass.: Belknap Press of Harvard University Press, 1963), p. 488. Letter to William Powell dated 1766. James Boswell also speaks of discussing such an acting book with Garrick.

[7]So called because David Garrick was 5 feet, 4 inches tall.

[8]Denis Diderot, *The Paradox of Acting*, and William Archer, *Masks and Faces* (both New York: Hill and Wang, 1958).

[9]James Boswell, *On the Profession of a Player*, reprinted from *The London Magazine* by Elkin, Mathews and Marrot, Ltd., London, 1929.

THE RESTORATION AND THE EIGHTEENTH CENTURY   221

Evidently it was not clear to these gentlemen that Diderot was speaking of control and not recommending a cold mechanical approach to a part. Certainly no actors of the status of Irving and Coquelin would deny that emotion must be used at some time in the acting process. In this book we have spent much time on that point.

ACTORS WITHOUT PLAYS

The teacher making lesson plans might wish that there were less congestion of great names in this section. History, not our wishes, must be arbiter in this. While few good plays were written, the eighteenth century gave a rich harvest of great actors and actresses. Names which would echo forever in green rooms and theatre foyers were first whispered in these candlelit playhouses: Mr. and Mrs. Betterton, Colley Cibber, Quin, Wilks and Mrs. Barry, Macklin, Garrick, the lovely actress with that fascinating name of Mrs. Bracegirdle, Mrs. Oldfield, Kitty Clive (who almost married Garrick), Nell Gwyn, Peg Woffington, Sarah Siddons, Edmund Kean; and on the continent, the romantic-looking Talma, Luigi and Francesco Riccoboni, the great German actor Schröder, the Russian Shtchepkin, whom Stanislavski called "our great law-giver," and the devastating

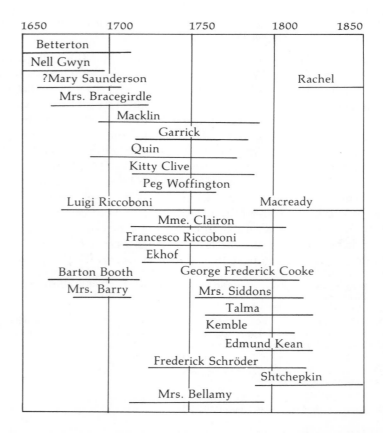

STYLES IN ACTING

Rachel in Paris. All of these thrilled and awed audiences of their day. Most of them came from humble beginnings, and through the magic of theatre were transformed into intimates of kings and queens. Great literary minds like Dr. Johnson, James Boswell, Pepys, Goldsmith, Hazlitt, and Leigh Hunt wrote of them. Reynolds, Gainsborough, and Hogarth immortalized them with brush and pen. They were the toasts of their age, the darlings of society. With little that was distinguished in plays, they popularized theatre and created some of the finest traditions in drama.

DAVID GARRICK

Among this constellation of stars, one — David Garrick — seems brighter than all the others. It has been claimed that Garrick completely reformed the art of acting by declining artificiality and cant.

This is somewhat refuted as our knowledge increases of Betterton and Charles Macklin. Macklin prepared his Shylock interpretation by methods which we have erroneously come to believe as exclusive to our time. He visited in the Jewish ghetto of London, absorbing attitudes, gestures, and inflections peculiar to Jews. His Shylock was the sensation of London; Alexander Pope declared, "This is the Jew that Shakespeare drew." In an effort to eliminate any bombast from his work, Macklin began rehearsals by merely reading, getting the sense of the lines and allowing them to be absorbed; then slowly and carefully, as convictions grew, so did his enlargement of the character.

Although Garrick's acting book has been denied us, we do know a good deal of his acting methods. He came from a nontheatrical family; in fact, he thought his brother might disown him for following the life of a player. The Garrick brothers had a little wholesale wine business and David had dabbled in amateur theatricals as a hobby. When he applied to Drury Lane and Covent Garden as an actor, he was quickly rejected. He finally hired himself to the Goodman's Field Theatre where, between acts of a concert, he performed *Richard III*. Billed as a "Young Gentleman who never appeared on any stage," Garrick was suddenly, unexpectedly, catapulted overnight into fame. Pope wrote that this new young man "never had been equalled as an actor" and that he "will never have a rival." Obviously, Garrick was in the right place at the right time. Within the next seven months he played eighteen widely different parts. Six short years later, he was not only leading player but also entrepreneur of Drury Lane, where he stayed for thirty years. Yes, Davy had luck — but also an indomitable will.

Garrick seemed equally adept at comedy or tragedy. Audiences howled with laughter at his Abel Drugger in *The Alchemist* and then cried at his King Lear. In fact, Garrick was the first to say that comedy was the proper schooling for tragedy. The Garrick Lear was carefully created, starting with his observation of a mentally ill old man. He was convinced that a good actor would always be in sympathy with the feelings of his character and be transformed beyond himself. Garrick also contended

GARRICK AS MACBETH. (COURTESY HARVARD COLLEGE LIBRARY THEATRE COLLECTION.)

that in the warmth of playing, with involvement in the character and the situation, the great actor might produce an electric inspirational moment, surprising even himself. Garrick was scholarly, thorough, and a very hard worker, with an apparently boundless energy. He would not tolerate any slipshod or slovenly habits in himself or in the casts he worked with. Declamation "revolted" him, and he believed that in an actor, "affectation should be marked as the blackest of all sins against nature." When bombastic old Quin saw Garrick act, he said, "If the young fellow is right, I and the rest of the players have been all wrong."

It is strange that Garrick never performed in any play by his contemporary, Richard Brinsley Sheridan, but by the time *School for Scandal,* and *The Rivals* appeared, Garrick had wearied of his many responsibilities and retired. Sheridan succeeded him as manager of Drury Lane.

Dr. Johnson wrote of Garrick:

> *It is amazing that anyone should be so ignorant as to think that an actor will risk his reputation by depending on the feelings that shall be excited in the presence of two hundred people — no, sir, Garrick left nothing to chance; every gesture, every expression of countenance and variation of the voice, was settled in his closet before he set foot upon a stage.*[10]

There is an oft-repeated remark of Garrick's to the effect that an actor should be able to make love to a table or chair as well as to a Juliet. I cannot take this seriously. Davy was a vain little man, fond of boasting and fun, and this remark was probably tossed off to amuse some people who expected the great entertainer to entertain. The sober record of his meticulous work habits and his brilliant achievements seem better foundations on which to determine his theories of acting than this single flippant remark.

An actor in Garrick's estimable position was bound to have envious detractors. One was no less than the King of England, who thought David "a great fidget," but Americans will discount this remark because the King's name was George III. But there may have been some truth in it. Others accused Garrick of using too many gestures and being forever busy while onstage. In a death scene, someone disliked the way he writhed about the floor clutching at the carpet; others noted how he kicked over a chair at the appearance of the Ghost in the Queen's Closet Scene of *Hamlet.* But remember that when such actions are coldly set down on paper, the essential element is eliminated — the life and personality of the actor. I believe that *the way Garrick performed* these pieces of business made them thrilling to most spectators. If we consider them just as mechanical actions, we deny the art of the actor, and Garrick was a great actor.

SALLY KEMBLE

Unlike Garrick, Sally Kemble was of a theatrical family. Eldest of twelve children, she trouped the little country towns with her family, who were

---

[10]Mrs. Clement Parsons, *Garrick and His Circle* (New York: G. P. Putnam's Sons, 1906).

strolling players. Often they would encounter a sign on the outskirts of a town, "No monkeys, marionettes, or actors," and they would have to detour. Mr. and Mrs. Kemble had plans; their children would not be players. John Phillip, two years younger than Sally, would study for the priesthood. They would find a good husband for Sally, and she would settle down to a quiet comfortable life far away from the turmoil of the stage. But at eighteen Sally married one of the actors in her father's company, William Siddons, who was twelve years older than she.

Mr. and Mrs. William Siddons continued to act in the provinces. News of her had come to Garrick's ear, and he sent a scout to witness a performance of the young actress. At fifty-eight, Garrick no longer had the patience to endure the constant bickerings of his three leading ladies, one of whom was the redoubtable Mrs. Abington. "Every one of them," he wrote, "considers herself at least equal to the queenly heroines she personates." He felt that a fresh young competitor would settle them. "If any lady begins to play tricks, I will immediately play off my masked battery of Siddons against them." Sarah, as she was now called, was twenty and in the final months of her second pregnancy. By now her brother John had given up all thoughts of the priesthood and was back acting. After being delivered of a little girl, Sarah Siddons opened in her first play in London at Drury Lane, *The Merchant of Venice.*

As Portia she was dressed atrociously; the other actresses had had the pick of wardrobe before her. She seemed awkward, her Portia had no humor, and there was something rural about her manner; but worst of all, she was not accustomed to such a big house. She could not be heard. The critics were unimpressed. "On the stage there is nothing so barren as cold correctness," one critic wrote. The others seemed to agree that the country actress was not for the city of London. But Garrick tutored her, and when she was not working, she sat in front, watching the great actor. Even so, when she played Lady Anne to his Richard III, she moved a critic to say that her performance was "lamentable." Her contract at Drury Lane was not renewed. Her former rival, Mrs. Abington, now became her defender. "You are all fools," she told the management and prophesied that they would regret the action.

The young actress wrote:

> It was a stunning and cruel blow. It was very near destroying me. My blighted prospects, indeed, induced a state of mind that preyed upon my health, and for a year and a half I was supposed to be hastening to a decline. For the sake of my poor children, however, I roused myself to shake off this despondency, and my endeavors were blessed with success, in spite of the degradation I had suffered in being banished from Drury Lane as a worthless candidate for fame and fortune.[11]

By sheer determination she was able to pull herself out of her depression. She would show London and Drury Lane what they had rejected. For five

[11]Thomas Campbell, *The Life of Sarah Siddons* (New York: Harper Brothers, 1834), p. 35, by permission.

THE RESTORATION AND THE EIGHTEENTH CENTURY 225

years she played every part that came her way. Suddenly, in a little watering place called Bath, her reputation skyrocketted.

In 1782, when she was twenty-seven, Sarah Siddons and family again made that trip to London. On her opening night, terror clutched her, "The awful consciousness that one is the sole object of attentions to that immense space—may perhaps be imagined but cannot be described," she wrote of her opening. But this night was more than just another opening. She had tasted bitter defeat on this very stage seven years ago. The play she was to act was *Isabella or The Fatal Marriage*, which she had played successfully at Bath. But London was not Bath. On the night before the opening, her voice disappeared, only to reappear miraculously "on the day."

The year 1782 became "the year of the Siddons." People remembered only one other debut to equal hers, the night young Garrick had brought an audience to its feet shouting his praises. The next day Sarah found that "the enthusiasm she excited had something idolatrous about it; she was regarded less with admiration than with wonder, as if a being of superior order had dropped from another sphere, to awe the world with the majesty of her appearance."[12] Sir Joshua Reynolds painted her as "The Tragic Muse" and signed his name on the border of the skirt. "I have resolved," he told her, "to go down to posterity upon the hem of your garment."

How did this shy country actress, so limited in acting range (she could not play comedy), convince all London that she was "a superior being"—a goddess? Mrs. Siddons possessed an incredible beauty—hawk-like nose[13] and piercing black eyes and great strands of glinting auburn hair. She moved slowly, majestically, molded in the grand, romantic style of acting, and she acted it on and off stage. They joked about the way she spoke to waiters in iambic pentameter, "You've brought me water, boy; I asked for beer." She is supposed to have patronized Edmund Kean who, like Garrick, was a small man, by saying, "You are a fine actor, but it's a pity there's so little of you." But Kean's name was to be linked with her own and Garrick's as the three greatest acting talents of the century.

EDMUND KEAN

Almost everything we know of Kean's acting is based on the writings of two critics who were the first to practice dramatic criticism as we know it today. "I have all along spoken freely of Mr. Kean's faults," Hazlitt wrote, "or what I considered such, physical, as well as intellectual."[14] This seems to bear out what we know of the actor's life. He had little or no

THE *TRAGIC MUSE* BY SIR JOSHUA REYNOLDS. (PHOTO OF THE ORIGINAL PAINTING NOW IN THE HUNTINGTON COLLECTION AND USED BY PERMISSION OF THE HENRY E. HUNTINGTON LIBRARY AND ART GALLERY.)

[12]William Archer and Robert Lowe, eds., *Hazlitt on Theatre* (New York: Hill and Wang, 1958).

[13]"My God, Madame, is there no end to your nose?" Reynolds asked as he painted her portrait. "The Tragic Muse" is now in the painting collection of the Henry E. Huntington Art Collection, San Marino, California.

[14]*Hazlitt on Theatre*, preface, p. xxxv.

STYLES IN ACTING

schooling, which was not unusual for the time, but there is no evidence of Kean's interest in any learning beyond his study of Shakespeare. We know that he suffered an injury to his leg when he fell from a horse as a circus performer, and thereafter walked with a limp. His voice was an unpleasant and unreliable instrument. Hazlitt said it was *"somewhat between an apoplexy and a cold."* Like Garrick he was not at all a handsome man, as was Kemble. Kean was addicted to drink, "my old complaint," he called it and was plagued all of his life by guilt because of his illegitimate birth. How then is it possible to class him with Garrick and Siddons? Mrs. Siddons' niece offered an explanation of Kean's magic in rousing an audience:

> *Kean is a man of decided genius, no matter how he neglects or abuses nature's good gift, he has it. He has the first element of greatness — power. No taste perhaps and no industry, perhaps; but, . . . he has the one atoning faculty that compensates for everything else, that seizes, rivets, electrifies all who see and hear him, and stirs down to their very springs the passionate elements of our nature. Only genius can do this.*[15]

EDMUND KEAN. (COURTESY OF THE HENRY E. HUNTINGTON LIBRARY AND ART GALLERY.)

This undoubtedly indicates that he was capable of amazing emotional surges which came to him on the spur of the moment and gave him the power to transport audiences along with him. Previously, we discussed the hazards of the emotions taking control of the actor; this was possibly Kean's great fault. Also, he was not intellectually equipped to plan an overall design in his work. He was all fire, exciting slapdash of bits and pieces, lacking the patience of the true artist. He could not discipline himself, either on or off stage. As Hazlitt said,

[15]Frances Ann Kemble, *Records of a Girlhood* (New York: Henry Holt & Co., 1879).

We miss in Kean, not the physiognomy, or the costumes, as much as the architectural building up of the part.

SOME FAMOUS PARTS

SIDDONS: Isabella in *The Fatal Marriage* (Southerne), Lady Macbeth, *Jane Shore* (Rowe), *The Fair Penitent* (Rowe), *Venice Preserved, Love Makes a Man* (Cibber), *The Orphan* (Otway), *Percy, the Suspicious Husband* (Hoadley), *The Mourning Bride* (Congreve), *The Grecian Daughter, The Stranger* (Kotzebue), *The Distressed Mother, The Devil To Pay*, Hamlet in *Hamlet, The Provoked Husband*.

GARRICK: Richard III, Lear, *Love Makes a Man* (Cibber), *The Fair Penitent, The Alchemist* (Jonson), *The Orphan* (Otway), *The Lying Valet, The Old Bachelor* (Congreve), *The School Boy* (Cibber), *Hamlet, The Rehearsal* (Buckingham), *The Suspicious Husband, Jane Shore, The Way of the World* (Congreve), Romeo.

EDMUND KEAN: Shylock, Othello, Lear, Richard III, Macbeth, Coriolanus, Giles Overreach in *A New Way to Pay Old Debts* (Massinger), *Every Man in His Humour* (Jonson), Harlequin, *The Suspicious Husband, Richard II*, Abel Drugger in *The Alchemist*, Duke Aranza in *Honey Moon*.

HIGH COMEDY

In the years preceding the French Revolution, France was arbiter for the world in cultural matters. There was a general shift toward lighter, gayer, more decorative types of expression in all the arts. In the English plays of this time, the acting was typically French. Its quintessence was a kind of elaboration, a rococo *flare*. It had tempo, a smartness and precision reminiscent of a minuet. Old actors called this "the manner," and indeed it is just that. Propriety is woven into the very texture of plays by Congreve and Sheridan. They are not properly acted without it. It gives color and authenticity to these pieces. It is properly artificial, bright, and vivacious.

To probe the inner life of a Mr. Tattle, Mrs. Candour, Lady Sneerwell, or a Charles Surface is to diffuse the bold outlines used in creating them. Searching such parts for "spine" and "truth" is to deny their distinctiveness. They are clean-cut, superficial *types* — and as such they are delightful.

The actor of the eighteenth century depended a great deal upon his body, his grace, his personal magnetism, and powers of expression. He used his voice as a biting, precise instrument to articulate the author's waxed and polished wit. No author of this time wrote with naturalism as his goal. Fashionable plays of the day were frivolous reflections of the mores of the upper class. Capable actors brightened them with a style that had high gloss and sophistication. In *The Flower in Drama*, Stark Young describes this style:

> *The voice (would) be clear, finished, the lips expert, the tongue striking well on the teeth; the tone would go up and down but always be sure of its*

place in the throat, be crisp, shining, in hand, like the satin and gold of the furniture and costumes, the rapier at the wrist, the lace over it, the worldliness and the wit.[16]

Preceding the Commedia scenario, we investigated the clown and his physical approach to playing farce. Now we approach a type of comedy that is mostly intellectual. This style is known as high comedy or drawing-room comedy. In serious plays, the actor attempts to move the emotions of his audience by means of re-creating a similar emotional experience in himself. But comedy is not supported by, and indeed has no affinity with, emotion. This style of playing is more cerebral than visceral. To be effective, both comedy and farce require a highly developed discipline and skill. Each movement, stance, inflection must be precise and studied. *Comedy is style at its height!* It should be easy, graceful—and above all, rehearsed to a technical precision. Nothing can be left to the inspiration of the moment. Wit is inspirational. It is sudden, an ingenious arrangement of words which bring merriment. But wit is not comedy. Comedy must be planned beforehand.

The Detachment Principle. In playing high comedy, the actor need not always stay within the confines of his character, but is most successful when he takes an attitude of standing outside it. In a way he detaches himself from the character and thus gains a perspective from which he can share the joke with the audience. For instance, let us take the old example of the man who slips on a banana peel and falls. It is far from comedy to the man, but to us, standing safely on the sidelines, it is comic. It is cruel perhaps, but then to a very sensitive person, all laughter may be cruel. Someone must always be the butt of a joke. The next time you hear a good storyteller delighting people with a joke, notice how he assumes a character for a particular gesture or effect and then figuratively steps outside the character to make comments *in his own identity.* From this viewpoint, he is able to editorialize, to share the joke with his listeners. *In playing comedy, the actor is both involved in his character and detached.* By another process, the actor attempts to cause the audience to laugh *at* the character. In using this approach, the actor stays within his character at all times, but this does not produce a true comedy effect. Other elements enter into it. The audience may feel sorry for the character, or hate him.

Audience-Actor Relationship. In comedy, the detachment of actor from character requires a more friendly relationship with the audience than is needed even for tragedy. The actor of comedy is, in a way, one of the audience. *He confides in them and is their contact with all that is happening.* He is sharing the joke with them. The great clowns and comedians are always likable, while some of our greatest tragic figures are despicable. Macbeth and Richard III are murderers and villains to the audience, but this does

[16]Stark Young, *The Flower in Drama* (New York: Scribner's, 1923), p. 88.

not destroy the excitement of the tragedies. Older actors knew that they must always, "keep their heads in comedy and lose their hearts in tragedy."

Distortion. As in tragedy, characters should be designed, created—but with an important difference. *One particular facet of the character must be selected, then enlarged and distorted.* Yet in the playing this exaggeration must seem to be almost unconsciously done. The comedic spirit is rooted in this overdrawn or underdrawn aspect of character. We know that Molière's invalid is hale and hearty and we laugh because his hypochondria is distorted out of proportion.

One of the favorite stunts used in college musicals is to dress up the burly football team as chorus girls. The more they try to imitate dainty femininity, the more awkward they seem and the greater are the laughs. It is all off-balance, distorted. But if a womanly man dresses as a woman, this is not so off-balance and is therefore less amusing. We may laugh out of embarrassment, but it is not pure comedy, because other elements enter into it.

This distortion we have been speaking about must always be rooted in the character. It is wrong to perform extraneous "bits" (such as slipping, voice tricks, or stumbling over one's feet) just for the purpose of getting laughs. But if your character is otherwise known as tipsy or clumsy or awkward, then such "bits" are connected and may very well fit into your characterization.

In the playing of farce, the overemphasis of an aspect of the character can be unreal, even completely absurd. A farce character can leave the stage to go some distance and pop back seconds later with mission accomplished. We accept such ridiculousness in farce, but in comedy everything must be made theatrically real and believable.

The Comedic Spirit. To summarize then, the successful playing of comedy calls for a principle of detachment, a closer audience-actor relationship, distortion of some facet of the character, and theatrical truth. Perhaps the most important task for the comedy actor is to convince the audience that he is also enjoying his character's eccentricities. This must be done genially; it must never seem rude, bitter, or mean. The best rule is: never attempt to play a comedy character unless you can find something in him to love.

REHEARSAL

THE WAY OF THE WORLD

A Comedy by William Congreve
An Adaptation
ACT IV SCENE i

1. Mrs. Millamant enters from USL in a huff. Mirabell follows her on but stops as she takes a position DC.

1 male, 1 female

1

MIRABELL: Do you lock yourself up from me to make my search more curious? Or is this pretty artifice contrived to signify that here the chase must end, and my pursuits be crowned? For you can fly no further.

MRS. MILLAMANT: There is not so impudent a thing in nature as the saucy look of an assured man, confident of success. The pedantic arrogance of a very husband has not so pragmatical an air.[2] Ah!, I'll never marry, unless I am first made sure of my will and pleasure.

2. Mrs. Millamant turns upstage.

MIRABELL: Would you have 'em both before marriage?

MRS. MILLAMANT: Mirabell, I'll lie abed in a morning as long as I please.

MIRABELL: Then I'll get up in a morning as early as I please.

MRS. MILLAMANT: I won't be called names after I'm married.

MIRABELL: Names?

MRS. MILLAMANT: [3]Aye, as wife, spouse, my dear, joy, love, sweetheart, and the rest of the nauseous cant in which men and their wives are so fulsomely familiar. Mirabell, don't let us be familiar or fond, nor kiss before folks, nor go to Hyde Park together the first Sunday in a new chariot, to provoke eyes and whispers, and then never to be seen together again; as if we were proud of one another the first week and ashamed of one another ever after. Let us never visit together, nor go to a play together; but let us be very strange and well-bred; let us be as strange as if we had been married a great while; and as well-bred as if we were not married at all.[4]

3. Turns back, facing him directly.

MIRABELL: Have you any more conditions to offer?

4. Walks upstage, as if she is finished with her requests.

MRS. MILLAMANT: [5]Liberty to pay and receive visits to and from whom I please; to write and receive letters without interrogatories or wry faces on your part; to wear what I please; and choose conversations with regard only to my own taste; to have no obligation upon me to converse with wits that I don't like, because they are your acquaintance: or to be intimate with fools, because they are your relations. Come to dinner when I please; dine in my dressing gown when I'm out of humor, without giving a reason. To have my closet inviolate; to be sole empress of my tea-table, which you must never pressure to approach without first asking leave. And lastly, wherever I am you shall always knock at the door before you come in. These articles subscribed, if I continue to endure you a little longer, I may by degrees dwindle into a wife.[6]

5. Again turns to him as if taking advantage of his receptivity.

6. These are her terms. She turns away with a "take it or leave it" attitude.

MIRABELL: Have I liberty to offer conditions — that when you are dwindled into a wife, I may not be beyond measure enlarged into a husband?

MRS. MILLAMANT: You have free leave. Speak and spare not.

MIRABELL: I thank you. Imprimis then, I covenant, that your acquaintance be general; that you admit no sworn confidant, or intimate of your own sex; no she-friend to screen her affairs under your countenance, and tempt you to make trial of a mutual secrecy. No decoy-duck to wheedle you a fop scrambling to the play in a mask — then bring you home in a pretended fright, when you think you shall be found out — and rail at

7. On hearing his first demand, she starts for UL, crossing in front of Mirabell but he stops her.

8. Again she starts for UL. He crosses before her, blocking her exit.

9. As he takes a step forward on each point, she steps back R.

10. Pushing him aside, she starts quickly for UL.

11. She hesitates. A faint smile of satisfaction as she turns front to audience.

12. He smiles and then takes her hand and kisses it. They both laugh as they embrace.

me for missing the play.[7] Item I article, that you continue to like your own face, as long as I shall; and while it passes current with me, that you endeavor not to re-coin it. To which end, together with all vizards for the day, I prohibit all masks for the night, made of oil-skins, and I know not what,—hog's bones, hare's gall, pig water, and the marrow of roasted cat.[8] I denounce against all strait lacing, squeezing for a shape, till you mold my boy's head like a sugar-loaf. Lastly, to the domination of the tea-table I submit—but with proviso, that you exceed not in your province; but restrain yourself to native and simple tea-table drinks,[9] as tea, chocolate, and coffee: as likewise to genuine and authorized tea-table talk—such as mending of fashions, spoiling reputations, railing at absent friends, and so forth—but that on no account you encroach upon the men's prerogative, and presume to drink healths, or toast fellows. These provisoes admitted in other things I may prove a tractable and complying husband.

MRS. MILLAMANT: [10]I hate your odious provisoes!

MIRABELL: Then we are agreed! Shall I kiss your hand upon the contract?

MRS. MILLAMANT: I shall never say it![11]

If Mirabell should not make a good husband—I am a lost thing, for I love him violently. I think I must have him.[12]

Well . . . I think . . . I'll endure you.

THE LIVING PLAYS OF WILLIAM CONGREVE

The Old Bachelor (1691)
The Double Dealer (1692)
Love for Love (1695)
The Way of the World (1700)

RICHARD BRINSLEY SHERIDAN (1751-1816)

No collection of classic dramatic literature would be representative without Richard Brinsley Sheridan's masterpiece, *The School for Scandal*. Sheridan had been a dramatist only two years when he wrote what has been called the greatest comedy in the English language. The famous screen scene in this play is thought to be the most skillfully constructed comedy scene ever written in our language. This play, which was George Washington's favorite, has outlived its own time and has consistently maintained its popularity. It is an archetype of high comedy and wit. Polished and dazzling, it moves swiftly to its climax.

PREPARATION FOR THE SCHOOL FOR SCANDAL

The abridged version used here differs from the one you will find in your library. It is an acting version—that is, it has been arranged by theatre practitioners, inspired comedians—to extract the most out of its lines and situations after playing it before hundreds of audiences.

All the actors in this play should work to develop precision both in movement and diction. There should be no trace of localized accents and the cast must be rehearsed tirelessly in order to achieve that teamwork known as ensemble playing.

THE CHARACTER OF LADY TEAZLE

The eminent drama critic of the 1890s, Mr. William Winter, has written of Ada Rehan's performance as Lady Teazle and in so doing has described what other actresses have achieved in the part. Concisely, he sets forth a blueprint for the character that might be of value to any young actress preparing the part.

> *Mrs. Abington,*[17] *the original representative of the part, made Lady Teazle entirely artificial, that being the temperament of the actress, and therein she obtained a brilliant success. Elizabeth Farren, who succeeded Mrs. Abington, embodied her with a natural refinement, making her an aristocrat by birth. Dora Jordan, who followed Elizabeth Farren, depicted her as a tantalizing compound of affectation and nature; the robes and manner were artificial; but the brown cheek, the cherry lips, the mischievous laughter, and the rustic freedom of the country girl were deliciously perceptible through the customs, airs, and trappings of fashion. This would seem to be the right method of playing the part, and this was the method pursued by Ada Rehan. Her impersonation of Lady Teazle pleased by its brilliancy, but it was her noble dignity and tender grief, at the close of the screen scene, that made the performance deeply impressive and commended it to an exceptional place in remembrance. She embodied Lady Teazle as a woman of self-respecting mind and tender heart—a sweet woman deeply touched and sharply wounded with a sense of misconduct and shame. The moral nature of the thoughtless young wife is aroused to the knowledge of duty, and she perceives her ingratitude and perverse unkindness, and she suffers in a spirit of profound contrition. Lady Teazle was shown to be a person of frank, downright moral sense, such as the insidious Joseph's sophistries were powerless to contaminate, and at the climax of the comedy every shred of dissimulation fell away from her and she stood forth an honest, natural, affectionate woman, humble, contrite, and more than ever lovely.*[18]

[17]Mrs. Frances Abington, previously referred to as defending Mrs. Siddons at Drury Lane. Regarding Mrs. Abington's performance as Lady Teazle, a contemporary, Tom King, wrote that her "every word stabbed."

[18]William Winter, *Ada Rehan, A Story* (privately printed for Augustin Daly, 1898), p. 123.

In characterizing Lady Teazle, the actress should not forget that Lady Teazle's sophistication and polish are acquired. At heart she is a country girl. The "tease" of Teazle may not be Sheridan's pun, but it would explain her visit to Joseph's flat.

Other Characters

Joseph. Sheridan uses this character to represent the society he is lampooning. Joseph is witty, quick, and malicious. He pretends to be pious but in reality is a hypocrite. (Contrast this character with Tartuffe.)

Charles. He is the opposite of his brother Joseph, being frank, honest, and basically good while pretending to be a rake.

Sir Peter Teazle. Although rich, Sir Peter is generous but believes in getting value. He is warmhearted and loyal although inclined to be somewhat cantankerous.

REHEARSAL

SIR JOHN GIELGUD AS JOSEPH SURFACE IN *THE SCHOOL FOR SCANDAL.* (RADIO TIMES HULTON PICTURE LIBRARY.)

THE SCHOOL FOR SCANDAL

ACT IV, SCENE iii
(the famous "Screen Scene")

CAST: JOSEPH SURFACE   LADY TEAZLE
SERVANT
SIR PETER TEAZLE
CHARLES SURFACE

SCENE: *The library in Joseph Surface's home. Necessary furniture: a divan, a screen covered with maps, and a chair. Divan is a little to right of dead center. Joseph is discovered. He turns to greet Lady Teazle as she enters.*

1. Lady Teazle crosses in front of Joseph to divan. When she is seated he comes level.

LADY TEAZLE: Have you been very impatient? I vow I couldn't come before.[1]

JOSEPH: O Madam, punctuality is very unfashionable in a lady of quality. *(Gestures to a place on divan.)*

2. Removes her gloves and settles herself.

LADY TEAZLE: Do you know, Sir Peter is grown so ill-natured of late, and so suspicious, when I know the integrity of my own heart — indeed 'tis monstrous![2]

JOSEPH: My dear Lady Teazle, when a husband entertains a groundless suspicion of his wife, she owes it to the honor of her sex to outwit him.

3. Joseph reacts politely to her every remark.

LADY TEAZLE: [3]The best way of curing his jealousy is to give him reason for it?

4. Still standing but in a position to ease onto divan next to her. She pauses as if weighing his advice.

JOSEPH: Once make a trifling faux pas, and you can't conceive how cautious you would grow —[4]

LADY TEAZLE: This is the oddest doctrine —

234   · STYLES IN ACTING

JOSEPH: Prudence,[5] like experience, must be paid for. Heaven forbid I should persuade you to do anything you thought wrong. I have too much honor to desire it.

LADY TEAZLE: [6]We may as well leave honor out of the argument.

JOSEPH: Ah,[6a] the ill effects of your country education still remain with you.

LADY TEAZLE: I doubt they do indeed; and I will own to you that if I could be persuaded to do wrong,[7] it would be by Sir Peter's ill humour — sooner than your *honourable* logic.

JOSEPH: Then, by this hand, which he is unworthy of — (*Taking her hand, about to kiss it as Servant enters.*) Blockhead! What do you want?

SERVANT: I beg your pardon, Sir, but I thought you would not choose Sir Peter to come up without announcing him.[8]

JOSEPH: Sir Peter! The devil — ?

LADY TEAZLE: Sir Peter![9] I'm ruined, — ruined! Now, Mr. Logic — Oh! mercy, he's on the stairs — I'll get behind here — and if I'm so imprudent again —

(She goes behind screen)[10]

JOSEPH: Give me that book. (*Sits, R of divan as Sir Peter enters*)

SIR PETER: Ah! [11]There he is — ever improving his mind — Mr. Surface, — Mr. *Surface!*

JOSEPH: (*Pretending to be startled, gets up, throws the book on divan*) O, my dear Sir Peter, I beg your pardon, I have been dozing over a stupid book.[12] (*Sir Peter looks about, circling above divan.*)

SIR PETER: Very neat indeed.[13] (*Stops at screen.*) Well, well, — and you even make your screen a source of knowledge — hung, I perceive, with maps.

JOSEPH: Oh yes, I find great use for that screen.[14] Here's a chair, Sir Peter — (*But Sir Peter sits on divan. Joseph places chair near him and sits*) [15](*Servant leaves*)

SIR PETER: There is a subject, my dear friend, on which I wish to unburden my mind.[16] Lady Teazle's conduct of late has made me very unhappy. I have pretty good authority to suppose that she has formed an attachment. I think I have discovered the man.[17]

JOSEPH: You alarm me.

SIR PETER: My dear friend —[18]

JOSEPH: Sir Peter, such a discovery would hurt me just as much as it would you.[19]

SIR PETER: Have you no guess who I mean? What do you say to Charles?

JOSEPH: My brother? Impossible.

SIR PETER: Oh, my dear friend,[20] the goodness of your own heart misleads you. You judge of others by yourself.

JOSEPH: Certainly, Sir Peter, the heart that is conscious of its own integrity

5. Joseph sits, putting his right arm back of divan.

6. Rising slowly, Lady Teazle smiles and looks knowingly at him. Ethel Barrymore made a memorable moment of this.

6a. Feeling his bird is escaping, Joseph rises.

7. She crosses to left toward door. Positions at this point Joseph, URC, Lady Teazle, ULC.

8. Servant exits, leaving door open.

9. Looks about, moving R.

10. Servant re-enters, picks up book from divan, hands it to Joseph who then comes down to divan, reclines on it with his back to upstage. Servant returns to place above entrance door.

11. Joseph pretends to be absorbed in the book, his back to Sir Peter, who taps him gently with his walking stick.

12. Servant is now arranging books and papers.

13. Sir Peter takes spectacles out of case and holds them out to see maps.

14. Joseph leads Sir Peter away from screen and motions that he sit on the divan as Joseph crosses back of it to DR.

15. Sir Peter glances at Servant and Joseph dismisses him with a nod as he walks front of divan to chair at L.

16. Sir Peter replaces glasses in case, then in pocket.

17. Joseph moves chair close so that he sits facing Sir Peter.

18. Puts hand on Joseph's knee.

19. Offers his hand and Joseph shakes it briefly.

20. Wags his finger at Joseph.

is ever slow to credit another's treachery.

SIR PETER: What noble sentiments![21] Ah Joseph—your brother has no sentiment—you never hear him talk so.

JOSEPH: Yet I can't but think Lady Teazle has too much principle.

SIR PETER: What is principle against the flattery of a handsome, lively young fellow? And then, you know, the difference in our ages—If I were to make it public, why the town would only laugh—at the foolish old bachelor,[22] who had married a young girl.

JOSEPH: You must never make it public.

SIR PETER: That the nephew of my old friend, Sir Oliver, should be the person to attempt such a wrong, hurts me.

JOSEPH: If it should be proved on Charles,[23] he is no longer a brother of mine. The man who can tempt the wife of his friend, deserves to be branded as a pest of society.

SIR PETER: What sentiments! What noble sentiments! What a difference there is between you.

JOSEPH: Yet I cannot suspect Lady Teazle's honor.[24]

SIR PETER: I'm sure I wish to think well of her! She has lately reproached me with no settlement on her—Here,[25] my friend, are two deeds, by one she will enjoy eight hundred a year independent while I live, and and by the other, the bulk of my fortune at my death.

JOSEPH: This conduct, Sir Peter, is truly generous.

(Enter Servant)

SERVANT: Your brother, Sir,[26] is speaking to a gentleman in the street, and says he knows you are within.

JOSEPH: I'm not within—I am out for the day!

SIR PETER: Stay. A thought has struck me; you shall be at home.[27] *(Joseph nods to Servant, who leaves.)* Let me conceal myself somewhere, then you tax him on the point we have been talking.

JOSEPH: Would you have me join in so mean a trick?

SIR PETER: You do him the greatest service by giving him an opportunity to clear himself. *(Looks at screen)* Here, behind the screen—Hey! What the devil! There seems to be one listener here already—I'll swear I saw[28]—a *petticoat!*

JOSEPH: Ha! ha! ha! Harkee![29]—'tis a little French milliner that having some character to lose, on your coming, Sir, she ran behind the screen.

SIR PETER: Here's a closet will do as well. Oh, you naughty boy! "A little French milliner," eh? *(Starts for screen; Joseph stops him and guides him to closet)* Oh, you sly rogue![30] *(Goes into closet.)*

JOSEPH: A curious situation I'm in,—to part man and wife in this manner.

LADY TEAZLE: *(Peeping around screen)* [31]Couldn't I steal off?

JOSEPH: Keep close, my angel!

SIR PETER: [32]Joseph, tax him home!

---

21. Sir Peter stamps his stick to make his point.

22. Takes out kerchief from sleeve and sniffs at it. He is feeling very sorry for himself.

23. Joseph rises and goes back of divan, placing hands on Sir Peter's shoulders as if to comfort him.

24. Joseph now moves DL in thought as he pretends to be defending Lady Teazle.

25. Sir Peter produces two deeds from inner pocket, buries face in kerchief as he reads. Joseph sits on his right and also produces a kerchief. They grope for hands, shake, turn heads to look at each and shake again. This business must be set and gauged to Sir Peter's lines.

26. At entrance of Servant, Joseph rises turns R and up behind divan to him. Sir Peter rises and goes to Joseph on his line.

27. Positions: Servant, UL, Joseph, ULC, Sir Peter, ULC (to Joseph's R.)

28. Joseph is fearful that Sir Peter is going to say "Lady Teazle."

29. Relieved, Joseph laughs nervously, regains his poise and passes it off as a man-to-man joke.

30. Wagging his finger at Joseph.

31. Pokes her head out one side of screen.

32. Sir Peter opens closet door a little.

STYLES IN ACTING

JOSEPH: Back, my dear friend.[33]

LADY TEAZLE: (*Peeping*)[34] Couldn't you lock Sir Peter in?

JOSEPH: Be still, my life.

SIR PETER: [35]The little milliner won't blab?

JOSEPH: In, in, Sir Peter.

(*Enter Charles*)[36]

CHARLES: Holla! (*Looking about*) What has made Sir Peter steal off?

JOSEPH: Hearing you were coming, he did not choose to stay.

CHARLES: What! [37]Afraid I wanted to borrow money of him?

JOSEPH: He thinks you are endeavouring to gain Lady Teazle's affections.

CHARLES: So the old fellow has found out that he has got a young wife, has he?[38]

JOSEPH: This is no subject to jest on, brother—

CHARLES: I never had the least idea of what you charge me, but if a pretty woman was purposely to throw herself in my way—and that pretty woman married to a man old enough to be her father—

JOSEPH: Well?

CHARLES: Why, I believe I should be obliged to—[39]

JOSEPH: What—?

CHARLES: To borrow a little of your morality,[40] that's all. But brother, I always understood *you* were her favorite.

JOSEPH: Brother, brother, a word with you[41]—Sir Peter has overheard all we have been saying—

CHARLES: Sir Peter? Where is he? (*Points to screen*) Here?

JOSEPH: (*Pointing to closet*) There!

CHARLES: Sir Peter, come forth![42] (*Opens door*)

JOSEPH: No, no—

CHARLES: (*Pulling in Sir Peter*) What! My old guardian! what—turn inquisitor?

SIR PETER: Give me your hand, Charles[43]—I believe I have suspected you wrongfully, but what I have heard has given me great satisfaction.

CHARLES: Then 'twas lucky you didn't hear any more. Wasn't it, Joseph? You might as well have suspected him, as me, mightn't he, Joseph?

(*Re-enter Servant and whispers to Joseph*)

SERVANT: Lady Sneerwell is below, and says she will come up.

JOSEPH: She must not come here.[44] (*Exit Servant*) (*Aside*) They must not be left together—(*Aloud*) I'll send Lady Sneerwell away, and return directly. (*As Sir Peter approaches the screen*) Sir Peter! (*Charles takes a step toward him*) Not you, Charles. Sir Peter—

CHARLES: Oh! (*Charles goes to screen and examines it*)

JOSEPH: (*Leading Sir Peter away from the screen*) Not a word of the French milliner.[45] (*Sir Peter laughs slyly. Then Joseph sees Charles at the screen and brings him to Sir Peter.*) Charles! Entertain Sir Peter—(*Exits*)

33. Closes door.

34. Pokes her head out the other side of screen.

35. Same business with door.

36. A breezy entrance. Charles moves easily and naturally. He punches Joseph on the shoulder as he passes him into room.

37. Charles has ended at divan. Joseph comes down to him.

38. Charles sits CL of divan.

39. These three lines may be repeated to heighten the comedy.

40. Charles rises.

41. Joseph goes to him and leads him to L away from closet. Speaks *sotto voce*.

42. The three are all above the divan and before the screen: Sir Peter, R, Charles, C, Joseph, L.

43. Like a child caught in the act, Sir Peter cannot look into Charles's eyes.

44. Back of Charles, to Servant.

45. Leads Sir Peter DL.

46. Joseph now leads Sir Sir Peter DL to Charles. Positions: Joseph, UL, then exits: Sir Peter, DCL, Charles, DL.

47. The "sentiment" line should be made important as it is repeated later.

48. Pointing to closet as he crosses to Sir Peter.

49. Pulls Charles close to him and speaks *sotto voce*.

50. A step toward screen. In panic, Sir Peter runs in front of divan to R.

51. Charles UCL, Sir Peter, UCR, Joseph, UL.

52. They open up to reveal Lady Teazle.

SIR PETER: Ah, Charles, if you associated more with your brother, one might indeed hope for your reformation. [46]There is nothing in the world so noble as a man of sentiment.[47]

CHARLES: Pshaw! He is too moral by half.

SIR PETER: Joseph is no rake—but he's no saint either. (*Chuckles as he whispers*) He had a girl with him when I called.

CHARLES: Joseph?

SIR PETER: Sh-h-h-h! A little French milliner. She's in the room now.

CHARLES: The devil she is—! There—?[48] (*Sir Peter makes a hissing sound three times, as he points to the screen*) What do you mean, s-ist, s-ist, s-ist—?[49] (*Sir Peter repeats sounds and gestures*) Behind the screen—? [50]Let's have her out—

SIR PETER: (*Trying to stop him*) No, no,—Joseph's coming—

CHARLES: Oh, we'll have a peep at the little milliner—

SIR PETER: Here he is![51] (*Just as Joseph re-enters, Charles throws down the screen*)

CHARLES: [52]Lady Teazle! By all that's wonderful.

JOSEPH: Lady Teazle! By all that's horrible.

SIR PETER: Lady Teazle! By all that's damnable!

A CONTEMPORARY PRINT OF THE FAMOUS SCREEN SCENE FROM THE ORIGINAL PRODUCTION. (VICTORIA AND ALBERT MUSEUM.)

53. Faces each as he questions them and waits in silence for their answers.

CHARLES: Sir Peter, this is one of the smartest French milliners I ever saw.[53] You seem all to have been diverting yourselves at hide and seek and I don't see who is out of the secret. Shall I beg your ladyship to inform me? Not a word? Brother, will you be pleased to explain? What, is morality dumb too? Sir Peter, though I found you in the dark, perhaps you are not so now! All mute? Well, I suppose you perfectly understand one another—so I'll leave you to yourselves.[54] (*Going*) Sir Peter, there's nothing in the world so noble as a man of sentiment. (*Exit*)

JOSEPH: Sir Peter,[55] I confess that appearances are against me—but I shall explain everything to—

SIR PETER: If you please, Sir!

JOSEPH: The fact is—Lady Teazle, knowing my pretensions to your ward, Maria—and knowing my friendship to the family—she, Sir, called here—in order that I explain these pretensions—but on your coming, being apprehensive of your jealousy, withdrew—and this, you may depend on it, is the whole truth of the matter.

SIR PETER: A very clear account, upon my word; and I dare swear the lady will vouch for every article of it.

LADY TEAZLE: [56]For not one word of it, Sir Peter. There is not one syllable of truth in what that gentleman has told you.

SIR PETER: I believe you, upon my soul, ma'am!

JOSEPH: (*Aside to her*) Madam, will you betray me?

LADY TEAZLE: Good Mr. Hypocrite, I'll speak for myself.

SIR PETER: Ay, let her alone, sir. She'll make out a better story than you, without prompting.

LADY TEAZLE: I came here on no matter relating to your ward. I came to listen to his pretended passion, if not to sacrifice your honour.

SIR PETER: I believe the truth is coming indeed!

JOSEPH: The woman's mad!

LADY TEAZLE: No, Sir; she has recovered her senses. Sir Peter, the tenderness you expressed for me,[57] when you could not think I was witness to it, has so penetrated to my heart, that had I left the place without the shame of discovery, my future life should have spoken the sincerity of my gratitude.[58] As for that smooth-tongued hypocrite, I behold him now so truly despicable that I shall never again respect myself for having listened to him.[59] (*Exit*)

JOSEPH: Sir Peter[60]—Heaven knows—

SIR PETER: That you are a villain! And so I leave you to your conscience.

JOSEPH: You are too rash, Sir Peter. The man who shuts out conviction by refusing to—[61]

SIR PETER: Oh, damn your sentiments!

(*Exit Sir Peter, still talking. Joseph collapses on the divan*)

THE LIVING PLAYS OF SHERIDAN

The Rivals (1777)
School for Scandal (1779)
The Critic (1779)

54. Crosses up to door L. Others "dress" stage. Sir Peter moves down before divan at R, motivated by his embarrassment.

55. Joseph moves down L., but on a line with Sir Peter.

56. Lady Teazle moves down between the men and takes stage at center in front of divan.

57. Joseph has moved DL a little on this speech.

58. Lady Teazle now steps to Joseph. Note: Be certain characters are not "bunched" or crowded, and all moves are properly motivated by the actors.

59. Sir Peter, now quite broken, uses kerchief to dab his eyes. This is comedy but must be done sincerely by the actor. Lady Teazle turns to Sir Peter as if to take his hands or to make some affectionate gesture—thinks better of it—bows dutifully near the door, then exits quickly.

60. As he steps to Sir Peter in defense of himself.

61. Sir Peter holds up his hand as if saying "no more" as he walks in front of Joseph to door; turns for last line, then exits.

FURTHER READING: RESTORATION AND EIGHTEENTH CENTURY DRAMA

Avery, Emmett, ed. *The London Stage.* Illinois: University of Southern Illinois, 1960. Vol. 1, 1660-1800, Vol. 2, 1700-1729.

Boas, Frederick S. *An Introduction to Eighteenth Century Drama: 1700-1780.* New York: Oxford University Press, 1953.

Brown, J. R. and Harris, B. *Restoration Theatre.* New York: Putnam, 1967.

Dobree, Bonamy. *Restoration Comedy, 1660-1720.* New York: Oxford University Press, 1962.

Fujimura, Thomas H. *Restoration Comedy of Wit.* New Jersey: Princeton University Press, 1952.

Gagen, Jean. *The New Woman, Her Emergence in English Drama 1600-1730.* New York: Twayne, 1954.

Hecht, J. J. *The Domestic Servant Class in Eighteenth Century England.* London: Routledge & Keegan Paul, 1951.

Hinshaw, N. W. "Graphic Sources for a Modern Approach to Acting Restoration Comedy." *Educational Theatre Journal* May 1968, pp. 157-170.

Holland, N. *The First Modern Comedies.* Cambridge, Massachusetts: Harvard University Press, 1959.

Krutch, J. W. *Comedy and Conscience after the Restoration.* New York: Columbia University Press, 1961.

Loftis, J. *Comedy and Society from Congreve to Fielding.* California: Stanford University Press, 1959.

MacCollum, John I., Jr. *The Restoration Stage.* New York: Houghton Mifflin, 1961.

Muir, Kenneth. *The Comedy of Manners.* London: Hutchinson University Library, 1970.

Nicoll, Allardyce. *A History of English Drama.* New York: Cambridge University Press, 1955. Vol. 1, Restoration Drama (1600-1700); Vol. 2, Early Eighteenth Century Drama (1700-1900).

Palmer, John. *The Comedy of Manners.* New York: Russell, 1962.

Payne, Rhoda. "Stage Direction During the Restoration." *The Theatre Annual,* 20 (1963): pp. 41-62.

Perry, Henry T. *Comic Spirit in Restoration Drama.* New York: Russell, 1962.

Underwood, Dale. *Etherege and the Seventeenth Century Comedy of Manners.* New Haven: Yale University Press, 1957.

Garrick

Barton, Mrs. Margaret. *Garrick.* London: Faber and Faber, n.d.

Burnam, Kalman. *David Garrick: Director.* Pittsburgh: University of Pittsburgh Press, 1961.

RECORDINGS

See Schwann Long Playing Record Catalog (see listings in catalog under "Sheridan").

18
Nineteenth-Century Drama

OSCAR WILDE (1856-1900)

The brilliant stage writing exemplified by Sheridan lay dead until Oscar Wilde brought the comedy of manners to life again in just three weeks' writing time. In 1900 Oscar Wilde was also dead, but not without a gibe: "If another century began and I was still alive it would be more than the English could stand." Wit has been called "educated insolence," and Wilde abounded in it.

PREPARATION FOR THE IMPORTANCE OF BEING EARNEST

This superfarce gives an audience nothing to think about, but a great deal to enjoy. It is a triumph of artificiality. Beginning with lies, entanglements pile one on another until it seems the whole structure will fall. Wilde's precarious plot contrasts amusingly with his precise, urbane, overcivilized characters who move politely among the snarls of deception and misunderstandings. It is all style, extravagantly absurd and amusing. This is the way an audience will enjoy it—and the way actors should play it.

    The characters are not "real," but they are very much alive. Usually when young actors are asked to enact sophistication, they tend to assume a bored, unattractive attitude. In contrast, the people of this play are devoted to polite, gracious manners. They are always charming, even when saying disagreeable things.

    They follow a definite pattern of behavior accepted as the correct way to live in a civilized society; any other way would be barbaric. Charm was greatly valued. Imagine a girl of today asking another's permission to look at her—and the other being refreshing enough to admit that she loves being looked at. In the comedy of manners, life is always pretended to be made up of the most exquisite demeanor. All men are wits and the ladies are engrossed with social amenities. Then, unexpectedly, the social mask drops and we see the ordinary and even quite primitive human being who has been wearing it. Some of the delight an audience finds is in witnessing this contrast between the ideal and the reality. It is typical of the comedy of manners that people are dressed beautifully in the mode of the day, that they are free of the economic pressures of making a living, and that they skirmish over trifles.

REHEARSAL

THE IMPORTANCE OF BEING EARNEST
An Excerpt from ACT II

CAST: CECILY   ALGERNON
          GWENDOLEN JACK

SCENE: *Garden of the Manor House. There is a metal table DRC and chairs with tea service set. There is a door to the interior UC.*

                                        STYLES IN ACTING

Discovered, Cecily sitting at table making an entry in her diary. Gwendolen enters from L. Cecily rises.

CECILY: Pray let me introduce myself to you.[1] My name is Cecily Cardew.

GWENDOLEN: Cecily Cardew?[2] What a very sweet name. Something tells me that we are going to be great friends. I like you already more than I can say. My first impressions of people are never wrong.

CECILY: How nice of you to like me so much after we have known each other such a comparatively short time.[3] Pray sit down.

GWENDOLEN: I may call you Cecily, may I not?

CECILY: With pleasure.[4]

GWENDOLEN: And you will always call me Gwendolen, won't you?[5]

CECILY: If you wish.

GWENDOLEN: Then that is all quite settled, is it not?

CECILY: I hope so.[6]

GWENDOLEN: Perhaps this might be a favorable opportunity for my mentioning who I am. My father is Lord Bracknell. You have never heard of papa, I suppose?

CECILY: I don't think so.

1. Cecily rises and advances to meet Gwendolen, offering her hand.

2. Moving to Cecily and shaking hands.

3. Indicating chair R of table.

4. Still standing: waits for Gwendolen to be seated.

5. Gwendolen sits at chair R of table.

6. Cecily sits, chair L of table.

SIR JOHN GIELGUD, DAME EDITH EVANS, AND MARGARET LEIGHTON IN *THE IMPORTANCE OF BEING EARNEST*. (RADIO TIMES HULTON PICTURE LIBRARY.)

GWENDOLEN: Outside the family circle, papa is entirely[7] unknown. I think that is quite as it should be. Cecily,—mama, who's views on education are remarkably strict, has brought me up to be extremely short-sighted; it is part of her system; so do you mind my looking at you through my glasses?

7. All through this speech, Gwendolen's eyes have been examining Cecily's dress, complexion, hands, manner, etc.

8. Using her lorgnette, Gwendolen has verified her worst fears that Cecily is young, attractive, and charming. There is a pause as she swallows the knowledge, then she speaks.

9. Rising, she walks a step to R in thought, then back to place.

10. She now saunters back of Cecily's chair to center, then turns to her.

11. Gwendolen walks in front of table to R.

12. Cecily rises, walks left, turns back to Gwendolen for question.

13. Gwendolen sits in Cecily's chair (R of table)

14. Looking front.

15. Cecily walks in front of table to R, turns, and leans over table to face Gwendolen.

16. Speaking shyly and confidentially; then sits in chair R of table.

17. Gwendolen rises politely.

18. Cecily also rises politely, then shows diary.

CECILY: Oh, not at all Gwendolen. I am very fond of being looked at.

GWENDOLEN: [8]You are here on a short visit, I suppose?

CECILY: Oh, no, I live here.

GWENDOLEN: Really? [9]Your mother, no doubt, or some female relative of advanced years, resides here also?

CECILY: My dear guardian, with the assistance of Miss Prism, has the arduous task of looking after me.

GWENDOLEN: Your guardian?

CECILY: Yes, I am Mr. Worthing's ward.

GWENDOLEN: Oh! [10]It is strange he never mentioned to me that he had a ward. He grows more interesting hourly. I am not sure, however, that the news inspires me with feelings of unmixed delight.
I am very fond of you Cecily; I have liked you ever since I met you. But I am bound to state that now that I know you are Mr. Worthing's ward, I cannot help but expressing a wish you were—well, just a little older than you seem to be—and not quite so very alluring in appearance. In fact, if I may speak candidly—

CECILY: Pray do! I think that whenever one has anything unpleasant to say, one should always be candid.

GWENDOLEN: Well, to speak with perfect candor, Cecily, I wish that you were fully forty-two, and more than usually plain for your age.[11] Ernest has a strong, upright nature. He is the very soul of truth and honor. But even men of the noblest possible moral character are extremely susceptible to the influence of physical charms.[12]

CECILY: I beg your pardon, Gwendolen, did you say Ernest?

GWENDOLEN: Yes.

CECILY: Oh, but it is not Mr. Ernest Worthing who is my guardian. It is his brother—his elder brother.

GWENDOLEN: Ernest never mentioned to me that he had a brother.[13]

CECILY: They have not been on good terms—

GWENDOLEN: Ah! That accounts for it. [14]And now that I think of it, I have never heard any man mention his brother. The subject seems distasteful to most men. Of course you are quite, quite sure that it is not Mr. Ernest Worthing who is your guardian?

CECILY: Quite sure. In fact,[15] I am going to be his.

GWENDOLEN: I beg your pardon?

CECILY: Dearest Gwendolen, there is no reason why I should make a secret of it to you.[16] Mr. Ernest Worthing and I are engaged to be married.

GWENDOLEN: My darling Cecily, I think there must be some slight error.[17] Mr. Ernest Worthing is engaged to me.

CECILY: [18]I am afraid you must be under some misconception. Ernest proposed to me exactly ten minutes ago.

GWENDOLEN: It is certainly very curious, for he asked me to be his wife yesterday afternoon at 5:30. If you would care to verify the incident, pray do so.¹⁹ I never travel without my diary. One should always have something sensational to read in the train.²⁰ I am so sorry, my dear, but I am afraid *I* have the prior claim.

CECILY: It would distress me more than I can tell you, dear Gwendolen, if it caused you any mental or physical anguish, but I feel bound to point out that since Ernest proposed to you, he clearly has changed his mind.

GWENDOLEN: ²¹If the poor fellow has been entrapped into any foolish promise I shall consider it my duty to rescue him at once, and with a firm hand.

CECILY: ²²Whatever unfortunate entanglement my dear boy may have got into, I will never reproach him with it after we are married.

GWENDOLEN: Do you allude to me, Miss Cardew, as an entanglement? You are presumptuous. On an occasion of this kind it becomes more than a moral duty to speak one's mind. It becomes a pleasure.

CECILY: Do you suggest, Miss Fairfax, that I entrapped Ernest into an engagement? How dare you? This is no time for wearing the shallow mask of manners. When I see a spade, I call it a spade.

GWENDOLEN: I am glad to say that I have never seen a spade.²³ It is obvious that our social spheres have been widely different.

CECILY: May I offer you some tea, Miss Fairfax?

GWENDOLEN: ²⁴Thank you. (*Aside*) Detestable girl! But I require tea!

CECILY: ²⁵Sugar?

GWENDOLEN: No thank you. ²⁶Sugar is not fashionable, any more.

CECILY: Cake, or bread and butter?

GWENDOLEN: Bread and butter, please. ²⁷Cake is rarely seen at the best houses nowadays.

CECILY: Miss Fairfax —

GWENDOLEN: ²⁸You have filled my tea with lumps of sugar and though I asked most distinctly for bread and butter, you have given me cake. I am known for the extraordinary sweetness of my nature, but I warn you, Miss Cardew, you may go too far.

CECILY: ²⁹To save my poor, innocent, trusting boy from the machinations of any other girl, there are no lengths to which I would not go.

GWENDOLEN: From the moment I saw you I distrusted you. I felt that you were false and deceitful. My first impressions of people are invariably right.

CECILY: It seems to me, Miss Fairfax, that I am trespassing on your valuable time. No doubt you have many other calls of similar character to make in the neighborhood.

(*Jack enters*)³⁰

19. Examines Gwendolen carefully through her lorgnette.

20. Producing her diary from her bag, holds it during the next move, but leaves bag on floor near chair R.

21. Meditating, she walks several steps to L.

22. Thoughtfully and sadly.

23. Satirically. Gwendolen now at LC, Cecily R of table.

24. "Thank you" is spoken with elaborate politeness. She then turns straight front for "Detestable girl."

25. Sweetly.

26. Superciliously Cecily looks angrily at her, takes up tongs, and puts four lumps of sugar into the cup.

27. As she moves in front of table to R, she returns diary to her bag. During this, Cecily is cutting a large piece of cake which she puts on Gwendolen's plate on table R.

28. Gwendolen smiles sweetly at her, sits R of table, takes up tea, sips, makes a grimace, puts down cup at once, reaches out her hand for bread and butter, looks at it and finds it is cake, rises in indignation—*then* speaks. (All this silent business should be done calmly and deliberately. It will hold the audience's attention without lines.

29. Rising.

30. From garden L, and seeing only their smiling faces is blissfully unaware of the mayhem the faces conceal.

31. Cecily gives to L on his entrance. He walks between girls, and offers to kiss Gwendolen; she draws back; holding up a restraining palm, then points to Cecily.

32. Laughing as if the very idea were preposterous.

33. Gwendolen now offers her cheek.

34. Sweetly. Really relieved.

35. Receding DL, Jack follows her.

36. From L.

37. Goes straight to Cecily DL without noticing anyone else, offering to kiss her. She repeats business of Gwendolen (as identically as possible). At this point, Gwendolen is DR with Jack to her L. Cecily is DL with Algernon to her R.

38. Looks about, sees that Gwendolen is the only other girl present, and laughs at the absurdity of it.

39. Repeats business of Gwendolen.

40. Gwendolen crosses Jack to front of table, then to C.

41. Algernon is now between the girls.

42. She moves in front of Algernon to Gwendolen at C.

43. The girls put their arms around each other's waists, as if for protection. Jack is now DL of table. Gwendolen is at C, Cecily to her L, and Algernon is DLC.

GWENDOLEN: Ernest! My own Ernest!

JACK: Gwendolen! Darling!

GWENDOLEN: A moment![31] May I ask if you are engaged to be married to this young lady?

JACK: To dear little Cecily?[32] Of course not! What could have put such an idea into your pretty little head?

GWENDOLEN: [33]Thank you. You may.

CECILY: I knew there must be some misunderstanding, Miss Fairfax.[34] The gentleman whose arm is at present around your waist is my dear guardian, Mr. John Worthing.

GWENDOLEN: I beg your pardon?

CECILY: This is Uncle Jack.

GWENDOLEN: Jack! Oh![35]

(*Enter Algernon*)

CECILY: Here is Ernest![36]

ALGERNON: My own love![37]

CECILY: A moment, Ernest! May I ask you—are you engaged to be married to this young lady?

ALGERNON: To what young lady? Good heavens! [38]Gwendolen!

CECILY: Yes, to good heavens, Gwendolen, I mean to Gwendolen.

ALGERNON: Of course not! What could have put such an idea into your pretty little head?

CECILY: Thank you.[39] You may.

GWENDOLEN: I felt there was some slight error, Miss Cardew. [40]The gentleman now embracing you is my cousin, Mr. Algernon Moncrieff.

CECILY: Algernon Moncrieff! Oh!

ALGERNON: [41]I cannot deny it.

CECILY: Oh!

GWENDOLEN: Is your name really John?

JACK: I could deny it. But my name is certainly John. It has been John for years.

CECILY: [42]A gross deception has been practiced on both of us.

GWENDOLEN: [43]My poor wounded Cecily!

CECILY: My sweet, wronged Gwendolen!

GWENDOLEN: You will call me sister, will you not?

CECILY: There is just one question I would like to be allowed to ask my guardian.

GWENDOLEN: An admirable idea! Mr. Worthing, there is just one question I would like to be permitted to put to you. Where is your brother Ernest? We are both engaged to be married to your brother Ernest, so it is a matter of some importance to us to know where your brother Ernest is at present.

JACK: [44]Gwendolen—Cecily—it is very painful for me to be forced to speak the truth. It is the first time in my life that I have ever been reduced to such a painful position, and I am really quite inexperienced in doing anything of the kind. However, I will tell you quite frankly that I have no brother Ernest. I have no brother at all. I never had a brother in my life, and I certainly have not the smallest intention of having one in the future.

CECILY: [45]No brother at all?

JACK: [46]None!

GWENDOLEN: [47]Had you never a brother of any kind?

JACK: [48]Never! Not even of any kind.

GWENDOLEN: I am afraid it is quite clear, Cecily, that neither of us is engaged to be married to anyone.

CECILY: [49]It is not a very pleasant position for a young girl suddenly to find herself in, is it?

GWENDOLEN: Let us go into the house.[50] They will hardly venture to come after us there.

CECILY: No, men are so cowardly, aren't they?

(The girls exit)

44. Coming up L, swings chair left of table and leans over it. He speaks slowly, hesitatingly.

45. Surprised.

46. Very pleased to say it.

47. More seriously.

48. More pleased than ever.

49. The girls are gloriously noble and proud through their tears.

50. They cast scornful looks at their respective beaux, and with arms around waists, retire into the house. The boys join each other at C and watch them disappear.

THE LIVING PLAYS OF OSCAR WILDE

Lady Windermere's Fan (1892)
An Ideal Husband (1892)
A Woman of No Importance (1893)
The Importance of Being Earnest (1895)
Salome (1896)

FURTHER READING

Harris, Frank. *Oscar Wilde.* New York: Dell, 1960.
Holland, Vyvyan. *Oscar Wilde, A Pictorial Biography.* New York: Viking, 1960.
Minney, Rubleigh James. *The Edwardian Age.* Boston: Little, Brown, 1965.
Pearson, Hesketh. *Oscar Wilde, His Life and Wit.* London: Grosset's, 1946.

NATURALISM, REALISM, AND THE FOURTH WALL[1]

Although Talma, Garrick, and even Mrs. Siddons were said to be "realistic," we must accept the term not as we use it today, but in its relationship to the accepted standard of acting that preceded it. As the old century closed and the nineteenth century began, the amateurs again stepped into prominence. André Antoine, a clerk in a gas company, joined an evening class in "Recitation and Diction" which inspired him to form a group[2]

[1]So called because the audience was considered as the "fourth wall" of a room.
[2]The Théatre Libre.

of other amateurs devoted to a new style of acting in a new style of play. They let it be known that they wanted only unpublished plays dealing with everyday subjects.

The quest for realism spread; it was established in Germany by Brahms' Freie Bühne, in England by the Independent Theatre (which found a new author with new ideas, George Bernard Shaw). Later in Ireland, the Abbey Theatre was established. In Russia, a rich man's dilettante son took the stage name of Stanislavski so as not to disgrace his family, and with Danchenko began the Moscow Art Theatre. All were amateurs. The professional actor could not, or cared not to, change his way of working. The amateurs, knowing little of acting (except that they wanted to act), set about the task of training themselves in a style suitable to the plays being submitted to them. Zola was busy in France writing novels and plays about common people. Although Ibsen began in romanticism with such plays as *Peer Gynt*, he was later to become the very cornerstone of the realistic movement. When Ibsen was compared to Zola, he readily admitted a similarity: "but with this difference," he added, "Zola descends into the cesspool to take a bath, I to cleanse it." In Russia, Gogol, Turgenev, Tolstoy, Chekhov, and Gorki were creating a new type of drama. With all this activity of fine minds working on plays that were different not only in development but also in conception, it was obvious that the old, flamboyant, declamatory style of acting had to be replaced by a new acting method.

Down through the centuries, we have seen how representative actors used the basic essentials in building characterization. Not only do we have their own words to that effect, but we have eyewitness accounts that these things were evidenced in their work. No one will deny that in this century we have made some developments out of our particular needs and we have given some new terminology to old processes, but we did not invent creative acting, and neither did Antoine or Stanislavski.

The plays of Sophocles, Shakespeare, and Moliére, while having certain intellectual content, do not attempt to alter radically the intellectual concepts of an audience. The plays written by Ibsen, Chekhov, and their contemporaries, however, do just that. This was an innovation of the "new" playwrights, and their plays required an intrinsically different type of acting. There was a need for acting which would more deeply probe the hidden depths of character, exploring internal values rather than accenting the previously accepted values of style, elegance, and theatricality. Voice and enunciation were no longer of importance; these new playwrights wrote the language of ordinary people, the speech heard in the marketplaces and streets. They did not use carefully selected and beautiful words, nor did they set them to meter.

The action in their plays was confined to that of ordinary or subordinary men and women. Such plays could be understood by the butcher and baker. It was no longer the daring of larger-than-life heroes facing insurmountable odds. Instead of fighting fate or an invading army, these new heroes fought existing social or economic mores.

Standards of acting based upon magnetism, stage presence, a trained body and voice, were discarded because the butcher and baker had none of these. They did not want to admire an artistic ideal; they wanted to look in a mirror. Stress was placed on the "real-life" aspects — the inner, not the outer man. Freudian theories were translated into acting terms. What appeared on the surface was only a part, or perhaps none, of the "real" meaning hidden underneath. No longer could an actor pick up a manuscript and interpret a character. It required time to get inside such characters. It was not wise to make snap judgments or depend upon tested and reliable devices of voice, gesture, or timing. The *need* had arrived for a new acting style. Once developed, this same method was to serve for subsequent plays to be written by such playwrights as O'Neill, Odets, Miller, and Williams.

HENRIK IBSEN (1828-1906)

Henrik Ibsen's influence on the theatre since his day has been monumental. His unique gift was in creating the so-called "well-made play," which stated in dramatic terms a number of social problems of significance to his generation. Most of these problems no longer concern us, but his dramatic skill was so great that his plays live on because of other qualities.

We can hardly imagine today just what was called a play before Ibsen began writing them. Early nineteenth-century plays were written to a set formula something on this order:

Act I.   Exposition, introduction of protagonists, and a struggle suggested.

Act II. ⎫
Act III. ⎭   Situations, given over to mounting tensions.

Act IV.   Spectacular ball or fête, stage filled with people, magnificent costumes and games, dances, etc., with an outburst, a quarrel, and a challenge. This was the climax. All must look bad for the hero.

Act V.   Everything resolved, all loose ends tied together (*denouement*).

Before Ibsen, no one expected a hero to be motivated by anything but heroic impulses. Ibsen discarded the fancy ornaments used in earlier plays, the strutting, posturing, ranting tirades, and the climactic scenes so loved by actors. It was Ibsen who won the first decisive victories for realism. His profundity and imagination, his special use of characterizations, his dialogue, and his play construction, are some of the elements for which he is known.

With Strindberg, he revolutionized playwriting. Existing drama was too sweet a confection for their tastes. Both worked in naturalism, and later both experimented with new forms. In 1880 the study of psychology was just beginning to interest authors. Ibsen used this knowledge to give depth to characters. He shifted emphasis to internal examination, in a search not so much aimed at greater realism but at greater truth. Before he dominated the stage, no one went to the theatre expecting to have the same experiences there that they had in everyday life.

In *The Master Builder*, the playwright was experimenting with symbolism. In the scene that follows, we see the furthest limit of his venture from realism into symbolism. We shall see later how Strindberg went far beyond Ibsen in this field, how he explored the hidden recesses of the soul, probing into dreams, even madness. Ibsen saw the road ahead, but was unable to follow it because his time was running out. In one of his last letters he wrote, "I shall not be able to absent myself from the old battle-fields. But if I return, I shall come forward with new weapons and new equipment." He was never to return to the battle. It was for younger men. But they would benefit by the old Norwegian's victories.

> *I will build me a cloud castle — Through the North its light shall fall.*
> *With two wings will I build it — a great wing and a small.*
> *In the larger shall inhabit a bard of deathless power;*
> *The lesser shall be given to be a maiden's bower.*
>
> (Ibsen, *Collected Poems*, 1871)

PREPARATION FOR THE MASTER BUILDER

EXERCISE 96

After a study of *The Master Builder* in its entirety, you should be able to answer the following questions:

1. This play has many symbols. Name three and specify what they mean to you. Why was the Master Builder convinced he must climb the tower? Is his fall symbol, fact, or both? Explain.

2. What price has Solness paid for his success and what threatens that success? Why does Solness refuse Ragnar a chance to be on his own? Solness believes he is mad; does anyone in this play agree with him?

3. Perform an improvisation in which Hilda stops to ask directions to Solness's house where she hopes to "claim her kingdom."

4. How does the scene between Solness and the Doctor contribute to Hilda's dramatic entrance?

5. Which character in this play is called "a bird of prey"? Who are "the helpers and servers"?

6. Frequently Ibsen uses a key word to describe Aline's character. What is that word? The author portrays a grown woman grieving over the loss of dolls. What do you think were his reasons for doing this? Mrs. Solness has been called "one of the living dead." Why?

7. What is the theme of this play? Can you write the plot development in two or three sentences? What is the climax? How does Kaia contribute to the plot?

8. Hilda comes to stay forever with Solness, then decides to leave. What causes her to change her mind? Do you believe it a wise decision? Do you believe Solness to be a religious man? Give reasons.

9. When Ibsen was writing this play, he was advising a wife who believed her husband had been hypnotized by another woman. Do you find any evidence of hypnosis in this play?

10. Hilda forces Solness to climb the tower, even though she knows there is a chance he may fall to his death. Obviously Ibsen wanted his audience to admire his leading woman, yet he has her gamble with another's life. If you were playing Hilda, what ways would you devise to make this acceptable to your audience?

11. Ibsen gives a word picture of Solness climbing the steeple. Work out an improvisation of this action using Ibsen's dialogue as a guide.

12. Can you think of any reasons why the playwright would bring Solness back on stage in Act III after he had taken him off carrying the wreath?

13. As there is so little physical action and so much talk, on what do you think the actors should concentrate in order to make this play absorbing to an audience?

Characterization

Hilda Wangle. Hilda is not the typical girl of Ibsen's century. He wrote almost prophetically of the girl of today. We now have many Hilda Wangles. They swoon over their latest crush, from Vallee to Sinatra to the Beatles. To some adults, such child-women may appear brash and undisciplined. Even so, none could deny that these *Hildas* live in an enchanted period of life.

But Ibsen's Hilda never grew up. She denies age, she is the eternal fresh breeze—so raw at times that we shudder; but she is forever invigorating us and renewing our own youth. Hilda is a romantic. She has that rare gift for believing and accepting. Life has not had time to teach her the bitter lessons of skepticism. She is brash, mercurial, unpredictable, generous, perhaps even foolish in giving of herself and her devotion. But whatever Hilda does impulsively, she also does with an open and trusting heart. She is the eagerness of youth, the impatience to get on with life and living, to drain the cup *now*, with no thought of tomorrow. This requires courage. An audience will excuse a dozen flaws of character if a protagonist has courage.

Halvard Solness. Solness is the opposite of everything Hilda represents. She comes into his life when he is beginning to feel the sour inactivity of age, and he basks in her youthful glow. It is neither her fault nor his that she has arrived late. The gallant effort they make to rise above time is the courageous and admirable element of this play. While we sense their defeat, we admire the indomitable human spirit in them that permits them to even dare. Solness knows he is no hero. He is even somewhat of a villain to himself. He regrets the many dishonorable actions he has taken in order to get ahead. But because Hilda believes him a hero, he tries to fulfill her dream of him—and dies in the attempt.

Nevertheless, Hilda's Master Builder lives on. Although this play is all too rarely performed, it should be a great favorite in high schools, for it tells us of the creative powers of youth and pleads with us to respect, to hold on to that power. Although Ibsen called his play "a tragedy," it is in reality a hymn to youth.

REHEARSAL

THE MASTER BUILDER

An Excerpt from ACT I

Translated by John C. Pearce, Ph.D.

CAST: HALVARD SOLNESS, MASTER BUILDER
HILDA WANGLE

SCENE: *Interior, Solness's house. Required, a table and chairs. At rise, Hilda is seated at table LC wearing a travelling suit. The student-actress should find a way to show the audience that she is a guest here, not a hostess. (Something might be done with her handbag, showing that her necessities are travelling with her.) Solness is bringing a tray to the table RC. It contains two cups. As he places one on the table before Hilda, she speaks.*

HILDA: Mr. Solness!

SOLNESS: Yes?

HILDA: Are you very forgetful?

SOLNESS: Forgetful?[1] No, not so far as I know.

HILDA: Then have you nothing to say to me about what happened—up there?

SOLNESS: (*In momentary surprise*)[2] Up at Lysanger? (*Indifferently*) Why—there's nothing much to talk about, it seems to me.

HILDA: (*Looking reproachfully at him*) How can you sit there and say such things?

SOLNESS: Well, then, why don't you tell me about it.

HILDA: [3]When the tower was finished, we had such a wonderful celebration in the town.

SOLNESS: Yes,[4] that day I'll never forget.

HILDA: (*Pleased*) You won't? How kind of you.

SOLNESS: Kind?

HILDA: There was music in the cemetery—[5]and many, many hundreds of people. We school-girls were dressed in white and we all had flags.

1. He smiles, places the other cup at his place, pulls out the chair and sits.

2. As he sips from the cup, he hesitates, then looks up at her.

3. She rises, strides deliberately upstage. Throughout the coming scene she ranges about as if she were unconsciously separating her dream of Solness from the reality of of the man sitting with her.

4. Musing pleasantly as he sips from his cup.

5. She begins to be caught up in her fantasy. She uses great sweeping, heroic gestures and movements.

STYLES IN ACTING

SOLNESS: Oh yes, those flags.[6] I certainly remember those.

HILDA: So then you climbed right up on the scaffolding—right up to the very top. And then you had a big wreath with you, and you hung that wreath right up on top of the weathervane . . .

SOLNESS: (*Interrupting*) Yes, I always used to do that—then. That's an old custom.

HILDA: It was so terribly thrilling—[7]to stand below and to look up at you! Just think. If he should fall—he—the Master Builder himself!

SOLNESS: (*As if to change the subject*) [8]Yes, yes, yes—it might very well have happened too, because one of those little imps in white, made such a commotion—shouting and screaming up at me . . .

HILDA: (*Sparkling with pleasure*). [9]"Hurrah for Master Builder Solness!" Yes!!

SOLNESS: And waved—and swung that flag around—that I—Well, I got giddy when I looked down at her.

HILDA: (*Seriously*) That little imp—[10]that was I.

SOLNESS: (*Looking steadily into her eyes*) I am sure of that now. It must have been you.

HILDA: (*Lively again*) Oh, it was so gloriously thrilling! [11]I couldn't imagine that there was a builder in the whole world who could build such a tremendously high tower. And there you stood, right on the very top of it as big as life! And that you didn't even get dizzy, not the least bit.[12] I just tremble when I think of it!

SOLNESS: You're quite sure I wasn't . . .

HILDA: (*Preposterous idea*) No, indeed! No! Oh, *no!* I knew that instinctively. If you *had* been, you never could have stood up there—and sung!

SOLNESS: (*Astonished*) [13]Sung? I sang?

HILDA: You certainly did.

SOLNESS: I've never sung a note in my life.

HILDA: You sang then. It sounded like harps in the air.

SOLNESS: (*Thoughtfully*) [14]That's strange, that is.

HILDA: (*She is silent for a little, then looks at him and speaks in a low voice*) But then—it was afterwards—that the real thing happened.

SOLNESS: [15]The real thing?

HILDA: (*Again sparkling*) Oh come now, I surely don't have to remind you of that, do I?

SOLNESS: Well, just remind me a little.

HILDA: You don't remember that they gave a big lunch in your honor at the Club?

SOLNESS: [16]Yes,—but it was dinner for me. I left next morning.

HILDA: And from the Club you were invited to our house for supper.

SOLNESS: You're right, Miss Wangle. It's wonderful how all these [17]little details impressed you.

6. To Solness, this story has no glamor, it is merely a recall of dear dead days.

7. Hilda is acting it all out— she is the wreath, the steeple, the hero—and all just as romantic as they were in King Arthur's day.

8. Pushing the cup away, he settles back contentedly in his chair. The actor might transmit this mood of comfort and mild amusement to us by smoking.

9. She comes down to him, leans over the table looking closely at him, somehow hoping he will recognize her.

10. As he does not, she must tell him.

11. Resuming her walk up and down.

12. Solness knows that he *was* dizzy.

13. He remembers some of her tall tale as fact, but *this* is preposterous.

14. Although he believes all this a complete fabrication, he is nevertheless flattered and amused.

15. Just a bit suspicious.

16. He is relieved.

17. "Little details" should be colored into insignificance.

18. Moving back of him to his L and leaning over, her face near his, she forces him to look squarely at her.

19. Very apprehensive.

20. Again resuming the walk.

21. She is now at C, and above the table, lost in her own dream. It will be quite effective if she can show us (without her own realization, of course) that her dream is hers alone and only remotely a part of the man seated at the table.

22. The realist.

23. A little upset with him because he has not accepted her enthusiasm. "*Orangia*" should be said as if it were Heaven. Oranges: then very rare in Norway and considered a great delicacy.

24. Back to her fantasy, straight front.

25. Pouting.

26. An awkward pause as Solness gathers his senses. This is what he has feared all along that he has misbehaved in some way.

27. As she throws up her hands in impatience and strides away from him.

28. Again leaning over the table and almost shouting into his face.

29. Very quickly but innocently.

30. Making her point even more definitely than before.

31. He slowly rises from the chair.

32. A fast turn away from him in utter disgust.

33. He approaches her timidly in voice and manner as she stands, her back to him, her feet far apart, and hands clasped behind in anger.

HILDA: [18]Little details! Well, I like that! Was it also just a little detail that I was alone in a room afterward when you came in?

SOLNESS: You were—[19]alone?

HILDA: (*Ignoring his question*) You didn't call me a little imp then.

SOLNESS: No? I didn't?

HILDA: You said I was beautiful in my white dress,[20] and you said I looked like a little princess—

SOLNESS: And I'm sure you did, Miss Wangle—and—besides, we were all feeling so gay and free that day.

HILDA: And that's when you said that when I grew up[21] I should become your princess.

SOLNESS: (*Laughing a little*) Dear, dear, did I say that too?

HILDA: Yes you did! And when I asked how long I should have to wait, you said that you would come again in ten years, like a troll, and carry me off—to Spain—or some fabulous place. And you promised you would buy me a kingdom there.

SOLNESS: Yes. Well, after a good meal one doesn't leave a small tip. (*With disbelief*) [22]Did I really say all that?

HILDA: You did. You even told me what the kingdom would be called.

SOLNESS: What was that?

HILDA: It was to be called "The Kingdom of Orangia."[23] That's what you said.

SOLNESS: That's an appetising name.

HILDA: Well, I didn't like it a bit.[24] It seemed as if you were making fun of me.

SOLNESS: Oh, I'm sure I didn't intend to do that.

HILDA: [25]Well, I should hope not—considering what you did next.

SOLNESS: (*With some trepidation*) [26]What did I do next?

HILDA: Well, that's just the end![27] If you've forgotten that too! I should have thought that no one could help remembering a thing like that!

SOLNESS: Why not give me just a hint, then—

HILDA: (*Looks steadily at him*) [28]You grabbed me and kissed me, Mr. Solness!

SOLNESS: (*Shocked*) [29]I did?

HILDA: [30]Indeed you did. You grabbed me with both your arms and you bent my head way back—and you kissed me—*many* times.

SOLNESS: [31]My dear, kind Miss Wangle!

HILDA: Surely you could never deny that?

SOLNESS: Ah, but I do! I feel I must deny it.

HILDA: (*Scornfully*) Oh, you wouldn't[32]—oh—how can you?

(*She turns, walks away, stands with her back to him angrily*)

SOLNESS: (*Pleadingly*)[33] Miss Wangle . . .

Brand (1866)
Peer Gynt (1867)
The League of Youth (1869)
The Pillars of Society (1877)
A Doll's House (1879)
Ghosts (1881)
An Enemy of the People (1882)

The Wild Duck (1884)
Rosmersholm (1886)
The Lady from the Sea (1888)
Hedda Gabler (1890)
The Master Builder (1892)
John Gabriel Borkman (1896)

FURTHER READING

Gassner, John. *A Treasury of the Theatre*, Vol. 2. New York: Simon & Schuster, 1951. pp. 10-14, 40-41.

————. *Masters of the Drama*. New York: Simon & Schuster, 1945. pp. 354-386.

Le Gallienne, Eva, trans. Introduction to *Six Plays*, by Henrik Ibsen. New York: Modern Library, 1957.

Tennant, P. F. D. *Ibsen's Dramatic Technique*. London: Albert Saifer, 1962.

Weigand, Hermann. *The Modern Ibsen: A Reconstruction*. New York: Dutton, 1960.

ANTON CHEKHOV (1860-1904)

Chekhov's style of playwriting brought out the quiet, uneventful character probing that has become synonymous with Stanislavski and the Moscow Art Theatre. Some theatregoers complain that his plays are aimless and depressing. But Chekhov's goals were not centered on plots, strong-willed characters, prepared climaxes. His remarkable achievement was that he was able to construct plays of enduring vitality without such aids. Although his plays are dramatically understated, acting can reveal complex themes and counterthemes, concluding with a crescendo of masterful orchestration. But if the acting fails to reveal the buried emotions and the hidden thoughts of the characters, then the dialogue might appear confusing, gloomy, or even boring.

The typical Chekhovian character has charm, a word we would hardly use to describe a character from Strindberg. Indeed Chekhov thought of his characters affectionately. They amused him. (See marginal notes in the excerpt.) They exist in a half-world between a nostalgic past and an illusory future.

The *Three Sisters*, the most frequently performed of Chekhov's plays has been called a "most richly textured play." In it we find examples of the celebrated Chekhovian dialogue, seemingly unimportant, even trivial on the surface, and yet revealing inner thoughts that expose the very soul of the character.

PREPARATION FOR THE THREE SISTERS

The following scene is not simple to act because there is so much to be contributed by the actors. Begin your preparation by reading the entire play, "not once but several times." When you feel you *know* the people of the Prozoroff household, then test yourself by answering the following questions dealing with atmosphere, theme, and characterization.

EXERCISE 97

1. Describe the atmosphere of this play as you imagine it.
2. Chekhov gives the ages of the three sisters in the dialogue. How old is Irina? Masha? Olga?
3. Masha is fond of quoting, "A green oak. . . ." Finish the sentence and state its significance.
4. Contrast the Solony-Irina scene in Act II with the Vershinin-Masha scene in Act I. Both are "love scenes," yet how do they differ?
5. In Act I, Masha cries constantly, and in Act II she says she has been laughing all day. Why?
6. What sort of life does Vershinin picture for his children's children?
7. What is Masha's philosophy of life?
8. What do you understand to be the theme of this play? Has it a protagonist?
9. Songs and music are used by Chekhov in Act I and in Act II, but in the third act he indicates a fire offstage. What is the dramatic use of each?

Characterizations

In your study of *The Three Sisters* you have come to know fourteen people. In our scene we shall concentrate on only four, but our knowledge of the others and our feeling of the play's atmosphere will help with the short scene. As you know, Andrey is the only son of the late General Prozoroff. Much has been expected of him as the male heir, and yet Andrey seems unable to climb out of a rut of ineffectuality. The more he struggles to rise, the more he sinks.

The middle sister, Masha, married to a mild but devoted teacher, finds love briefly with an army officer who is himself plagued by a miserable but permanent marriage.

Even in the following short scene, we can appreciate the engrossing picture Chekhov paints of Russian life in a small town. If the people who frequent the Prozoroff living room are not cheerful, they are lively, friendly, and talkative. Even if their talk is only "whistling in the dark," it provides them with the courage to go on. Chekhov has one of his characters talking about the migration of birds in the autumn, "They will always go on flying. It doesn't matter what thoughts they are thinking, high thoughts or low ones, they just go on flying, not knowing where they are going, or why. They just go right on flying."

STANISLAVSKI AS VERSHININ. (COURTESY OF SOV-PHOTO.)

SIR JOHN GIELGUD AS LT. COL. ALEXANDER VERSHININ IN HIS PRODUCTION OF CHEKHOV'S *THE THREE SISTERS*, LONDON, 1935. (RADIO TIMES HULTON PICTURE LIBRARY.)

STYLES IN ACTING

It was for the plays of Chekhov that "Stanislavski's system" was developed and no method is more effective when producing a play of realism such as *The Three Sisters*. Begin by placing yourself in the atmosphere of the play, remembering that it is Russia in the late nineteenth century. An immediate consideration for this scene is to become conscious of the social levels existing in the Russia of that time.

REHEARSAL

THE THREE SISTERS*

An Excerpt from ACT II

Translated by Elisavete Fen

CAST: MASHA   ANDREY
               FERAPONT
               VERSHININ

SCENE: *The house of the three sisters. A sitting room. Required: a table R of center, chairs, and an entrance DL.*

At rise, Andrey reading a book at the table. Ferapont steps timidly into the room, wearing a tattered old coat with the collar up. His ears are muffled. This could be the only time he has ever been permitted to enter the living room of General Prozoroff's house and he is awed. When Andrey becomes conscious that he is not alone, he looks up from his book and goes to the old man. The class distinction might be shown as Ferapont quickly snatches his cap off his head and bobs up and down with the serf's respectful attitude toward a landowner.

ANDREY: Hullo, old chap![1] What did you want to see me about?

FERAPONT: The Chairman's sent you the register and a letter or something. Here they are. (*Hands him the book and the letters.*)

ANDREY: Thanks. That's all right. Incidentally, why have you come so late?[2] It's past eight already.

FERAPONT: What's that?

ANDREY: (*Raising his voice*) I said, why have you come so late?[3] It's past eight already.

FERAPONT: That's right. It was still daylight when I came first, but they wouldn't let me see you.[4] The master's engaged, they said. Well, if you're engaged, you're engaged. I'm not in a hurry. (*Thinking that Andrey has said something*) What's that?

ANDREY: Nothing. (*Turns over the pages of the register*)[5] Tomorrow's Friday,

*Used with the kind permission of Mr. Gillian M. Jones of Penguin Books Ltd., England.

1. "Old chap" is merely a polite term of veneration.

2. Andrey is not really concerned that Ferapont is late. He is glad to see the old servant and is trying to make conversation.

3. Andrey guides him into the room.

4. Ferapont turns to go but Andrey guides him back.

5. Positions at this point: Andrey ULC at table, Ferapont at L.

6. This is "inner dialogue"; it should not be considered as "speech" or conversation, but revelations of his desires and ambitions, and it will take time to find the words to express such thoughts, he will need to hunt for them.

7. He motions for the old man to sit in the chair L of table. Ferapont does so, but reluctantly. Here again, Andrey is not talking to Ferapont but to himself.

8. Tyestov's and The Great Moscow were fine old restaurants in old Moscow. Ferapont looks uncomfortable because of the difference in social positions, and also he does not hear too well.

9. In contrast to Andrey, the old man is making conversation, but he is so inept at it that he cannot contribute any fresh thought—only disconnected utterances from his memory.

A SCENE FROM *THE THREE SISTERS* WITH IRINA (MARIANNE FAITHFUL) CENTER, TRYING TO COAX BROTHER AUDREY PROZOROV (GEORGE COLE) TO HAVE SOME FUN. THE OTHER SISTERS ARE OLGA (LEFT) PLAYED BY AVRIL ELGEE, AND MASHA PLAYED BY GLENDA JACKSON. (COURTESY OF HER BRITANNIC MAJESTY'S CONSULATE-GENERAL.)

10. He *finishes* the story on "and died," *then* remembers the addition. It is an anti-climax meaning nothing, but it does reveal the character of the old man. Here we have a typical example of Chekhovian "comedy," all too frequently neglected in his plays. He meant that there should be a great deal of comedy in his plays, but it is not of the "funny" kind. He deals with ironic comedy very much in this sense as Chaplin did.

11. Ferapont has heard only a word here and there not only because he is hard-of-hearing but mostly because he is so ill-at-ease that he is unable to concentrate on what is being said. As Andrey turns to him, he realizes that he is expected to talk. He rises and continues with his stale old story.

12. At this point Ferapont decides to do something about his discomfiture and ask permission to leave.

13. As quickly as Andrey releases the old man, he turns to his book. Ferapont leaves on the line indicated by Chekhov. Andrey is

there's no meeting, but I'll go to the office just the same—do some work. I'm so bored at home. (*A pause*) Yes, my dear old fellow, how things do change, what a fraud life is! So strange! Today I picked up this book, just out of boredom, because I hadn't anything to do.[6] It's a copy of some lectures I attended at the University—Good Heavens! Just think—I'm secretary of the local council now, and Protopopov's chairman, and the most I can ever hope for is to become a member of the council myself! I—a member of the local council! I, who dream every night that I'm a professor in Moscow University, a famous academician, the pride of all Russia!

FERAPONT: I'm sorry, I can't tell you. I don't hear very well.

ANDREY: If you could hear properly I don't think I'd be talking to you[7] like this. I must talk to someone, but my wife doesn't seem to understand me, and as for my sisters—I'm afraid of them for some reason or other, I'm afraid of them laughing at me and pulling my leg—I don't drink, and I don't like pubs, but how I'd enjoy an hour or so at Tyestov's,[8] or the Great Moscow Restaurant! Yes, my dear old fellow, I would indeed!

FERAPONT: The other day at the office a contractor was telling me about some business men who were eating pancakes in Moscow.[9] One of them ate forty pancakes and died.[10] It was either forty or fifty, I can't remember exactly.

ANDREY: You can sit in some huge restaurant in Moscow without knowing anyone, and no one knowing you; yet somehow you don't feel that you

STYLES IN ACTING

don't belong there—Whereas here you know everybody, and everybody knows you, and yet you don't feel you belong here, you feel you don't belong at all—You're lonely and you feel a stranger.

FERAPONT: What's that? (*A pause*)[11] It was the same man that told me—of course, he may have been lying—he said that there's an enormous rope stretched right across Moscow.

ANDREY: Whatever for?

FERAPONT: I'm sorry, I can't tell you. That's what he said.

ANDREY: What nonsense. (*Reads the book*) Have you ever been to Moscow?

FERAPONT: (*After a pause*) No. It wasn't God's wish. (*A pause*)[12] Shall I go now?

ANDREY: Yes, you may go. Good bye.[13] (*Reading*) (*Ferapont goes*) Come in the morning and take some letters—You can go now. (*A pause*) He's gone. (*A bell rings*) Yes, that's how it is—(*Stretches and slowly goes to his room. Singing is heard offstage; a nurse is putting a baby to sleep. Enter Masha and Vershinin*)

MASHA: I don't know.[14] (*A pause*) I don't know. Habit's very important, of course. For instance, after Father died, for a long time we couldn't get accustomed to the idea that we hadn't any orderlies to wait on us. But, habit apart, I think it's quite right what I was saying. Perhaps it's different in other places, but in this town the military certainly do seem to be the nicest and most generous and best-mannered people.

VERSHININ: I'm thirsty.[15] I could do with a nice glass of tea.

MASHA: (*Glances at her watch.*)[16] They'll bring it in presently. You see, they married me off when I was eighteen. I was afraid of my husband because he was a schoolmaster, and I had only just left school myself.[17] He seemed terribly learned then, very clever and important. Now it's quite different, unfortunately.

VERSHININ: Yes[18]—I see—

MASHA: I don't say anything against my husband—I'm used to him now—but there are such a lot of vulgar and unpleasant and offensive people among the other civilians. Vulgarity upsets me, it makes me feel insulted. I actually suffer when I meet someone who lacks refinement and gentle manners, and courtesy.[19] When I'm with the other teachers, my husband's friends, I just suffer.

VERSHININ: Yes, of course. But I should have thought that in a town like this the civilians and the army people were equally uninteresting.[20] There's nothing to choose between them. If you talk to an educated person here, civilian or military, he'll generally tell you that he's just worn out. It's either his wife, or his house, or his estate, or his horse, or something—[21] We Russians are capable of such elevated thoughts—then why do we have such low ideals in practical life? Why is it? Why?

MASHA: Why?

speaking to himself (stream of consciousness). Warn bell offstage.

14. Masha precedes Vershinin into the room, speaking as they walk on stage. She carries a small flower which she has picked during the walk. This is a continuance of a conversation started before we see them. The actress must create the first part of the conversation herself.

15. Up to this point, Vershinin has been an interested contributor to the dialogue, but now that he is in the room, he associates it with comfort—refreshments, happiness, etc. Also the walk has made him thirsty.

16. Her watch is pinned on her blouse. Masha is disinterested in tea. She is absorbed in the conversation and sits R of table.

17. Here we have a revealing confession that is very near her heart. She is beginning to love Vershinin, but is struggling with a sense of guilt because she is married to a boring but kind man.

18. Vershinin knows what she is confessing. He also knows that he is powerless to do anything about it.

19. There should be no doubt in our minds that Masha is in love—we should see it in the way she looks at Vershinin. She describes the army man as her ideal, everything she desires in a man, and Vershinin is an army man.

20. He sits L of table. Without arguing, he does nevertheless disagree with her, but it is so gentle and polite that it reveals his tender attitude toward her. He hopes to keep the conversation in general, not personal, terms. In effect, he is saying that all men have their problems.

21. Now Vershinin succeeds in getting the conversation centered upon one of his favorite topics: "a better life—and why can't we achieve it?"

22. She looks adoringly at him, then smiles with great compassion and love.

23. He is expressing the pain of the deep wound in his heart.

24. Masha is apprehensive and nervously touches the flower on the table in front of her. Vershinin notices this, picks up her hand, and impulsively kisses it. She cannot speak. She rises, walks, trying to find some trivial matter to talk about.

25. Her eyes fall upon the stove, and she speaks of it, walks back to the same chair and sits, resuming her nervous fiddling of the flower.

26. She implies much more than just a belief in superstition.

27. This should be spoken slowly, almost reverently. Vershinin must hunt for each word as it is difficult for him and the words he finds are inadequate, little more than clichés and repetitions. Even so, we must accept these as a sincere declaration of his love for Masha.

28. Under no circumstances should this be interpreted as a mocking laugh. It is the frightened laugh of a pathetic little child. She is laughing because she dare not give way to tears. Far from laughing at Vershinin, she is feeling the futility and sadness of their situation. With great effort she regains her composure, deciding to be honest with herself and to encourage his love, no matter what the consequences. But her shame stays with her, as she covers her face.

VERSHININ: Yes, why does his wife wear him out, why do his children wear him out? And what about *him* wearing out his wife and children?

MASHA: [22]You're a bit low-spirited today, aren't you?

VERSHININ: Perhaps. I haven't had any dinner today. I've had nothing to eat since morning. One of my daughters is a bit off color, and when the children are ill, I get so worried. I feel utterly conscience-stricken at having given them a mother like theirs.[23] Oh, if you could only have seen her this morning! What a despicable woman! We started quarreling at seven this morning and at nine, I just slammed the door and walked out.[24] (*A pause*) I never talk about these things in the ordinary way. It's a strange thing, but you're the only person I feel I dare complain to. (*Kisses her hand.*) Don't be angry with me. I've nobody, nobody but you—[25] (*A pause*)

MASHA: What a noise the wind's making in the stove![26] Just before Father died, the wind howled in the chimney just like that.

VERSHININ: Are you superstitious?

MASHA: Yes.

VERSHININ: How strange. (*Kisses her hand.*) You really are a wonderful creature, a marvellous creature! Wonderful, marvellous![27] It's quite dark here, but I can see your eyes shining.

MASHA: (*Moves to another chair.*) There's more light over here.

VERSHININ: I love you, I love you, I love you—I love your eyes, I love your movements—I dream about them. A wonderful, marvellous being!

MASHA: (*Laughing softly*)[28] When you talk to me like that, somehow I can't help laughing, although I'm afraid at the same time. Don't say it again, please. (*Half audibly*) Well no—go on. I don't mind—(*Covers her face with her hands*) I don't mind—Someone's coming. —Let's talk about something else.

THE LIVING PLAYS OF ANTON CHEKHOV

Ivanov (1887)   *The Three Sisters* (1900)
The Seagull (1896)   *The Cherry Orchard* (1904)
Uncle Vanya (1897)

FURTHER READING

Buford, W. H. *Chekhov and His Russia.* London: Keegan Paul, 1947. Social and intellectual life of the late nineteenth century in Russia.

Krutch, Joseph Wood. *"Modernism" in Drama.* Ithaca, N.Y.: Cornell University Press, 1953. See chapter headed (of all things!) "Pirandello."

Magarshack, David. *Chekhov the Dramatist.* New York: Hill & Wang, 1950.

Simmons, Ernest J. *Chekhov, A Biography.* Boston: Little, Brown, 1962.

AUGUST STRINDBERG (1849-1912)

Revolution in the Making

It may be that August Strindberg lacked Ibsen's self-control, accuracy of detail, and skill at play making, but he had a more penetrating insight into underlying experiences that almost bordered on mysticism and the occult. The difference between the characters of Ibsen and Strindberg is the difference between a photograph and x-ray.

Strindberg shared with both Ibsen and Chekhov a mastery at probing the human soul. But Strindberg was able to take reality and spin it through the air until it seemed more like an exciting theatrical illusion than reality. Strindberg referred to his characters as "my souls"; they were not people to him, but the substance inside people. His "souls" had the look of people—they ate and loved—but they existed in a rarefied Strindbergian atmosphere, and they had the power and vigor of madness. Strindberg seems nearer to Poe than to Ibsen.

Fame came to Strindberg because of his realistic plays, *Miss Julie* and *The Father*. The master Antoine produced his plays. But today interest seems to focus upon the plays of his later period, for in these he delved into a deeper reality. They have the validity of dreams. This involvement with dreams and the dream state was later to become known as surrealism. The plays have a contagion of death about them, but pain and death are treated as healing agents, which purify like fire. They were written with a conscious naïveté but still maintain a kind of sophistication. They are what is called in painting "primitives" or, in play terms, development of medieval morality plays. These are very personal plays, written to release the author's own tortures.

Others were working for a time with symbolism—Maeterlinck, Hauptmann, even Ibsen—but Strindberg has far more influence today.

In *The Dance of Death* Strindberg placed two people in an old tower. Although utterly weary of each other, they are nevertheless bound together forever by time and custom. The old man is maddened because he has never been promoted. These two failures try to live out their days by creating for themselves an illusionary world of glamor and status. This play, written in 1901, has certain similarities to *The Chairs* by Ionesco, written in 1952; both are called "tragic farces."

Ibsen closed the door on nineteenth century realism. He said masterfully all there was to say in the "peephole theatre"; but Strindberg opened another door. He is the rightful father of the theatre of illusion. As Eugene O'Neill wrote, "Strindberg still remains among the most modern of moderns, the great interpreter in the theatre of the characteristic spiritual conflicts which constitute drama."

Three distinct periods of dramatic activity are recognized in the works of August Strindberg. He began by writing traditional little romantic dramas. Then about 1887, with *The Father* and *Miss Julie*, he entered into

NINETEENTH-CENTURY DRAMA

a period in which he produced ultrarealistic plays which established him as a serious playwright. But the plays of his later period, after the turn of the century, strike our generation as most portentous and relevant to our times — the esoteric and symbolic pieces like *The Dream Play* and *The Ghost Sonata*.

In *The Ghost Sonata*, Strindberg pioneered a style of drama never before attempted in the theatre. Pirandello, de Ghelderode, Brecht, Beckett, Genet, and many lesser-known, latter-day playwrights are Strindberg's beneficiaries. In *The Theatre of the Absurd*, Martin Esslin writes" . . . the first to put on stage a dream world in the spirit of modern psychological thinking was August Strindberg. The three parts of *To Damascus* (1898-1904), *A Dream Play* (1902), and *The Ghost Sonata* (1907), are masterly transcriptions of dreams and obsessions and direct sources of the Theatre of the Absurd."

PREPARATION FOR THE GHOST SONATA

It is significant, in the writing of *The Ghost Sonata*, that Strindberg digressed from many traditional rules of dramaturgy and evolved a style in which theme and images in motion prevailed over plot and characterizations. *The Ghost Sonata*, his most famous play, was written in 1907 from the pit of Strindberg's private inferno, demonstrating his scorn for the world, but also showing his deep sympathy for the deluded creatures who are born into it. The play abounds in striking visual and aural effects, and it is set in a kind of limbo or purgatory, where humans are doomed to exist before they reach the peaceful realm of the dead. The plot, slight as it is, begins with an evil Old Man enlisting the aid of an idealistic young Student to gain entry into a mystery house where he seeks vengeance on its inhabitants. The scenes of the play have been compared to the movements of a sonata, the first scene an allegro, the second the largo. An excerpt from the second scene which follows will be incomprehensible without knowing how it fits into the entire play. In this scene, known as the "Ghost Supper," the Old Man exposes the deceit and betrayal of the other guests, and he demolishes them by showing how he has them all in his power. But the mood changes quickly when the Old Man himself is proved to be a murderer and is left defenseless.

THE GHOST SONATA*

An Excerpt from SCENE II

3 males, 1 female

UL is a porcelain stove, its mantle holds a mirror, a pendulum clock and a candelabrum.
In the rear wall is a door to the hyacinth room and above that is concealed a door

*From the book *The Chamber Plays* by August Strindberg. Trans. by Evert Sprinchorn and Seabury Quinn, Jr. Copyright © 1962 by Evert Sprinchorn and Seabury Quinn, Jr. Published by E. P. Dutton & Co., Inc. and used with their permission.

STYLES IN ACTING

THE *GHOST SONATA* AS PRODUCED BY IRA ZUKERMAN FOR NORTH
CAROLINA SCHOOL OF THE ARTS. COSTUMES AND SETTINGS BY CHRIS-
TINA GIANNINI. (COURTESY NORTH CAROLINA SCHOOL OF THE ARTS.)

*to a closet. UR leads to a hallway, and down from that is a statue with a curtain
which can be drawn to conceal it. Baron Skanskorg and The Fiancée are already
seated but they have no lines in this excerpt.*

Chairs are arranged in a semicircle.

THE COLONEL: Polly![1]

THE MUMMY:[2] Cluck, cluck! Dumb-cluck!

THE COLONEL: Shall we invite the young people, too?

THE OLD MAN: No! Not the young people! They shall be spared.

[3]

THE COLONEL: Shall I ring for the tea?

THE OLD MAN: Why bother? No one cares for tea. Why play games?

1. In the doorway to the
hyacinth room. Speaks off.

2. The *Mummy* enters.

3. They seat themselves in
a semicircle. Silence.

NINETEENTH-CENTURY DRAMA

4. Pause.

5. Slowly, deliberately, and with frequent pauses.

6. Pause. All look at each other in silence.

7. Long silence.

8. Another long silence.

9. Pointing to the hyacinth room.

10. He refers to the fire and how the *Student* saved many lives.

11. Pause.

12. The clock can be heard preparing to strike the hour.

13. *The Old Man* strikes the table with his crutch.

14. *The Mummy* goes over to the clock and stops its pendulum. Then speaks in her normal voice, seriously.

15. Approaches *The Old Man*.

THE COLONEL: Then perhaps we should start a conversation?

THE OLD MAN: About the weather? Which we know. [5]Ask each other how we're feeling? Which we also know. I prefer silence . . . in which one can hear thoughts and see the past. Silence cannot hide anything—which is more than you can say for words. I read the other day that the differences in languages originated among the primitive savages who sought to keep their secrets from the other tribes. Languages are therefore codes, and he who finds the key can understand all the languages of the world. But that doesn't mean that secrets cannot be discovered without a key. Especially in those cases where paternity must be proved. Legal proof is of course another matter. Two false witnesses provide complete proof of whatever they agree to say. But in the kind of escapades I have in mind one doesn't take witnesses along. Nature herself has planted in man a blushing sense of shame, which seeks to hide what should be hidden. But we slip into certain situations without intending to, and chance confronts us with moments of revelation, when the deepest secrets are revealed, the mask is ripped from the imposter and the villain stands exposed. . . .[6]

Extraordinary, how silent you all are![7]

Take this house, for example. In this estimable house, in this elegant home, where beauty, wealth, and culture are united . . .[8] All of us sitting here, we know who we are, don't we? . . . I don't have to tell you. . . . And you know me although you pretend ignorance. . . . Sitting in that room is my daughter,[9] yes mine, you know that too . . . She has lost all desire to live, without knowing why . . . She was withering away because of the air in this house, which reeks of crime, deception, and deceits of every kind. . . . That is why I had to find a friend for her, a friend from whose very presence she would apprehend the warmth and light radiated by a noble deed. . . .[10] That was my mission in this house. To pull up the weeds, to expose the crimes, to settle the accounts, so that these young people might make a new beginning in this home, which is my gift to them![11]

Listen to the ticking of the clock, like a deathwatch beetle in the wall! Listen to what it's saying: . . . "time's-up, time's-up! . . ." When it strikes—in just a few moments—your time is up. Then you may go—not before. But the clock raises its arm before it strikes. [12]—Listen! It's warning you: "Clocks can strike!"—[13] And I can strike too! Do you understand?

[14]

THE MUMMY: But I can stop time in its course. I can wipe out the past, and undo what is done. Not with bribes, not with threats—but through suffering and repentance.

[15]

STYLES IN ACTING

We are poor miserable creatures, we know that. We have erred, we have transgressed, we, like all the rest. We are not what we seem to be. At bottom we are better than ourselves, since we abhor and detest our misdeeds. But when you, Jacob Hummel,[16] with your false name, come here to sit in judgement over us, that proves that you are more contemptible than we! And you are not the one you seem to be! You are a slave trader, a stealer of souls! You once stole me with false promises.[17] You murdered the Consul who was buried today, you strangled him with debts. You have stolen the student and shackled him with an imaginary debt of his father's, who never owed you a penny . . .

But there is one dark spot in your life, which I'm not sure about— although I have my suspicions . . . I think that Bengtsson might help us.[18]

THE OLD MAN: No! Not Bengtsson! Not him![19]

THE MUMMY: Then it is true? He does know!

Bengtsson, do you know this man?

BENGTSSON: Yes, I know him and he knows me. Life has its ups and downs, as we all know, and I have been in his service, and once he was in mine. To be exact, he was a sponger in my kitchen for two whole years. Since he[20] had to be out of the house by three o'clock, dinner had to be ready at two, and those in the house had to eat the warmed-up food left by that ox. Even worse, he drank up the pure soup stock and the gravy, which then had to be diluted with water. He sat there like a vampire, sucking all the marrow out of the house, and turned us all into skeletons. And he nearly succeeded in putting us into prison, when he accused the cook of being a thief. . . . Later I met this man in Hamburg under another name. He had become a usurer or bloodsucker. And it was there that he was accused of having lured a young girl out onto the ice in order to drown her, for she was the only witness to a crime which he was afraid would come to light. . . .

THE MUMMY: [21]That is the real you! Now empty your pockets of the notes and the will![22] Pretty bird! Where's Jacob!

THE OLD MAN: Jacob's here!

23

THE MUMMY: Can clocks strike?

THE OLD MAN:[24] Clocks can strike!

Coo-coo! Coo-coo! Coo-coo! . . .[25]

THE MUMMY: [26]Now the clock has struck! Stand up, and enter the closet where I have sat for twenty years, crying over our misdeeds. You'll find a rope in there, which can represent the one you strangled the Consul with, and with which you intended to strangle your benefactor. . . . Go in!

27

16. Pointing to *The Old Man.*

17. He has tried to rise and speak but has collapsed in his chair and shriveled up and, like a dying insect, shrivels more and more during the following dialogue.

18. She rings the bell on the table.

19. She rings again. The little *Milkmaid* appears in the door to the hall, unseen by all except *The Old Man,* who shies in terror. The *Milkmaid* disappears when Bengtsson enters.

20. Sponger: one who lives off others.

21. Approaches *The Old Man.* Passes her hand over his face.

22. Johansson appears in the door to the hall, knowing his slavery to *The Old Man* is ended. *The Old Man* produces a bundle of papers which he throws on the table. *The Mummy* strokes *Old Man's* back.

23. Like a parrot, then crows like a rooster.

24. Making clucking noises.

25. Imitates a cuckoo clock.

26. The *Mummy* opens the concealed door to the closet.

27. *The Old Man* goes into the closet as the *Mummy* closes the door.

28. Bengtsson places the screen in front of the door.

Bengtsson! Put up the screen! The death screen![28] It is over!—May God have mercy on his soul!

ALL: Amen!

THE LIVING PLAYS OF AUGUST STRINDBERG

Master Olof (1872)
The Father (1877)
Miss Julie (1888)
The Creditor (1890)
The Link (1897)
To Damascus, I (1898)

Gustavus Vaga (1899)
There are Crimes and Crimes (1899)
The Dance of Death (1901)
The Dream Play (1902)
The Ghost Sonata (1907)

FURTHER READING:

Bjorkman, Edwin. *Introductions to Plays by August Strindberg.* New York: Scribner's, 1928. 4 vols. *The* authority.

Clark, Barrett, and Freedley, George. *A History of Modern Drama.* New York: Appleton-Century Crofts, 1947.

Gassner, John. *Masters of the Drama.* New York: Simon & Schuster, 1945. pp. 388-395.

Mortensen, Brita, and Downs, Brian. *Strindberg, An Introduction to His Life and Work.* New York: Cambridge University Press, 1949. Paperback.

Sprigge, Elizabeth. *The Strange Life of August Strindberg.* New York: Macmillan, 1949. Excellent.

Valency, Maurice. *The Flower and the Castle.* New York: Macmillan, 1963. About Ibsen and Strindberg.

GEORGE BERNARD SHAW (1856-1950)

It might be said that George Bernard Shaw straddled both the nineteenth and twentieth centuries like a colossus. G. B. S. has been criticized for peopling his plays with characters who were little more than speakers for Shavian wit and raillery. However, Shaw could develop characterizations which were vivid and highly entertaining, such as Caesar, Androcles, Major Barbara, Higgins, Liza, and Candida.

When Shaw began to write plays he was unable to get producers to read them, and so he published them himself. In substituting books for theatre, he assumed somewhat more than the playwright's rightful function. Shaw took on the jobs of scene designer, director, actors, and, at times, producer and audience. Sometimes there seem to be more directions than lines in his plays. I have known actors who automatically started work on a Shaw play by running a blue pencil through every word of narrative so that they might better concentrate on the job at hand; namely, *to contribute to the character themselves as creative artists.* Shaw does explore the background and goals of his characters rather imaginatively. If this exploration inspires you as an actor or can be blended into your conception, all well and good to use his comments.

PREPARATION FOR PYGMALION

In *Pygmalion,* we are concerned with a specific English dialect which is spoken by a particular class in a particular section of London. (See also discussion of dialects, Appendix 2.) Cockney, like American, is a localized version of English. Nothing upsets an Englishman more than to be told by an American that he speaks "with an English accent." In *Pygmalion,* Shaw uses the subject of phonetics as a bond to hold his story together. Eliza speaks a "gutter language," and Professor Higgins sets about to reform her speech. When he does so, the play is over, the story told — except for showing the audience how Eliza's character changes with her change in speech. In the excerpt we are to use, Eliza's cockney is not so important as it is earlier in the play. However, she reverts to it when she is off-guard, tired, or angry, as she is in our scene.

STYLES IN ACTING

PYGMALION*

An Excerpt from ACT IV

CAST: ELIZA

HIGGINS

SETTING: *Higgins's study, midnight. Required for this exercise: Sofa at LC. On the floor in front of it are some men's soft slippers. At RC is Higgins's desk and chair. Door UL.*

Immediately preceding this moment we have had a long scene of very high spirits. They have all returned from the Embassy Ball, which has been a triumph. Higgins and Pickering have been elated, complimenting each other as Eliza has sat silently and inconspicuously waiting for someone to admit she had some part in the success. From a first amazement, her mood has grown to anger, and now she is fighting back her tears of rage. Pickering has just left, as has Mrs. Pearce. Higgins is in stocking feet, very smug and content with his victory.

At rise, Higgins is walking from his desk at L to door L, intending to call Mrs. Pearce. Eliza is on the sofa, looking like a beaten puppy.

HIGGINS: (*Following Pickering to the door*) Goodnight. (*Over his shoulder, at the door*) Put out the lights, Eliza;[1] and tell Mrs. Pearce not to make coffee for me in the morning: I'll take tea. (*He goes out.*)

> 1. Not looking at her; she is just a part of the furniture.

Eliza tries to control herself and feel indifferent as she rises and walks across to the hearth to switch off the lights. By the time she gets there she is on the point of screaming. She sits down in Higgins's chair and holds on hard to the arms. Finally she gives way and flings herself furiously on the floor, raging.

HIGGINS: (*In despairing wrath outside*) What the devil have I done with my slippers? (*He appears at the door*)

LIZA: (*Snatching up the slippers, and hurling them at him one after the other with all her force*) There are your slippers.[2] And there. Take your slippers; and may you never have a day's luck with them![3]

> 2. Pitches them at him, not so hard that they cannot be found later.
>
> 3. She beats on the floor like a child in a tantrum.

HIGGINS: (*Astounded*) [4]What on earth—! (*He comes to her.*) What's the matter? Get up. (*He pulls her up*) Anything wrong?

LIZA: (*Breathless*) Nothing wrong—with you. Ive won your bet for you, havnt I? Thats enough for you. I dont matter, I suppose.

> 4. He starts back to get the slippers, but stops as she speaks.

HIGGINS: You won my bet! You! Presumptuous insect! *I* won it. What did you throw those slippers at me for?

LIZA: Because I wanted to smash your face.[5] I'd like to kill you, you selfish

> 5. Eliza standing at C, Higgins at LC. She is in a towering rage, alternately crying and storming.

*From which was made the award-winning musical film, My Fair Lady. Excerpt by permission of The Public Trustee and The Society of Authors, London.

6. He wheels her upstage before him and into the sofa, not the "easy-chair." Higgins is now C facing her.

7. He paces up and down back of sofa, stopping to throw questions at her like a prosecuting attorney.

8. Stops suddenly, then asks incredulously. Resumes his pacing. Now patronizing her.

9. She moves L to sofa and eases into it as she sniffles.

10. Back of sofa.

11. Eliza moves to UR and he follows her on his line.

brute. Why didnt you leave me where you picked me out of—in the gutter? You thank God it's all over, and that now you can throw me back again there, do you? (*She crisps her fingers frantically.*)

HIGGINS: (*Looking at her in cool wonder.*) The creature is nervous, after all.

LIZA: (*Gives a suffocated scream of fury, and instinctively darts her nails at his face*)!!

HIGGINS: (*Catching her wrists*) Ah! would you? [6]Claws in, you cat. How dare you shew your temper to me? Sit down and be quiet. (*He throws her into the easy-chair*)

LIZA: (*Crushed by superior strength and weight*) Whats to become of me? Whats to become of me?

HIGGINS: How the devil do I know whats to become of you?[7] What does it matter what becomes of you?

LIZA: You dont care. I know you dont care. You wouldnt care if I was dead. I'm nothing to you—not so much as them slippers.

HIGGINS: (*Thundering*) T h o s e slippers.

LIZA: (*With bitter submission*) Those slippers. I didnt think it made any difference now.

A pause. Eliza hopeless and crushed. Higgins a little uneasy.

HIGGINS: (*In his loftiest manner*) Why have you begun going on like this? May I ask whether you complain of your treatment here?

LIZA: No.

HIGGINS: Has anybody behaved badly to you? Colonel Pickering? Mrs. Pearce? Any of the servants?

LIZA: No.

HIGGINS: [8]I presume you dont pretend that *I* have treated you badly?

LIZA: No.

HIGGINS: I am glad to hear it. (*He moderates his tone.*) Perhaps youre tired after the strain of the day. Will you have a glass of champagne? (*He moves toward the door*)

LIZA: No.[9] (*Recollecting her manners*) Thank you.

HIGGINS: (*Good-humored again*) This has been coming on you for some days. I suppose it was natural for you to be anxious about the garden party.[10] But thats all over now. (*He pats her kindly on the shoulder. She writhes.*) Theres nothing more to worry about.

LIZA: No. Nothing more for y o u to worry about. (*She suddenly rises and gets away from him by going to the piano bench, where she sits and hides her face*) Oh God! I wish I was dead.[11]

HIGGINS: (*Staring after her in sincere surprise*) Why? In heaven's name, why? (*Reasonably, going to her*) Listen to me, Eliza. All this irritation is purely subjective.

LIZA: I don't understand. I'm too ignorant.

HIGGINS: It's only imagination. Low spirits and nothing else. Nobody s hurting you. Nothing s wrong. You go to bed like a good girl and sleep it off. Have a little cry and say your prayers: that will make you comfortable.

LIZA: I heard your prayers. "Thank God its all over!"

HIGGINS: (*Impatiently*) Well, dont you thank God it's all over? Now you are free and can do what you like.

LIZA: (*Pulling herself together in desperation*) What am I fit for? What have you left me fit for? Where am I to go? What am I to do? Whats to become of me?

HIGGINS: (*Enlightened, but not at all impressed*) Oh, thats what's worrying you, is it? [12](*He thrusts his hands into his pockets, and walks about in his usual manner, rattling the contents of his pockets, as if condescending to a trivial subject out of pure kindness*) I shouldnt bother about it if I were you. I should imagine you wont have much difficulty in settling yourself somewhere or other, though I hadnt quite realized that you were going away. (*She looks quickly at him: he does not look at her, but examines the dessert stand on the piano and decides that he will eat an apple*) You might marry, you know. [13](*He bites a large piece out of the apple and munches it noisily.*) You see, Eliza, all men are not confirmed old bachelors like me and the Colonel. Most men are the marrying sort (poor devils!); and youre not bad-looking: its quite a pleasure to look at you sometimes—not now, of course, because youre crying and looking as ugly as the very devil; but when youre all right and quite yourself, youre what I should call attractive. That is, to the people in the marrying line, you understand. You go to bed and have a good nice rest; and then get up and look at yourself in the glass; and you wont feel so cheap.

Eliza again looks at him, speechless, and does not stir.

The look is quite lost on him: he eats his apple with a dreamy expression of happiness, as it is quite a good one.

HIGGINS: (*A genial afterthought occurring to him*) I daresay my mother could find some chap or other who would do very well.

LIZA: We were above that at the corner of Tottenham Court Road.[14]

HIGGINS: (*Waking up*) What do you mean?

LIZA: I sold flowers. I didnt sell myself. Now youve made a lady of me and I'm not fit to sell anything else. I wish youd left me where you found me.

HIGGINS: (*Slinging the core of the apple decisively into the grate*) Tosh, Eliza.[15] Dont you insult human relations by dragging all this cant about buying and selling into it. You neednt marry the fellow if you dont like him.

LIZA: What else am I to do?

HIGGINS: Oh, lots of things. What about your old idea of a florist's shop? Pickering could set you up in one: he's lots of money. (*Chuckling*) He'll have to pay for all those togs youve been wearing today; and that, with the hire of the jewellery, will make a big hole in two hundred pounds.

12. He breaks the mood by walking to back of desk. He does not sit. (He is too interested in what he has to say.)

13. This business with the apple is excellent for the comedy points as it is audible as well as visual and also it shows his insensitivity to others. In a subtle way it is matching "the action to the words."

14. With some bitterness.

15. Moves to the R where we pretend there is a fireplace, and in passing tosses the core into it.

Why, six months ago you would have thought it the millennium to have a flower shop of your own.[16] Come! youll be all right. I must clear off to bed. [17]I'm devilish sleepy. By the way, I came down for something. I forget what it was.

LIZA: Your slippers.

HIGGINS: Oh, yes, of course. You shied them at me.[18] (*He picks them up, and is going out when she rises and speaks to him*)

LIZA: Before you go, sir —

HIGGINS: (*Dropping the slippers in his surprise at her calling him Sir*) Eh?

LIZA: Do my clothes belong to me or to Colonel Pickering?

HIGGINS: (*Coming back into the room as if her question were the very climax of unreason*) [19]What the devil use would they be to Pickering?

LIZA: He might want them for the next girl you pick up to experiment on.

HIGGINS: (*Shocked and hurt*) Is that the way you feel toward us?

LIZA: I dont want to hear anything more about that. All I want to know is whether anything belongs to me. My own clothes were burnt.

HIGGINS: But what does it matter? Why need you start bothering about that in the middle of the night?

LIZA: I want to know what I may take away with me. I dont want to be accused of stealing.

HIGGINS: (*Now deeply wounded*) Stealing! You shouldnt have said that, Eliza. That shews a want of feeling.

LIZA: I'm sorry.[20] I'm only a common ignorant girl; and in my station I have to be careful. There cant be any feelings between the like of you and the like of me. Please will you tell me what belongs to me and what doesnt?

HIGGINS: (*Very sulky*) You may take the whole damned houseful if you like. Except the jewels. Theyre hired. Will that satisfy you? [21](*He turns on his heel and is about to go in extreme dudgeon*)

LIZA: (*Drinking in his emotion like nectar, and nagging him to provoke a further supply*) Stop, please.[22] (*She takes off her jewels.*) Will you take these to your room and keep them safe? I dont want to run the risk of their being missing.

HIGGINS: (*Furious*) Hand them over. (*She puts them into his hands*). If these belonged to me instead of the jeweller, I'd ram them down your ungrateful throat. (*He perfunctorily thrusts them into his pockets, unconsciously decorating himself with the protruding ends of the chains*)

LIZA: (*Taking a ring off*) This ring isnt the jeweller's: its the one you bought me in Brighton.[23] I dont want it now. (*Higgins dashes the ring violently into the fireplace, and turns on her so threateningly that she crouches over the piano with her hands over her face and exclaims*) Dont you hit me![24]

HIGGINS: Hit you! You infamous creature, how dare you accuse me of such a thing? It is you who have hit me. You have wounded me to the heart.

---

16. Crossing up to door UL.

17. Moves to door, stops, turns, and over shoulder, he asks:

18. Finds slippers, repeats business of going and the over-the-shoulder question.

19. She is now facing upstage before the sofa. *Before* his line regarding Pickering, he takes a deliberate walk down to her R.

20. The scene should now begin to build in emotion.

21. To UL.

22. He is now at her L, as she has "given" a few steps to her R as he has moved.

23. She holds it out to him. There is a moment as he looks at it silently. Then he steps to her, snatches it, and throws it at her feet. (Remember, Eliza must be able to find it quickly, later on.)

24. She is in mortal terror and covers her head to avoid the blows she fully expects.

STYLES IN ACTING

LIZA: (*Thrilling with hidden joy*) I'm glad. Ive got a little of my own back, anyhow.

HIGGINS: (*With dignity, in his finest professional style*) You have caused me to lose my temper: a thing that has hardly ever happened to me before.[25] I prefer to say nothing more tonight. I am going to bed.

LIZA: (*Pertly*) Youd better leave a note for Mrs. Pearce about the coffee; for she wont be told by me.[26]

HIGGINS: (*Formally*) Damn[27] Mrs. Pearce; and damn the coffee; and damn you; and damn my own folly in having lavished hard-earned knowledge and the treasure of my regard and intimacy on a heartless guttersnipe. (*He goes out with impressive decorum, and spoils it by slamming the door savagely*).

    Eliza smiles for the first time.[28]

25. Higgins is indignant.

26. Like a child.

27. Each "damn" should be timed with some movement.

28. Eliza is pleased at the way things have gone. She struts about in satisfaction, decides to find the ring, does so, and puts it on with admiration.

THE LIVING PLAYS OF GEORGE BERNARD SHAW

Arms and the Man (1894, Source of the musical, *The Chocolate Soldier*)
Candida (1895)
The Devil's Disciple (1897)
The Man of Destiny (1897)
Mrs. Warren's Profession (1898)
You Never Can Tell (1899)
Caesar and Cleopatra (1899)
The Admirable Bashville (1901)

Man and Superman (1903)
Major Barbara (1905)
The Doctor's Dilemma (1906)
Androcles and the Lion (1913)
Pygmalion (1913, Source of the musical *My Fair Lady*)
Heartbreak House (1919)
Back to Methuselah (1921)
Saint Joan (1923)

FURTHER READING

Henderson, Archibald. *George Bernard Shaw, Man of the Century.* New York: Appleton-Century Crofts, 1956. The authorized biography.

EUGENE O'NEILL (1888-1953)

The high cultural standards Eugene O'Neill set for himself as a playwright were different from those of other playwrights of his time. "Most modern plays," he said, "are concerned with the relation between man and man, but this does not interest me at all. I am interested in the relation between man and God." For the first time in American dramaturgy, O'Neill made it possible that plays written by an American deserved to be compared with other literature, even to the great plays of the past written by Sophocles and Shakespeare. This had always been an ambition of O'Neill's and he fulfilled it with *Lazarus Laughed, Strange Interlude,* and *Mourning Becomes Electra.* By the use of masks, he was able to revive in contemporary form, the use of the Greek chorus and the Restoration aside. During the ten-year period of his retirement beginning in 1935, he disavowed some of these earlier ambitions and returned to the use of modern realism, which resulted in two major works: *The Iceman Cometh* and *Long Day's Journey into Night*.

Although Bernard Shaw once called O'Neill, "a banshee Shakespeare," he left us a priceless legacy in American drama by consistently demonstrating how human destiny affects an individual. His dedication to his chosen art and his driving ambition eventually gained O'Neill four Pulitzer Prize awards[1] and he remains America's only Nobel Prize dramatist.

PREPARATION FOR LONG DAY'S JOURNEY INTO NIGHT

This autobiographical play, written in 1940, was not produced until 1956, after O'Neill's death. It is a play of "old sorrow, written in tears and blood," according to his dedication, in which he was able "to face my dead at last" and to "write it with deep pity and understanding and forgiveness for all the four haunted Tyrones."

Working with a conventional family premise, O'Neill was able to permeate his play with more profound dimensions by comparing youthful dreams and ambitions with the tragic realities of life. Family relationships are not stable in this play but alternate between love and sharp painful condemnations. Characters are masterfully drawn and developed. Critic Henry Hewes has said, "Each of the quartet (the Tyrones) advances from morning's surface jocularity into evening's soul-shaking revelations of self-truth."[2]

Long Day's Journey into Night may be Eugene O'Neill's finest play and some believe it the greatest tragedy ever written by an American playwright. The following excerpt from Act III is revealing of the mother character in this play.

Mary is described by O'Neill as being fifty-four, of medium height, and still in possession of her young graceful figure, although her hair has turned white. Her hands are never still, rheumatism has knotted her fingers and she is sensitive about them. Her voice is soft and musical, contributing to her simple unaffected charm as well as to her unworldly innocence brought about by being isolated and bereft of all but conventional wifely protection. As a child she was sheltered and convent-schooled; it was not until after her marriage that she was exposed to a world of cheap hotel rooms, alcohol, tobacco; her husband's drunken cronies, his penuriousness, and his former mistress.

O'Neill conferred upon this character (for which his own mother served as model) a kind of pathetic and tragic dignity. From the agonies of childbirth, increased because of her husband's stinginess in hiring a

---

[1]Pulitzer prizes were awarded O'Neill for *Beyond the Horizon* (1920), *Anna Christie* (1921), *Strange Interlude* (1928), *Long Day's Journey into Night* (1956). The Nobel Prize for literature was awarded him in 1936.

[2]From *Saturday Review*, November 24, 1956.

cheap doctor, she experiences her first release — through morphine. Dope is her way back into her girlish dreams and the security of the convent life.

The other character in this excerpt is the serving girl, Cathleen, who is ignorant and bumptious, although cheerful, hearty, and loyal. She stands left of the table which is just off center stage, an empty whiskey glass in her hand, and shows the effects of her drinks. Mary is pale, but her eyes shine with an unnatural brilliance. As she sits at the table RC she alternates a mood of gay youthfulness with a dark introspective detachment. They have returned from town where they have made an important purchase.

REHEARSAL

LONG DAY'S JOURNEY INTO NIGHT*

An Excerpt from ACT III
(Pulitzer Prize Play for 1957)

2 females

CATHLEEN: The way the man in the drugstore acted when I took in the prescription for you.

Indignantly.

The impidence of him!

MARY: *With stubborn blankness.*

What are you talking about? What drugstore? What prescription?

Then hastily, as Cathleen stares in stupid amazement.

Oh, of course, I'd forgotten. The medicine for the rheumatism in my hands. What did the man say?[1]

Then with indifference.

Not that it matters, as long as he filled the prescription.

CATHLEEN: [2]It mattered to me, then! I'm not used to being treated like a thief. He gave me a long look and says insultingly, "Where did you get hold of this?" and I says, "It's none of your damned business, but if you must know, it's for the lady I work for, Mrs. Tyrone, who's sitting out in the automobile." That shut him up quick. He gave a look out at you and said, "Oh," and went to get the medicine.

MARY: *Vaguely.*

[3]Yes, he knows me.

LONG DAY'S JOURNEY INTO NIGHT, AN OUTSTANDING SUCCESS OF THE NATIONAL THEATRE OF GREAT BRITAIN. LAURENCE OLIVIER STARRED AS JAMES TYRONE. (PHOTO BY ZOE DOMINIC, COURTESY OF THE NATIONAL THEATRE.)

1. Mary walks to screen door at R.

2. Puts down glass.

3. Looking out the screen door.

TWENTIETH-CENTURY DRAMA   275

She sits in the armchair at right rear of table. She adds in a calm, detached voice.

I have to take it because there is no other that can stop the pain—*all* the pain—I mean, in my hands.

She raises her hands and regards them with melancholy sympathy. There is no tremor in them now.

Poor hands! You'd never believe it, but they were once one of my good points, along with my hair and eyes, and I had a fine figure, too.

Her tone has become more and more far-off and dreamy.

They were a musician's hands. I used to love the piano. I worked so hard at my music in the Convent—if you can call it work when you do something you love. Mother Elizabeth and my music teacher both said I had more talent than any student they remembered. My father paid for special lessons. He spoiled me. He would do anything I asked. He would have sent me to Europe to study after I graduated from the Convent. I might have gone—if I hadn't fallen in love with Mr. Tyrone. Or I might have become a nun. I had two dreams. To be a nun, that was the more beautiful one. To become a concert pianist, that was the other.

She pauses, regarding her hands fixedly. Cathleen blinks her eyes to fight off drowsiness and a tipsy feeling.

I haven't touched a piano in so many years. I couldn't play with such crippled fingers, even if I wanted to. For a time after my marriage I tried to keep up my music. But it was hopeless. One-night stands, cheap hotels, dirty trains, leaving children, never having a home—

She stares at her hands with fascinated disgust.

See, Cathleen, how ugly they are! So maimed and crippled! You would think they'd been through some horrible accident!

She gives a strange little laugh.

So they have, come to think of it.

She suddenly thrusts her hands behind her back.

I won't look at them. They're worse than the foghorn for reminding me—

Then with defiant self-assurance

But even they can't touch me now.

She brings her hands from behind her back and deliberately stares at them— calmly.

They're far away. I see them, but the pain has gone.

CATHLEEN: *Stupidly puzzled.*

You've taken some of the medicine? It made you act funny, Ma'am.[4] If I didn't know better, I'd think you'd a drop taken.

MARY: *Dreamily.*

It kills the pain. You go back until at last you are beyond its reach. Only the past when you were happy is real.

STYLES IN ACTING

4. Cathleen walks a step UL, then returns as an afterthought.

She pauses—then as if her words had been an evocation which called back happiness she changes in her whole manner and facial expressions. She looks younger. There is a quality of an innocent convent girl about her, and she smiles shyly.

If you think Mr. Tyrone is handsome now, Cathleen, you should have seen him when I first met him. He had the reputation of being one of the best looking men in the country. The girls in the Convent who had seen him act, or seen his photographs, used to rave about him. He was a great matinee idol then, you know. Women used to wait at the stage door just to see him come out. You can imagine how excited I was when my father wrote me he and James Tyrone had become friends, and that I was to meet him when I came home for Easter vacation. I showed the letter to all the girls, and how envious they were![5] My father took me to see him act first. It was a play about the French Revolution and the leading part was a nobleman. I couldn't take my eyes off him. I wept when he was thrown in prison—and then was so mad at myself because I was afraid my eyes and nose would be red. My father had said we'd go backstage to his dressing room right after the play, and so we did.

5. Cathleen chuckles from interest and sympathy.

She gives a little excited, shy laugh.

I was so bashful all I could do was stammer and blush like a little fool. But he didn't seem to think I was a fool. I know he liked me the first moment we were introduced.

Coquettishly.

I guess my eyes and nose couldn't have been red, after all. I was really very pretty then, Cathleen. And he was handsomer than my wildest dream, in his make-up and his nobleman's costume that was so becoming to him. He was different from all ordinary men, like someone from another world. At the same time he was simple, and kind, and unassuming, not a bit stuck-up or vain. I fell in love right then. So did he, he told me afterwards. I forgot all about becoming a nun or a concert pianist. All I wanted was to be his wife.

She pauses, staring before her with unnaturally bright, dreamy eyes, and a rapt, tender, girlish smile.

Thirty-six years ago, but I can see it as clearly as if it were tonight! We've loved each other ever since. And in all those thirty-six years, there has never been a breath of scandal about him. I mean, with any other woman. Never since he met me. That has made me very happy, Cathleen. It has made me forgive so many other things.

THE LIVING PLAYS OF EUGENE O'NEILL

Bound East for Cardiff (1916)
In the Zone (1917)
Long Voyage Home (1917)
Ile (1917)
Beyond the Horizon (1920)
Anna Christie (1921)
Emperor Jones (1920)
The Hairy Ape (1922)

Desire under the Elms (1924)
The Great God Brown (1926)
Lazarus Laughed (1927)
Strange Interlude (1928)
Mourning Becomes Electra (1931)
Ah, Wilderness! (1933)
Long Day's Journey into Night (1940)
The Iceman Cometh (1946)

FURTHER READING

Alexander, Doris. *The Tempering of Eugene O'Neill.* New York: Harcourt, 1962.

Clark, Barrett. *Eugene O'Neill, The Man and his Plays.* New York: Dover, 1947.

Gelb, Arthur, and Gelb, Barbara. *O'Neill.* New York: Harper, 1962. Recommended.

Leech, Clifford. *Eugene O'Neill.* New York: Grove Press, 1963.

BERTOLT BRECHT (1898-1956)

It may seem that just as we are getting an acting style established in our minds, someone comes along who says, "No, no, that's not the way to act. *I* will show you how." We have gone from Classical to Commedia, to Elizabethan, to Restoration, to Realism, to—will it never end? Probably not; an art cannot remain static and live.

Expressionism

Early in this century, the theatre was almost completely dominated by naturalism. There was Stanislavski in Russia, André Antoine in France, Granville Barker in England, and, in middle Europe, Saxe-Meiningen and Brahm. But after the First World War, there began a revolt against this style. In such expressionistic plays as Toller's *Man and Masses,* Kaiser's *Morn to Midnight,* Rice's *Adding Machine,* and O'Neill's *Hairy Ape* and *Emperor Jones,* naturalism was replaced by a style that was frankly theatrical. In writing, acting, and producing, the aim was to express certain impressions; for instance, in *The Hairy Ape,* there was no attempt to make people walking along Fifth Avenue look or behave like real people. They walked like automatons and wore masks; they were created to express a thought and not imitate nature. However, the emotional content was similar to the realistic theatre.

At the end of another world war, there appeared the "lost generation" of disillusioned young artists, among them a German poet named Bertolt Brecht. Realism was all wrong for his day, Brecht maintained. His would be a "scientific" theatre, for a scientific age. It was his belief that the lives of individuals could no longer be portrayed on the stage apart from social and economic conditions. He contended that the theatre should dispense with vulgar emotionalism and that it should be a "learning theatre."

Brecht was a Marxist, but he was openly denounced by the U.S.S.R. To make matters worse, the Russian theatre officially approved and adopted the Stanislavski system that represented everything of which Brecht disapproved; that is, the transfigured actor, the emotionally moved audience, and the naturalism of the presentation.

Brechtian Theories

Brecht's theory of acting was based on the concept of *Verfremdung* or "Alienation," the so-called A effect. (The German word *Verfremdung* might be translated as "seeming odd to.") This did not imply that he wanted the audience to be alienated from the play or the players; rather, he wished to create in the audience and the actors a detached attitude toward the performance. He proposed the opposite of the realistic theory, which sought to create an empathy between actor and audience, audience and play.[3]

In preparing one of Brecht's plays using his acting theories, our first step will be to purge our minds of every effort to reproduce reality.[4] Our accent must be on how events happen, and not on the emotions of the people they happen to. The acting approach needs to be abstract and objective, with only one timid finger touching reality.

The "A effect" eliminates the magic along with what Brecht calls the "hypnotic tensions" of emotionalism. In our attitude toward our audience, we must not try to create any empathy. We must dehumanize our bodies and personalities. We *don't want the audience to "feel" for our characters—indeed, as actors, we are not going to feel for them ourselves. We are going to stand back and observe them!* We must keep in mind that his plays are "learning plays," that his is a theatre of instruction. As actors we are going to be surprised at our characters. Always there will be the shock of recognition. As Brecht himself explains, "To see one's mother as a man's wife, one needs the 'A effect'—for instance, when one acquires a stepfather."[5]

Actors are to become *demonstrators*, such as an eyewitness describing an event who does not become personally involved in it. We are reporters. It is the difference between seeing a riot on TV and hearing a newscaster tell about it.

Brecht often attempted to make this point clear by giving an illustration. Let us try to find his meaning by means of an experience.

[3]Peter Demitz, *Brecht* (Englewood Cliffs, N.J.: Prentice-Hall, 1962), pp. 106-116.
[4]John Willet, *Brecht on Theatre* (New York: Hill and Wang, 1959), p. 136.
[5]Ibid., p. 144.

One of our players pretends that he has been an eyewitness to an accident. Two other players are to be police officers questioning him about the circumstances.

The incident: An old man was standing on the curb, apparently trying to decide whether or not he would cross the street. A passing motorist saw him, but the old man, perhaps because of poor eyesight, did not see the approaching car. The driver of the car thought perhaps the old man had decided not to cross and proceeded ahead at the same time as the old man crossed. There was an instant when both seemed to know what was going to happen, but nothing could be done to prevent the tragedy. The old man was killed and the driver has been taken away for emergency treatment.

Attitude of the eyewitness: He has not been actively involved in the accident, being merely a spectator. He speaks of it in the past tense. The dramatic moment has passed. Therefore he is in a position to relate and make comment without bias. He acts out the limping old man, the moment of terror, the motorist's subsequent disturbances, what was said by each man, *all as he remembers them.* It has not been *his* tragedy. *He himself has not been or is not now emotionally involved.*

Attitude of policemen: The accident and the report are simply in their line of duty. Questions are asked according to a set form. One policeman fills out this form as answers are given. They do not suspect the man of being involved and do not accuse him. They are polite but insistent.

Our three actors should improvise dialogue for this exercise after becoming familiar with the above facts.

As we rehearse a play by Brecht, we study our characters in a critical, not in a sympathetic way. We see the character's folly or virtue, but we do not become involved; *we do not identify with him.*

As practical working actors, we begin by reading his play. Brecht asks us to be astounded and question not only the incidents in the play but the behavior of the character we are to play.[6] The actor must never *be*— he must *show* the character. To aid us, he suggests that we:

1. Transpose our characters into the third person.
2. Reset the action and incidents from present to past tense.
3. Speak aloud all of our stage directions during rehearsals.

From the start we have been seeking a method of detachment, or "Alienation." Asides are to be spoken directly to the audience. We will not try for any illusion that these asides are anything but information we are frankly giving to the audience. We will *show*, not *re-create* a particular incident, and we must above all avoid being "universally human."[7]

---

[6]Ronald Gray, *Brecht* (Edinburgh and London: Oliver and Boyd, 1961), pp. 65-70.
[7]See Martin Esslin, *Brecht, The Man and His Work* (New York: Doubleday, 1960), pp. 141-42, for comparison to the villain in old melodramas.

Assume that we have prepared our play earnestly and sincerely along these lines and are now ready to show it to an audience. *Remember, from the first we have been to great pains to prevent our audience from any empathy toward the play or the characters.* What happens? They cry for *Mother Courage.* Their hearts break for the plight of *The Jewish Wife. They are deeply moved!*[8]

If the "Alienation" effect is to be given a fair chance, it may be that we will need plays which do not involve everyone so much. To the end of his life, Brecht lamented that his plays were being misunderstood, that spectators should not be emotionally involved. But Bertolt Brecht was a brilliant man of the theatre. He filled the stage with his originality in lighting, projections, signs, symbols, poetry, music, masks—in other words, he had a genius for creating Theatre. Although he tried to avoid the beautiful, the lyrical, or anything directly moving, we are fortunate that he failed. The English theatrical critic, Kenneth Tynan, was "unmoved by what Brecht had to say but overwhelmed by the way in which he said it."[9]

PREPARATION FOR THE GOOD WOMAN OF SETZUAN

In this play, Brecht uses a device which served Robert Louis Stevenson years ago when writing *The Strange Case of Dr. Jekyll and Mr. Hyde.* In most dramas, conflict is expressed by a hero struggling against a villain, or fate, or "the system," or some other force. But in *Dr. Jekyll* and *Good Woman,* the conflict is within one character. The evil alter-ego becomes an *actual physical embodiment.* In both these plays, the physical transference from good to bad and from bad to good is witnessed by the audience.

Duality in characters has become a favorite device of the so-called avant-garde playwright. Such roles are challenging to an actor. Actual physical changes must be made so that there is no confusion in the minds of the audience as to which character is occupying their immediate attention. And yet the change must not seem pat or contrived. There is a constant danger that an audience will recognize the device *as a device*— and if they do, the tendency is to laugh.

It is easy—too easy—to characterize a hard, practical businessman by relying upon memories of other actors in similar parts. There is only one solution—personal observation. Find a man you know who is more interested in money than in his fellow-man, and observe at first hand how he behaves. His greed will be shown in some way. Similarly, does a "good woman" really talk in saccharine tones and mince about with hesitant steps? Learn from your own *observation*—then *select, adapt, and develop these two characterizations imaginatively.*

Shen Te, the "Good Woman" of Setzuan, befriends three shabby little gods and is rewarded with riches. But Shen Te cannot bear the sight of human suffering and begins to share her good fortune. Her unselfishness does not come from any sense of moral obligation but is a spontaneous expression of her kind nature. However, others take advantage of it,

[8]Esslin, *Brecht,* p. 234.

[9]Kenneth Tynan, *Curtains* (New York: Atheneum, 1961), p. 389.

and she is surrounded by a wolf pack of spongers, so that she cannot continue. It is painful for her to be unkind to others, and so she invents a male "cousin," Shui Ta, a calculating profit-minded businessman. The theme according to John Willet is "that in a competitive society goodness is often suicidal."[10] But time after time, Brecht's expressed intentions are defeated by his extraordinary gift for writing vivid and moving drama; the "message" is lost. We find only admiration for Shen Te's courage and her devotion towards her fellow-man.

The physical disguise of Shen Te as Shui Ta must meet two requirements: (1) the actress must be able to change quickly in full view of the audience, and (2) the audience must believe that other characters would be fooled by the disguise.

The solution reached in the photograph shown meets both requirements admirably. The actress wears a long Chinese robe which might be worn by a male or female. A hard hat and mask complete the change. The rest is left to the actress's imagination. But she must manage convincing interpretations for both Shui Ta and Shen Te.

In Brecht's own production, Shui Ta was in European clothes, mask, and stilts (similar to the Greek *cotherni*). I mention all this about costumes, not because we are concerned with them in this exercise, but because everyone (including the audience) should be *aware* of them.

THE GOOD WOMAN OF SETZUAN AS PERFORMED AT THE STUDIO THEATRE, MUNICH. PRODUCED BY HANS SCHWEIKART, SETTINGS BY CASPER NEHER. (FROM *THE THEATRE IN GERMANY.* REPRINTED BY PERMISSION OF F. BRUCKMANN VERLAG.)

[10]John Willet, *Brecht on Theatre.*

STYLES IN ACTING

THE GOOD WOMAN OF SETZUAN*

An Excerpt from SCENE x

Translated by Eric Bentley

CAST: SHUI TA ⎱ ONE PERSON   MR. SHU FU
       SHEN TE ⎰   YANG SUN
       MRS. MI TZU   WONG, THE CARPENTER
       MRS. YANG   GRANDFATHER
       THE NIECE   THE OLD MAN
       MRS. SHIN   THE POLICEMAN
       THE OLD WOMAN   THE UNEMPLOYED MAN
       SISTER-IN-LAW   THREE GODS (AS JUDGES)

SCENE: *Courtroom. Groups: Shu Fu, the Barber, and Mrs. Mi Tzu; Yang Sun and Mrs. Yang; Wong, the Carpenter, the Grandfather, the Niece, the Old Man, the Old Woman; Mrs. Shin, the Policeman; the Unemployed Man, the Sister-in-Law.*

At rise: The Three Gods sit UBC in their regal judges' robes. Groups as indicated above are behind ropes to the L. There is a stool at RC. The Policeman leads in Shui Ta who walks with lordly steps from down left. The crowd whistles and jeers. Shui Ta turns up and sees the Judges for the first time. He is shocked, nearly faints, then regains control of himself. The Policeman raps his staff to open the proceedings.

FIRST GOD: Defendant Shui Ta, you are accused of doing away with your cousin Shen Te in order to take possession of her business. Do you plead guilty or not guilty?

SHUI TA: Not guilty, my lord.

FIRST GOD: (*Thumbing through the documents of the case*) The first witness is the policeman. I shall ask him to tell us something of the respective reputations of Miss Shen Te and Mr. Shui Ta.

POLICEMAN: [1]Miss Shen Te was a young lady who aimed to please, my lord. She liked to live and let live, as the saying goes. Mr. Shui Ta, on the other hand, is a man of principle. Though the generosity of Miss Shen Te forced him at times to abandon half-measures, unlike the girl he was always on the side of the law, my lord. One time, he even unmasked a gang of thieves to whom his too trustful cousin had given shelter. The evidence, in short, my lord, proves that Mr. Shui Ta was *incapable* of the crime of which he stands accused!

1. He stands in place to the L of the Gods, but turns to them when addressed.

FIRST GOD: I see. And are there others who could testify along, shall we say, the same lines?

(Shu Fu rises)

POLICEMAN: (Whispering to Gods) Mr. Shu Fu—a very important person.

FIRST GOD: (Inviting him to speak) Mr. Shu Fu![2]

SHU FU: Mr. Shui Ta is a businessman, my lord. Need I say more?

FIRST GOD: Yes.

SHU FU: Very well, I will. He is Vice President of the Council of Commerce and is about to be elected a Justice of the Peace.

(He returns to his seat. Mrs. Mi Tzu rises)

WONG: Elected! He gave him the job![3]

(With a gesture the First God asks who Mrs. Mi Tzu is.)

POLICEMAN: Another very important person, Mrs. Mi Tzu.

FIRST GOD: (Inviting her to speak) Mrs. Mi Tzu!

MRS. MI TZU: My lord, as Chairman of the Committee on Social Work, I wish to call attention to just a couple of eloquent facts: Mr. Shui Ta not only has erected a model factory with model housing in our city, he is a regular contributor to our home for the disabled.[4] (She returns to her seat)

POLICEMAN: (Whispering) And she's a great friend of the judge that ate the goose!

FIRST GOD: (To the Policeman) Oh, thank you. What next? (To the Court, genially) Oh, yes.[5] We should find out if any of the evidence is less favorable to the defendant. (Wong, the Carpenter, the Old Man, the Old Woman, the Unemployed Man, the Sister-in-Law, and the Niece come forward)

POLICEMAN: (Whispering) Just the riffraff, my lord.

FIRST GOD: (Addressing the "riffraff") Well, um, riffraff—do you know anything of the defendant, Mr. Shui Ta?

WONG: [6]Too much, my lord.

UNEMPLOYED MAN: What don't we know, my lord.

CARPENTER: He ruined us.

SISTER-IN-LAW: He's a cheat.

NIECE: Liar.

WIFE: Thief.

BOY: Blackmailer.

BROTHER: Murderer.

FIRST GOD: Thank you. We should now let the defendant state his point of view.[7]

SHUI TA: [8]I only came on the scene when Shen Te was in danger of losing what I had understood was a gift from the gods. Because I did the filthy jobs which someone had to do, they hate me. My activities were restricted to the minimum, my lord.

SISTER-IN-LAW: He had us arrested!

2. Shu Fu already standing behind the ropes.

3. Shu Fu is pushed back into the crowd by Mrs. Mi Tzu, Shen Te's landlady.

4. Mrs. Mi Tzu is threatened. She fights back, and is pushed to the rear as Wong, the carpenter, and others come forward to the front to the limits of the ropes.

5. As soon as order has been restored, the Gods look at each other and smile in satisfaction. Then the first God turns and smiles at the mob.

6. Wong has been waiting this chance. He does not speak but explodes, and the others are caught up in his fury as they shout their accusations. Wong has a bandaged hand.

7. The God smiles. There is a pause. We know he hasn't heard a word or refuses to be concerned with their accusations.

8. He speaks in calm, soothing tones.

SHUI TA: Certainly. You stole from the bakery!

SISTER-IN-LAW: [9]Such concern for the bakery! You didn't want the shop for yourself, I suppose!

SHUI TA: I didn't want the shop overrun with parasites.

SISTER-IN-LAW: We had nowhere else to go.

SHUI TA: There were too many of you.

WONG: What about this old couple: Were *they* parasites?

OLD MAN: We lost our shop because of you!

OLD WOMAN: And we gave your cousin money!

SHUI TA: My cousin's fiancé was a flyer. The money had to go to *him*.[10]

WONG: Did you care whether he flew or not? Did you care whether she married him or not? You wanted her to marry someone else! (*He points at Shu Fu*)

SHUI TA: The flyer unexpectedly turned out to be a scoundrel.

YANG SUN: (*Jumping up*) Which was the reason you made him your manager?[11]

SHUI TA: Later on he improved.

WONG: And when he improved, you sold him to her? (*He points out Mrs. Mi Tzu*)

SHU TA: She wouldn't let me have her premises unless she had him to stroke her knees!

MRS. MI TZU: What? The man's a pathological liar. (*To him*) Don't mention my property to me as long as you live! Murderer![12] (*She rustles off in high dudgeon.*) ·

YANG SUN: (*Pushing in*) [13]My lord, I wish to speak for the defendant.

SISTER-IN-LAW: Naturally. He's your employer.

UNEMPLOYED MAN: And the worst slave driver in the country.

MRS. YANG: That's a lie! My lord, Mr. Shui Ta is a great man. He . . .

YANG SUN: He's this and he's that, but he is not a murderer, my lord. Just fifteen minutes before his arrest I heard Shen Ti's voice in his own back room.

FIRST GOD: Oh?[14] Tell us more!

YANG SUN: I heard sobbing, my lord!

FIRST GOD: But lots of women sob, we've been finding.

YANG SUN: Could I fail to recognize her voice?

SHU FU: No, you made her sob so often yourself, young man!

YANG SUN: Yes. But I also made her happy. Till he (*pointing at Shui Ta*) decided to sell her to you!

SHUI TA: Because you didn't love her.

WONG: Oh, no; it was for the money, my lord!

SHUI TA: And what was the money for, my lord? For the poor! And for Shen Te so she could go on being good!

WONG: [15]For the poor? That he sent to his sweatshops? And why didn't

9. She turns to the others for support—and gets it.

10. Mrs. Mi Tzu again has worked her way through the crowd to the ropes.

11. Yang Sun snarls at Shui Ta, shaking his fist and trying to get at him under the ropes. The Policeman steps forward and gets him back in place.

12. She again disappears into the group.

13. Mrs. Yang is Yang Sun's mother.

14. A beat, as the Gods look at each, wondering about this new evidence.

15. The angry Wong finally gets through the crowd again to the ropes.

you let Shen Te be good when you signed the big check?

SHUI TA: For the child's sake, my lord.

CARPENTER: What about *my* children? What did he do about them? (*Shui Ta is silent*)

WONG: The shop was to be a fountain of goodness. [16]That was the gods' idea. You came and spoiled it!

SHUI TA: If I hadn't, it would have run dry!

MRS. SHIN: There's a lot in that, my lord.

WONG: What have you done with the good Shen Te, bad man? She *was* good, my lords, she was, I swear it! (*He raises his hand in an oath*)

THIRD GOD: What's happened to your hand, water seller?

WONG: (*Pointing to Shui Ta*) It's all his fault, my lord, *she* was going to send me to a doctor — (*To Shui Ta*) You were her worst enemy!

SHUI TA: I was her only friend!

WONG: Where is she then? Tell us where your good friend is![17] (*The excitement of this exchange has run through the whole crowd*)

ALL: Yes, where is she? Where is Shen Te? (*Etc.*)

SHUI TA: Shen Te . . . had to go.

WONG: Where? Where to?

SHUI TA: I cannot tell you! I cannot tell you!

ALL: Why? Why did she have to go away? (*Etc.*)

WONG: (*Into the din with the first words, but talking on beyond the others*) Why not, why not! Why did she have to go away?

SHUI TA: (*Shouting*) Because you'd all have torn her to shreds, that's why! My lords, I have a request. Clear the court! When only the judges remain, I will make a confession.

ALL: (*Except Wong, who is silent, struck by the new turn of events*) So he's guilty? He's confessing! (*Etc.*)[18]

FIRST GOD: (*Using the gavel*) Clear the court!

POLICEMAN: Clear the court!

WONG: Mr. Shui Ta has met his match this time.

MRS. SHIN: (*With a gesture toward the judges*) You're in for a little surprise. (*The court is cleared. Silence.*)

SHUI TA: Illustrious ones![19]

   (*The Gods look at each other, not quite believing their ears*)

SHUI TA: Yes, I recognize you!

SECOND GOD: (*Taking matters in hand, sternly*) What have you done with our good woman of Setzuan?

SHUI TA: I have a terrible confession to make: I am she! (*He takes off his mask, and tears away his clothes. Shen Te stands there.*)

SECOND GOD: Shen Te![20]

SHEN TE: Shen Te, yes. Shui Ta *and* Shen Te. Both.
 Your injunction

16. This scene must build in tempo and vehemence. There must be give and take between the Gods and Shui Ta against the group. Within the group itself there is fighting. There is one clique within the group who agree and support each other. But the group should be constantly agreeing or disapproving of the proceedings. The First God quiets them with his gavel or the Policeman threatens. When there is silence, the God speaks in a high, sustained tone of calm.

17. This is the climax. The scene should start calmly, but little by little build to this point.

18. Now satisfied that Shui Ta will confess, they hurry out to discuss it outside.

19. This is the salutation used by Shen Te when she befriended them. They are surprised at Shui Ta using it in Shen Te's voice and with her manner.

20. Shui Ta changes into Shen Te before their eyes. For a moment the Gods cannot speak.

To be good and yet to live
Was a thunderbolt;
It has torn me in two
I can't tell how it was
But to be good to others
And myself at the same time
I could not do it
Your world is not an easy one, illustrious ones!
When we extend our hand to a beggar, he tears it off for us
When we help the lost, we are lost ourselves
And so
Since not to eat is to die
Who can long refuse to be bad?
As I lay prostrate beneath the weight of good intentions
Ruin stared me in the face
It was when I was unjust that I ate good meat
And hobnobbed with the mighty
Why?
Why are bad deeds rewarded?
Good ones punished?
I enjoyed giving
I truly wished to be the Angel of the Slums
But washed by a foster-mother in the water of the gutter
I developed a sharp eye
The time came when pity was a thorn in my side
And, later, when kind words turned to ashes in my mouth
And anger took over
I became a wolf
Find me guilty, then, illustrious ones,[21]
But know:
All that I have done I did
To help my neighbor
To love my lover
And to keep my little one from want
For your great, godly deeds, I was too poor, too small.

(Pause)

FIRST GOD: (*Shocked*) Don't go on making yourself miserable,[22] Shen Te! We're overjoyed to have found you!

SHEN TE: [23]I'm telling you I'm the bad man who committed all those crimes!

FIRST GOD: (*Using—or failing to use—his ear trumpet*) The good woman who did all those good deeds?

SHEN TE: Yes, but the bad man too!

21. The Gods smile at each beatifically. All is right with the world.

22. Soothingly, with paternal assurances.

23. Trying hard to convince them of her guilt.

FIRST GOD: (*As if something had dawned*) Unfortunate coincidences! Heartless neighbors!

THIRD GOD: (*Shouting in his ear*) But how is she to continue?

FIRST GOD: Continue? Well, she's a strong, healthy girl . . .

SECOND GOD: You didn't hear what she said!

FIRST GOD: I heard every word! She is confused, that's all![24] (*He begins to bluster*) And what about this book of rules—we can't renounce our rules, can we? (*More quietly*) Should the world be changed? How? By whom? The world should *not* be changed![25] (*At a sign from him, the lights turn pink, and music plays*)

> [26]And now the hour of parting is at hand.
> Dost thou behold, Shen Te, yon fleecy cloud?
> It is our chariot. At a sign from me
> 'Twill come and take us back from whence we came
> Above the azure vault and silver stars. . . .

SHEN TE: No! Don't go, illustrious ones!

FIRST GOD:

> Our cloud has landed now in yonder field
> From whence it will transport us back to heaven,
> Farewell, Shen Te, let not thy courage fail thee. . . .

(*Exeunt Gods*)[27]

THE LIVING PLAYS OF BERTOLT BRECHT

Baal (1918-1920)	*Mother Courage* (1939)
In the Jungle of the Cities (1921-1923)	*Galileo* (1938-1939)
A Man's a Man (1924-1925)	*The Good Woman of Setzuan* (1938-1940)
Three Penny Opera (1928)	*The Caucasian Chalk Circle* (1944-1945)
Saint Joan of the Stockyards (1929-1930)	

FURTHER READING:

Brecht, Bertolt, *Parables for the Theatre.* Translated by Eric Bentley. Minneapolis: University of Minnesota Press, 1961.

Esslin, Martin. *Brecht, the Man and His Work.* New York: Doubleday, 1960.

Gray, Ronald. *Brecht.* New York: Grove Press, 1961.

Munk, Erica, ed. *Stanislavski and America.* New York: Hill & Wang, 1966. See Eric Bentley's article "Stanislavski and Brecht," pp. 116-123.

Willet, John. *Brecht on Theatre.* New York: Hill & Wang, 1959.

Weideli, Walter. *The Art of Bertolt Brecht.* New York: New York University Press, 1963.

24. Confident and sure of himself.

25. She feels all alone, pleading with them on her knees.

26. Almost a benediction.

27. Shen Te looks about helplessly as she rises; there is no one to help her. She sinks into the chair in despair.

STYLES IN ACTING

20
Theatre Today

The "new theatre" is known by many names. Some call it the theatre of the Absurd, the Underground theatre, others refer to it as off-off Broadway, the theatre of Protest, or the New Wave. Those who do not care for it call it just another art fraud. Playwrights connected with it subscribe to none of these labels, preferring to have their work considered individually, apart from any movement or trend. Harold Pinter has been called the leading British playwright of the Absurd school and yet, in this connection, he has said, "I don't see any placards on myself, and I don't carry any banners. Ultimately, I distrust any definitive labels."[1] Whatever name modern playwrights go by, their plays seem influenced by the nineteenth century existentialist Sören Kierkegaard and the subsequent writings of Kafka and Joyce. The movement's association with the theatre might be said to have begun with Strindberg's "dream plays"; certainly Strindberg influenced these new playwrights. A closer relationship is perhaps found in the Ubu plays by Alfred Jarry produced in 1896. But the theatre of the Absurd got off to a real start in 1950 when Ionesco's *Bald Soprano* opened in Paris.

THE THEATRE OF THE ABSURD: "PANTOMIME OF PLACES," IMPROVISATION BY THE BAUHAUS STAGE, WEIMAR, 1924. (COURTESY FRAU OSKAR SCHLEMMER.)

[1]Harold Pinter, "Writing for Myself," *Twentieth Century*, 169, 1008 (February 1961): pp. 172-175.

STYLES IN ACTING

The leading characters in these plays are in marked contrast to the protagonists of old. Ibsen's heroes had goals to reach, or they wanted dignity; but the undignified characters of the Absurd can find nothing to attain. They drag aching feet as they move listlessly through a mental vacuum. Unlike O'Neill's ape man, they do not even want "to belong." Beckett's vagrant "heroes" of *Waiting for Godot* subject an audience to two hours of despair and self-pity, and the play ends exactly as it began, with nothing gained, nothing lost. How many of us could sit in that existential hell of a hotel room with the characters Sartre has invented for his *No Exit* and not feel a little ashamed of being human? Where other plays we have studied seek to free the spectator's mind of the petty or mean and elevate his thoughts by lofty themes and heroic achievements, the absurd theory of playwriting seems to depend upon the element of shock and sensation, rather than morality and human stature. Would you consider it enlightening to spend an evening with people who live in garbage cans and spout case histories from Jung and Freud? As Esslin has pointed out, these playwrights have done what Brecht failed to do—they have succeeded in alienation.

WHY "ABSURD"?

With advances in science and technology and the subsequent decline in formerly respected moral values, man seems more and more lost in the smog of the jet age. He feels estranged, separated from the standards of yesterday. Having lost all rapport with the world and himself, he is beset with a feeling of isolation and futility. He sits, waiting for someone to help, to give him answers; he is "waiting for Godot." The playwrights of this "school" ask that we see the utter ridiculousness of this absurd situation; perhaps they are even trying to "laugh us out of it," just as the would-be suicide in *Luv* is laughed out of his intention. They seem to be telling us that nothing can ever be fully explained and that this is the mystery of life. So we should relax, learn to accept things as they are; that this is the only way we will find out who we are and what we are doing here. The danger in this philosophy of disengagement is that the cure might become part of the disease.

We might conclude after examining the theatre of the Absurd that these plays deal with dehumanized characters set into plays which are not plays at all, and that they offer themes based on variations of a philosophy of futility. But if we are to be consistent in our policy of considering the pros and cons of each of our subjects, we shall be required to explain the reasons for the loud acclaim given these plays in every theatrical capital of the world—except New York. Even after admitting that there is a certain intellectual snob appeal toward anything new in art, we shall need to find other reasons for such popularity.

EUGENE IONESCO (1912-   )

PREPARATION FOR THE BALD SOPRANO

France has always been receptive to, and led the world in, art innovations. Several years ago Parisian audiences showed their disinterest in theatre as it was being presented. Thirty-two theatres closed, and box office receipts dropped to nearly two-fifths. But one small theatre was "packing them in." A new author, Ionesco, had a fresh kind of theatre. Realism was not enough for him.

Ionesco has been called an anti-playwright. He disliked the theatre, but while learning English, he copied out phrases from a copy book and arranged some of these fossilized words into a "play" and read it to some friends. He thought he was writing a tragedy of the breakdown in communication for which people substitute hollow slogans, dreary social clichés, and status phrases. To Ionesco's horror, his friends thought his play very funny.

In the excerpt we are using from this same play, *The Bald Soprano*, two people are trying to find identity. By use of embalmed speech, Ionesco is able to add an absurdity, a special rhythmic brightness, to the surface of what is basically a very human and comic situation. The scene becomes a caricature of reality, pointing up the ridiculousness of our everyday social conversation. It is a paradox, absurd, and a classic example of avant-garde playwriting.

The Bald Soprano is certainly not a well-made play; it is not even a play, but it is a startling piece of theatre. This play, and particularly this scene, was one of the opening salvos of the avant-garde revolution.

You will note in the author's directions that he frequently asks that his actors appear bored. He states, "The dialogue which follows must be spoken in voices that are drawling, monotonous, a little singsong without nuances." He wishes to convey to the audience the thought that communication between humans is difficult. Fine. The author's wish should also be the actor's. But in the first place, he has written monotony into his lines and it would seem to belabor the point to ask the actors to act bored. How much better it would be had he explained to his actors what he wished, then be respectful enough to permit them the means of accomplishing it! It is one thing to convey boredom and another thing to become boring to an audience.

But then Ionesco is not an actor, and never was. An actor knows primarily that he must interest his audience and that this audience has heretofore been reached by use of movement and word coloring. This is the language they understand. It would make an interesting exercise to first play the scene as Ionesco directs, then to play it again by coloring lines with everything that can be added by the players' imaginations and individualities. There is so little physical movement in the scene that an actor may "feel" the necessity of finding some means to interest his

STYLES IN ACTING

audience. One suggestion would be to show the thought process which results in a certain line being spoken, the reasons for saying the line before it is said.

REHEARSAL

THE BALD SOPRANO*

An Excerpt

Translated by Donald M. Allen

CAST: MRS. MARTIN
       MR. MARTIN

SETTING: *"A middle-class English Interior."* Needed: *two chairs placed at center stage, set at angles to give proper sight lines and a clock chime that can be loud or soft.*

At rise: *Mr. and Mrs. Martin sit facing each other without speaking. They smile timidly at each other.*

MR. MARTIN: Excuse me, madam, but it seems to me, unless I'm mistaken, that I've met you somewhere before.

MRS. MARTIN: I, too, sir. It seems to me that I've met you somewhere before.

MR. MARTIN: Was it, [1]by any chance, at Manchester that I caught a glimpse of you, madam?

MRS. MARTIN: That is very possible. I am originally from the city of Manchester. But I do not have a good memory, sir. I cannot say whether it was there that I caught a glimpse of you or not!

MR. MARTIN: Good God, that's curious! I, too, am originally from the city of Manchester, madam!

MRS. MARTIN: That is curious!

MR. MARTIN: Isn't that curious![2] Only I, madam, I left the city of Manchester about five weeks ago.

MRS. MARTIN: That is curious! What a bizarre coincidence! I, too, sir, I left the city of Manchester about five weeks ago.

MR. MARTIN: Madam, I took the 8:30 morning train which arrives in London at 4:45.

MRS. MARTIN: That is curious! How very bizarre! And what a coincidence! I took the same train, sir, I too.

1. Suggestion: Try awkward pauses between each new thought as Mr. Martin tries to think of something to make conversation.

2. By beginning this scene slowly and filling it with embarrassed looks and hesitations, the audience will become interested. Remember, this play's asset is its novelty.

MR. MARTIN: Good Lord, how curious! Perhaps then, madam, it was on the train that I saw you?

MRS. MARTIN: It is indeed possible; that is, not unlikely. It is plausible and, after all, why not![3]—But I don't recall it, sir!

MR. MARTIN: I travelled second class, madam. There is no second class in England, but I always travel second class.

MRS. MARTIN: That is curious! How very bizarre! And what a coincidence! I, too, sir, I travelled second class.

MR. MARTIN: How curious that is! Perhaps we did meet in second class, my dear lady!

MRS. MARTIN: That is certainly possible, and it is not at all unlikely. But I do not remember very well, my dear sir!

MR. MARTIN: [4]My seat was in coach No. 8, compartment 6, my dear lady.

MRS. MARTIN: How curious that is! My seat was also in coach No. 8, compartment 6, my dear sir!

MR. MARTIN: How curious that is and what a bizarre coincidence! Perhaps we met in compartment 6, my dear lady?

MRS. MARTIN: It is indeed possible, after all! But I do not recall it, my dear sir!

MR. MARTIN: To tell the truth, my dear lady, I do not remember it either, but it is possible that we caught a glimpse of each other there, and as I think of it, it seems to me even very likely.

MRS. MARTIN: Oh! truly, of course, truly, sir!

MR. MARTIN: How curious it is![5] I had seat No. 3, next to the window, my dear lady.

MRS. MARTIN: Oh, good Lord, how curious and bizarre. I had seat No. 6 next to the window, across from you, my dear sir.

MR. MARTIN: Good God, how curious that is and what a coincidence! We were then seated facing each other, my dear lady! It is there that we must have seen each other!

MRS. MARTIN: How curious it is! It is possible, but I do not recall it, sir!

MR. MARTIN: To tell the truth, my dear lady, I do not remember it either. However, it is very possible that we saw each other on that occasion.

MRS. MARTIN: It is true, but I am not at all sure of it, sir.

MR. MARTIN: Dear madam, were you not the lady who asked me to place her suitcase in the luggage rack and who thanked me and gave me permission to smoke?

MRS. MARTIN: But of course, that must have been I, sir. How curious it is, how curious it is, and what a coincidence!

MR. MARTIN: How curious it is, how bizarre, what a coincidence![6] And well, well, it was perhaps at that moment that we came to know each other, madame?

3. As Mrs. Martin agrees, Martin nods and smiles his approval, but then when she fails to recall, he immediately is crestfallen.

4. Martin hopefully attacks each fresh new thought.

5. At first crestfallen, then thinks of another possibility.

6. This has now become a refrain. It is spoken because there is a silence which should be filled with some sound.

STYLES IN ACTING

MRS. MARTIN: How curious it is and what a coincidence! It is indeed possible, my dear sir![7] However, I do not believe that I recall it.

MR. MARTIN: Nor do I, madam. (*A moment of silence. The clock strikes twice, then once.*) Since coming to London, I have resided in Bromfield Street, my dear lady.

MRS. MARTIN: How curious that is, how bizarre![8] I, too, since coming to London, I have resided in Bromfield Street, my dear sir.

MR. MARTIN: How curious that is, well then, well then, perhaps we have seen each other in Bromfield Street, my dear lady.

MRS. MARTIN: How curious that is, how bizarre! It is indeed possible, after all! But I do not recall it, my dear sir.

MR. MARTIN: I reside at No. 19, my dear lady.

MRS. MARTIN: How curious that is. I also reside at No. 19, my dear sir.

MR. MARTIN: Well then, well then, well then, well then, perhaps we have seen each other in that house, my dear lady?

MRS. MARTIN: It is indeed possible but I do not recall it, dear sir.

MR. MARTIN: My flat is on the fifth floor, No. 8, my dear lady.

MRS. MARTIN: How curious it is, good Lord, how bizarre! And what a coincidence! I too reside on the fifth floor in flat No. 8, dear sir!

MR. MARTIN: (*Musing*) How curious it is, how curious it is, how curious it is, and what a coincidence! You know, in my bedroom there is a bed, and it is covered with a green eiderdown. This room, with the bed and the green eiderdown is at the end of the corridor between the w.c.[9] and the bookcase, dear lady!

MRS. MARTIN: What a coincidence, good Lord, what a coincidence! My bedroom, too, has a bed with a green eiderdown and is at the end of the corridor, between the w.c., dear sir, and the bookcase!

MR. MARTIN: How bizarre, curious, strange! Then, madam, we live in the same room and we sleep in the same bed, dear lady. It is perhaps, there that we have met!

MRS. MARTIN: How curious it is and what a coincidence! It is indeed possible that we have met there, and perhaps even last night. But I do not recall it, dear sir!

MR. MARTIN: I have a little girl, my little daughter, she lives with me, dear lady. She is two years old, she's blond, she has a white eye and a red eye, she is very pretty, her name is Alice, dear lady.

MRS. MARTIN: What a bizarre coincidence! I, too, have a little girl. She is two years old, has a white eye and a red eye, she is very pretty, and her name is Alice, too, dear sir!

MR. MARTIN: (*In the same drawling, monotonous voice*)[10] How curious it is and what a coincidence! How bizarre! Perhaps they are the same, dear lady!

7. *Warn Clock.*

8. The refrain again, but once the pattern is established, it may be amusing to the audience to alter the reading. For instance, this time it could be read as if what she said solved everything and was indeed a great discovery.

9. w.c.: English expression for water closet, or bathroom.

10. Again the author reminds us that he expects the scene to be flat and colorless.

MRS. MARTIN: How curious it is! It is indeed possible, dear sir. (*A rather long moment of silence. The clock strikes 29 times. Mr. Martin, after having reflected at length, gets up slowly and, unhurriedly, moves toward Mrs. Martin, who, surprised by his solemn air, has also gotten up very quietly.*)

11. And again.

MR. MARTIN: (*In the same flat, monotonous voice, slightly sing-song*) [11]Then, dear lady, I believe that there can be no doubt about it, we have seen each other before and you are my own wife . . . Elizabeth, I have found you again! (*Mrs. Martin approaches Mr. Martin without haste. They embrace without expression. The clock strikes once, very loud. This striking of the clock must be so loud that it makes the audience jump. The Martins do not hear it.*)

MRS. MARTIN: Donald, it's you, darling! (*They sit together in the same armchair, their arms around each other, and fall asleep. The clock strikes several more times . . .*)

REHEARSAL

A NIGHT OUT*

Harold Pinter

An Excerpt from ACT II, SCENE ii

1 female
1 male

The kitchen. Mrs. Stokes is asleep, her head resting on the table, the cards disordered. The clock ticks. It is twelve o'clock.

Albert enters, closes the door softly, stops, looks at his mother and begins to creep up the stairs at back. Her voice stops him.

MOTHER: Albert!

1. He stops.

Albert! Is that you?

2. She goes to the kitchen door.

What are you creeping up the stairs for? Might have been a burglar. What would I have done then?

3. He descends slowly.

Creeping up the stairs like that. Give anyone a fright. Creeping up the stairs like that. You leave me in the house all alone . . .

4. She stops and regards him.

Look at you! Look at your suit. What's the matter with your tie, it's all

*From *A Night Out, Night School, Revue Sketches, Early Plays* by Harold Pinter. (New York: Grove Press, 1967), pp. 31-33. Copyright © 1961 by Harold Pinter. Reprinted by permission of Grove Press, Inc.

For an analysis of *A Night Out*, see Martin Esslin, *The Peopled Wound* (New York: Doubleday, 1970), pp. 91-95.

STYLES IN ACTING

crumpled, I pressed it for you this morning. Well, I won't even ask any questions. That's all. You look a disgrace.

5

What have you been doing, mucking about with girls?

6

Mucking about with girls, I suppose. Do you know what the time is? I fell asleep, right here at this table, waiting for you. I don't know what your father would say. Coming in this time of night. It's after twelve o'clock. In a state like that. Drunk, I suppose. I suppose your dinner's ruined. Well, if you want to make a convenience out of your own home, that's your business. I'm only your mother, I don't suppose that counts for much these days. I'm not saying any more. If you want to go mucking about with girls, that's your business.

7

Well, anyway, you'll have your dinner. You haven't eaten a single thing all night.

8

I wouldn't mind if you found a really nice girl and brought her home and introduced her to your mother, brought her home for dinner, I'd know you were sincere, if she was a really nice girl, she'd be like a daughter to me. But you've never brought a girl home here in your life. I suppose you're ashamed of your mother.

9

Come on, it's all dried up. I kept it on a low light. I couldn't even go up to Grandma's room and have a look round because there wasn't any bulb, you might as well eat it.

10

What's the matter, are you drunk? Where did you go, to one of those pubs in the West End? You'll get into serious trouble, my boy, if you frequent those places, I'm warning you. Don't you read the papers?

11

I hope you're satisfied, anyway. The house in darkness, I wasn't going to break my neck going down to that cellar to look for a bulb, you come home looking like I don't know what, anyone would think you gave me a fortune out of your wages. Yes. I don't say anything, do I? I keep quiet about what you expect me to manage on. I never grumble. I keep a lovely home, I bet there's none of the boys in your firm better fed than you are. I'm not asking for gratitude. But one thing hurts me, Albert, and I'll tell you what it is. Not for years, not for years, have you come up to me and said, Mum, I love you, like you did when you were a little boy. You've never said it without me having to ask you. Not since before your father died. And he was a good man. He had high hopes of you. I've never told you, Albert, about the high hopes he had of you. I don't know what you do with all your money. But don't forget what it cost us to rear you, my boy, I've never told you about the sacrifices we made, you wouldn't care, anyway. Telling me lies about going to the

5. He walks past her into the kitchen, goes to the sink and pours himself a glass of water. She follows him.

6. She begins to pile the cards.

7. She takes his dinner out of the oven.

8. She places a plate on the table and gets a knife and fork. He stands by the sink, sipping water.

9. Pause.

10. He stands.

11. Pause.

12. Albert lunges to the table, picks up the clock and violently raises it above his head. A stifled scream from the Mother.

firm's party. They've got a bit of respect at that firm, that's why we sent you there, to start off your career, they wouldn't let you carry on like that at any of their functions. Mr. King would have his eye on you. I don't know where you've been. Well, if you don't want to lead a clean life it's your lookout, if you want to go mucking about with all sorts of bits of girls, if you're content to leave your own mother sitting here till midnight, and I wasn't feeling well, anyway, I didn't tell you because I didn't want to upset you, I keep things from you, you're the only one I've got, but what do you care, you don't care, you don't care, the least you can do is sit down and eat the dinner I cooked for you, specially for you, it's Shepherd's Pie . . . ₁₂

EXPERIMENTAL THEATRE IN AMERICA

In his book *Theatre of Protest and Paradox,* Wellwarth remarks that the avant-garde movement has failed to produce any coherent body of work in America.[2] While our actors, directors, and producers are not indifferent to new developments, producing costs here are much higher than in Europe. Productions are always a gamble, even in the best of circumstances; American audiences support only the plays they wish to see. If *Waiting for Godot* and *Rhinoceros* had been commercial successes on Broadway, there would have been an avalanche of plays of the Absurd. They were not.

When costs made it impossible to experiment with untried plays on Broadway, smaller theatres were engaged in lower-rent districts, mostly in Greenwich Village. This movement became known as Off Broadway; there were regularly scheduled performances in licensed theatres, employing union actors and stage hands and inviting newspaper and magazine critics. In other words, it was little Broadway, complete with box office and regular ticket sales. Then, after it became established, rents were raised, unions became more demanding, and ticket prices soared.

This change created a need for another movement which became known as "off-off Broadway." These groups operate in lofts, cellars, churches, and libraries but, because of restrictions, are not allowed to sell tickets so they must rely on "membership fees" or grants to support their work. Usually, the actors are theatre students, novices, or at any rate, those who have other means of support. On off-off Broadway, a play's "run" is restricted by the unions to no more than nine performances.

With the question of economics solved, these groups allow new playwrights the opportunity to see their plays performed before audiences. If not directly influenced by the plays of the Absurd, the work of these young American playwrights might, at least, be considered of the same genre. They are certainly not structured plays in a traditional sense.

[2]George Wellwarth, *Theatre of Protest and Paradox* (New York: New York University Press, 1964).

STYLES IN ACTING

They reject plot, dealing only in situation. Out of the hundreds produced, I know of only one play that presents a memorable character. They are *types*—often identified only as General, Second Protestor, or Man—following Ionesco's example of calling his leading actors Berenger. Dialogue is undistinguished, given over to nonsequiturs; when a theme is apparent it is usually pessimistic; expressing dissent from life and/or society.

But off-off Broadway has opened doors for aspiring playwrights. These groups have also mounted the first full-scale attack upon realism, which has for too many years stifled fresh new forms and ideas in the theatre. These devoted professional-amateurs attempt to say things in a different way, choosing metaphors, not only authentic to interior and exterior patterns but also theatrically true. In many productions, startling effects have been achieved—by improvisation, through multimedia—films, swirling lights, blatant sounds, gigantic mannekins, masks, acrobatics—using stylization, imagination, and an impudent but exciting theatricality.

But the most important contribution of all the new movements is the return to older, purer forms of theatre. These movements have recaptured the marvelous, the illusion, that spirit of Shakespeare, Moliére, and the Commedia dell'Arte. Once again we may pay homage to the clown, that ancient symbol of man, bumbling about in a world he never seems to understand. Once again the stage has become an enchanted place, Alice's Wonderland, the abode of dwarfs and monsters and divine nonsense. This new theatre has given other dimensions to language. Characters speak gibberish or say what they do not mean, or mean what they never say because they distrust ordinary language as a means of communication. It has been called a theatre of reflecting mirrors, where reality blends almost imperceptibly into fantasy. It has proved that illusion does exist and that it cannot thrive in a climate of rationality and naturalism. But most important, from an acting standpoint, these theatres have demonstrated that characters can be vividly alive *without any human emotion or motivation.*

These playwrights have the avowed intent of tearing down realism and once again giving us Theatre. For this we can only admire their courage. If their work shocks us into getting up off our park benches and realizing that it is not in man's nature to quit but to survive, to meet every challenge and re-create values—then it has been a most worthwhile venture.

Acting in the Experimental Theatre

The foregoing discussion has been given to provide the actor with a few definitions, objectives, and also the pros and cons of the theatre of the Absurd. It is always part of the actor's preparation to be informed about the aims of his author.

The question is often asked, "How does one apply 'the method' to the plays of the avant-garde, to the poetic theatre of Shakespeare, to the 'epic' theatre of Brecht, and to the Restoration theatre?" The question itself presupposes that the Stanislavski system[3] is a kind of Lydia E. Pinkham cure-all. In fact, it evolved from requirements of the *realistic* theatre. *If swallowed whole, it is only applicable to that theatre.* But Stanislavski based his work on tested creative processes of older actors he had studied. This process includes an in-depth understanding of play and period, observation, concentration, motivation, imagination, a trained body and voice, and an examination of the inner drives of character. These are parts of Stanislavski's system and also part of the working technique of many fine actors long before he was born. Obviously the developments made for the particular requirements of realism serve little purpose in other types of drama.

It is not generally known that in 1905, Stanislavski himself predicted the break with realism when he wrote:

> . . . realism, and (depicting) the way of life have outlived their age. The time has come to stage the unreal. Not life itself, as it occurs in reality, must be depicted, but rather life as it is vaguely perceived in fantasies and visions at moments of lofty emotion. This is the spiritual situation that must be transmitted scenically, in the way that painters of the new school use cloth, musicians of the new trend write music, and the new poets, poetry. The works of these painters, musicians, and poets have no clear outlines, definite and finished melodies, or precisely expressed ideas. The power of the new art lies in its combinations of colors, lines, musical notes, and the rhyming of words. They create general moods that carry over to the public unconsciously. They create hints that make the most unobservant person create with his own imagination." [4]

It is much easier to explain *how not to act* the new plays than *how to act* them. The texture of each play is so different that it is impossible to generalize. Not only is each author unlike any other, but each play he writes may approach the absurd thesis from a different point of view. The creative acting process for de Ghelderode's *Women at the Tomb* would be different from the approach to the same author's *Pantagleize*. The first might be called a modern morality play; the second is more in the spirit of the Commedia. *It is the particular author's conception of a particular play which must be translated into acting terms by actors and director.*

Perhaps you are by now convinced that the actor of today needs to know many different styles of acting. Most actors resist this thought. *But all acting cannot be rolled into one single miracle pill.* Indeed, this is the great dilemma of today's actor. He has learned how to be intense with inner values, to explore minutiae, and he has learned his lessons well. But now

[3]Quite a difference has developed between "the method" and Stanislavski's system. Two actresses, highly publicized as being Method have never read Stanislavski. See Lewis Funke and John E. Booth, *Actors Talk about Acting* (New York: Random House, 1961), pp. 169 and 453.

[4]Konstantin Stanislavski *Moia zhizn' v iskusstve*, p. 501, as quoted in Nikolai A. Gorchakov, *The Theatre in Soviet Russia*, trans. by Edgar Lehrman (New York: Columbia University Press, 1957), p. 44.

he sees that playwrights and audiences are moving away from the depressing little rooms of realism in which he has specialized. Only the most insensitive will deny that audiences have become bored with the constant diet of box sets and "just plain folks." Broadway moves within the periphery of its own private world so much that perhaps it cannot see what is happening in the rest of the world and indeed in other cities of its own country. Another theatrical revolution has begun, and it is no longer practical for an actor to be a specialist in a single acting technique. *The new actor must have an integrated knowledge of basic creative fundamentals from which he can move easily with changes as they occur.*

This makes us wonder if older actors, trained and practiced for three decades in naturalism, can ever meet the challenge of today and tomorrow. It is difficult to abandon settled working habits once they become firmly entrenched. But it is not so difficult for younger minds and bodies to acquire new techniques; they have nothing to unlearn. Antoine could not get established professionals to abandon their old romantic style of acting and had to train amateurs in realism. Conditions today may represent a pendulum swing in the opposite direction.

These new plays need people who can project an idea more than an emotion, who know that there is a difference between style and "stylistic." The theatre of the Absurd demands acting that is conventionalized in form and actors who do not need to rely on emotion or spontaneity. Where are such actors to be found today?

The American commercial stage, TV, and films are such costly and ponderous industries that they seldom venture into experimentation. As a result, new plays, along with new actors, may find their hearing in the low-budget stages or in the educational theatre. It would seem to follow that a beginning actor, who has had some experience in acting the plays of Ionesco, van Itallie, or Pinter, might find an open door in the experimental theatres.

PREPARATION FOR "INTERVIEW" FROM AMERICA HURRAH!

In our next excerpt, from *America Hurrah!*, you will notice the author's use of short repetitious dialogue, the cliché phrase, and the constant defensive apology. Quite apart from the obvious comic effect these produce, they are typical devices to be found in the plays of Ionesco, Beckett, and the most successful of the absurdists, Harold Pinter.

Such repetition demonstrates the preoccupation of the characters with themselves and their own thoughts.

Itallie's "Interview" is reminiscent of one of Pinter's early revue sketches called "Applicant,"[5] except that in Pinter's writing the roles are somewhat characterized. The lack of any background, coloration, or personality kinks prevents Itallie's First Interviewer or Second Applicant

[5]Harold Pinter, "Applicant" in *The Dwarfs and Eight Revue Sketches* (New York: Dramatists Play Service 1965).

from being anything but *types*. This makes it difficult for actors to begin even the most primary construction of characters. The excerpt has been chosen because it can be an effective exercise in the use of timing and ensemble playing, which has become so important in working in contemporary plays.

REHEARSAL

AMERICA HURRAH!*

Jean-Claude van Itallie (1935-
An Excerpt from "Interview"

(A Best American Play and winner of the Vernon Rice Award, 1966)

For 4 females and 4 males

The First Inverviewer for an employment agency, a young woman, sits on stage as the First Applicant, a Housepainter, enters.

1. Standing.	FIRST INTERVIEWER:[1] How do you do?
2. Sitting.	FIRST APPLICANT:[2] Thank you, I said, not knowing where to sit.
3. The characters will often include the audience in what they say, as if they were being interviewed by the audience.	[3] FIRST INTERVIEWER:[4] Won't you sit down?
4. Pointedly.	FIRST APPLICANT:[5] I'm sorry.
5. Standing again quickly, afraid to displease.	FIRST INTERVIEWER:[6] There. Name, please?
	FIRST APPLICANT: Jack Smith.
6. Busy with imaginary papers, pointing to a particular seat.	FIRST INTERVIEWER: Jack what Smith?
	FIRST APPLICANT: Beg pardon?
	FIRST INTERVIEWER: Fill in the blank space, please. Jack blank space Smith.
7. Pointing.	FIRST APPLICANT: I don't have any.
8. Sitting.	FIRST INTERVIEWER: I asked you to sit down.[7] There.
	FIRST APPLICANT:[8] I'm sorry.
	FIRST INTERVIEWER: Name, please?
	FIRST APPLICANT: Jack Smith.
	FIRST INTERVIEWER: You haven't told me your MIDDLE name.
9. Suspicious, but writing it down.	FIRST APPLICANT: I haven't got one.
	FIRST INTERVIEWER:[9] No middle name.
10. Second Applicant, a woman Floorwasher, enters.	[10] FIRST INTERVIEWER: How do you do?

STYLES IN ACTING

SECOND APPLICANT:[11] Thank you, I said, not knowing what.

FIRST INTERVIEWER: Won't you sit down?

SECOND APPLICANT:[12] I'm sorry.

FIRST APPLICANT: I am sitting.

FIRST INTERVIEWER:[13] There. Name, please?

SECOND APPLICANT:[14] Jane Smith.

FIRST APPLICANT: Jack Smith.

FIRST INTERVIEWER: What blank space Smith?

SECOND APPLICANT: Ellen.

FIRST APPLICANT: Haven't got one.

FIRST INTERVIEWER: What job are you applying for?

FIRST APPLICANT: Housepainter.

SECOND APPLICANT: Floorwasher.

FIRST INTERVIEWER: We haven't many vacancies in that. What experience have you had?

FIRST APPLICANT: A lot.

SECOND APPLICANT: Who needs experience for floorwashing?

FIRST INTERVIEWER: You will help me by making your answers clear.

FIRST APPLICANT: Eight years.

SECOND APPLICANT: Twenty years.

FIRST INTERVIEWER: How do you do?[15]

SECOND APPLICANT: I'm good at it.

FIRST APPLICANT: Very well.

THIRD APPLICANT:[16] Thank you, I said, as casually as I could.

FIRST INTERVIEWER: Won't you sit down?

THIRD APPLICANT:[17] I'm sorry.

SECOND APPLICANT: I am sitting.

FIRST APPLICANT:[18] I'm sorry.

FIRST INTERVIEWER:[19] There. Name, please?

FIRST APPLICANT: Jack Smith.

SECOND APPLICANT: Jane Smith.

THIRD APPLICANT: Richard Smith.

FIRST INTERVIEWER: What *exactly* Smith, please?

THIRD APPLICANT: Richard F.

SECOND APPLICANT: Jane Ellen.

FIRST APPLICANT: Jack None.

FIRST INTERVIEWER: What are you applying for?

FIRST APPLICANT: Housepainter.

SECOND APPLICANT: I need money.

THIRD APPLICANT: Bank president.

FIRST INTERVIEWER: How many years have you been in your present job?

THIRD APPLICANT: Three.

SECOND APPLICANT: Twenty.

11. Sitting.

12. Standing.

13. Pointing.

14. Sitting.

15. Third Applicant, a Banker, enters.

16. Sitting.

17. Standing again.

18. Standing again.

19. Pointing to a particular seat.

	FIRST APPLICANT: Eight.
20. Fourth Applicant, a Lady's Maid, enters.	FIRST INTERVIEWER: How do you do?[20]
	FOURTH APPLICANT: I said thank you, not knowing where to sit.
	THIRD APPLICANT: I'm fine.
	SECOND APPLICANT: Do I have to tell you?
	FIRST APPLICANT: Very well.
	FIRST INTERVIEWER: Won't you sit down?
	FOURTH APPLICANT: I'm sorry.
21. Sitting again.	THIRD APPLICANT:[21] Thank you.
22. Standing again.	SECOND APPLICANT:[22] I'm sorry.
23. Sitting.	FIRST APPLICANT:[23] Thanks.
24. Pointing to a particular seat.	FIRST INTERVIEWER:[24] There. Name, please?
25. Fourth Applicant sits.	[25]
	ALL APPLICANTS: Smith.
	FIRST INTERVIEWER: What Smith?
	FOURTH APPLICANT: Mary Victoria.
	THIRD APPLICANT: Richard F.
	SECOND APPLICANT: Jane Ellen.
	FIRST APPLICANT: Jack None.
	FIRST INTERVIEWER: How many years' experience have you had?
	FOURTH APPLICANT: Eight years.
	SECOND APPLICANT: Twenty years.
	FIRST APPLICANT: Eight years.
	THIRD APPLICANT: Three years four months and nine days not counting vacations and sick leave and the time both my daughters and my wife had the whooping cough.
	FIRST INTERVIEWER: Just answer the questions, please.
	FOURTH APPLICANT: Yes, sir.
	THIRD APPLICANT: Sure.
	SECOND APPLICANT: I'm sorry.
	FIRST APPLICANT: That's what I'm doing.
26. Second Interviewer, a young man, enters and goes to inspect Applicants. With the entrance of each Interviewer, the speed of the action accelerates.	SECOND INTERVIEWER: How do you do?[26]
	FIRST APPLICANT:[27] I'm sorry.
	SECOND APPLICANT:[28] Thank you.
	THIRD APPLICANT:[29] I'm sorry.
27. Standing	FOURTH APPLICANT:[30] Thank you.
28. Sitting.	SECOND INTERVIEWER: What's your name?
29. Standing.	FIRST INTERVIEWER: Your middle name, please.
30. Sitting.	FIRST APPLICANT: Smith.
	SECOND APPLICANT: Ellen.
	THIRD APPLICANT: Smith, Richard F.
	FOURTH APPLICANT: Mary Victoria Smith.
	FIRST INTERVIEWER: What is your exact age?

STYLES IN ACTING

SECOND INTERVIEWER: Have you any children?

FIRST APPLICANT: I'm thirty-two years old.

SECOND APPLICANT: One son.

THIRD APPLICANT: I have two daughters.

FOURTH APPLICANT: Do I have to tell you that?

FIRST INTERVIEWER: Are you married, single, or other?

SECOND INTERVIEWER: Have you ever earned more than that?

FIRST APPLICANT: No.

SECOND APPLICANT: Never.

THIRD APPLICANT: Married.

FOURTH APPLICANT: Single, now.

THIRD INTERVIEWER: How do you do? [31]

FIRST APPLICANT:[32] Thank you.

SECOND APPLICANT:[33] I'm sorry.

THIRD APPLICANT:[34] Thank you.

FOURTH APPLICANT:[35] I'm sorry.

FOURTH INTERVIEWER: How do you do? [36]

FIRST APPLICANT:[37] I'm sorry.

SECOND APPLICANT:[38] Thank you.

THIRD APPLICANT:[39] I'm sorry.

FOURTH APPLICANT:[40] Thank you.

31. Third Interviewer, a woman, enters.
32. Sitting.
33. Standing.
34. Sitting.
35. Standing.
36. Fourth Interviewer, a man, appears on the heels of the Third Interviewer.
37. Standing.
38. Sitting.
39. Standing.
40. Sitting.

PREPARATION FOR MARIGOLDS

This play was the critic's choice for the Best American Play award in 1970, as well as a Pulitzer Prize winner in 1971 and a winner of the Obie Award. The play's theme parallels the effects of Cobalt 60 on marigold seeds with the effects of a flighty and self-indulgent mother on her daughters. The character of this acid-tongued Beatrice dominates not only her daughters but the action of this fine comedy-drama.

Having survived her own childhood poverty, an unhappy marriage, she remains indomitable and ambitious. The family lives in genteel squalor, which is supported by caring for an old lady who lives with the mother and her daughters, Ruth and Tillie. Ruth is subject to mental seizures and Tillie is a vague and indeterminate child whose high-school teacher has encouraged her to experiment with atomic energy on marigold seeds. As this scene begins Beatrice, the mother, is sitting watching Tillie fondle her beloved rabbit.

THE EFFECT OF GAMMA RAYS
ON MAN-IN-THE-MOON MARIGOLDS*

Paul Zindel
An Excerpt from ACT I

Ruth enters at a gallop, throwing her books down and babbling a mile a minute.

RUTH: Can you believe it? I didn't until Chris Burns came up and told me about it in Geography, and then Mr. Goodman told me himself during the eighth period in the office when I was eavesdropping. Aren't you so happy you could bust? Tillie? I'm so proud I can't believe it, Mama. Everybody was talking about it and nobody . . . well, it was the first time they all came up screaming about her and I said, "Yes, she's my sister!" I said it, "She's my sister! My sister! My *sister!*" Give me a cigarette.

BEATRICE: Get your hands off my personal property.

RUTH: I'll scratch your back later.

BEATRICE: I don't want you to touch me!

RUTH: Did he call yet? My God, I can't believe it, I just can't.

BEATRICE: Did who call yet?

RUTH: I'm not supposed to tell you, as Mr. Goodman's private secretary, but you're going to get a call from the school.

BEATRICE: [1]What is she talking about?

TILLIE: I was in the Science Fair at school.

NEW YORK TELEVISION THEATRE'S PRODUCTION OF *MARIGOLDS* WITH EILEEN HECKART (STANDING) AS BEATRICE AND JUDITH LOWRY AS HER BOARDER. (COURTESY WNET, EDUCATIONAL BROADCASTING CORP.)

1. To Tillie.

STYLES IN ACTING

RUTH: Didn't she tell you yet? Oh, Tillie, how could you? She's fantastic, Mama! She's a finalist in the Science Fair. There were only five of them out of hundreds and hundreds. She won with all those plants over there. They're freaks! Isn't that a scream? Dr. Berg picked her himself. The principal! And I heard Mr. Goodman say she was going to be another Madam Pasteur and he never saw a girl do anything like that before and . . . so I told everybody, "Yes, she's my sister!" Tillie, "You're my sister!" I said. And Mr. Goodman called the Advance and they're coming to take your picture. Oh, Mama, isn't it crazy? And nobody laughed at her, Mama. She beat out practically everybody and nobody laughed at her. "She's my sister," I said, "She's my sister!"

That must be him! Mama, answer it—I'm afraid. [2]

Answer it before he hangs up! [3]

Mama! He's gonna hang up! [4]

Hello? . . . Yes . . . [5]

It's him! . . . Just a minute, please . . .[7] [6]
He wants to talk to you.

BEATRICE: Who?

RUTH: The *principal!*

BEATRICE: Hang up.

RUTH: I told him you were here! Mama![8]

BEATRICE:[9] Yes? . . . I know who you are, Dr. Berg . . . I see . . . Couldn't you get someone else? There's an awfully lot of work that has to be done around here, because she's not as careful with her home duties as she is with man-in-the-moon marigolds . . .

Me? What would you want with me up on the stage? . . . The other mothers can do as they please . . . I would have thought you had enough in your *history* without . . . I'll think about it . . . Goodbye, Dr. Berg . . .

I said I'd think about it! [10]

RUTH: What did he say? [11]

BEATRICE:[12] How could you do this to me? How could you let that man call our home!

I have no clothes, do you hear me? I'd look just like you up on that stage, ugly little you!

Do you want them to laugh at us? Laugh at the two of us?

RUTH:[13] Mother . . . aren't you proud of her? Mother . . . it's an *honor.*

[14]

2. The telephone rings.

3. Ring.

4. Ring.

5. Ruth grabs the phone.

6. Aside to Beatrice.

7. Covering the mouthpiece.

8. Beatrice gets up and shuffles slowly to the phone.

9. Finally, into the phone.

10. Pause, then screaming.

11. She hangs up the phone, turns her face slowly to *Ruth*, then to *Tillie*, who has her face hidden in shame in the rabbit's fur.

12. Flinging her glass on floor.

13. Disbelievingly.

14. *Tillie* breaks into tears and moves away from *Beatrice*. It seems as though she is crushed, but then she halts and turns to face her mother.

15. *Through tears.*

16. *Beatrice's* face begins to soften as she glimpses what she's done to *Tillie.*

17. *Tillie* starts toward her. *Beatrice* opens her arms to receive her as music starts in and lights fade. A chord of finality punctuates the end of Act I.

TILLIE:[15] But . . . nobody laughed at me.

BEATRICE: Oh, my God . . .
[16]

[17]

FURTHER READING: THEATRE TODAY

Abel, Lionel. *Metatheatre.* New York: Hill & Wang, 1963.

Armstrong, William, ed. *Experimental Drama.* London: Bell & Sons, 1963.

Barrault, Jean-Louis. *Rabelais, A Dramatic Game in Two Parts.* Translated by Robert Baldick. London: Faber & Faber, 1971.

Bentley, Eric. *The Playwright as Thinker.* Cleveland: World, 1955.

Brown, John R. and Bernard, Harris. *Contemporary Theatre.* London: Edward Arnold Ltd., 1962.

Brustein, Robert. *Theatre of Revolt, An Approach to Modern Drama.* Boston: Atlantic Monthly Press, 1964.

———. *Revolution As Theatre, Essays on the Radical Style.* New York: Liveright, 1971.

Chiari, Joseph. *Landmarks of Contemporary Drama.* London: Herbert Jenkins, 1965.

Coe, Richard. *Eugene Ionesco.* New York: Barnes & Noble, 1965.

Esslin, Martin. *Absurd Drama.* London: Penguin, 1965.

———. *The Peopled Wound, The Work of Harold Pinter.* New York: Doubleday, 1969.

Gascoigne, Bamber. *Twentieth Century Drama.* London: Hutchinson & Co. Ltd., 1962.

Grossvogel, David. *Brecht, Ionesco, Beckett, Genet: Four Playwrights and a Postscript.* Ithaca: Cornell University Press, 1962.

Hayman, Ronald. *Contemporary Playwrights: Harold Pinter.* London: Heinemann Educational Books Ltd., 1968. Also in same series, Samuel Beckett & John Osborne.

Hinchcliffe, Arnold P. *Harold Pinter.* New York: Twayne Publications, Inc., 1967.

Lahr, John, ed. *Showcase #1.* New York: Grove Press, 1969. Plays from the O'Neill Foundation by Hailey, Horovitz, Gagliano, Guare.

Smith, Michael. *More Plays from off-off Broadway.* Indianapolis: Bobbs-Merrill, 1968.

———. *Theatre Trip.* Indianapolis: Bobbs-Merrill, 1969. Author's visit to European New Theatres.

Styan, J. L. *The Dark Comedy.* New York: Cambridge University Press, 1962.

Taylor, John R. *Anger and After.* London: Methuen, 1962.

Tynan, Kenneth. *Tynan on Theatre.* London: Penguin, 1964.

Wellworth, George, and Benedickt, Michael. *Theatre of Protest and Paradox. 2d ed. New York: New York University Press, 1968.*

A SELECTION OF TODAY'S PLAYS AND PLAYWRIGHTS

Ionesco

The Bald Soprano (1948)
The Lesson (1950)
Jack, or the Submission (1950)
The Chairs (1950)
Amédée (1954)
Rhinoceros (1954)

Pinter

The Birthday Party (1957)
A Slight Ache (1958)
A Night Out (1958)
The Caretaker (1960)
The Dumbwaiter (1960)
The Collection (1962)
The Homecoming (1965)
Old Times (1971)

van Itallie

I'm Really Here (1 Act)
The Serpent (1969)
America Hurrah! (1967)

Osborne

Look Back in Anger (1950)
The Entertainer (1957)
Luther (1961)
Inadmissible Evidence (1964)
A Patriot for Me (1965)

Albee

The Sandbox (1959)
The Zoo Story (1958)
Who's Afraid of Virginia Woolf?
   (1962)
A Delicate Balance (1966)
*Box, and Quotations from Chairman
   Mao Tse tung* (1969)

Zindel

Let Me Hear You Whisper
And Miss Reardon Drinks a Little
*The Effect of Gamma Rays on Man-
   in-the Moon Marigolds* (1970)
   Pulitzer Prize Play 1971

APPENDIX 1
Questions and Answers

When speakers finish their prepared talks, it is the custom to allot some time in which the speaker answers questions put to him by his listeners. No matter where a speaker travels or to whom he speaks, he can be sure that certain questions will always be asked. These may be phrased differently, but in essence they will be similar. The recurring questions about acting deal mostly with very practical matters and usually relate to the person asking them. Here are a few — with answers.

---

1. *Can Acting Be Taught?*

This question has been asked for three-hundred years, and actors from Siddons to Stanislavski have answered it. The consensus of opinion is that *acting cannot be taught; that an actor can be trained, but that talent is a gift.* It may be that the question is still asked in the hope that someone will disagree. Well, I agree. That is, I agree that an actor can be trained, but that part about "gift" and "talent" is ambiguous for a journeyman actor.

There was a time when I considered myself an infallible judge of acting talent; one good reason why I relinquished that avocation happened during the filming of a George Arliss picture in which I was playing opposite a young actress whom Universal had "let go" as a stock player. This left her free-lancing, and at the time we were making this picture, she was not at all sure of a Hollywood future. Although I found her attractive personally, I remember also thinking that she had little chance of reaching any notable success. Her eyes were too large, and she had affected speech and mannerisms. If anyone had asked me "Will she make it?" I would certainly have answered in the negative. The young lady's name was Bette Davis, future winner of ten Academy Award nominations.

Even Mr. Arliss could make an error in judging "talent." During the tryout of *Green Goddess,* he decided that one of his supporting players was

310

BETTE DAVIS AND HARDIE ALBRIGHT IN THE MOVIE *SO BIG*. (WITH PERMISSION OF CREATIVE MANAGEMENT ASSOCIATES.)

ineffectual, and he gave Ronald Colman his notice. Shirley Booth was almost replaced in *Come Back, Little Sheba* because she was *"shuffling through the part, giving a stock company performance"* according to the author, William Inge, and the director, Daniel Mann.[1] Miss Booth's characterization was acclaimed and is still considered one of the classics of modern acting. During rehearsals of *Death of a Salesman*, it was doubtful if Lee Cobb would ever be allowed to open in the part.

The decision you must make as to whether or not to become an actor should not depend entirely upon the opinions given by those in, or on the fringes of, the theatre. Even critical judgments of professionals are notoriously poor. This may be explained if we accept that our emotions are completely independent of our critical faculties. In your own experience, you know that often when seeing a poor TV show or reading a trashy novel, somehow you get caught up and are moved in spite of the fact that your critical judgment is constantly telling you that the material is trash.

So much for "talent" and judgments of it. If you can recognize it, you are more perceptive than I—or less experienced. As for that other word, "gift," the dictionary describes it as "endowed with talent" and so by circuitous reasoning, if you know "talent," you will have no difficulty in knowing who is "gifted."

---

2.   *Aren't certain people born with an instinct for acting?*

David Garrick had no training at all. One day he was a wine salesman, and the next the outstanding actor of his generation. But let's not

[1]Richard Maney, *Fanfare, The Confessions of a Press Agent* (New York: Harper and Row, 1957), p. 86. Quoted by permission.

QUESTIONS AND ANSWERS   311

overlook some other qualities he had. *Garrick, the wine merchant, believed wholeheartedly in Garrick, the actor.* A Greek philosopher once said that a man could never step into the same river twice, for the second time, the river would be different. Right now you are what you are, but it is not what you were, nor what you will be tomorrow. If you believe as much in yourself as did Garrick, you also can become a fine actor. Sarah Bernhardt believed, "Will-power is a fundamental condition of success for every man; for the actor it is a condition to which all others are subordinate."[2] Naturally, you'll have moments of doubt when you'll think seriously of giving up the idea and settling down to a nice, steady, unglamorous job. Just be positive that you want to act so much that you can survive a sense of ineptitude, bitter criticism, and long periods of apparent failure. You'll not be the first with doubts or reasons for them. Here is a notice about a young lady's first appearance in a good part in a great city:

> *On before us tottered, rather than walked, a very pretty, delicate, fragile-looking creature dressed in a most unbecoming manner in a faded salmon-colored sack and coat, and uncertain whereabouts to fix either her eyes or her feet. She spoke in broken, tremulous tone and at the close of her sentences her words generally lapsed into a horrid whisper that was absolutely inaudible.*[3]

That's enough to put anyone out of show business, isn't it? It was written by a London critic reporting the first appearance there of Sarah Siddons, and she was not rehired for the next season. As we have seen, this failure in London made such a scar that she very nearly gave up the theatre; but she went back to the provinces and saturated herself in work. Work seems to be the magic ingredient of outstanding acting. In my research on great actors of the past, and in professional association with the best of my time, I cannot think of one who did not earn his fame by love of the art and indomitable labor. And labor it is; it entails years of tedious craft training, conditioning of body and voice, development of instinct and intellect, plus constant execution of the art. How much easier it would be to be "gifted" and thus avoid all this back-breaking effort. Yes, Garrick was "gifted," *but he also exhausted everyone around him — working!*

Another attribute of the fine actor is the possession of *an indomitable drive to be great. Quand même* ("in spite of everything") was Sarah Bernhardt's motto, which she kept constantly before her. Although she entered the Conservatoire at sixteen, she was twenty-two before her career really began and twenty-five before her first success. This should be a useful lesson to those who expect overnight stardom. In his book, *Seven Daughters of the Theatre,* Wagenknecht tells of the celebrated American actress, Julia Marlowe, who as a girl,

[2]H. J. Stemming, trans., *The Art of Sarah Bernhardt* (New York: Dial Press, 1925).
[3]W. Clarke Russell, *Representative Actors* (London: Frederick Warne and Co., 1888).

*studied in seclusion for three solid years the five roles in which she had
decided to prepare herself. To keep her body supple she took up fencing.
She was willing to practice half a day if necessary on the tone quality of
a single word. Her texts she studied in the light of all commentaries,
reading as widely as possible in the backgrounds of the period involved.
She made herself a miniature theatre, with dolls for actors, so that she
might visualize the entire production from start to finish, giving it actual
body before her eyes. In all this she was aided notably by unusual powers
of concentration, frequently becoming so absorbed in her task that she
would be oblivious to everything else going on around her.*[4]

JULIA MARLOWE AS JULIET. (FROM THE KATH-
ERINE GREY COLLECTION.)

Like Julia Marlowe, you must plan your work intelligently. Work is
the *only* way to develop body and voice. Reading will not accomplish this;
neither will sitting around discussing "show biz." *And no one can do it for
you!* It requires regular and systematized planning; so much time for
dancing—folk, ballet; so much for fencing—broadswords and foil; then
singing—classical, modern; breath control; diction—and so, on and on.

Edwin Booth wrote,

*I have barely time to swallow my dinner hastily and go to work—work.
Never since I began my theatrical career did it seem so truly to resemble
downright bodily, mental, and spiritual "hammer and tongs."*[5]

If you live in a small town and feel you have no place to study such
things, or couldn't afford all those lessons, remember that if you want
something badly enough, you'll work out your problems. If not—it's wiser
to stop wishing now! There is a library in your town. Get some books with
exercises in them. (See end of chapter.) Anything and everything you do
to prepare yourself is accumulating force within you. When your chance
comes, nothing will be able to resist that power within you. Dedicated
study and training should be considered as your investment in your future.

---

3. *How much has luck to do with an actor's success?*

I'm afraid it must be admitted that luck has quite a bit to do with success.
Hardly anyone who has been around show business for any length of
time will deny the importance of being in the right place at the right time.
To an actor, it can mean the difference between stardom and being a good
reliable player the rest of his life. This whole area of "luck" is not a premise
to which I subscribe easily; I have never believed in rabbits' feet or "never
whistle in a dressing room," or "never wish anyone good luck on an
opening," or any such theatrical superstitions. But I do believe in the
lucky break.

[4]From *Seven Daughters of the Theatre*, by Edward Wagenknecht. Copyright 1964 by the
University of Oklahoma Press.
[5]Edwina Booth Grossman, *Edwin Booth*. Copyright 1894 by D. Appleton-Century Co.,
p. 161.

QUESTIONS AND ANSWERS

Yet I say again, when that chance comes, an actor had better be ready. It may never come again. The actor who will benefit from that lucky break will be the one who can carry on, who is equipped to follow one success with another. No matter how handsome or magnetic an actor may be, he must never neglect his training. Training and experience will sustain him when his youthful appearance is gone.

4.   *How important is appearance to an actor?*

Some thirty years ago, looks were very important. There were 900 to 1,000 players under contract to studios.[6] A few were "types," but the majority were handsome youngsters chosen because they were photogenic. The box office names at that time were all glamorous women and handsome men. With the advent of the gangster pictures came the elevation of the "mug." Even the pretty boys began talking out of the sides of their mouths, trying to be tough. Mugs were "box office" and the uglier they were, the more tickets they sold. Thus ended an old movie tradition. Today, a girl may have a shape like a banana, but if she can act or is skilled at comedy she is given consideration, especially if she has been a success on the stage or in night clubs. Although physical requirements are not what they were, there are other positive qualities which young people must have. I mean particularly training and experience. Each year thousands of hopefuls with no training and no experience come to Hollywood and New York and try to break into the profession, then, finally broke and disillusioned, go back home without once being inside a casting office. A straight line is not always the shortest distance to Broadway or Vine Street. Keep away from the big time until you have an education and some experience. When they want you they will surely find you.

5.   *What about personality?*

Individuality is a better word; "personality" connotes someone who is "on" all the time—a show-off. That sort doesn't seem to get anywhere. People suspect that they are covering up inadequacies. But magnetism is a great asset to an actor. I'm sure you have seen the kind of person who is quiet and reserved but who attracts others. People seem to respect him, feel that he is not a surface person but has interesting depths. He is challenging, and we want to learn more about such a person.

[6]Today there are only some 200 contract players and, for the most part, these are contracted for certain TV series. When the show is finished, so is the contract.

6. How does a young actor get experience?

In previous centuries the theatre trained its own by the time-honored apprentice method, and this system survived until the demise of repertory and stock companies. This was on-the-job training consisting of much practice and only such theory as an apprentice might obtain when some older member of the company volunteered information. There were certain dialectical advantages, of course. Pupils could communicate by that unique language never fully understood by any but actors. The apprentice could also watch his master practice what he preached. But the process was instruction by osmosis, and at best, more incidental than planned or systematically progressive.

Today neither the professional theatre nor the trade unions make any provision for the training of young people who wish to enter the acting profession. This task has dropped into the laps of our educational institutions.

7. Is it possible to combine training and college education?

Education is of primary importance to an actor. A good education will give him a background in literature, psychology, philosophy, an appreciation of related arts, and a fuller understanding of people. Few of us realize that training of actors in colleges is an innovation of our century; a great deal might be said of its progress, which has not been easily won. Even as late as 1914, when Thomas Wood Stevens led Andrew Carnegie into the newly built Carnegie Tech theatre, he found it wise to explain it to the bene-factor as a "lecture hall." Mr. Carnegie never realized he was supporting a drama department. Had the Puritan-minded old Scot observed the "To be, or not to be" carved on the entrance doors he might have realized he was getting the old theatrical, "Nothing is, but what is not."

The problem which university drama departments had to solve was how to include practical theatre training when their charters provide only for a liberal arts education. Each step in progress needed to be carefully planned and cautiously executed. But now college theatres seem to be generally accepted and respected. Many professionals today have degrees from such institutions.

The vastly expanded audience for all the arts has been almost exclusively developed by colleges and universities. And this has come at a most opportune time, when the taste of the Broadway-oriented mass audience has declined to a disturbingly low cultural level. Today our universities are housing not only the scholar and the artist but also an exclusive and discerning audience. Certainly this should portend an upgrading in the cultural values of tomorrow's mass audience. Colleges have gathered professional artisans as instructors, and for these artists the college has assumed the position of patron once held by the church or the court.

The curriculum offered by most American colleges, universities, and some of the more advanced high schools allows the student an invaluable opportunity to become part of a group of equally enthusiastic young people learning the art and craft of acting. A violinist may practice alone with his instrument, but the actor must have other actors and an audience to reach his full learning potential.

Unlike the apprentice system, the university provides a well-ordered and constructively planned series of courses in such important allied skills as dancing, voice production, and fencing, as well as the academic studies which encourage mental development.

College drama gets the beginner into roles of importance much sooner than did the apprentice method. If this seems somewhat like teaching the baby to swim by throwing it into the lake, it might also be said that the method is quick and decisive. Either the baby swims or drowns immediately.

Of course the college "star" will one day face the inevitable move into professional ranks, where he must content himself with parts of much less importance. At such a time he is apt to wonder about the value of his degree. But the wonder should be only temporary. I have firsthand experience in this, as I entered the profession holding one of the first degrees ever awarded in drama. Once a novice gets a small part, the university-trained actor is much more apt than the self-taught novice to demonstrate the knowledge he has acquired. If his training has been practical, it will soon be obvious that he can be entrusted with better parts. In all probability he will also be more familiar with audiences and audience psychology, a very important matter.

---

8. *Should an actor work in a play he knows is trash?*

Not if he can write home for money. But if he is a professional and there is nothing better, he does. An acting job is not easy to find, and a poor play cannot last forever. But it may lead to getting a part in a good play. Try not to be too critical. Don't assume the job of unhired and unpaid critic. Accept responsibility without question and perform tasks to the best of your ability. Subordinate your personal prejudices. Concentrate that energy on the job at hand. Use your actor's discipline. The world is full of critics, and they are mostly amateurs. That's why excavation companies put peepholes in fences—so that sidewalk foremen can watch workers work.

9. *What about little theatre training?*

Even avocational acting, while far from ideal, is better than no acting at all. In little theatres, however, far too much time is apt to be spent socializing and too little in study and rehearsal. The result is a superficial, imitative, or a vanity-oriented performance. Acting experience must have certain standards or it is more destructive than constructive.

It is important to get before an audience any time in any place, even though the "theatre" be nothing more than Lope de Vega's "Three boards, two actors, and a passion."

One means of getting before an audience is by being a guest at local clubs, banquets, civic groups, and so forth. Readings should be selected that may be delivered standing at a table without benefit of props or scenery. Prepare these for ten or fifteen minute presentations only, and choose the material apropos the club, holiday, or particular occasion. You should not expect any reimbursement; you will be repaid in experience. Once established as a solo performer, you can easily use your club contacts to present short scenes with other actors. By booking an advance itinerary, your group can have the advantage of getting traveling expenses on weekends and holidays and obtaining valuable experience acting before a variety of audiences. Simplicity should be the watchword in such ventures. Select scenes that are unpretentious; place your emphasis upon careful study of your scenes and characters, the ensemble work, and communication with your audiences.

10. *Suppose I am trained and have experience; how do I get my first professional work?*

Directors, casting offices, or producers prefer to see you act before they will believe you can handle a part before an audience. It is the old truism all over again—you can't get a job unless you have experience and you can't get experience unless you have a job. You won't be hired by making the rounds of casting offices alone. Just as you learn to act by acting you find work by working. If you work diligently enough as an amateur, you should be able to get into the profession.

The best way to obtain employment is to create it yourself. Start your own group. When you feel yourselves prepared, invite an audience. Work any time, any place and don't be concerned about being paid. *Once you have been paid, you can never act again without remuneration.* You will then be a member of a union. The only exception would be voluntary appearances for charity or patriotic causes. But membership in a union is no guarantee of getting a job. Our unions do not obtain jobs for members; they protect the actor's interests once he gets a job.

QUESTIONS AND ANSWERS   317

11. *What are these unions?*

There are six important unions:

1. *Actors' Equity Association* (AEA, or *Equity*), 226 West 47th Street, New York City. This is the oldest performer's union (formed in 1914), and its realm of interest is the legitimate stage.
2. *Screen Actors Guild,* or SAG, 7750 Sunset Blvd., Hollywood, Calif. This is the motion picture union. This includes filmed TV.
3. *American Federation of Television and Radio Artists,* or AFTRA, 1551 N. LaBrea, Hollywood, Calif. Live TV and radio.
4. *The American Guild of Musical Artists,* or AGMA. Offices in most major cities. Opera, ballet dancers, and concert artists.
5. *The American Guild of Variety Artists,* or AGVA. Vaudeville, circus, and night club performers.
6. *Screen Extras Guild.* Motion picture extra's union. Together these unions form *The Associated Actors and Artistes of America,* which is chartered by the AFL-CIO.

Keep in touch with Equity or SAG even though you are not yet a member. You'd be surprised at the information all these unions give non-members. They might suggest places a young actor can stay on a limited amount of money or inform you as to which summer companies are accepting apprentices. In addition to these unions there is *Central Casting,* a nonprofit, non-union employment agency run by the larger film studios for the benefit of extra players.

On the subject of expenses: in Hollywood or New York it will cost about $80 a week to live modestly. So you must think about developing some part-time skill which will sustain you while you are waiting for that big break. During the thirties, Lloyd Bridges and Russell Conway were part-time package stampers in the New York Post Office.

12. *What are the qualifications for joining these unions?*

All have similar qualifications; to become a member of SAG you must be either (1) a paid-up member in one of the other "four A's," or (2) have a proffered contract from a producer of a motion picture. (This must not be an extra role.) Initiation fee is $250, plus quarterly dues of $15. There are nine classifications of dues depending upon annual income of the member.

Actors' Equity Association provides an alternative program for those who wish to gain experience before deciding to become members. A young actor may serve for two seasons as an apprentice in summer stock, provided it is a professional Equity company. At the end of his apprentice period, he may become a regular union member. Equity's initiation fee is $250 and dues are $36 for the minimum bracket, payable semi-annually.

Most professionals pay dues to two or three unions, as few actors today can depend upon any one medium.

Many beginners feel that getting a union card is a big step in their careers. My advice is don't be in a hurry. Many acting opportunities not available to a professional are open to you as an amateur. Amateur is a French word, meaning "for love." If you love the theatre, remember that becoming a professional will be like coming home from a honeymoon to marriage. You will be assuming the responsibility of making your love practical, and this will take time.

While you are making a living and "making the rounds" of casting and production offices, your training must not be neglected. Even professionals are constantly rehearsing and acting, when not being paid. Actors' Equity approves of this, provided the audience does not pay. In fact, Equity itself contributes a small producing cost to a program set up in New York called Equity Library Theatre. Previously produced plays are cast competitively from Equity members "in good standing" and these casts rehearse and perform for no wage, as do director, producer, costumer, and stagehands. Such ventures not only keep the actor at his trade but also serve as "showcases" where he can be seen. Many actors have been cast in commercial stage plays, films, and TV because they were seen in Equity productions. Other "workshops" or "showcase theatres" vary from the greatly publicized New York studios where "young professionals practice their art" to humble stages set up in vacant stores. There are some forty such little groups operating in Hollywood alone. These groups, unlike the theatre which Equity sponsors, are supported by the actors themselves, who pay a fee to cover operating expenses. Sometimes the charge is as little as $15 a month, but the more elaborate New York workshops may cost the actor $100 or more per month. This may all sound very discouraging indeed, but you need to be very sure that acting is to be your life's work.

---

13. *Isn't it easier to get into TV commercials?*

This is the most difficult field of all, even for established professionals, because it is well paid for the time expended. I have seen forty or fifty well-known actors sitting outside an agency office waiting to be called in for an interview for a two- or three-line part in a commercial. Someone named these "cattle calls," and the resemblance is striking.

Many have an erroneous impression that people with no acting experience make commercials and receive fortunes for it. For the most part, people giving endorsements of TV products are professionals who are skillful enough to make you believe they are just ordinary office workers or housewives. Manufacturers are very careful of their public image and would not dare to endanger sales by hiring non-union actors. There are, however, some fly-by-night agencies who place ads in the classified columns offering to pay for endorsements of a product. Space is hired in an office building, camera and sound are hidden, and as applicants are interviewed, they are recorded and photographed. Those chosen are given a small check and sign a complete release. In other words, there are no residual payments, and it is from residuals that the professional makes his money; each time a commercial is rescreened, the actor ordinarily receives a small percentage of his original pay. This is the reason actors endure "cattle calls."[7]

---

14. *How much does an established actor make per year?*

Forty thousand, three thousand, or five hundred dollars — it depends entirely on the individual. I believe SAG once made an income survey of its members. You might write the Guild for information.

---

15. *What about agents?*

There are almost two hundred agents franchised by the Guild in Hollywood, and even the smallest agent is not apt to take on a new client without seeing him perform. Here is another reason for you to keep working and acting. Some agents will, however, accept a "Broadway name" on reputation alone. Years ago it was customary for agents to have six or eight clients and do very well with them. But that was in the days of the "B" pictures. Today, in spite of the fact that the number of pictures produced in Hollywood has dropped, agents have considerably increased the number of clients they handle. The hope is that by having more clients who work less, the agent can stay in business. This reasoning helps the agent but not the individual actor.

In Hollywood an agent is almost a necessity. He is in a much better position to know which studios have films ready for casting. Usually he has been in the business for years and has many acquaintances among producers, writers, directors, and casting agents. In New York, however, casting information is more readily available to the actor. Such publications as *Variety* and *Player's Guide* publish current "Legit" news. An actor can consult the bulletin board at the Equity office as to casting and pick up bits of hearsay when making the rounds. Also producers, directors, and casting people are much more available in New York than in Hollywood.

[7]Initial payment for one commercial is "scale" or minimum salary, as determined by the union.

When you are on your rounds in New York or visiting studios in Hollywood, it is wise to carry photographs which can be left with producers or casting offices.

16. *What sort of photographs?*

These should be eight-by-ten-inch glossy prints. They must be *theatrical portraits* taken by a photographer who understands the particular style. An enlarged snapshot or high school graduation portrait simply will not do. Wait until you get to New York or Hollywood and consult the yellow pages for *Theatrical Portrait Photographers.* SAG, Equity, or your agent may be able to suggest a reliable photographer. Pick four of the best shots and have them made into a composite, then have reproductions made. You may order twenty-five or fifty of these reproductions for six to ten cents each. Your resume should be pasted on back of each.

17. *What is the form of a résumé?*

It should be typed double spaced, and may be mimeographed. Limit information about yourself to one page or less. At the top of the page type your name, address, height, weight, coloring, and other pertinent information. List various phone numbers where you can be reached. Your training and education should be listed next. Broadway, films, and television are headings you might use, if possible. Keep to facts which can be proved. Information should be simple, direct, and honest. Leave something to talk about at interviews. When you do get in to see a producer or director, *don't put on an act.* Don't try to be something you are not. If you are to be interviewed about a play which is published, read it beforehand. Dress simply. Don't appear in jeans or any dress that might give the impression you are eccentric. Remember names, shake hands when dismissed, thank the interviewer for considering you, *and leave at once.* Be neither obsequious nor impudent but friendly and respectful. Try to leave your prospective boss with the impression that you are intelligent, cooperative, studious, *and a worker;* in other words, that you would be a valuable and pleasant person to have around. Follow this advice and you will receive only courtesy and consideration.

18. *What about auditions?*

Should you be asked to read, it may be in an office or in a dark empty theatre, and in all probability the reading will be "cold"; that is, you will be given a few minutes only to leaf through the play and concentrate upon the lines you are expected to read. Read for *sense*. It is dangerous to try for a characterization or emotion. Generally such readings are to find an actor whose voice and personality match a particular character. A director or producer is ready to use his imagination.

When we were casting *All the Living,* an actor we were considering haughtily informed us "I never *read*—I *act.*" When he realized I was adamant, he did read for us, but his reading reflected his resentment and petulance —which was exactly the feeling I was hoping to find. He was given the part at once. Later, during rehearsals, he added the "acting" he had mentioned and lost the attitude I had visualized when writing the part.

No one will expect you to give a performance at a reading. It *is* important that you remain calm and assured and that you show an intelligence and an eagerness at reading. Just try to make sense of the lines and to give a hint of some overall concept of the part.

It is very important that you become a good sight reader. You should be able to pick up reading matter which you have never seen before and read it aloud with meaning and intelligence. You must not hesitate or stumble over words, and your voice should convey meaning to the listener in a vivid and interesting manner. Make it a point to read aloud to yourself or others at least once every day. Clip out articles from newspapers and magazines which you have found interesting and practice reading these to your family. As you do, retain eye contact with your listeners. Consider one person as an entire audience and remember you must always hold the interest of your audience. Study facial expressions and if you see evidence of disinterest, do something quickly to regain it. How is this done? Usually, an audience's lack of interest begins when the actors' voice betrays his own disinterest. Believe every word you are reading. Make the words personal to your listeners. Never give up eye contact. Glance down at your paper quickly, photograph a phrase or sentence, and return to that invaluable eye contact, for you will find it a sensitive barometer of your audience's interest.

Drilling of this kind will also be useful if you have an opportunity to work in radio.[8] The same contact you have developed with listeners can be transferred to work with the microphone. Imagine it to be a living person and not a little metal box. As a matter of fact, it is the hearing aid of many living persons. When I first did radio work, I was impressed when I saw more experienced radio actors' attitude toward the mike. They seemed to treat it as another human. They smiled, winked, and frowned at it. Of course they realized that none of these things were making any impression on the device, but it gave them the sense of being in contact with other humans.

---

[8]Radio is far from dead. Many young people have found it receptive to new talent and a steppingstone to other media.

YOUR FUTURE IN THE THEATRE

The next twenty years of the theatre are going to be exciting. All of you have the chance to take part. Perhaps one day you may come to believe that our work together saved you some time and heartbreak.

You are going into a theatre which has greater possibilities than the one I entered in 1926. Then everyone was searching. O'Neill and Rice were dabbling in expressionism, George Kelly was writing kitchen drama, Reinhardt was producing his spectacular and thrilling *Miracle*. There seemed no positive direction in America. Great European actors came to us; the Moscow Art Players from Russia, Guitry from France, Duse from Italy. Then the Depression swept art aside. All that mattered was existing. Bread lines angered Americans; they were determined that these would never happen again. Revolt and anger exploded in the theatre. At last we seemed to have a direction. For the next twenty years we *preached* to audiences. We crammed our plays with "isms,"—ideology and propaganda. We gave them psychiatry and intellectual dialogues, better read than acted. We treated theatre as a place to think, whereas it should be a place to feel, to experience, to contact the infinite. We lost the skill of older theatre-workers to produce the remarkable and amazing.

To compound the felony, our unions raised prices—while we continued to torture audiences. At last, they realized that we of the theatre were nothing but high-priced bores, and they deserted us. Like every other audience since time began, they wanted excitement in the theatre. They wanted to feel the magic and the illusion of it. They found these things in the musicals.

But now all over America there are signs of a vast renaissance of legitimate theatre, not localized on Broadway. In the years ahead we shall once again find the skill to act and produce the remarkable and the amazing. Once again we shall create the magic of make-believe. The theatre will once again be a place which excites and thrills. You can be an actor on such a stage. Do you know what it is to be an actor?

Every page in this book has been devoted to explaining just what makes an actor. It has taken thousands of words. A great writer, John Steinbeck, has done it with just a few, in his eulogy to John Emery, a man admired by both Steinbeck and myself as actor and cherished friend. On the opening night of *The Three Sisters* at the Civic Repertory Theatre, John Emery and I walked on stage together for the first time as professionals. We shared a dressing room for the next forty weeks and during the subsequent years we were in constant contact. Here is what Mr. Steinbeck thought of John Emery, actor:

> He was an actor, a member of that incorrigible peerage against which, along with gypsies and vagabonds, laws once were made, lest they cause living to be attractive, fear unthinkable, and death dignified, thereby robbing church and state of their taxes on unhappiness.
>
> An actor, a player, not the product of make-up and publicity, but an actor in his blood, six generations back, brother and son of the great and, may

we please hope, the permanent fellowship of Burbage, and Garrick, of Booth and Joe Jefferson, of Toto and Emmett Kelly. This was his company, an actor. He played many parts well, whereas most of us play only one — badly.

Sometimes he seemed a child, easily hurt and wryly smiling, but he was wise in friendship and inept in hatred.

He was consistent — professional — responsible — gallant. (A footnote here: Please to remember the time he broke his ankle on stage and played unlimping to his curtain.)

Because of his profession, his life was exposed, down stage, lighted, but none but the stupid, the vain or the vengeful could charge him with ungentleness.

He played larger than life — bravura — and he played small as a mouse. His profession was himself. May all of us hope to come to our curtain as unstained and worthily as he.[9]

FURTHER READING

Play Guides

Cartnell, Van H., ed. *Plot Outlines of 100 Famous Plays.* New York: Doubleday, 1926.

Dury, F. K. W., *Dury's Guide to Best Plays.* New York: Scarecrow Press, 1953.

Mersand, Joseph, ed. *Guide to Play Production.* New York: Appleton-Century-Croft, 1953. For directors, teachers. Descriptions of plays and problems.

Shank, Theodore, ed. *A Digest of 500 Plays.* New York: Crowell-Collier, 1963. Plot outlines and production notes.

Indexes

Write to Drama Bookshop, 150 West 52nd St., New York 10019, for lists of indexes of one-act plays, as well as monologues and dialogues.

Thompson, Ruth G., *Index to Full Length Plays* (1926-1944), 1946, and *Index to Full Length Plays* (1895-1925). Boston: F. W. Faxon Co., 1956.

West, Dorothy, and Peake, Dorothy. *Play Index* (1949-1952). New York: H. W. Wilson, 1953. Lists authors, subjects, and gives analyses, cast and production requirements, etc.

Reference Books

Bowman, Walter, ed. *Theatre Language.* New York: Theatre Arts Books, 1961. A dictionary of terms and phrases from fourteenth to twentieth century.

Hartnoll, Phyllis, *Oxford Companion to the Theatre,* 2d ed. New York: Oxford, 1957. One volume on all theatre people and subjects. Recommended.

[9]Reprinted with the permission of John Steinbeck and *Equity Magazine,* January 1965.

Lounsbury, Warren. *Backstage from A to Z*. Seattle: University of Washington Press, 1959. A glossary of stage terms.

Rae, Kenneth, ed. *An International Dictionary of Technical Theatre Terms*. New York: Theatre Arts Books, 1960.

Roach, Helen. *Spoken Records*. New York: Scarecrow Press, 1963. A digest of over 200 spoken records.

Employment

Dalrymple, Jean. *Careers and Opportunities in the Theatre*. New York: Dutton, 1969.

Moore, Dick. *Opportunities in Acting*. New York: Universal, 1963. Former Equity staff member and actor gives authoritative tips on the profession. Recommended.

Savan, Bruce. *Your Career in the Theatre*. Garden City, New York: Doubleday, 1961. Useful information on the New York theatrical profession.

U.S. Department of Labor. *Employment Outlook in the Performing Arts*. Bureau of Labor Statistics Bulletin No. 1300-65, Washington 25, D.C.

Self-instruction

Dancing (Text, Diagrams, Exercises)

Lifar, Serge. *Lifar on Classical Ballet*. London: Allan Wingate, 1951. Illustrations, definitions, positions, *battements, ronds-de-jambes,* preparations, and point work. Recommended.

Martin, John. *Introduction to the Dance*. New York: W. W. Norton, 1939.

Fencing

Washington, D.C.: American Association for Health, Physical Education and Recreation, Washington, D.C. *Pamphlet on Fencing* ($1.00). n.d.

Bernhardt, Frederica, and Edwards, Mrs. Vernon. *How to Fence*. Dubuque, Ia.: W. C. Brown, 1961. Paperback.

Editors of *Sports Illustrated*. *Book of Fencing*. New York: Lippincott, 1962. Foils, épée, sabre. Beautifully illustrated drawings of positions. Excellent.

Lidtstone, R. A., *Fencing, A Practical Treatise on Foil, Epée and Sabre*. London: Witherby, 1952.

Singing

Bachner, Loris. *Dynamic Singing*. New York: Hill & Wang, 1944.

Bairstow, Edward C. and Greene, Harry Plunket. *Singing Learned from Speech*. New York: St. Martins, n.d.

Dodds, George. *Voice Placing and Training Exercises*. New York: Oxford, 1927.

Trusler, Ivan, and Ehret, Walter. *Functional Lessons in Singing*. Englewood Cliffs, N.J.: Prentice-Hall, 1960. Paperback.

Trade Publications

Backstage, 165 West 46 St., New York, N. Y. 10036.

Show Business, also publishers of *Summer Theatre*, 136 West 44th Street, New York, N. Y. 10036.

Variety, 154 West 46th Street, New York, N. Y. 10036.

FILMSTRIPS FOR USE IN TEACHING DRAMA

There are many filmstrips available, some of which can be helpful to theatre arts teachers. Choices depend entirely upon the instructor's curriculum. The following lists may be helpful:

Butler, James H., and Work, William. "Filmstrips for Use in Teaching Drama and Theatre," *Educational Theatre Journal*, Vol. 15, No. 1 (March 1963), pp. 66-74.

Filmstrip Guide, 3d ed. New York N.Y. 10052: H. W. Wilson, Co. 950 University Ave., 1954.

Work, William, Kahan, Gerald, and Quinn, Robert S. "16 mm Films for Use in Teaching Drama and Theatre," *Educational Theatre Journal*, Vol. 15, No. 3 (October 1963), pp. 259-275.

You may write to the following sources for lists of filmstrips or information concerning your special needs for films:

Educational Film Sales Department, University Extension, University of California, Los Angeles.

Eye Gate House, Inc., 2716 41st Ave., Long Island City, N. Y.

Paramount Theatre Supplies, 32 W. 20th St., New York, N. Y.

Stanley Bowmar Co., 513 W. 166th St., New York, N. Y.

Advanced Voice and Speech

DIALECTS AND ACCENTS

Dialects and accents are not properly respected by young players. There are far too many high school Pygmalions whose cockney consists of a few "Aih-eee" sounds interspersed like clashing cymbals in a symphony of Midwestern "r-r-r's." It is a mistake to disparage the use of dialects. When convincing, they contribute much to a characterization. Just as study is needed to acquire a new language, nearly the same diligence should be given to the study of dialect. It would be better not to attempt a dialect at all unless you are willing to devote time, research, and practice to its perfection. Offhand, clumsy attempts will hurt, not help, a characterization. In the professional theatre, the dialect problem is usually sidestepped by employing actors who speak in broken English or who have backgrounds in another language.

The word *accent* means primarily stress or emphasis; it can apply to speaking, to music, and to other forms of expression. The importance of the music or melody factor in language becomes obvious when we realize that if a foreign student were to carry over his native intonations into American English, he would speak with a foreign sound *even though he were speaking his phonemes perfectly.*

Dialect has several meanings. It can refer to the result of superimposing a foreign language on a primary language—a mixture of two languages. When a foreigner comes to America, his existence may depend upon his being understood. His native speech—whether cultured or patois—must be changed to fit new needs. He must not only learn a new language, but unlearn another. While doing so, he may use words and phrases from the old language while using the new incorrectly. The most important change will be in the melodic rhythms.

Dialect is also a local or provincial form of some basic language. It can include a special vocabulary and word usage as well as distinctive intonations. We would more properly refer to a Southern dialect than to a Southern "accent."

In the study of dialects for stage use, most beginners either (1) study from the words respelled by the author to convey his idea of a particular dialect, or (2) choose some model and imitate his speech in parrotlike imitation. Both approaches are superficial. Your concern should not be with words or lines alone, but with an in-depth understanding of the feeling and melody of the other language.

To illustrate the first study method, let us take four different versions of "Mary Had a Little Lamb,"[1] which has been used by students for many years in the practice of dialects.

Chinese

> Was gal name Moll had lamb,
> Flea' all samee white snow;
> Evly place Moll gal walkee
> Ba-ba hopee 'long too.

German

> Dot Mary haf got ein leddle schaf
> Mit hair youst like some vool;
> Und all der place dot gal did vent
> Das schaf go like some fool.

French

> La petite Marie had le jeune muttong,
> Ze wool was blanche as ze snow;
> And everywhere la Belle Marie went
> Le Jeune mottong was zure to go.

Irish

> Begorry, Mary had a little shape,
> And the wool was white entoirely.
> An' wherever Mary wad sthir her sthumps
> The young shape would follow her completely.

Obviously, in *reading* such lines, the dialect and interpretation depend entirely upon what the author has written — and his interpretation of dialect may be right or wrong. Some early plays of this century illustrate how naively dialect can be written and show that it is a mistake to depend upon *words* in acquiring convincing dialects. Also this method allows no latitude for the actor's creativity, no opportunity to incorporate dialect into characterization. The actor is little more than a reader.

Dialect and accent are more than syllabification; they are *sounds*, and sounds are not easily or accurately captured in words. It is the melody of their speech which expresses the very soul of a people.

---

[1]From Gertrude E. Johnson *Dialects for Oral Interpretation* (New York: The Century Company, 1922), p. 25.

As for the second method, of parroting a speech model, there are hidden dangers which make this not altogether desirable. The actor could very well acquire the model's idiosyncrasies of personality and speech as well as his dialect. If you use this method, be quite certain that your model has no speech impediment, or you might end by speaking a German dialect with a lisp. While it is true that imitation can be used to some extent, a really convincing dialect is best accomplished by first learning the correct sounds by aid of the International Phonetic Alphabet (see p. 331). Correct sounds, spoken in sequence, will give you a familiarity with the melody of the language. Even the most difficult of dialects can then be managed so that they sound authentic and are completely convincing to an audience.

Melody and intonation are interchangeable terms describing an overall pattern of the primary language. Included in this are variations in pitch; for example, Scandinavian and Oriental dialects tend to modulate from a higher key than ours, while German, in contrast, is lower and more guttural. Vocal quality is also part of the music, as are stress, elisions ("gang" for going), substitutions of vowels and consonants, and native emphases. We may not be aware of the melody in our own speech.

EXERCISE 99

We have many variations in pitch, such as

Using other familiar words, draw a few graphs of your own different intonations, then try some common phrases; for example,

When an acquired language is superimposed over a primary language, we have another element to consider. The graph of an English-American speaker might look like this:

think
I ——————————————⟍ so.

But Mexican-American's might look like this:

If we were able to hear another language without words — but by musical inflections alone — it would still seem foreign to our ears.

Certain performers have made a speciality of dialects. Danny Thomas, an American of Lebanese extraction, has perfected Yiddish so well that he is frequently mistaken for a Jew. Mr. Thomas has gone directly to Hebrew, the source of Yiddish. When characterizing an

ADVANCED VOICE AND SPEECH

American-Jew in one of his stories, he remembers first how the phrase would sound in Hebrew, adapts to Yiddish, then adds American-Yiddish variations.

Space does not permit a more detailed study of dialects, but these few hints may serve as a guide by which the actor with a particular dialect problem will be able to begin his study in the right direction. There are books specializing on the various aspects of this subject, but it will be most successful and gratifying if the student is able to work beyond the written word into *sounds*, where he will make his own discoveries.

FURTHER READING

Wise, Claude M. *Applied Phonetics.* Englewood Cliffs, N.J.: Prentice-Hall, 1957. Applies the International Phonetic Alphabet to varieties of American and English speech.

Chriest, Fred M. *Foreign Accent.* Englewood Cliffs, N.J.: Prentice-Hall, 1964.

Herman, Lewis, and Lewis, Marguerite. *Foreign Dialects.* New York: Theatre Arts Books, 1958.

————. *American Dialects,* New York: Theatre Arts Books, 1947.

A SYSTEM FOR CORRECT PRONUNCIATION

The many divergencies in our spelling are well known. For example, the first "k" in knock has no sound, and yet in "king," it sounds like a "k." "A" is pronounced in many ways but always spelled "a." Indeed, our spelling has little relation to pronunciation; for instance check the spelling against the sound of the following: *go, do, dove, women, woman, not.*

Hardly one of the sounds in our language is represented by a single symbol. This is but one reason why I recommend the International Phonetic Alphabet (IPA). This system employs symbols, each symbol representing a single sound and each sound representing a single symbol. The IPA can be of great help in eliminating substandard speech and dialectical variations and in detecting mispronunciations and improving articulation. It encourages accurate hearing. Kenyon warns that "There are few subjects on which educated Americans are so ready to pass judgement and give advice on the basis of so little sound knowledge as the pronunciation of the English we use."[2] The IPA system is authoritive; when you use it, you may be assured you are right. It will give you the confidence an actor must have.

Modern dictionaries represent sounds by respelling words and using alphabetical symbols, with dots and marks to indicate pronunciation. These *diacritical marks* may be adequate for the layman, but for those who specialize in speech, the IPA system is more effective. The publishers of dictionaries have devised different systems, no two exactly alike.

[2]John Samuel Kenyon, *American Pronunciation* (Ann Arbor, Mich.: George Wahr Publisher, 1935).

IPA SYMBOLS AND DIACRITICAL MARKS[3]

	Phonetic Symbol	Key Word		Webster	Funk & Wagnalls	American College
1.	[i]	*eat*	[it]	ē	ī	ē
2.	[ɪ]	*it*	[ɪt]	ĭ	i	ĭ
3.	[e]	*chaos*	[keɒs]	â	—	ā
4.	[ɛ]	*ever*	[ɛvɹ]	ĕ	e	ĕ
5.	[æ]	*at*	[æt]	ă	a	ă
6.	[a]	*ask*	[ask]	ȧ	ɛ	—
7.	[u]	*moon*	[mun]	o͞o	ū	o͞o
8.	[ʊ]	*book*	[bʊk]	o͝o	u	o͝o
9.	[o]	*obey*	[obeɪ]	ô	o	ō
10.	[ɔ]	*all*	[ɔl]	ô	ө̄	ô
11.	[ɒ]	*often*	[ɒfn]	ŏ	ө	ŏ
12.	[ɑ]	*father*	[faðɹ]	ä	ā	ä
13.	[ʌ]	*up*	[ʌp]	ŭ	ʊ	ŭ
14.	[ə]	*about*	[əbaʊt]	ȧ	ɔ	ə
15.	[ɝ]	*bird*	[bɝd]	ûr	Ūr	ûr
16.	[ɜ]	*bird*	[bɜd]	û	Ū	û
17.	[ɹ]	*weather*	[wɛðɹ]	ē	—	ər
18.	[aɪ]	*time*	[taɪm]	ī	aɪ	ī
19.	[ɔɪ]	*boy*	[bɔɪ]	ɵi	ɵi	oi
20.	[aʊ]	*sound*	[saʊnd]	ou	aʊ	ou
21.	[eɪ]	*day*	[deɪ]	ā	ē	ā
22.	[oʊ]	*go*	[goʊ]	ō	ō	ō
23.	[ɛɹ]	*air*	[ɛɹ]	âr	ãr	âr
24.	[m]	*may*	[meɪ]	m	m	m
25.	[n]	*no*	[noʊ]	n	n	n
26.	[ŋ]	*ring*	[rɪŋ]	ng, ŋ	ŋ	ng
27.	[p]	*pay*	[peɪ]	p	p	p
28.	[b]	*bay*	[beɪ]	b	b	b
29.	[t]	*time*	[taɪm]	t	t	t
30.	[d]	*dime*	[daɪm]	d	d	d
31.	[k]	*come*	[kʌm]	k	k	k
32.	[g]	*go*	[go]	g	g	g
33.	[f]	*feel*	[fil]	f	f	f
34.	[v]	*veal*	[vil]	v	v	v
35.	[θ]	*think*	[θɪŋk]	th	th͡	th
36.	[ð]	*them*	[ðɛm]	t̶h̶	t̶h̶	t̶h̶
37.	[s]	*soon*	[sun]	s	s	s
38.	[z]	*zoo*	[zu]	z	z	z
39.	[ʃ]	*ship*	[ʃɪp]	sh	sh͡	sh
40.	[ʒ]	*measure*	[mɛʒɹ]	zh	ʒ	zh
41.	[h]	*how*	[haʊ]	h	h	h
42.	[w]	*water*	[watɹ]	w	w	w
43.	[j]	*yes*	[jɛs]	y	y	y
44.	[r]	*red*	[rɛd]	r	r	r
45.	[l]	*leap*	[lip]	l	l	l
46.	[tʃ]	*church*	[tʃɝtʃ]	ch	ch͡	ch
47.	[dʒ]	*judge*	[dʒʌdʒ]	j	j	j

[3]From Elise Hahn and others, *Basic Voice Training for Speech* (New York: McGraw-Hill Book Company, 1957), pp. 24-55.

Should you become familiar with a particular system and find that dictionary not at hand, then you must try to puzzle out the pronunciation symbols in another dictionary, based on another system (often a trying experience). The IPA has the additional advantage of being international. Its symbols represent the same sounds in any language, an asset when an actor is working with foreign phrases and dialects. By use of the IPA system he will be able to write speech phonetically, just as he hears it when listening to a speech model or studying tapes of his own voice when following a course of speech self-improvement.

Look now at the IPA chart. You already know from your own alphabet many of the symbols and the sounds they indicate; therefore you are well on your way to memorizing the IPA system.

VOWELS

A speech teacher has made the excellent suggestion that vowels be renamed "tones," a word which denotes *sounds* rather than *letters*. Vowels are the main vehicles of speech. All vowel sounds are voiced.[4] Their characteristic is that the outward stream of breath is not stopped or interrupted. The tone is generally believed to be influenced by the laryngeal, oral, and nasal cavities. Because of the position of the tongue when making sounds, the pure vowels are classified as front, middle, and back. The tongue is a much larger and more influential instrument in speech than most people imagine. Pure vowels are made by a single position of the mouth, whereas a diphthong is a combination of two vowels with the tongue gliding smoothly from one position to another position, which it may not necessarily reach. Old actors referred to a diphthong as "a vowel and a vanish."

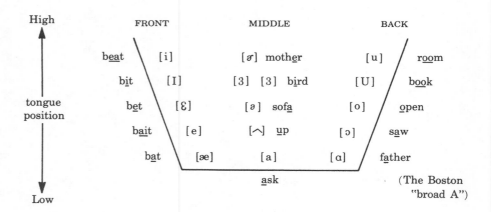

[4]Some experts disagree. Touch your throat and *whisper* a, e, i, o, and u. Can you do it and not use voice?

332   APPENDIX 2

EXERCISE 100

With the vowel chart before you, follow the line from left to right as you read aloud, first the word, then the isolated vowel sound as underlined.

Using a mirror, watch the adjustments made by your lips, jaw, and especially your tongue as you perform this exercise. Practice saying the words below, and note in the mirror the adjustments made by your lips, jaw, and tongue, and where the sounds are made.

late, hat, yes, calm, ask (general American); ask (English or Bostonian), seem, hit, reap

In the following list, practice the complete word, then isolate the vowel sound.

feet, women, fatal, ever, plaid, true, put, protrude, aunt

EXERCISE 101. SUSTAINING TONES

Only vowels may be sustained. Consonants cannot. Stand and relax. Next place both palms on the abdomen, just under the rib cage. Inhale. Imagine a fist is being aimed at your middle. Tighten the muscles. Exhale as you *shout* "HAH!" Relax. Again inhale. As you exhale, shout *"HAY!"* Again, assume the same position and conditions, but shout *"HEE!"* Again, *"HOH!"* Relax. Assume the same position and the same conditions, but this time conserve breath in order to sustain the vowels:

1. HAH h-h-h-h-h!
2. HAY a-a-a-a-a!
3. HEE e-e-e-e-e!
4. HOH o-o-o-o-o!
5. HI i-i-i-i-i!

Note that in preparation for each sustained tone, you are first filling your lungs with an adequate supply of air to "motorize" the long tone. In such exercises, we develop the fellows of the instrument. The normal breathing cycle is altered. We actually take more breath than the body requires. This is a necessity in sustaining tones.

Here are some vowels to practice:

language, luscious, hair, eat, tear, care, grieve, machine, receive, mend, friend, manager, statue, dashing, task, half, glance, dance, grass, earnest, learn, first, tomb, noon, lose, took, book, torn, nook, lawn

DIPHTHONGS

In sounding a diphthong, the tongue, lips, and jaw take a vowel position and then glide to another sound where the sound either stops at once or glides on to another sound. Examples: twice, how, soil, bait, boat, mouse,

ADVANCED VOICE AND SPEECH

prone, wore, cheer, hour. There are five main diphthongs,[5] but other combinations may be called diphthongs when they have similar glide movements.

CONSONANTS

Unlike vowels, which are made by breath traveling through *uninterrupted* passages to become tones, consonants are hewn and shaped into crisp, clean sounds by tongue, lips, and teeth.[6] A less fanciful and more accurate definition is given by Hahn:

> To produce consonants, the breath stream is stopped momentarily at a particular place in the mouth, or made to flow through a narrow passageway, or diverted through the nose. The positions for the articulation of consonants are therefore much more definite than for vowels.

Some consonants are voiceless, as in *p, t, k, s, f, h;* others are voiced, as in *b, d, g, v, w, n,* and *l.* "Voiced" sounds are the results of actions or movements of the vocal folds and the vibrations of air in the resonating cavities. "Voiceless" is the opposite of "voiced." You may always check the difference by placing your fingers on your Adam's apple as you speak a word.

Consonants require fast and efficient adjustments of lips, tongue, and cheek. They carry the main burden of speech, giving it clarity, vigor, and beauty. Common faults in the phonation of consonants are either a tendency to be overprecise, or to slur the sounds so that they are unintelligible. Consonants should be spoken so that there is no doubt as to the sound. Never expose an audience to such sounds as "Bra'way" for Broadway, "belong'inks" for belongings, or "may-an" for man unless these pronunciations are contributing to your characterization.

If you intend to work at self-improvement (and no one is perfect), it will help you if you start by determining: (1) whether you have proper breathing and control of it, (2) where and how sounds are made, (3) whether you hear accurately and are able to echo sounds correctly, and (4) whether you are able to bring meaning to lines by use of stressed syllables, pauses, and contrasts between weak and strong words.

SELF-IMPROVEMENT

The proper procedure for improving speech skills begins with an analysis. Adequate survey will reveal to both instructor and student areas in which work is needed. The tape recording of each student's speech can be used as training proceeds and later to show progress. Material for the recording should be varied. Begin with a little informal conversation, then perhaps

[5]From *Basic Voice Training for Speech* by Elise Hahn and others (New York: McGraw-Hill Book Company, 1957). Used by permission.

[6]For detailed descriptions of consonants, see Margaret McLean, *Good American Speech* (New York: E. P. Dutton, 1952), Ch. 3.

some formal verse, and certainly some lines or speeches from plays. Plays selected should be both modern and classic and each period should be represented by serious and comic excerpts. The recording should be studied and the checklist below filled out and preserved for future comparison with later recordings.

CHECKLIST ON VOICE AND SPEECH

Name_____ Date_____
_____
_____

RELAXATION
         Student has ability to relax_____
         Needs work___ Tense___ Distracted___ Indifferent___
Remarks_____

BREATHING   Type: Clavicular___ Upper Thorax_____ Medial_____
               Diaphragmatic-Abdominal_____
Remarks_____

PROJECTION Excellent___ Good___ Needs work_____
  VOLUME: Too loud___ Too weak___ Muffled___
           Lacks variety_____ General, needs correction___
Remarks_____
  TIMING:

	Good	Average	Needs work
Phrasing_____			
Intensity_____			
Ability to amplify sounds_____			
Variety_____			

RESONATION
  PITCH:
         General level: Too high____ Too low_____
         Uncertain_____
Remarks_____
  QUALITY:
         Sincere___ Nasal___ Tense___ Breathy (aspirate)_____
         Emotional___ Colorless___ Warm, friendly_____
         Thin___ Indifferent___ Metallic___ Husky_____ Harsh_____
         Portentous_____ Slurred (meaning unclear)_____
         Strident (strained)_____ Flat (lack of vibrato)_____
Remarks on quality of tones_____

INSTRUMENTS:	Clear	Obstructed	
Nose_____			
Mouth_____			
Throat_____			

Remarks_____

ARTICULATION
         Ease at manipulation of articulars_____
         Needs correction_____
Proper action of Tongue_____ Needs work_____
               Lips_____ Needs work_____
               Teeth_____ Needs work_____

ADVANCED VOICE AND SPEECH   335

PRONUNCIATION

Hearing: Accurate___ Faulty___ Incorrect___
Suggestions to improve_____

DICTION:

SOUND PRODUCTION:

Ability to enunciate vowels
Good___ Needs work___
Ability to articulate consonants
Good___ Needs work___
Ability to stress important words
Good___ Needs work___
Ability to stress syllables
Good___ Needs work___
Enunciation (General)
Satisfactory___ Needs correction___
Omissions?___ Substitutions?___Additions?___
Ability to use IPA symbols
Good_____ Needs practice_____

ACCENT:

Foreign___ "General American"_____
Classification of General American, localized accents.
Eastern
"Yankee"_____ Bostonian_____ New York_____
Southern
"General Southern"____ Rural or mountain____
Texas_____ Florida_____
Midwestern
Chicago____ Ohio____ Pennsylvania____ Iowa____
Western
Oklahoma____ Wyoming____ Other, not listed_____
Northwestern____ Southwestern____
San Francisco____

Remarks_____

FURTHER READING

In addition to readily available references for pronunciation, such as Funk and Wagnall's, Webster International, and New College dictionaries, there are others which most actors use:

Bender, J. F. *NBC Handbook of Pronunciation,* New York: Crowell, 1955.

Jones, Daniel. *An Outline of English Phonetics.* London: Albert Saifer, 1957. For English as spoken by Londoners.

Kenyon, John S., and Knott, Thomas A. *A Pronunciating Dictionary of American English,* Springfield, Mass.: Merriam, 1944. Uses IPA symbols.

Thomas, Charles. *Phonetics of American-English.* New York: Ronald Press, 1958. For American dialects.

Index

INDEX

INDEX

Student's Rehearsal Notes

Student's Rehearsal Notes

Student's Rehearsal Notes

Student's Rehearsal Notes

Student's Rehearsal Notes

Student's Rehearsal Notes

Student's Rehearsal Notes

Student's Rehearsal Notes

Student's Rehearsal Notes

Student's Rehearsal Notes

Student's Rehearsal Notes

Student's Rehearsal Notes

Student's Rehearsal Notes

Student's Rehearsal Notes

Student's Rehearsal Notes

Student's Rehearsal Notes

Student's Rehearsal Notes

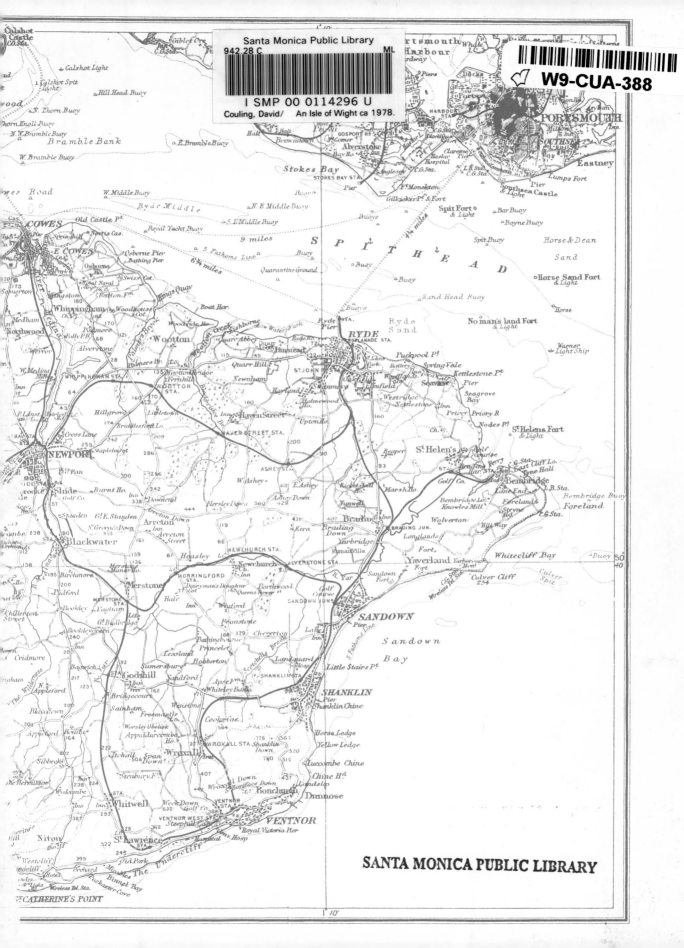

AN ISLE OF WIGHT CAMERA

The endpapers show a map of the Isle of Wight
drawn in 1914

AN ISLE OF WIGHT CAMERA

1856~1914

David Couling

The Dovecote Press

FOR RUTH

Be to her virtues very kind;
Be to her faults a little blind.
Mathew Prior

Text © David Couling 1978
First Published in Great Britain 1978 by
The Dovecote Press
Stanbridge, Wimborne, Dorset
in association with
The Compton Press Ltd
The Old Brewery, Tisbury, Wiltshire
and printed offset by
Unwin Brothers, The Gresham Press, Old Woking,
Surrey
ISBN 0 9503518 2 2

Contents

Introduction

The Isle of Wight has often been regarded as a micro-cosm of southern England, but there are two factors which make it unique: its mild climate and the fact that it is surrounded by water. Nowhere could the benefits of these two features be more apparent than in the pages of this book. For in the early nineteenth century the Isle of Wight – 'The Island' as it has always been affectionately known by its residents – was a quiet and undisturbed rural backwater. The signs of progress were few, for none of its coastal towns and villages had as yet become a fashionable 'watering place'. There was no regular packet service to the Island; those who wished to visit it completed the voyage in open wherries and were carried by cart over the mud that then covered the northern foreshore. Its economy was dependent on fishing and farming. In winter it was often impossible to reach the Island for days at a time. Yet, despite its isolation, the Island was beginning to gather a reputation as a retreat for writers, poets and artists. Keats lived and wrote for a time at Newport and Shanklin; Swinburne spent his childhood at East Down, later returning to the Island; and Thomas Arnold, historian, theologian and greatest of English schoolmasters, was born in East Cowes.

In 1852 Tennyson came to live in the peace of Farringford, remaining for more than thirty years and writing much of his best known work whilst living on the Island. Seven years earlier, in 1845, Queen Victoria and Prince Albert had bought the 2,000 acre Osborne estate from Lady Isabella Blachford. It was intended as a country retreat, a place where the Queen and her family might scape from the duties and pomp that surrounded them on the mainland. But, unwittingly, the Queen's action was to turn the Island into the most popular of Victorian seaside resorts. As an increasing number of visitors crossed the Solent to tour the island where the Queen chose to spend so much of her time, the Isle of Wight's character began to change.

The start of a regular packet service and the arrival of the railways made the Island increasingly accessible and led, in turn, to the influx of tourists so deplored by Tennyson. Indeed, many visitors made a special pilgrimage to Farringford to see the poet. The development of the Island railway system was a gradual process, largely taking place in the twenty years that followed the formation of the Isle of Wight Railway Company in 1864. By 1876 Ryde, Ventnor and Newport were all connected by railway. Shanklin, Sandown and Ventnor had developed into popular resorts whose commercial season extended throughout much of the winter. For, as one guide-book wrote, 'there is none of the risks which lurks round almost every corner of the Riviera of encountering the icy winds which visit it in the winter; there is practically no dust, which is such a potent cause of disease; and there are none of the characteristic foreign smells which often point to defective sanitation.' In other words, it was respectable, wholesome and a perfect place to spend a holiday. Tourists flocked to it. It had sandy beaches, superb scenery, a romantic history and was home for both the Queen and the greatest of nineteenth-century poets.

The first recorded regatta was held off the Island in 1776, forerunner of a yachting season which begins at Cowes in May and reaches its climax in the first week of August. As yachting grew fashionable, thanks partly to the patronage of Prince Albert and King Edward VII, it brought additional prosperity to the Island and its boat yards. Whereas the latter built and maintained the yachts, the former provided the large professional crews needed to man them.

As the paddle steamer service developed, links between the Island and mainland grew closer. Day trips could be taken between one resort and the next, excursions be taken to view the Needles. Indeed, for many visitors the Needles summed up everything the Island stood for. A foreign visitor once wrote: 'We approached the Needles. The spectacle was grand. Our officers gazed in admiration. The very men who swarmed upon the deck made a pause to look upon the giddy height. The most exact steerage seemed necessary to save the ship from the sharp rocks that compress the waters into the narrow straights below. There is something imposing in entering England by this passage'.

Most of the photographs included in this book have never been published before, and it is worth remembering that at the time they were taken photography was not the simple matter that it is today. The photographer had to carry a large amount of equipment, including heavy glass plate negatives, which were sometimes as large as 12 inches by 10 inches. PLATES 78, 79 and 80 were contact-printed directly from such negatives. Considerable patience must have been needed to obtain such superb results, especially as all three photographs were taken from a moving boat. But such photographs are rare, and today, more than at any time in the past, the collecting of Victorian and Edwardian photographs has become of paramount importance to local libraries and archive departments. In the case of the Isle of Wight they afford a valuable insight into the way of life of its people and provide a remarkable document of the changes that took place on the Island during the latter part of the nineteenth century.

Many people have unwittingly contributed to this book. They are those who have recognized the importance of their old photographs and have made them available to public bodies. One can only hope that this enlightened trend will continue in the future.

Acknowledgements

I am most grateful to the following for allowing me to include their photographs in this book: The County Records Office, Newport: photograph numbers 1, 6, 7, 9, 10, 11, 12, 13, 15, 16, 18, 19, 21, 23, 24, 25, 26, 27, 28, 29, 30, 31, 32, 35, 38, 39, 41, 46, 51, 53, 55, 56, 58, 59, 61, 64, 65, 68, 69, 77, 84, 89, 92, 93, 95, 96, 98, 102, 106, 107, 109, 111, 113, 118, 119, 121, 123; R. E. Brinton: 8, 14, 17, 33, 34, 43, 45, 54, 57, 62, 66, 99, 101, 104, 105, 108, 120; Frank Cheverton Ltd., Newport: 40, 122; D. Couling: 72, 80, 87, 94, 112; The Cowes Maritime Museum: 37, 52, 88, 97; The Cope Collection: 42, 49, 50, 60, 63, 67, 71, 103, 114, 115, 116, 117; The Bernard Cox Collection: 3, 4, 110; L. J. Daly: 20, 22, 100; J. A. Haysom: 5; The National Motor Museum, Beaulieu: 36; The National Maritime Museum, Greenwich: 86, 124; The Royal Naval Museum, Portsmouth: 91; The City of Southampton, Civic Records Office: 5; Roger M. Smith of Cowes: 2, 44, 47, 70, 73, 74, 75, 76, 78, 79, 81, 82, 83, 85, 90; Dorothy Woodhouse: 48.

I should like to express my debt to the following for their assistance and kindness in helping me in my research; without their help, this book would not have been possible: L. J. Mitchell, Director of Cultural Services, The Isle of Wight; Mrs. H. Scammell and the staff of The County Records Office, Newport; Mrs. Harrison and the staff of The Cowes Maritime Museum; G. Hampson, Sub Librarian Special Collection, The Cope Collection; Miss S. D. Thomson, City Archivist, The City of Southampton, Civic Records Office; Commander S. G. Clark, M.B.E. R.N. (Retd), Director, The Royal Naval Museum, Portsmouth; Mr. Gully, Frank Cheverton Ltd., Newport; Bernard Cox.

I should also like to express my gratitude to those who assisted in resolving problems in the production of this book: R. E. Brinton, for supplying and dating many of the photographs; Keith Turner, a valued assistant in my research; and Graham Davis for checking the text.

Lastly I should like to thank David Burnett of The Dovecote Press: his advice and encouragement have been invaluable.

Departure

2. (*Overleaf.*) The SS *Brighton Queen* travelling between Southampton and Ryde in about 1905. The *Brighton Queen* was built in 1899. After the outbreak of war in 1914 she became a mine-sweeper and a year later was sunk by a mine off the Belgian coast. The first steam packet service between the Isle of Wight and the mainland was started in 1826. Twenty years later, Queen Victoria bought the Osborne estate and from then on the Island's popularity as a summer resort was assured.

Isle of Wight Steamer, Portsmouth Harbour.

4. Lymington harbour, 1890. The two paddle steamers shown in the photograph are the *Mayflower* and *Solent*. The Lymington ferry went to Yarmouth. Throughout the nineteenth century schemes were discussed and companies formed for the construction of a tunnel under the Solent between the two towns. Thankfully, the tunnel has yet to become a reality.

3. The *Duchess of Edinburgh* docked at
Portsmouth in 1900.

5. The Royal Pier, Southampton, in about 1890.

Arrival

6. Ryde Pierhead in 1899. The first pier was built in 1814, before which the packets were met by wherries and their passengers driven across the beach in carts. The pier was later lengthened and a horse-drawn tram service started. The horses were replaced by electric trams in 1885. The railway pier was built in 1879. Note the line of amusement machines in the foreground.

7. Victoria Pier, Ryde, in about 1880. The pier was built in 1859 but was never a commercial success and has since been demolished. At the end of the century hot and cold ozone baths were built near the pierhead for those suffering from rheumatism.

8. Yarmouth in 1890. The Square was almost the first place visitors went to after disembarking from the Lymington ferry. In 1890 a passenger ticket on the ferry cost 4d.

9 Shanklin Pier in about 1900. A notice to the left of the
entrance gives details of paddle steamer departures to
Cherbourg, Brighton, Southsea, Bournemouth, the Needles,
Southampton and round the Island.

11. Seaview beach in 1912. Note
that the bathing machines have
been replaced by changing
tents.

10. The *Brighton Queen* alongside Cowes Pier in 1903.

Beside the Sea

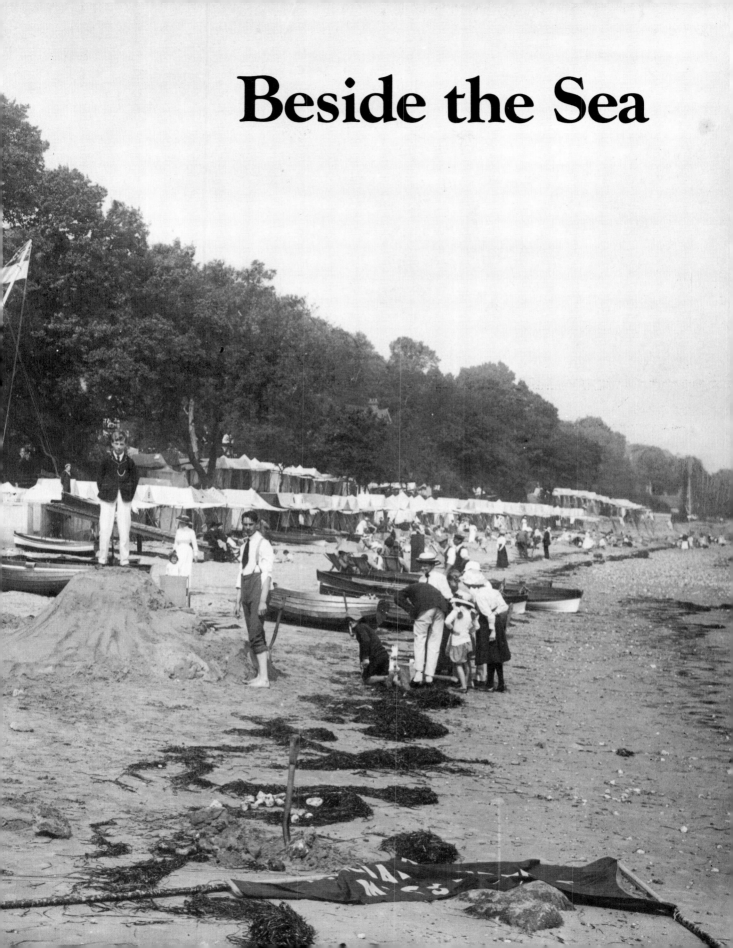

12. Seaview Sands in the summer of 1912.

13. Seaview Sands and Pier in 1892. The 1,000 foot pier was modelled on the chain pier at Brighton and was built between 1879 and 1881 at a cost of £6,000. In December 1951 it was wrecked by storms.

14. Sandown from the cliffs in about 1890. The development of the town was typical of most Island resorts. In 1850 it boasted only a few fishermen's huts, by 1890 it had nearly 5,000 residents. For a while it was the most fashionable resort in England and in 1874 four European monarchs spent part of the summer in the town.

15. Sandown seafront from the pier in 1891. The pier was built in 1878.

16. Pierrots performing on the sand at Sandown in the early 1900s.

17. 'The Orchids' playing at the Kursaal, Sandown Pier in about 1905. Though its name has since been changed the Kursaal is still in use as a dance hall.

18. Looking west along the mile long length of Sandown esplanade, 1896.

19. (*Overleaf.*) Shanklin beach in 1910, looking west from the pier. No other photograph sums up so superbly the popularity of the Isle of Wight as a summer resort. Indeed, Shanklin was so crowded during the summer months that a local guide-book complained that 'trippers come more often than is desirable, that its beauties are shorn, its glories departed.'

20. Holiday makers on the sands at Shanklin in the summer of 1860.

21. Shanklin from the pier in 1900. The pier was completed in 1891 at a cost of £24,000. Facing the pier was a pump-room where the waters could be tasted at 1d. a glass. Note the hydraulic cliff-lift.

22. Sampson's Baths, Shanklin Chine, in about 1860.

23. Shanklin Sands in the early 1900s. The clock tower was built to commemorate Queen Victoria's Diamond Jubilee.

24. Ventnor from the beach in 1878. In the early nineteenth century Ventnor consisted of an inn, mill and a few fiishermen's cottages. In 1829 Sir James Clark (later Queen Victoria's physician) wrote a paper on *Organic Diseases* in which he described the Undercliff as 'a highly favourable residence for invalids throughout the year.' The town's future was assured and by 1878 it boasted hotels, an esplanade, Town Hall, theatre and Consumptive Hospital.

25. Ventnor beach in 1892. The bathing machines lined up at the water's edge were for use by women only and could be hired for 4d. a day.

26. Ventnor looking east, 1890.

27. Ventnor, looking west, in the early 1900s.

28. Ventnor Pier in 1887. The town's first two piers were both destroyed by storms.

30. Gentlemen's bathing machines on the beach at Ventnor, 1908.

29. Two visitors to the Island on Cripples Path, Blackgang Chine, in 1856. Once a notorious smuggling haunt – hence its name – Blackgang Chine has since developed into one of the main tourist attractions on the Island.

34. Totland Bay in 1890, ten years after the opening of both the pier and hotel. As one Victorian guide-book told its readers, and as this photograph suggests, 'the *clientele* of this modest watering-place is of a distinguished kind.'

36. (*Overleaf.*) A Milnes Daimler motor bus in Queen's Road, Ryde, in about 1910. Note the wickerwork on the top deck.

35. Ryde Esplanade and Pier in 1867.

Transport

37. The Wight No. 2 Navyplane in flight off Cowes in September 1913. The plane, made by Wight & Sons of Cowes, had made its maiden flight in the previous month. After modifications it was tested by the Admiralty. After the outbreak of war it was used for training purposes at Calshot and was eventually 'written-off' in May 1915.

38. A coach-and-four outside the 'Old Times' coach booking office in Ryde High Street in about 1880.

39 A coach-and-four about to disembark from the floating bridge which carried passengers between Cowes and East Cowes over the River Medina, in about 1900.

40. An Argyle 4 cylinder tourer. In the early days of motoring it was difficult to take cars to the Island. Most were loaded on to barges at Lymington and towed across by tug. In 1912 the fare for a car was 10/-.

41. A 14 cwt wagonette, built by the East Cowes firm of Liquid Fuel Engineering Co in 1899. With a 40 gallon oil tank sufficient for an 80 mile journey and an 80 gallon water tank, enough for 25 miles, the wagonette could reach a top speed of 18 mph.

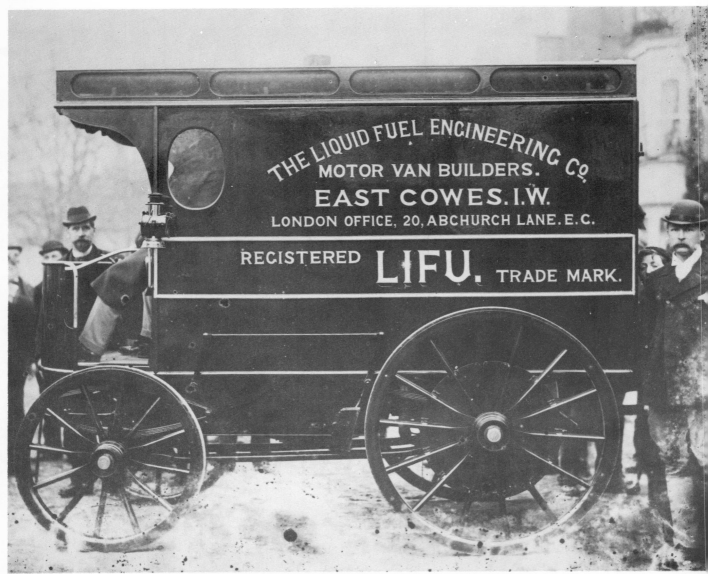

42. The start of the Isle of Wight Motor Bus Service, April 1906. The service operated from Ryde and covered most of the Island. Each bus was equipped with a postbox and handled the delivery of newspapers to each of the villages on its route. The lack of business during the winter months and the poor condition of the roads led to the company failing in the following year.

43. Work on the last section of the Ryde to Ventnor railway line, after emerging from the tunnel under St Boniface Down. The line was finally opened in September 1866.

44. (*Overleaf*.) A superb photograph of the 'Terrier' (0-6-0T No. 12) of The Isle of Wight Central Railway crossing the level-crossing at Shide in 1904. The 'Terrier' was built in 1880 and was used on the Island from 1903 to 1936.

47. A mid-morning break for shipwrights at an East Cowes yard in 1888.

45. The first train into Shanklin Station. 1864. This train is reputed to have been driven by 'Hell-Fire Jack', a legendary Island train-driver who paid little attention to speed limits. By the end of the century the Island rail network had been completed and you could buy a 13/- ticket which enabled you to travel anywhere you liked for a week.

46. A coach leaving Shanklin Station in 1864. Until the completion of the line to Ventnor the coach acted as a link between the two towns.

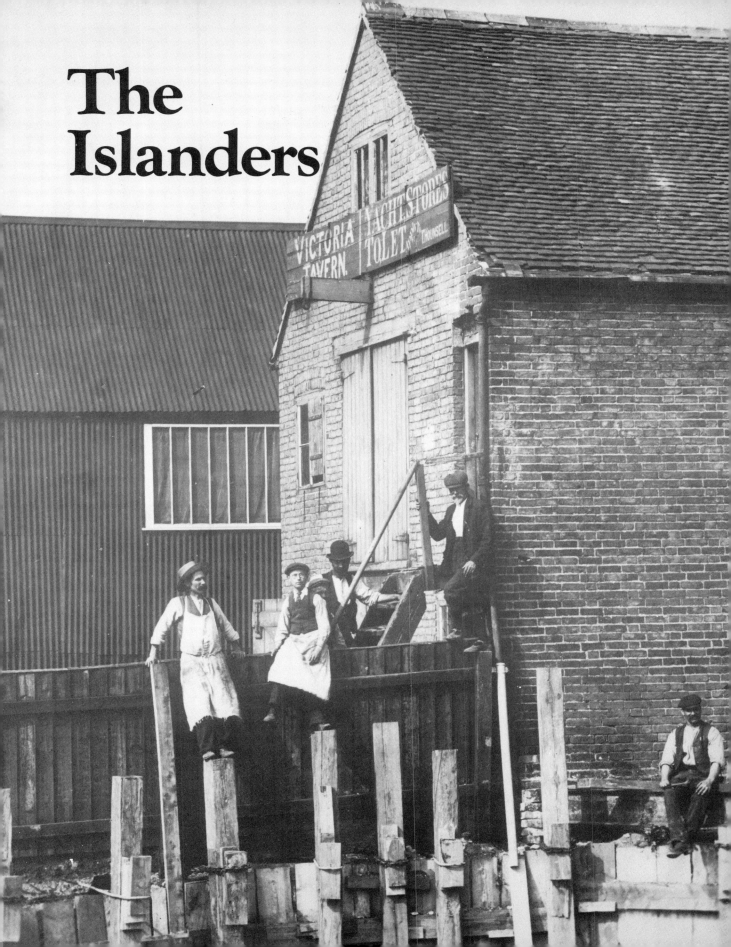

The Islanders

49. A group of Islanders standing outside Whitwell Post Office in 1908.

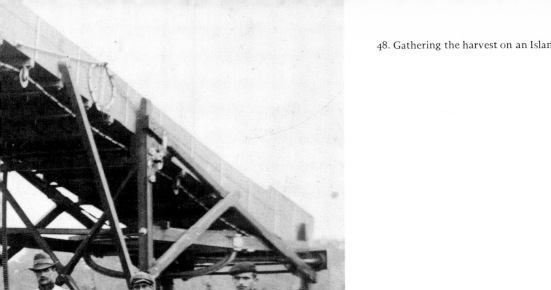

48. Gathering the harvest on an Island farm in 1900.

50. A. H. Couldrey outside his Bembridge hardware store in 1905.

51. Fishermen with their boats, nets and pots on Luccombe beach in about 1880.

52. Mr H. White aboard his steam-powered wildfowler's punt in the early 1900s. The noise of the engine can hardly have been much assistance when stalking wildfowl.

53. A group of fishermen taking mackerel from a seine net in 1911.

54. A soldier of the Isle of Wight Rifle Volunteers holding a standard issue flint-lock muzzle loading rifle in about 1859.

55. A group of Bandsmen at Newtown Camp in the summer of 1912.

56. The Shanklin Bazaar in about 1858.

57. A fine display of Christmas fare, by G. A. Burt, a Ventnor butcher, in 1900.

58. The Inn at Old Shanklin, before the fire in 1869 which left it a charred wreck. In describing the fire, *The Shanklin Journal* wrote: 'While all praise is due to those who worked so energetically in endeavouring to subdue the flames, we cannot too strongly condemn the conduct of others, who might have rendered valuable assistance, but who preferred to look on, and criticise the actions of those engaged.' The inn was owned by the Prouten family, represented here by the man and two women on the left. On the right are the town crier, William Clayton, in a top hat, and Francis Cooper, the town's leading builder, in a smart white suit.

59. James Horlock, bailiff of the Shanklin Estate. Horlock was disliked in the village and in 1848 he informed his employer that 'Michaelmas at Shanklin (when servants were hired) is nothing but a scene of drunkenness.' The estate's legal advisers once described him as 'useful, but . . . too busy praying.' He died in 1866.

60. Yaverland Manor in 1900 when it belonged to a family of farmers called White.

61. George Tullege, shepherd at Shanklin Farm. Tullege's house, Ash Cottage, was demolished in 1874 when the Upper Chine was being built. He was born in 1793, the year the Napoleonic Wars started, and died in 1877.

62. A group of Islanders gathered in an unidentifiable lane in 1900. This photograph was sent out as a Christmas card.

63. Canine competitors being rowed out to sea before the start of the Dog Race at Gurnard Regatta in 1910. The dogs were dropped overboard and the race won by the first to reach shore.

64. A gathering of Islanders for the presentation of £300, a photograph album and other gifts to the Reverend and Mrs Barry Cole on the occasion of their golden wedding anniversary in July 1899.

65. An excursion of the Mothers Meeting at Haylands, Ryde in 1904.

66. The Victorian love of sentiment is illustrated in this early photographic study, taken in Bonchurch graveyard in the late 1850s. The inscription reads:
'To The Memory of
    Little Jane
who died 30th Jan 1799
    in her fifteenth
    year of her age'

67. A girl shrimping at St. Helens in 1905.

68. 'The Young Shipbuilders', a typical example of the late-Victorian postcards sold in the Island resort towns.

69. A group of children gathered round a rowing-boat at Chine Hill, Shanklin. The boat belonged to John Prouten, landlord of the Chine Inn.

▷ 70. (*Overleaf.*) A group of visiting gentry gathered outside Osborne House. Though none of their names are known it seems possible that they may have included members of various European royal families.

The Gentry

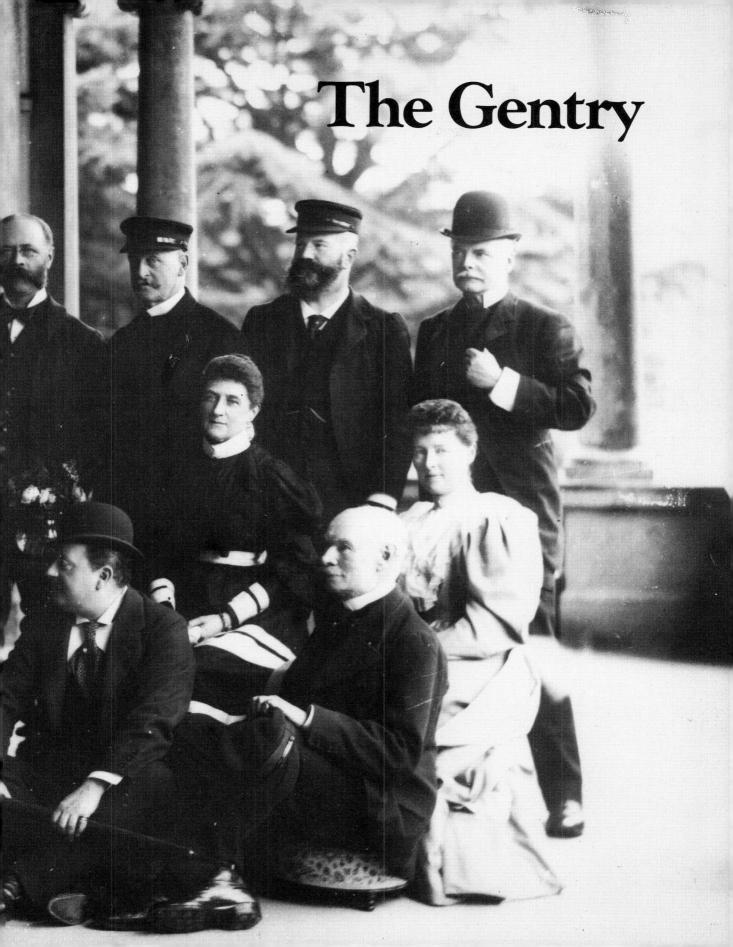

71. Yaverland Vicarage in about 1880, when William Malland was Rector. The tricycle on the left was a two-seater.

73. A view of the Harbord-Johnstone wedding reception at Cowes in the summer of 1898.

72. This fine portrait of an unnamed Island lady was taken in about 1860.

74. A Sixth Term official portrait of the cadets at the Royal Naval College, Osborne, in 1911.

75. A society wedding group photographed on the lawns of the Royal Yacht Squadron, Cowes, in about 1890.

76. A group of visiting gentry on board their
yacht in Cowes Harbour in 1901.

77. Margaret Cameron's famous portrait of Alfred, Lord Tennyson. For many years Margaret Cameron's collection of photographs (recently saved for the nation after a special appeal) hung in the waiting room on Lymington Pier. In 1852 Tennyson bought Farringford House. It was his home for the next thirty years and much of his work, including *Maud* and *Idylls of the King* was written in an attic he called his 'fumitory'. Near to the house, on Tennyson Down, a cross was constructed after the poet's death, for it was here, 'in fair days and foul, that Tennyson was accustomed to make a daily pilgrimage, declaring that the air on the Downs was worth "sixpence a pint." He would sit for hours gazing out to sea, his big, black, broad-rimmed hat and his military-looking cloak wrapped about the tall, bent firm, making him a picturesque figure, familiar to everyone in the vicinity of his beloved home.'

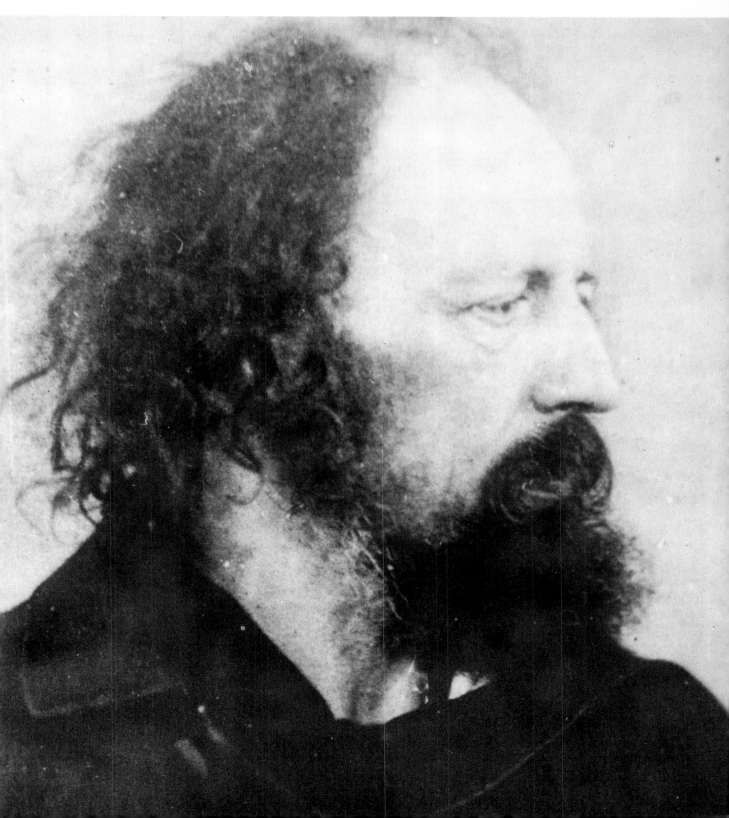

Yachts &
Shipbuilding

78. (*Overleaf.*) The Royal Yacht *Britannia* in about 1900. Built for Edward, Prince of Wales (later King Edward VII), the 122 foot racing cutter won a record total of 208 prizes between 1893 and 1924. She was manned by a professional crew of 35 and boasted 17,000 feet of canvas when under full sail. After King George V's death the *Britannia* was taken out to sea and scuttled, in accordance with his wishes.

79. A motor boat taking part in an early powerboat race off Cowes in about 1900.

80. The tug *Irishman* leaving Cowes Harbour in 1905.

81. *Shamrock II*, dismasted off Cowes during trials in 1901 when King Edward VII was on board. The 265 ton yacht was the second of the same name to be owned by Sir Thomas Lipton.

82. The steam yacht *Gladys* being repainted in an East Cowes boat yard in 1895.

83. The view from Lallows Yard, West Cowes, towards East Cowes, in about 1890.

84. The American yacht *Xarifa* berthed at Cowes in 1894.

85. Archduke Charles Stephen of Austria (standing on the right in a white cap) aboard his steam yacht *Ui* at Cowes in about 1890.

86. The Royal Yacht *Victoria and Albert*, the third with the same name. The yacht was built in 1899, and, after being broken-up in the 1950s, was replaced by the present Royal Yacht *Britannia*. The *Victoria and Albert* was made entirely of wood, weighed 5,500 tons and was 380 feet long. One of her last official duties was to carry Queen Elizabeth II for the Coronation Review of the Fleet at Spithead.

87. A gaff-rigged ketch sailing past the holiday makers on Victoria Pier, Cowes, in 1900.

88. The destroyer HMS *Brooke* off the Isle of Wight in 1912. The *Brooke* was built on the Island by White's in 1896. In 1917 she rammed and sank a German destroyer and after the war was sold to the Chilean Navy.

89. The paddle steamer *Valiant* on trials off Cowes in 1902, before sent to Africa for use on the River Niger. This stern-wheeler was one of a succession of paddle steamers built by White's at Cowes and even when loaded had a draught of only 2 feet.

90. A fleet of 15 metre yachts during a race off Cowes in the summer of 1913. The first recorded regatta took place at Cowes in 1776. Although the Yacht Club was formed in 1815 it became the Royal Yacht Club in 1820 and was named the Royal Yacht Squadron in honour of William IV in 1833. The racing season began in May and finished at the end of September, but the most important races took place during Cowes Week in early August.

91. A posed photograph of the only two survivors of HMS *Eurydice*, Ordinary Seaman Sydney Fletcher and Able Seaman Benjamin Cuddiford. The *Eurydice*, a 900 ton 26 gun frigate first commissioned in 1877, was returning to Portsmouth from a training cruise in the West Indies when she was struck by a sudden squall two-and-a-half miles off Sandown in March 1878. She suddenly capsized and foundered; out of a total crew of 300, Fletcher and Cuddiford were the only survivors. This photograph was presented to the two men by a Ventnor doctor who gave them first aid when they were first brought ashore.

Wrecks

92. An attempt to right HMS *Eurydice* in
Sandown Bay, 1878. Seven of those who died
when the ship went down are buried in Christ
Church, Sandown.

93. A coastguard on patrol on an Island beach
in 1858.

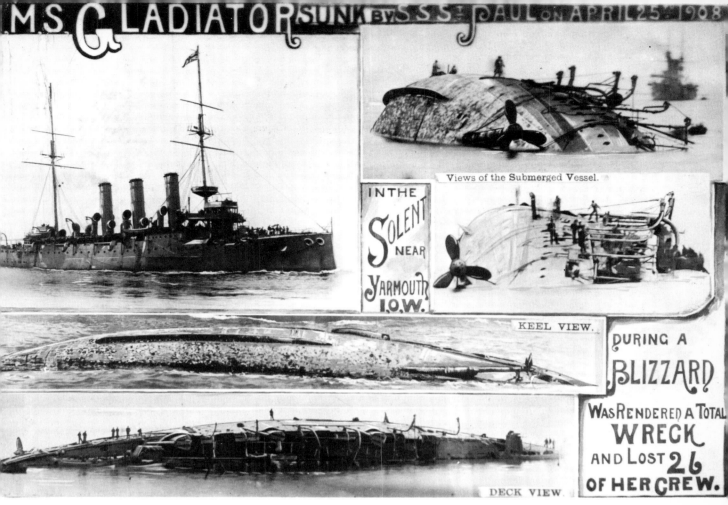

MS GLADIATOR SUNK BY SSS PAUL on APRIL 25th 1908

Views of the Submerged Vessel.

IN THE SOLENT NEAR YARMOUTH I.O.W.

KEEL VIEW.

DURING A BLIZZARD WAS RENDERED A TOTAL WRECK AND LOST 26 OF HER CREW.

DECK VIEW.

94. A postcard commemorating the loss of HMS *Gladiator* on April 25th 1908. The *Gladiator* collided with the American liner *St Paul* during a freak snowstorm off Yarmouth, and although her captain managed to run her onto the sands 26 lives were lost in the accident.

95. A party of sightseers being rowed round the half-submerged HMS *Gladiator* on 26 April 1908. Note the diver in the centre of the photograph.

96. A group of HM Coastguards in about 1860. Each man was armed with a musket, bayonet, two sea-service pistols, a sword, powder and ammunition. They were housed in beached hulks and amongst the furniture issued to each coastguard were an iron bedstead, four Windsor chairs and a half-bushel coalbox.

98. Newport High Street, in about 1906.

97. The ill-fated paddle steamer *Chancellor* aground at Ventnor after her second voyage in July 1863. Ventnor pier was then still being built and, on her maiden voyage, the *Chancellor's* passengers had to be taken ashore in rowing boats. To avoid further discomfort to the passengers the *Chancellor's* owners decided that in future she should berth alongside the pier. The operation was a success, but during the night she was blown broadside on to the beach and broke in half.

Places

102. The road to Godshill. This photograph, taken in 1890, captures the unspoilt character of the Island in the nineteenth century.

99. Bonchurch in 1859. Dr Thomas Arnold, the Head-master of Rugby School who was born in East Cowes, once described the village 'as the most beautiful thing on the sea coast on this side of Genoa'; whilst another Victorian thought 'that heaven itself can scarcely be more beautiful.'

100. Godshill in about 1870. The village is now a noted tourist attraction.

101. Shanklin village in about 1859. In 1846 it was described as 'small and scattery, all mixed up with trees, and lying among sweet airy falls and swells of ground.' Between 1851 and 1871 the population of the town rose from 355 to nearly 3,000.

103. The Parade, Cowes, during Cowes Week in 1912.   104. Cowes High Street in 1904.

107. (*Overleaf.*) Ryde esplanade and gardens, 1898.

105. Castle Street, Carisbrooke in 1890, 'as charming, clean-looking, and delightfully situated as any village in the interior of the Island.'

106. The gateway to Carisbrooke Castle in 1862. Leaning against the gate is a blind guide; a card, explaining his disability, hangs round his neck. A visit to Carisbrooke was almost compulsory for all visitors to the Island; by 1860, twenty horse buses a day plied between the castle and Newport during the summer months.

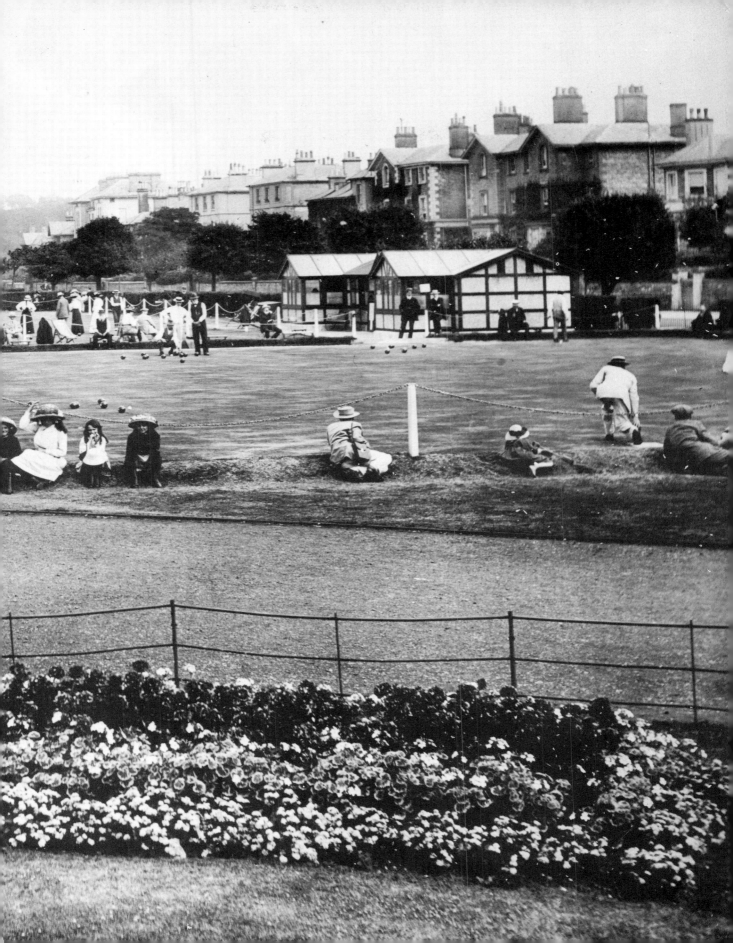

111. The 2nd Wessex Howitzer Brigade riding through Ryde High Street in 1900. Horses were brought over to the Island from Portsmouth in barges and landed at the Horse Boat slip on Ryde esplanade.

112. The scene at a Newport Market Day in 1900. The market was held every Tuesday in St James Square. In 1927 it was moved to the South Street Cattle Market. It was traditionally the most important of all the markets held on the Island.

113. The eastern end of Ventnor in 1902. An open air concert is taking place on the right.

114. The Point Hotel, Bembridge,
later the Pilot Boat Inn, in about
1880. A late nineteenth-century
guide-book described the village
as a place where 'the scenery
is not sublime; the smaller shops
are still rather primitive; and
we are not even sure that the
older cottages conform to the
very latest requirements of
civilization.' Such sentiments
seem to have kept many visitors
away, for Bembridge never
developed into a fully-fledged
resort; even today, much of
its character is still preserved.

115. Stanwell Farm, Bembridge,
in about 1900.

116. The Royal Spithead Hotel, Bembridge, in 1898. The hotel was the headquarters of the Royal Isle of Wight Golf Club, and when this photograph was taken full board cost about 73/- a week.

117. Lane End, Bembridge, 1890. Once a separate hamlet, Lane End is now a suburb of Bembridge.

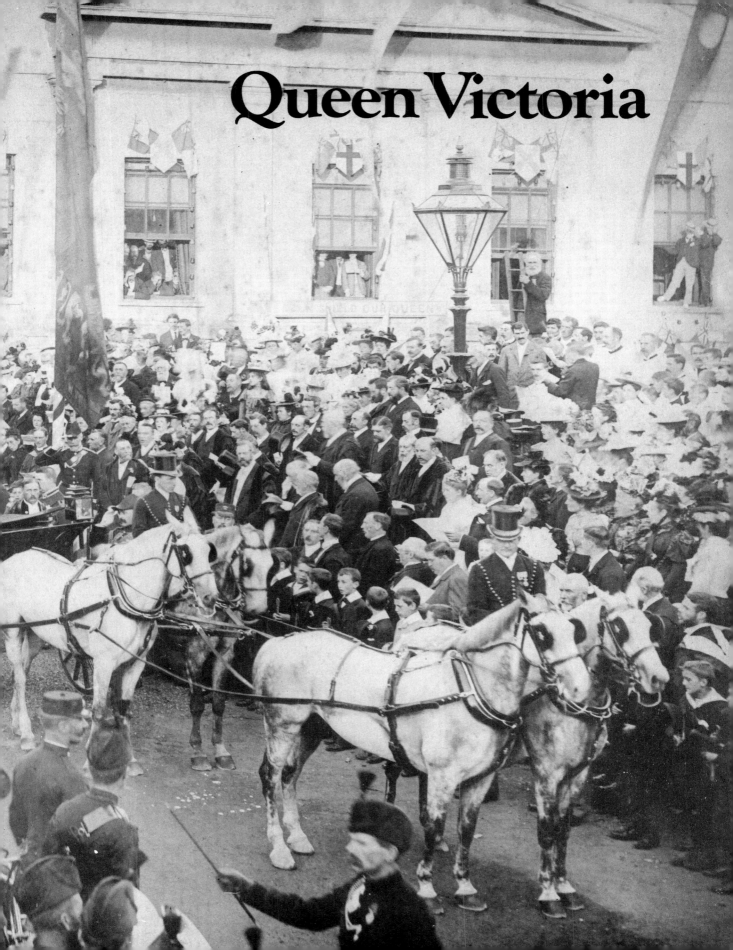

Queen Victoria

118. (*Overleaf.*) Queen Victoria being greeted by the Mayor and Corporation of Newport on the occasion of her Diamond Jubilee in 1897.

119. Osborne House in 1900. Queen Victoria and Prince Albert bought the Osborne estate in 1845 for £26,000. She always thought of it as her 'little paradise' and after Albert's death spent much of her time in seclusion at the house. Between 1845 and 1848 Prince Albert and Thomas Cubitt redesigned the existing house and added on additional wings. After his mother's death, King Edward VII, for whom Osborne had unhappy memories, presented the house and its 2,000 acre estate to the nation.

OSBORNE HOUSE.

120. One of the only three known photographs
of Queen Victoria laughing, taken by a Newport
photographer in about 1880.

121. Queen Victoria arriving in Cowes to receive a loyal address in commemoration of her Diamond Jubilee of 1897.

122. Queen Victoria opening the Victoria Ward (now the childrens' ward of Ryde County Hospital) in 1899. The landua in which the Queen is sitting was made by R. B. Cheverton & Co, a Ryde firm still in existence.

123. A stereoscope showing Queen Victoria's funeral cortège leaving Osborne on 1 February 1901. The Queen died at Osborne on 22 January. Her body lay in state for a week in the house before being placed on a gun carriage for the journey to Windsor. The white and gold pall on the coffin was embroidered with a cross and the Royal Arms, and the coffin was carried by the Queen's Company of the 1st Grenadiers. King Edward VII can be seen behind the gun carriage.

124. The end of an age. The body of Queen Victoria being carried between Cowes and Portsmouth on the Royal Yacht *Alberta*. The *Alberta*, accompanied by three other royal yachts, passed through a 10 mile line of warships on the journey, each of which saluted the coffin with a minute gun as the *Alberta* passed. The late Uffa Fox recounted that as the *Alberta* left Cowes a shaft of sunlight broke through the heavy cloud, shining on the yacht and illuminating it throughout the fleet.